# Exploring the Heritage
## of
# John Calvin

# Exploring the Heritage
## of
# John Calvin

*David E. Holwerda, Editor*

**Baker Book House**
Grand Rapids, Michigan

Copyright 1976 by
Baker Book House Company
Grand Rapids, Michigan

ISBN 0-8010-4146-5
Library of Congress Catalog Card Number: 76-3919

*Printed in the United States of America*

**John H. Bratt**

These essays are published to honor John Bratt on the occasion of his retirement from Calvin College. He has taught in the Department of Religion and Theology almost twenty-eight years, and for twenty-one years has served as its chairman. The publication of these essays is an expression of the esteem and affection of his colleagues.

John Harold Bratt was born on August 23, 1909 in Holland, Michigan. From early childhood he was molded by the Calvinist environment of his family, his church, and his school. His family attended the historic Ninth St. Christian Reformed Church of Holland, and his early formal education was received in the Christian elementary and secondary schools of that city. He graduated from Calvin College in 1933 and from Calvin Theological Seminary in 1937. During the following two years he earned two Master's degrees. The first was received in 1938 from Columbia Seminary in Decatur, Georgia, for a thesis which developed a historical comparison of the Christian Reformed and the Southern Presbyterian churches. The second Master's degree was received from Harvard Divinity School in 1939. In 1955, he was awarded the Th.D. degree by Union Seminary of Richmond, Virginia, for the thesis "The Rise and Development of the Missionary Consciousness in the Christian Reformed Church."

John Bratt has been a teacher most of his life. He began his career as a teacher of Bible in the Grand Rapids Christian High School from 1939-1942. For four years, 1942-1946, he served as pastor of the Dorr Christian Reformed Church; but apart from this brief interlude his entire professional career has been spent as a teacher in academic institutions. In 1946 he received an appointment to Calvin College as an assistant in English and Speech. Appointed to the Bible Department in 1947, he has served as its chairman from 1954 through 1975.

John Bratt has made a significant contribution to the life of Calvin College and the Christian Reformed Church. He was first of all a teacher who loved the classroom and the stimulating contact with young people. His lectures were always well organized and articulate, and his humor gentle and kind. As a historian and teacher, he has had a love for the Reformed tradition and has continually promoted interest in the heritage of John Calvin. Aware of the richness of that tradition, he has always been open to the need for testing new ideas in new situations. Although he held a deep appreciation for his own denomination, his loyalty was never parochial. Standing in the tradition of John Calvin, his spirit has always been ecumenical.

As a teacher and writer, John Bratt has helped to shape and gently stimulate the mind of the church. He is recognized for his wisdom and good judgment, and he has served efficiently on important committees for both the college and the church. His leadership has always been kind, his authority always exercised with a view to serving others, and his patience limitless. His desire was for the unity of the church.

We, his colleagues, honor him for his gracious demeanor, his wise counsel, and his Christian charity. Our prayer for him and his wife, Gladys, is that God may richly bless them in their years of retirement.

# CONTENTS

# Preface

The following essays on the heritage of John Calvin were written by people who are, or who have been, members of the Department of Religion and Theology of Calvin College. Two of these are currently members of the faculty of Calvin Theological Seminary: Andrew J. Bandstra, Professor of New Testament, a member of the Department of Religion from 1957-1963; and Theodore Minnema, Professor of Ethics and Apologetics, a member of the Department of Religion from 1962-1975. One present member of the Department, Mr. Henry Hoeks, was regrettably unable to contribute an essay due to the pressures of completing a doctoral thesis.

Unless noted otherwise, quotations from the works of Calvin are taken from the following editions: *Calvin: Institutes of the Christian Religion,* J. T. McNeill, ed., F. L. Battles, trans.; *The Library of Christian Classics,* vol. 21 (Philadelphia: Westminster Press, 1960); *Calvin's New Testament Commentaries,* eds. D. W. and T. F. Torrance (Grand Rapids: Eerdmans); and the Calvin Translation Society edition (1844-1855) of *Calvin's Commentaries on the Old Testament,* reprint edition (Grand Rapids, Eerdmans). Quotations from the Bible are from the Revised Standard Version.

*Andrew J. Bandstra*

# CHAPTER 1 LAW AND GOSPEL

## IN CALVIN AND IN PAUL

### The problem

It is easy to amass quotations that appear to set Calvin in direct opposition to Paul on the subject of law and gospel. Calvin, for example, says: "With respect to doctrine we must not imagine that the coming of Christ has freed us from the authority of the law; for it is the eternal rule of a devout and holy life, and must, therefore, be as unchangeable as the justice of God, which it embraced, is constant and uniform."[1] Again, in commenting on the "new covenant" spoken of in Jeremiah 31:31-34, Calvin states: "It being new, no doubt refers to what they call the form... but the substance remains the same. By substance I understand the doctrine; for God in the Gospel brings forward nothing but what the Law contains."[2] And because the law is regarded by Calvin as being the heart and core of Scripture, he regards not only the priests, prophets, and psalmists but also the apostles as interpreters and expounders of the law.[3] Indeed, even the role of Christ Himself is said to be simply that of a "faithful interpreter" of the law.[4]

Paul, on the other hand, frequently extols the great change that has come about with the advent of Christ. He says, for example: "Therefore, if any one is in Christ, he is a new creation; the old has passed away, behold, the new has come" (II Cor. 5:17). Again, Paul

1. *Comm.* on Matt. 5:17 (Pringle trans.); cf. *Comm.* on Rom. 6:15; *Comm.* on Gal. 3:25; and *Inst.*, II.vii.14.

2. *Comm.* on Jer. 31:31 f.

3. Cf. *Inst.*, IV.viii.6-9.

4. *Comm.* on Matt. 5:21.

11

affirms that in Christ and His Spirit we have been freed from the
bondage of the law, "for the law of the Spirit of life in Christ Jesus
has made me free from the law of sin and death" (Rom. 8:2). And in
what sounds like an absolute statement, the apostle proclaims: "sin
will have no dominion over you, since you are not under law but
under grace" (Rom. 6:14).

How can the above judgments of Calvin be squared with the ac-
cents of Paul's proclamation? It has often been affirmed that Luther
and Lutheranism on this subject have a better insight into Paul than
did Calvin. For in Lutheran thought, law and gospel are often set
over against one another in dialectical tension rather than in any kind
of teleological unity. Werner Elert represents one strain of Lutheran
thought when he says: "For Paul, as well as for Luther, the law and
gospel stand in substantive dialectical opposition to each other. When
the law speaks, the gospel is silent. When the gospel speaks, the law
must hold its peace."[5] Over against Calvin,[6] who affirmed that law
and gospel (or old and new covenants—which in many respects were
synonymous terms to Calvin) were one in substance but differed
only in the form of administration, Elert argues that for both Luther
and Paul the law and gospel stand in *substantive* antithetical relation
to each other.

It is not the purpose of this essay to address the Lutheran-Re-
formed debate on the subject of law and gospel, nor directly to investigate the differences between Luther and Calvin. Certainly it is not
the aim of the article to attempt to demonstrate that Calvin is always
a better interpreter of Paul than is Luther. But it is the contention of
this essay that when Calvin is properly understood he is a more faithful interpreter of Paul than has often been thought. Specifically, a
contemporary Calvin scholar, Ira John Hesselink, has recently
argued that Calvin's position on law and gospel has not been fully
articulated. He has shown that it is inadequate to deal with the law-
gospel theme in Calvin under the two rubrics of *unity of substance*
but *difference in form of administration,* which has frequently been
the case; to these two must be added the third rubric, in a sense later
to be defined, the *antithesis between law as "letter" and gospel as*

---

5. *Law and Gospel,* trans. E. H. Schroeder (Philadelphia: Fortress, Facet Books,
Social Ethics, Series # 16, 1967), p. 1.

6. Elert takes issue not only with Calvin but also with Karl Barth who spoke of the
law as nothing other than the necessary form of the gospel, whose content is grace;
cf. "Gospel and Law," *Community, State, and Church: Three Essays,* ed. W. Her-
berg (New York: Doubleday, Anchor Books, 1960), especially p. 80. This treatise
was originally published in 1935 and has sparked a lively debate, particularly on the
part of Lutheran scholars.

*"Spirit."* [7] If Calvin does indeed speak of the *antithesis* between letter and Spirit, it will be easier to see him as an accurate interpreter of the Pauline statements on "law and gospel."

The question can be raised how this inadequate presentation of Calvin's position on law and gospel has persisted in both popular and (to some extent) scholarly circles. It is perhaps understandable that Lutheran scholars have tended to overlook Calvin's statements on the antithesis of law and gospel as letter and spirit and have spoken only of Calvin's insistence on the unity of substance and differentiation of form. Because of this they tend to say that Calvin coordinates law and gospel, with quantitative but no qualitative differences between them, and thus levels off the distinction between law and gospel. [8] But Reformed scholars may also have contributed to this improper understanding of Calvin. Hesselink makes the following pertinent judgment: "Concerning this point, viz., the *antithesis* between the law and the gospel, many presentations of Calvin's thought by Reformed scholars are partially responsible for the continuing suspicions and apprehensions of their Lutheran brethren. Too often in the enthusiasm—and rightly so—for Calvin's thesis that the substance of the covenants is the same, only the form differs, Calvin's utterances concerning law and gospel in the traditional Lutheran sense have been noted only incidentally, if at all." [9] In addition to his interpreters, whether Lutheran or Reformed, Calvin himself—as we will see later—may have to shoulder some of the responsibility for contributing to this misunderstanding. But in one way or another, the abbreviated form of Calvin's position on the law and gospel theme has contributed in its own way to what J. I. Packer calls the "Calvin of legend" in distinction from the "Calvin of fact." [10]

In this essay, after a section devoted to the definition of the terms

7. *Calvin's Concept and Use of the Law* (unpub. diss., Basel, 1961), chap. 7, especially pp. 9 f. and 42 ff. A copy of this dissertation, along with a later revised edition (also in typed form), is available in the "Calvin Collection" of the Calvin Theological Library (Grand Rapids, Mich.). This set of three rubrics to describe Calvin's view of law and gospel is also used by Werner Krusche, *Das Wirken des Heiligen Geistes nach Calvin* (Göttingen: Vandenhoeck & Ruprecht, 1957), pp. 184-201; but Hesselink significantly modifies the construction under "Distinction of Form" and "Antithesis of Letter and Spirit."

8. See, e.g., Helmut Thielicke, *Theological Ethics,* trans. Wm. H. Lazareth (Philadelphia: Fortress, 1966), I: 94-125, especially pp. 120 ff.; and W. Elert, *Law and Gospel,* pp. 44 ff.

9. *Calvin's Concept and Use of the Law,* chap. 7, fn. 33.

10. J. I. Packer, "Calvin the Theologian," *John Calvin: A Collection of Distinguished Essays,* ed. G. E. Duffield (Grand Rapids: Eerdmans, 1966), pp. 149 ff.

"law" and "gospel" in Calvin and in Paul, we will take up the three rubrics mentioned above: the unity of substance between law and gospel, the distinction in form of administration between the two, and the antithesis between the law as letter and the gospel as Spirit. In each of these an attempt will be made to assess the extent to which Calvin correctly or adequately interprets Paul.[11]

## Toward a definition of terms

*Calvin's use of the terms "law" and "gospel"*

Calvin used the word "law" as a flexible term expressing a wide range of ideas and concepts. The law basically is an expression of the will of God. "In the Law of God a perfect standard of all righteousness is presented to us which with good reason can be called the eternal will of the Lord."[12] In this essay we are concerned with the "written law" as the expression of the will of God and not directly with the "law of nature."[13] Even in regard to this written law, however, the term "law" may have a variety of meanings in Calvin and it is therefore difficult to give a succinct definition of the term. Even Calvin's attempts at summarizing the meanings that he assigns are not always helpful nor identical since much depends on the context in which he is writing. At the beginning of his discussion of the law in the *Institutes*, he affirms: "I understand by the term 'law' not only the Ten Commandments, which set forth a godly and righteous rule of living, but the form

11. For Calvin's view of law and gospel, I am especially indebted to Hesselink's dissertation (see above, fn. 7). As Hesselink notes in his introductory chapter, very little has been written that is specifically devoted to Calvin's conception of the law. Since his dissertation was presented (1961), at least one other dissertation has appeared on the subject, Ralph Roger Sundquist, Jr., *The Third Use of the Law in the Thought of John Calvin: An Interpretation and Evaluation* (Columbia University, 1970; available through University Microfilms, A Xerox Co., Ann Arbor, Mich.). Since this book is devoted to Calvin's third use of the law, it does not deal extensively with the problem of law and gospel, though the subject is treated on pp. 223 ff. On the topic of "letter and Spirit," Sundquist speaks of "difference" rather than "antithesis," pp. 232 ff.

12. *Instruction in Faith (1537)*, trans. P. T. Fuhrmann (Philadelphia: Westminster, 1949), p. 24; cf. *Inst.*, I.xvii.2 and II.viii.5. R. A. Gessert points out that "in many places, particularly when speaking of man's need for the revelation of Scripture, Calvin tends to identify Law with the Word of God" ("The Integrity of Faith: An Inquiry into the Meaning of Law in the Thought of John Calvin," *S.J.T.* 13 [1960], p. 251); cf. *Inst.*, I.vi.

13. For Calvin the *content* of the Mosaic law and the law of nature are the same; cf. *Inst.*, IV.xx.16 and II.viii.1. Yet the latter has proved to have failed and has been inadequate with respect to the love of God and neighbor.

of religion handed down by God through Moses.''[14]

John T. McNeill has identified three referents of the term "law" in Calvin: "(1) the whole religion of Moses . . . ; (2) the special revelation of the moral law to the chosen people, i.e., chiefly the Decalogue and Jesus' summary . . . ; or (3) various bodies of civil, judicial, and ceremonial statutes . . . . ''[15] Certainly the distinction between the "moral law" (chiefly the Ten Commandments and directly related materials) and the "supplements" (various ceremonial and political laws) is important in understanding Calvin, for the latter have as their purpose "merely to aid us in observing the moral law" in which " God has briefly but comprehensively summed up the rule of a just and holy life.''[16] This distinction becomes especially significant for understanding how or in what ways the law was "abrogated" with the coming of Christ.

But perhaps more important for the purpose of understanding the law and gospel motif in Calvin is the definition of law as "the form of religion handed down by Moses." This designation is described more extensively in another place. In so doing Calvin makes an important distinction in the ministry or office of Moses, in an effort to make plain how Paul could in Romans 10:5-10 make the law agree with faith and yet set the righteousness of the law in opposition to the righteousness of faith. Says Calvin: "The word law is used in a twofold sense. At times it means the whole doctrine taught by Moses, and, at times, that part of it which belonged peculiarly to his ministry, and is contained in its precepts, rewards and punishments.''[17] The "whole doctrine of Moses" is then related to "the universal office" of Moses, which was to preach both repentance and faith. This, in turn, meant that Moses proclaimed both precept and promise, for faith is peculiarly related to promise, and repentance is especially related to precept. Therefore in proclaiming the law in this broader sense Moses preached the gospel which led men "to flee to the haven of divine goodness—to Christ himself.''[18]

In this sense the precepts are combined with the free promises of divine mercy. But it is also possible to speak of a "restricted" sense

14. *Inst.*, II.vii.1. In another place he says: "The law consists chiefly of three parts: first, the doctrine of life; second, threatenings and promises; third, the covenant of grace, which being founded on Christ, contains within itself all the special promises" (*Comm.* on Isa., "Preface").

15. McNeill-Battles, *Inst.*, II. vii. 1, fn. 1.

16. *Comm. Harm. Pent.*, "Preface."

17. *Comm.* on Rom. 10:5.

18. Ibid.

of law and a "peculiar" ministry of Moses. How Calvin understands this requires an extensive quotation:

> The promises of the Gospel, however, are found only here and there in the writings of Moses, and these are somewhat obscure, while the precepts and rewards, appointed for those who observe the law, frequently occur. The function, therefore, of teaching the character of true righteousness is, with justification, properly and peculiarly attributed to Moses, as is also the function of showing the nature of remuneration which awaits those who observe it, and what punishment awaits those who transgress it. For this reason Moses himself is contrasted with Christ by John when he says: "The law was given by Moses; grace and truth came by Jesus Christ" (John 1:17). Whenever the word *law* is used in this restricted sense, Moses is implicitly contrasted with Christ. We are then to see what the law contains in itself when separated from the Gospel. I must, therefore, refer what I say here of the righteousness of the law not to the whole office of Moses, but to that part of it which was peculiarly entrusted to him.[19]

The distinction between the "whole office of Moses" and his "peculiar office" is comparable to another distinction that Calvin makes in reference to the law: the law in its setting of the covenant of grace and the law as "bare law" or "bare commandments of the law." One meaning of the law for Calvin is: "the covenant of grace, which, being founded on Christ, contains within itself all the special promises."[20] In this sense the law includes not only precept but also promise; it is not only a rule of life but also includes the adoption of Israel.[21] Concerning law considered from this aspect, W. Niesel's judgment is certainly correct: "Calvin's understanding of divine law is based on the recognition that the law of God is covenantal law."[22] In this broad sense of law the term is almost a synonym for the old covenant or testament. But Calvin also frequently refers to the law in a more restricted sense of "bare precepts" or "bare law." In commenting on the delight and comfort of the law expressed in Psalm 119:142, Calvin states: "As this could not be true of the *bare commandments* which, so far from alleviating us rather fill us with anxiety, there is no doubt that by 'commandments' he comprehends

19. Ibid. In other places also Calvin speaks of the "office" that was "peculiarly imposed upon him of setting forth precept and reward," and that one must "distinguish between the general doctrine which was delivered by Moses and the special commission which he received" (*Comm. Harm. Pent.* on Exod. 19:1; cf. *Comm.* on II Cor. 3:6 f.).

20. *Comm.* on Isa., "Preface."

21. Cf. *Comm.* on Ezek. 20:12 f.: *Comm.* on Jer. 11:10; *Inst.*, II.vii.1 and II.v.7,10.

22. *The Theology of Calvin*, trans. H. Knight (Philadelphia: Westminster, 1956), p. 92.

in a word the whole doctrine of the law in which God not only requires what is right but in which also, calling his elect ones to the hope of eternal salvation, he opens the door of perfect happiness."[23]

Paul, Calvin asserts, in an attempt to refute the error of his opponents, "was sometimes compelled to take the *bare law in a narrow sense,* even though it was otherwise graced with the covenant of free adoption."[24] The "bare law" is the law in the narrower sense, removed from its context of free promises in the covenant of grace. "Although the covenant of grace is contained in the law, yet Paul removes it from there, for in opposing the Gospel to the law he regards only what was peculiar to the law itself, viz., command and prohibition, and restraining transgressors by the threat of death." This bare law, "considered in itself, can do nothing but bind those who are subject to its wretched bondage by the horror of death as well, for it promises no blessing except on condition, and pronounces death on all transgressors."[25]

The reference to "no blessing except on condition" in the law recalls the distinction Calvin makes between "evangelical promises" or "promises of grace" which are included in the law as broadly defined and the "promises of the law" in the narrower sense. Calvin asseverates: "I call 'promises of the law' not those sprinkled everywhere in the books of Moses, since in them many evangelical promises also occur, but those properly pertaining to the ministry of the law. Promises of this sort, by whatever name you wish to call them, declare there is recompense ready for you if you do what they enjoin."[26]

Much more could be written on the question of the meaning of the term "law" in Calvin, but this should be sufficient to see the importance of and the widespread evidence for a basic twofold meaning of the law in Calvin's thought. On the one hand, there is the wider meaning of the whole office and ministry of Moses in which law becomes practically synonymous with the covenant of grace in the Old Testament and which contains not only precepts and rewards, that is, "promises of the law," but also promises of free grace with all its benefits. On the other hand, there is law in the narrower sense, the peculiar ministry and office of Moses, the "bare law," with its precepts and rewards—namely, the promises of the law which are

23. *Comm.* on Ps. 119:142; cf. *Comm.* on Acts 7:38; *Comm.* on Ps. 111:9; and *Comm.* on Ps. 19:7, 8.

24. *Inst.,* II.vii.2.

25. *Comm.* on Rom. 8:15.

26. *Inst.,* III.xvii.6.

conditional because they demand perfect obedience, and which
threaten, frighten, and kill.

With reference to the meaning of the term "gospel" in Calvin we
can be brief. In the light of the twofold definition of law, it is not
surprising that Calvin could also recognize a twofold definition of
gospel. He clearly delineates this:

> Some extend the word Gospel to all the free promises of God
> scattered even in the Law and the Prophets. And it cannot be
> denied that whenever God declares that He will be propitious
> to men and forgive their sins, He sets forth Christ at the same
> time, whose property it is to shed abroad the rays of joy wherever
> He shines. I admit therefore that the fathers partook of the same
> Gospel as ourselves, so far as the faith of free salvation is con-
> cerned. But because the Spirit is wont to say in the Scriptures
> that the Gospel was first proclaimed when Christ came, let us
> keep to this manner of expression. Let us also hold to the defini-
> tion of the Gospel that I have given, that it is a solemn proclama-
> tion of the grace revealed in Christ.[27]

Thus the gospel in the broad sense is contained in the law in the
broad sense; but for the gospel thus contained in the Law and the
Prophets Calvin prefers to use the term "promises" or "promises of
free remission of sins" or "promises of free mercy." Ruled by Scriptural and common usage, Calvin prefers to use the term "gospel"
in its narrower (or "higher") sense and to reserve it for the proclamation of the grace manifested in Christ, with John the Baptist as the
"dividing line" between the law and the prophets on the one hand
and the gospel of the grace in Christ on the other.

These definitions of law and gospel in Calvin's thought are important for understanding the relationship he posits between the two.
But before we investigate more extensively that relationship, we
must attempt to set forth, briefly, Paul's usage of these terms.

*Pauline usage of "law" and "gospel"*[28]

It is generally agreed that though the Greek word for law *(nomos)*
does not mean the same as the Hebrew *Torah*, the point of departure

27. *Comm.* on John, "The Theme of the Gospel of John"; cf. *Comm.* on Mark 1:1;
and *Inst.*, II.ix.2.

28. It is difficult to speak of *the* Pauline conception of law, not only because there is
scholarly dispute as to which epistles are authentically Pauline but also because it has
been argued that within the Pauline corpus of writings there is a sharp distinction
between the earlier "apostolic" view of the law and the "early Catholic" view in the
so-called later Paulines (e.g., Col., Eph., and the Pastorals). It is alleged that in the
"early Catholic" view there is a high regard for the principle of law in the Christian
life, while in the "apostolic" view the principle of law was altogether abandoned. But
a variety of emphases appears even in the earlier epistles. See John W. Drane, "Tradition, Law, and Ethics in Pauline Theology," *Nov. Test.* 16 (1974): 167-78. Yet even
in the midst of this variety, a discernible pattern is evident.

for Paul is the *Torah*, God's law in the Old Testament.[29] Pauline usage can be classified under the following headings:[30] (1) The law is the revelation of God to His people that is stamped by the name of *Moses*. In this sense it is called the "law of Moses" (I Cor. 9:9) and the name "Moses" can stand for the written law of the old covenant (II Cor. 3:15). (2) The law is the *Scriptures* of the old covenant which testify to the revelation given on Mount Sinai. As Scripture, law may be distinguished from "the prophets" (Rom. 3:21), but may also include "the prophets" (I Cor. 14:21) and evidently also "the prophets and the psalms" (Rom. 3:19; cf. Luke 24:44). (3) The law in Paul refers especially to the *demands* which are contained in the revelation given to Moses. Paul does not make any formal distinction between the "moral" and the "ceremonial" law—indicated in part by the persistent use of the singular and never the plural of *nomos*—but he may place emphasis on the ethical side of the law (Gal. 5:14; Rom. 13:8-10), or at another time on the ceremonial prescriptions (Gal. 4:10; 5:3 ff.; I Cor. 10:18). (4) In a modified and derivative sense it may refer (a) generally to a "norm," "principle," or even "constraint" (Rom. 3:27; 7:21, 23, 25), or (b) to the "law of Christ" or the "law of the Spirit of Life" (Gal. 6:2; Rom. 8:2; cf. I Cor. 9:21).

The first three meanings as given above are obviously the most important in considering the problem of law and gospel. These meanings do not coincide precisely with the terms as used by Calvin, and yet the first two do come close to what Calvin calls the broader meaning of the law in that they refer to the whole Old Testament revelation as related to Moses. Furthermore, the third rubric of law as demand comes close to what Calvin wished to designate as law in the narrower sense, namely, the law in itself with its precepts and rewards. Interestingly, Paul uses the broader and narrower meaning of the term within the space of one verse, which parallels Calvin's twofold distinction. Paul announces in Romans 3:21, 22: "But now the righteousness of God has been manifested apart from the law,

29. Cf. W. Gutbrod, *"nomos," TDNT* IV: 1061. For two recent excellent surveys of Paul's understanding of the law, see George Eldon Ladd, *A Theology of the New Testament* (Grand Rapids: Eerdmans, 1974), pp. 495-510, and Herman Ridderbos, *Paul: An Outline of His Theology,* trans. J. R. De Witt (Grand Rapids: Eerdmans, 1975), pp. 130-58 and 278-88.

30. Those given here are an adaptation and enlargement of the list given by C. Maurer, *Die Gesetzlehre des Paulus* (Zollikon-Zürich: Evangelischer Verlag, 1941), pp. 81 ff. For comments see A. J. Bandstra, *The Law and the Elements of the World: An Exegetical Study in Aspects of Paul's Teaching* (Kampen: Kok, 1964), p. 76. Cf. also the description in R. Bultmann, *Theology of the New Testament,* vol. I, trans. K. Grobel (London: SCM Press, 1952), pp. 259 ff.; and the grouping given by C. E. B. Cranfield, "St. Paul and the Law," *SJT* 17 (1964): 44.

although the law and the prophets bear witness to it, the righteousness of God through faith in Jesus Christ, for all who believe." The phrase "apart from the law" refers to the fact that salvation through Christ is apart from the "works of the law" (Rom. 3:20, 28) and therefore all "boasting" is excluded (3:27). Indeed through the law in this sense men only "know sin" (3:20) and experience the wrath of the law (4:15). Yet God's righteousness—namely, His eschatological saving activity in Christ—is witnessed to in the law and the prophets. In this broader sense of law, continuity between the old and new is affirmed.

The gospel for Paul centers in Jesus Christ; or as Joseph A. Fitzmyer states: "For him, Jesus Christ is the gospel."[31] Paul uses the term "gospel of Christ" (I Thess. 3:2; Gal. 1:7; Phil. 1:27; etc.) as with other designations which emphasize Christ's death and resurrection (I Cor. 15:1-7; Rom. 1:1-5). This usage, of course, fits Calvin's narrower sense of the term "gospel."

But Paul has some distinctive emphases in his use of the term. He regards the gospel as a power, "the power of God" (Rom. 1:16—therefore also "God's gospel"; I Thess. 3:2, etc.); it is a gospel for all, both Jew and Greek (Rom. 1:16; etc.); and the gospel is a "mystery" (*mystērion*—I Cor. 2:7; Rom. 11:25; 16:25; Col. 1:26, 27; 4:3; etc.). This last designation might appear to conflict with Calvin's broader view of the gospel by which he refers also to those "free promises" contained in the law and the prophets. It appears to be in conflict because gospel as mystery is explained as "the mystery hidden for ages and generations but now made manifest to his saints" (Col. 1:26; cf. I Cor. 2:7 and Rom. 16:25). This might seem to say that the Old Testament saints did not know the gospel.[32] It is true that elsewhere Paul affirms that "the scriptures... preached the gospel beforehand to Abraham" (Gal. 3:8) and describes the gospel as that which God "promised beforehand through his prophets in the holy scriptures" (Rom. 1:2). But does this apply also to the gospel as "mystery"? In some way it does, for Paul combines the ideas of gospel as mystery and testimony of the prophets. So in Rom. 16:25 he refers to the gospel "according to the revelation of the mystery which was kept secret through long ages" and then adds in verse 26: "but now is disclosed and through the prophetic writings is made known to all nations." Thus whatever the full implica-

---

31. Joseph A. Fitzmyer, *Pauline Theology: A Brief Sketch* (Englewood Cliffs: Prentice-Hall, 1967), p. 19; see his fine survey on pp. 18-23, to which the above description is indebted.

32. Calvin notes this problem in the *Inst.*, II.ix.4 as well as in his *Comm.* on Rom. 16:25 f.

tion of the idea of gospel as "mystery," it is clear that Paul does not wish to preclude its being preached, promised, and made known in the Old Testament Scripture as a whole and especially in the prophetic writings.

This brief delineation of Paul's use of the terms "law" and "gospel" does not get us directly into the law-gospel problem in Paul. Paul never explicitly juxtaposes the terms "law" and "gospel" and never directly contrasts them. When speaking of the contrast, Paul uses such terms as "works of the law" as opposed to "the hearing of faith" or "righteousness of law" as opposed to "spirit," and so forth. These, however, will come up for consideration in the next section. This survey of usage is perhaps sufficient to show that when Calvin speaks of the law and gospel he is using terminology in a way similar to that of Paul.

### The relationship between law and gospel

In discussing Calvin's thought on law and gospel, it is important to keep in mind the twofold definition of the law given by him. "For most of the time Old Testament-New Testament or old covenant-new covenant is equivalent to law-gospel for Calvin. Law in this comprehensive sense is usually identical with the old covenant. In this case the substance of the covenants (or law and gospel) is the same. Only the form of administration differs."[33]

But Calvin does not define law in this way when he speaks of the *antithesis* of law and gospel. Then he means law in the "narrower" sense as described earlier; it is the peculiar office or ministry of Moses, the "bare law" with its precepts and rewards. Or, to use another phrase from Calvin, it is the law *insofar as* it is opposed to the gospel.[34] With this distinction in mind, we give consideration to the three main assertions concerning the relationship between law and gospel.

#### *The unity of substance or reality*

It is difficult to speak seriatim of "unity of substance" and "difference of form," since Calvin almost always discusses the two together. The classic statement by Calvin is: "The covenant made with all the patriarchs is so much like ours in substance and reality

---

33. Hesselink, *Calvin's Concept and Use of the Law,* chap. 7, p. 9. Yet it is not entirely accurate to imply that when Calvin used the term "Old Testament" or "old covenant" he was always using it in the broad sense of precept plus the promises of free mercy. Sometimes, when the old covenant is contrasted with the new, he seems to understand the term "old covenant" also in the narrower sense of law, viz, law with its precepts and rewards. Cf. *Inst.* II.xi.7.10.

34. Cf. e.g., his *Comm.* on II Cor. 3:6.

that the two are really one and the same. Yet they differ in the mode of dispensation."[35] Yet for the sake of orderly presentation, we will first ask what belongs to the unity of substance or reality. Much could be written about this, but since this subject is so well known, the following items may suffice.[36]

1. The unity of substance means that there is a *unity of doctrine* between the law and the gospel. Calvin affirms that "by substance I understand the doctrine; for God in the Gospel brings forward nothing but what the law contains. We hence see that God has so spoken from the beginning, that he has not changed, no not a syllable, with regard to the substance of the doctrine."[37] The unity of doctrine roots in the fact that "God is never inconsistent with himself, nor is he unlike himself."[38] So for Calvin, even though the Bible speaks of an old and a new covenant, there is basically or essentially only one covenant of grace that is common to both the Old and New Testaments. In the light of Christ and His teachings it is clear to Calvin that "God has never made any other covenant than that which he made formerly with Abraham, and at length confirmed by the hand of Moses."[39] Indeed the "newness" of the new covenant pertains only to the form, or to what Calvin calls "the outward mode of the teaching."[40]

2. The unity of substance is a *unity of faith* between Old Testament and New Testament believers. The fathers under the old covenant shared with us—though only in part and imperfectly—the same adoption into the hope of immortality, a common salvation bestowed solely by the mercy of God, and the same grace through the one Mediator, Jesus Christ.[41] Many other points of identity between the faith of the old and new covenant are mentioned throughout Calvin's works.[42] Calvin emphasized this point over against the

35. *Inst.*, II.x.2. This comparison of unity of substance and difference of form appears frequently in the commentaries also.

36. A recent work is devoted to this subject: H. H. Wolf, *Die Einheit des Bundes: Das Verhältnis von Altem und Neuem Testament bei Calvin* (Neukirchen, Kreis Moers: Verlag Erziehungsvereins, 1958).

37. *Comm.* on Jer. 31:31 f.

38. Ibid. Cf. *Comm.* on Isa. 2:3; *Comm.* on Gal. 3:12; and *Comm.* on Heb. 1:1 f.

39. *Comm.* on Jer. 31:31 f.; cf. *Inst.*, II.x.1.

40. *Comm.* on Jer. 31:31 f.

41. These are stated in *Inst.*, II.x.2 and elaborated in that chapter.

42. For a summary, see *Comm.* on Gal. 4:1; see further, I. John Hesselink, "Calvin and Heilsgeschichte," *Oikonomia: Heilsgeschichte als Thema der Theologie*, ed. F. Christ (Hamburg-Bergstedt: Reich, 1967), p. 166.

"wonderful rascal, Servetus, and certain madmen of the Anabaptist sect," who regarded the "Israelites as nothing but a herd of swine" to whom the Lord promised "nothing but a full belly"[43]—that is, nothing but earthly, material, natural blessings and not the spiritual blessings of the new covenant.

3. The unity of substance finds central expression as a *unity in Christ*. The heart of the "one doctrine" and the "common faith" is none other than Christ Himself.[44] More specifically, it is "Christ clothed in his own promises."[45] As Hesselink reminds us, Calvin repeatedly refers to the fact that "Christ is the 'fundamentum,' 'anima,' 'vita,' 'spiritus,' 'scopus,' 'finis,' and 'perfectio' of the law."[46] Even though the types point forward to Christ in His manifestation in the flesh, Calvin affirms that Christ did not first begin to be manifested in the gospel. As the eternal Son of God, He was active in the Old Testament and was the "fountain" from which the Old Testament men of faith drank.[47] As Henry Stob well says:

> Calvin, accordingly, finds Christ no less in the book of James than in the book of Romans, no less in the Old Testament than in the New, no less in the law than in the gospel. Christ is what the Bible is about from first to last. What to some may appear, therefore, to be Calvin's undue orientation to Old Testament motifs or his sub-Christian legalism, is in fact his Christo-centrism, his conviction that it is the whole of Scripture and the entire fabric of revelation *was Christum treibet*.[48]

Calvin never tires of underscoring this truth concerning the unity of substance between the law and gospel. His zeal for stressing this unity has contributed to the assessment that Calvin levels off the distinction between the old and new covenants. Sometimes Calvin's rhetoric is extreme in this regard. When he says that "not one syllable" in doctrine has changed in the gospel,[49] he does lay himself open to that kind of charge. When he says that the apostles and even Christ Himself are "only interpreters" of the law,[50] he comes

43. *Inst.*, II.x.1.

44. *Inst.*, II.x.2; in II.x.23 Calvin also observes that another aspect of identity is the same Christ as pledge and object of faith.

45. *Inst.*, II.ix.3; cf. III.ii.6.

46. "Calvin and Heilsgeschichte," *Oikonomia*, p. 166.

47. Cf. *Inst.*, IV.viii.5.

48. "Justification and Sanctification: Liturgy and Ethics," *Marburg Revisited: A Reexamination of Lutheran and Reformed Traditions*, ed. P. C. Empie and J. I. McCord (Minneapolis: Augsburg, 1966), p. 106.

49. *Comm.* on Jer. 31:31 f.

50. Cf. introductory paragraph of this article, with fns. 3 and 4.

perilously close to asserting that the New Testament is only an interpretation or application of the Old.[51]

Yet the unity of the two is important to him as a theological issue, since, as was noted above, it is related to the unity and unchangeableness of God Himself. In addition, Calvin was no doubt impelled to underscore so strongly the unity of the covenant because of certain movements in the church of his day. He felt constrained to make this emphasis over against the "catabaptists and other monstrous rascals,"[52] that is, the Anabaptists or those whom we would designate as antinomians.[53] In that particular historical situation, it was necessary to place emphasis on the unity of the covenant.

In comparing Calvin with Paul on this point, it would be fair to say that this insistence on the *unity* of law and gospel in Calvin is a nuance that is not particularly accented by Paul. Not that Paul does not know of the unity or continuity between the old and the new covenants. Indeed he does. Paul insists that the law and prophets testify to the righteousness of God now revealed in Christ (Rom. 3:21), that faith does not nullify but confirms the law (Rom. 3:31), that God never intended for man under sin to be saved by the works of the law (Rom. 3:20; Gal. 2:16),[54] that the principle of receiving the inheritance by faith is related to the "oneness" of God (Rom. 3:30; Gal. 3:20), that Christ was present in the old covenant and was the "rock" from which the Old Testament fathers drank (I Cor. 10:1-4),[55] and so on.

Paul seems to have assumed the unity of the old and new dispensations and implicitly speaks of it in a variety of ways. Yet he certainly does not emphasize this theme as does Calvin. Rather Paul's emphasis, also no doubt in part due to the opposition he was contesting in his ministry, was on the newness of the new situation ushered in by Christ: "If any one is in Christ, he is a new creation; the old

51. Hesselink (*Calvin's Concept and Use of the Law*, chap. 3, fn. 113) doubts whether Calvin would go so far as to make the above assertion; Calvin's rhetoric, however, almost implies this.

52. *Inst.*, "Prefatory Address," McNeill-Battles, I, p. 28.

53. Sundquist, *The Third Use of the Law*, pp. 38 ff., argues that Calvin developed his idea of law as the way between two extremes: the Roman Catholic hierarchy on the right (as legalists) and the Anabaptists on the left (as antinomians). In *Inst.*, II.x.1., Calvin mentions the "rascal Servetus and certain madmen of the Anabaptist sect" as the occasion for stressing the similarity of the Old and New Testament.

54. See Bultmann's comments on Gal. 2:16, *Theology*, I, p. 263.

55. Cf. A. J. Bandstra, "Interpretation in I Corinthians 10:1-11," *CTJ* 6 (1971): 9-14. If A. T. Hanson is correct, Paul (and other NT writers) often asserted or assumed Christ's preexistent activity in the OT; cf. *Jesus Christ in the Old Testament* (London: SPCK, 1965), pp. 10 ff.

has passed away, behold, the new has come" (II Cor. 5:17), and on the surpassing glory of the new covenant and its ministry (II Cor. 3:7 ff.). In his situation Paul was impelled or constrained to stress the radical newness of the gospel; and at just these points, Calvin is prone to temper the idea of "newness" by insisting on the unity of substance. He does this in such a way that Calvin himself raises the question whether, after such great insistence on the unity of substance, one can truly speak of differences between the two.[56] Thus the accent in Calvin falls on the unity of law and gospel while for Paul the radical newness of the gospel is stressed.

This difference in accent sometimes leads Calvin to misinterpret some of Paul's statements on the law. This can be illustrated from some of Calvin's comments on Galatians 3. In verses 22 and 23, Paul explains that the "scripture consigned all things to sin" and that "before faith came, we were confined under the law." In this connection, Calvin states that the Old Testament believers "were besieged on every hand by the curse; but against this siege there were built the prison walls which protected them from the curse. So that he shows the prison of the law to have been in fact beneficent in spirit."[57] But the law as "beneficent in spirit" is precisely not in view here; much rather the negative aspect is stressed. In the next verse (Gal. 3:24), Paul says that "the law was our custodian until Christ came." Calvin understands this not only in the law functioning in the negative sense, as a "mirror"[58] to show us our unrighteousness so as to constrain us to seek the grace of Christ, but he also understands Paul to be speaking of the law in the positive manner of bringing people to Christ. He says: "And certainly the ceremonies had the power not only of alarming and humbling consciences, but of exciting them to faith in the coming Redeemer.... The whole law, in short, was nothing but a manifold variety of exercises in which the worshippers were led by the hand to Christ."[59] But this more positive view of the law is precisely not in view here; for bondage, being shut up under sin and the curse of the law, is Paul's concern in this context.[60] Calvin understands Paul to refer to the gospel as con-

56. *Inst.,* II.xi.1.

57. *Comm.* on Gal. 3:23.

58. On the different uses of the "mirror" image in Calvin, see Wm. F. Kiesecker, "John Calvin's Mirror," *Theol. Today* 17 (1960): 288 f.

59. *Comm.* on Gal. 3:24.

60. Cf. Herman Ridderbos, *The Epistle of Paul to the Churches of Galatia,* trans. H. Zylstra (Grand Rapids: Eerdmans, 1953), p. 144. More broadly on this subject, cf. G. C. Berkouwer, *Sin,* trans. P. C. Holtrop (Grand Rapids: Eerdmans, 1971), pp. 167 ff.

tained in the law although the context does not support such an interpretation.

### The difference of form or mode of administration

In the consideration of the difference of form between the law and gospel, Calvin has in mind basically the larger concept of the law, that is, the "whole law" in distinction from the "bare law." As was already evident in the quotation given in the preceding section, the difference lies in the "form,"[61] or in the "mode of dispensation," or in "manner of teaching."

In the *Institutes,* Calvin specifically enumerates five differences between the old and new covenant:[62] (1) In the Old Testament, spiritual blessings are represented under the figure of earthly blessings; whereas in the New this inferior mode of revelation is superseded. (2) In the old covenant, truth is expressed in types, images, and ceremonies; whereas in the new the very substance of truth is revealed openly in Christ. (3) The old can be and is described as "literal" or as "letter": it was carved on tablets of stone and brings condemnation and death; the new is described as "Spirit": it is written on men's hearts and brings righteousness and life. (4) Arising out of the third difference is the fourth: the old brings "bondage," the bondage of fear; the new brings "freedom," the freedom of trust and assurance. (5) The old covenant is confined to one nation, Israel; the new has reference to all nations, containing the calling of the Gentiles.

Actually the third and fourth differences are of a slightly different nature than the other three. For, seen especially in the light of Calvin's statements in his commentaries, they represent a part of Calvin's position on the antithesis between the law and the gospel. Although this antithesis is not absolute, the break between law and gospel on these two items is much sharper than with the other three. These two, therefore, will be considered in the next section. The other "differences" are more a matter of a quantitative difference, a

---

61. Ronald S. Wallace not only devotes a chapter to "Unity of Revelation—Unity of Substance" but also a chapter to "Unity of Revelation—Unity of Form," *Calvin's Doctrine of the Word and Sacraments* (Grand Rapids: Eerdmans, 1957), pp. 27 ff. Wallace recognizes the "differences of form" in Calvin, which subject he discusses under "unity of substance" (pp. 32 ff.). Nor can it be denied that there is in Calvin a continuity of the "form" of Christ in the old and new covenant. But two questions can be raised about the formulation "Unity of Revelation—Unity of Form": (a) does it do justice to Calvin's *terminology;* and (b) does it permit adequate room for the *concept* of actual difference in form, to say nothing of Calvin's view of the antithesis between letter and Spirit?

62. What follows is a summary of *Inst.,* II.xi.

question of "more or less," a matter of degree.[63] Calvin's statement in regard to the sacraments of the old and new covenant illustrates this matter of degree: "For both [law and gospel] attest that God's fatherly kindness and graces of the Holy Spirit are offered us in Christ, but ours are *clearer and brighter*. In both Christ is shown forth, but in ours *more richly and fully*, that is, in accordance with the difference between the Old and New Testament, which we have discussed above."[64]

Calvin describes this "more" of the gospel (and the "less" of the law) in many different ways throughout the *Institutes* and his commentaries. A variety of images and metaphors is used to make the point. He speaks of the law "veiling" the truth that is openly given in the gospel.[65] He writes of the law hiding the gospel under "signs," "figures," and "types."[66] Following especially the terminology of Hebrews, he speaks of the law being the "shadow," which is contrasted with the reality and substance found in Christ.[67]

Other imagery also appears. The law is like the "first sketch" of the painter—rough, obscure, and unpolished; the gospel presents the "true likeness" of Christ, in "life-like colours."[68] The fathers under the old covenant had only a "slight taste"[69] of the grace that we enjoy fully: "For we know that under the Law they had only a scanty taste of the benefits of God; and when Christ was revealed in the flesh, the blessings were poured out, as it were, with a full hand, even to satisfaction."[70] In addition to the metaphors of "painting" and "eating," Calvin uses the analogy of "childhood" and "maturity": "It was the Lord's will that this childhood be trained in the elements of this world and in little external observances, as rules for children's instruction, until Christ should shine forth, through whom the knowledge of believers was to mature."[71] Again, he uses

63. Cf. Hesselink, *Calvin's Concept and Use of the Law*, chap. 7, pp. 23 ff.

64. *Inst.*, IV.xiv.26 (italics added).

65. *Comm.* on Heb. 2:1; cf. *Comm.* on Heb. 7:12; and *Comm.* on John 5:39.

66. *Comm.* on I Cor. 10:3; *Comm.* on Col. 2:11; *Comm.* on Heb. 8:1; *Inst.*, IV.xx.15; and II.ix.3.

67. *Comm.* on Heb. 4:8, 10; *Comm.* on Heb. 8:5; *Comm.* on Heb. 10:19; and *Comm.* on Col. 2:17.

68. *Comm.* on Col. 2:18; cf. *Comm.* on Heb. 10:1.

69. *Inst.*, II.ix.1.

70. *Comm.* on John 1:16; cf. *Comm.* on Heb. 11:13 where Calvin points out that this slight taste did "satisfy" the OT saints, though they continued to long for Christ.

71. *Inst.*, II.xi.5; cf. *Comm.* on Gal. 4:2.

the idea of "light," comparing the situation under law as the dawn to the midday of the gospel, or as "nothing more than little sparks of that light of life whose full brightness lightens us today."[72]

In this connection, Hesselink calls attention to an often overlooked aspect of Calvin's thought, namely, the idea of "suspended" grace or "suspended" faith.[73] That is, though the grace of Christ, as the eternal Son, was afforded to the fathers under the old cultus, yet this grace or faith was contingent on the coming of Christ in the flesh. The old covenant was "wrapped up in the shadowy and ineffectual observance of ceremonies and delivered to the Jews; it was temporary because it remained, as it were, *in suspense* until it might rest upon a firm and substantial confirmation. It became new and eternal only after it was consecrated and established by the blood of Christ."[74] But this "suspension" of grace does not mean that the Old Testament saints did not participate efficaciously in the substance of the covenant of grace, even while participating in the shadowy ceremonies: "Paul does not make the ceremonies shadowed because they have no reality, but because their fulfillment has been, so to speak, *held in suspense* until the appearance of Christ. Then I say that this must be understood not of efficacy but rather of mode of signification. For until Christ was manifested in the flesh, all signs foreshadowed him as if absent, however much he might make the presence of his power and himself inwardly felt among believers."[75]

The idea of "suspension" is here interpreted to refer to Christ "as if absent," a concept Calvin further describes when he says that the Old Testament believers "possessed Him [Christ] as one hidden, and as it were absent; I say absent not in power of grace, but because he was not yet manifest in the flesh."[76] In that sense the real blessings under the law were all *contingent on* the historical manifestation of Christ in the flesh. So not only was the *faith* of the believers under the law "so to speak in a state of suspense, until Christ appeared,"[77] but even the *revelation* pertaining to Christ was held in suspension: "God, therefore, was silent at that time, because

---

72. *Comm.* on John 1:18. Calvin maintains that this difference is not absolute but a comparison between minor and major.

73. See Hesselink, *Calvin's Concept and Use of the Law*, chap. 7, pp. 36 ff.; also his "Calvin and Heilsgeschichte," *Oikonomia*, pp. 168 ff.

74. *Inst.*, II.xi.4 (italics added).

75. *Inst.*, IV.xiv.25 (italics added).

76. *Comm.* on I Peter 1:12; cf. *Comm.* on Gal. 3:23.

77. *Comm.* on Acts 13:32.

He held in suspense the revelation of these things concerning which he desired His servants to prophesy."[78] Indeed Calvin even goes so far as to say that *grace* was held in suspension: "Grace was in a manner suspended until the advent of Christ; not that the Fathers were excluded from it, but they had not a present manifestation of it in their ceremonies."[79] By speaking of "suspended" grace in this way, Calvin seeks to maintain the basic continuity of grace in law and gospel and at the same time underscore the extreme difference of degree between the two, in order that the "newness" of the new covenant might receive its due.

Does this emphasis on the difference of form or mode of administration reflect an authentic Pauline concept? Does this idea of difference of degree, of more or less, between the old and the new covenant coincide with a part of the Pauline proclamation? Is there a difference of degree in the form within the unity of substance which explicates a genuine Pauline idea?

To be sure, one finds something like this in the Pauline kerygma. There is the argument, for example, from the less-to-the-greater in II Corinthians 3:7-11. The ministry of Moses, though a ministry of condemnation and death, is a ministry of glory. Yet its glory, when compared to that of the new covenant, is almost nil. The exceeding greatness of the glory of the new overshadows the old. Four things can be said of this comparison. First, the identity of the God who deals with Moses and the God who acts in Christ is assumed by Paul. Second, the "glory" of the new covenant is so radically new and so exceedingly great that the two can hardly be compared. Third, in spite of the great difference between them, the two are brought into positive relationship again, with the central unity in Christ (cf. II Cor. 3:14, 16). Fourth, behind this great diversity in unity stands God as the Lord of the history of revelation and redemption.[80]

Also instructive is the comparison made in Colossians 2:17. Speaking of matters pertaining to food and drink laws, to festivals, new moons, and sabbaths as ordered by the law, Paul says: "These are only a shadow of what is to come; but the substance belongs to Christ." The imagery of "shadow" and "substance" (or "reality," or "body") presents a positive correlation between the law and

78. *Comm.* on Rom. 16:21 ff.

79. *Comm.* on Col. 2:14. In his *Comm.* on Dan. 9:25, it is said that *true expiation* was "suspended" until Christ's manifestation; cf. *Comm.* on Heb. 9:15.

80. See C. Maurer, "Der Schluss 'a minore ad majus' als Element paulinischer Theologie," *TLZ* 85 (1960): 149 ff.

Christ.[81] The shadows (following the most likely interpretation) were a projection of the "coming things"—considered as future from the Old Testament vantage point—which are now a reality in Christ. Just as Christ is the true food and drink present under the old covenant (I Cor. 10:3, 4; cf. I Cor. 11:23 ff.) and the substance of the Passover feast (I Cor. 5:7), so Christ here is the real substance present in shadowy form in the ceremonial and cultic regulations of the law.[82] The main emphasis in Colossians 2:16 and 17, of course, is that since Christ has been manifested, these practices should no longer form the criterion for evaluating the Christian life. But precisely in this negative setting the positive correlation is all the more striking.[83] In fact, there are many allusions in Paul's writing to religious institutions of the old covenant, which all imply a contrast of some sort with the realities of the new, but which also form a positive analogy to what has happened or will happen in the new covenant.[84]

So this accent of difference in form, with the more glorious and greater reality of the new, is not absent from Paul. Yet it would be more correct to say that this emphasis is more consistently reflected in the Epistle to the Hebrews than in the writings of Paul. In Hebrews the thought is governed by the concept of "covenant" and the "old" is limited to the concept of "old covenant," while the "law" is primarily the law which governs cultic and ceremonial regulations. Consequently, there is in Hebrews a more positive relationship between the old and new covenants, even though the contrast is

81. H. J. Schoeps recognizes very little positive evaluation of the law here, for he interprets the phrase as "mere shadows" and "practically therefore of negligible quantity" (*Paul: The Theology of the Apostle in the Light of Jewish Religious History,* trans. H. Knight [London: Lutterworth, 1961], p. 198). But this evaluation does justice neither to the shadow-body metaphor in Plato, Philo, and Hebrews, nor to the positive parallels between the Old and New Testaments in Paul.

82. On the "sabbath question" in this passage, see W. Rordorf, *Sunday,* trans. A. A. K. Graham (Philadelphia: Westminster, 1968), pp. 101 ff.

83. Herold Weiss argues that in Col. the "law" does not appear as Mosaic law and that the Mosaic law is no longer functioning as a recognizable entity ("The Law in the Epistle to the Colossians," *CBQ* 34 [1972]: 294-314, especially 311). But this argument does not seem to give a satisfactory account of Col. 2:16, 17, a passage that Weiss all but neglects.

84. Cf. N. A. Dahl, "Christ, Creation, and the Church," *The Background of the New Testament and Its Eschatology;* in honour of C. H. Dodd, ed. W. D. Davies and D. Daube (Cambridge, 1956), pp. 425-29. Dahl lists some nine ways in which this correlation comes to expression. See also E. E. Ellis, *Paul's Use of the Old Testament* (Grand Rapids: Eerdmans, 1957), pp. 130 ff. For the exegetical presuppositions which undergirded the early Christian's understanding of the relationship of the old and the new, see R. Longenecker, *Biblical Exegesis in the Apostolic Period* (Grand Rapids: Eerdmans, 1975), pp. 93 ff.

resolved in terms of the vast superiority of the new covenant.[85] But in Paul's writings the characteristic aspect of his eschatology is that of the two ages, which has a cosmic setting and in which the two ages are related in an *antithetical* manner.[86] The old age is dominated by such forces as the "god of this world," by sin, death, and the flesh. Insofar as the law is associated with these forces of the old age, the law contributes to the "reign" or "power" of sin which brings death.[87] In this sense, the law in Paul is characteristically related more negatively or antithetically to the gospel. It is to this aspect of Paul's thought that consideration is given in the following section.

### The antithesis of law as "letter" and gospel as "Spirit"

In beginning this discussion on the antithesis of letter and Spirit in Calvin, we must call to mind certain things that have been stated previously in this essay. First of all, the specific concerns of this section are those places in Calvin where he speaks of the *antithesis* between law and gospel,[88] or (as he does more frequently) where he speaks of the law *insofar as* it (or Moses) is said to be *opposed* to the gospel (or Christ).[89] Second, when Calvin contrasts the two in this manner he is referring to the law in its restricted or narrower sense, namely, the bare law with its precepts and rewards. Third, this "antithesis" or "opposition" comes to clear expression in what Calvin refers to as the distinction between the law as "letter" and the gospel as "Spirit," and between the "bondage" of the law and the "freedom" of the gospel. Though these distinctions are described in the *Institutes*,[90] they are more clearly developed as antitheses in the commentaries on II Corinthians 3:6 and following and on Romans 8:15.

In II Corinthians 3:6 the apostle speaks of his ministry as coming from God, "who has qualified us to be ministers of a new covenant, not in a written code [or, 'letter'] but in the Spirit; for the written code [or, 'letter'] kills, but the Spirit gives life." In verse 7, Paul goes

85. On this see especially Geerhardus Vos, "Hebrews, the Epistle of the Diatheke," *Princeton Theol. Rev.* 13 (1915): 587-632, and 14 (1916): 1-61.

86. Cf. G. Vos, *The Pauline Eschatology* (Grand Rapids: Eerdmans, 1961) pp. 10 f.

87. See Rom. 5:20; 6:12-23; 7:4-6; I Cor. 15:56. For a good summary, see V. P. Furnish, *Theology and Ethics in Paul* (Nashville/New York: Abingdon, 1968), pp. 115-18 and 135-43; also G. Bornkamm, *Paul,* trans. D. M. G. Stalker (New York/Evanston: Harper & Row, 1971), pp. 120-29.

88. As he does, e.g., in *Comm.* on John 1:17; *Comm.* on II Cor. 3:6 f.; and *Comm.* on Jer. 31:31 f.

89. E.g., in *Comm.* on II Cor. 3:6 f.; *Comm.* on Rom. 8:15; etc.

90. *Inst.,* II.xi.7-10.

on to state that this written code or letter was a "dispensation of death," was "carved in letters of stone," and was temporary, like the "fading" of Moses' glory.

Calvin's discussion of law and gospel on this passage is important because he feels that Paul does not bring up the subject in response to the error of the false apostles at Corinth. In other places Calvin notes that Paul's language is adapted to the particular circumstance of dealing with "perverse interpreters of the law, who separated it from the grace and Spirit of Christ."[91] But Calvin thought that the false prophets at Corinth did not confound the law and gospel, so that Paul's purpose in comparing the two here was "to show them the chief excellence of the Gospel and the chief recommendation of its ministers, which is the efficacy of the Spirit." Whatever the precise purpose, Calvin states that "there is no doubt that by *letter* he means the old testament and by the *Spirit* the Gospel."[92]

Calvin goes on to inveigh against the interpretation of Origen who said that the "letter" referred to the grammatical and natural, or "literal," sense of Scripture and that the "spirit" referred to the "allegorical" sense. Paul, Calvin correctly observes, was not here giving us a key for interpreting Scripture; rather he was showing how the prophecy of Jeremiah 31:31-34 was being fulfilled also in his preaching at Corinth. Calvin then states:

> But the question arises whether under the old testament God only sounded forth with an external voice and never also spoke inwardly to the hearts of the godly by His Spirit. My first answer is that Paul is here considering what belonged peculiarly to the Law, for although God was at that time working through His Spirit, that did not come about through the ministry of Moses but through the grace of Christ, as is said in John 1:17, "The law was given by Moses but grace and truth by Jesus Christ." Certainly God's grace was not inactive all that time, but it is sufficient for this comparison that it was not the peculiar blessing of the Law. For Moses fulfilled his office when he had delivered the doctrine of life with its added promises and threats. That is why he calls the Law the letter because it is in itself dead preaching, but he calls the Gospel Spirit because its ministry is living and indeed life-giving. My second answer is that these things are not affirmed absolutely of the Law or of the Gospel, but only insofar as the one is contrasted with the other, for even the Gospel is not always Spirit. But when the two are being compared, it is true and proper to affirm that it is of the nature of the Law to teach men literally so as not to penetrate beyond

91. *Comm.* on Ps. 19:7 f.; cf. *Comm.* on Rom. 5:20; *Comm.* on Rom. 8:15; *Comm.* on Gal. 3:19; *Inst.*, II.xi.7; etc.

92. *Comm.* on II Cor. 3:6.

their ears but it is of the nature of the Gospel to teach them spiritually because it is the instrument of Christ's grace.[93]

Calvin sharpens this antithesis between law and gospel when he considers the description of the law in verse 7 as the "dispensation of death." After analyzing various aspects of the comparison, he says:

> We must now examine briefly these attributes of Law and Gospel, bearing in mind that he is not speaking of the whole doctrine contained in the Law and the prophets nor of what happened to the fathers under the old testament but is taking note only of what belongs peculiarly to the ministration of Moses. The Law was engraved on stones and thus it was literal teaching. This defect had to be corrected by the Gospel, since the Law was bound to be transitory *(fragilis)* as long as it was consigned only to tablets of stone. Thus the Gospel is a holy and inviolable covenant because it was promulgated under the guarantee of the Spirit of God. From this it follows that the Law was a ministration of condemnation and death, for when men are taught of their duty and are told that all who do not satisfy God's righteousness are accursed, they are convicted and found guilty of sin and death. Thus from the Law they receive nothing but this condemnation for there God demands what is due to Him, and yet gives no power to perform it. But by the Gospel men are regenerated and reconciled to God by the free remission of their sins, so that it is the ministration of righteousness and so of life.[94]

After acknowledging that even the gospel, like the law, can be "a fragrance of death unto death" (II Cor. 2:16), Calvin affirms that in a sense the function of a "dispensation of death" is only "accidental" to the law, arising not because of any defect in the law, but because of our sins. Yet Paul calls the law, not the gospel, the dispensation of death. The reason for this fact Calvin explains as follows:

> For although the Gospel is an occasion of death to many, it is still rightly called the doctrine of life because it is the means of regeneration and freely offers reconciliation with God. But because the Law only prescribes a rule for good living without reforming men's hearts into the obedience of righteousness and threatens transgressors with everlasting death, it can do nothing but condemn. Or, to put it another way, it is the function of the Law to show us the disease without offering any hope of cure, and it is the function of the Gospel to provide the remedy for those in despair. Since the Law abandons a man to himself it consigns him to inevitable death, while the Gospel leads him to Christ and thus opens the gates of life. To kill is thus a perpetual and inevitable accident *(accidens)* of the Law for, as the apostle says elsewhere, "All that remain under the Law are subject to

93. Ibid.          94. *Comm.* on II Cor. 3:7.

its curse" (Gal. 3:10), but the Gospel does not always kill for in it "is revealed the righteousness of God from faith to faith" and therefore it is "the power of God unto salvation to everyone that believeth" (Rom. 1:16-17).[95]

Furthermore, Calvin observes that Paul, in speaking of the temporary character of the law, was not referring simply to the ceremonial law. "I for my part," says Calvin, "take the abolition of the Law which is in question here, to apply to the whole of the old testament insofar as it is opposed to the Gospel, so as to agree with the statement that the Law and the prophets are until John [Matt. 11:13], for that is what the context requires."[96]

We have quoted extensively from Calvin's commentary on II Corinthians 3:6 and following in order to get something of the flavor of this important section. It is clear that Calvin had a very penetrating view of the condemning and killing function of the law. Many other passages from his commentaries could also be cited;[97] but for the purposes of this article, only one more will be given.

In Galatians 2:19, Paul says: "I through the law died to the law, that I might live unto God." Calvin sees here also a sharp contrast between the law in the narrower sense and Christ:

> *To die to the law* is to renounce it and to be freed from its dominion, so that we have no confidence in it and it does not hold us captive under the yoke of slavery. Or it might mean that, as it gives us all up to destruction, we find no life in it. This latter view fits in better. For he denies that Christ is the author of evil, because the law is more hurtful than helpful. The law bears within itself the curse which slays us. Hence it follows that the death brought about by the law is truly deadly. With it is contrasted another kind of death, in the life-giving fellowship of the cross of Christ. He says that he is crucified along with Christ that he might begin to live.[98]

Arising out of the antithesis between law as "letter" and the gospel as "Spirit," is the related antithesis of the "bondage" of the law and

95. Ibid. Note that the law is death-dealing only "accidentally," that is, in relationship to man's sin (cf. also *Comm.* on Acts 7:38). But because man after the Fall is sinner, "to kill is thus a *perpetual and inevitable accident* of the Law." For this idea further, see W. Krusche, *Das Wirken des Heiligen Geistes nach Calvin*, pp. 196 ff. Calvin often sees the correlation between the nature of law and the nature of man. This is important to keep in mind also in connection with the third use of the law—for the law can function positively only in the lives of those who have been justified and sanctified. On this see R. Sundquist, *The Third Use of the Law*, pp. 169 ff.

96. *Comm.* on II Cor. 3:7.

97. Cf. *Comm.* on Ps. 19:7 f.; *Comm.* on John 1:17; *Comm.* Acts 7:38; *Comm.* on Rom. 4:15; *Comm.* on Rom. 5:20; *Comm.* on I Cor. 15:56; *Comm.* on Gal. 3:19; and *Comm.* on Heb. 9:15.

98. *Comm.* on Gal. 2:19; cf. *Comm.* on Rom. 7:4-6.

the "freedom" of the gospel. This distinction is elaborated in Calvin's remarks on Romans 8:15: "For you did not receive the spirit of slavery [or, 'bondage'] to fall back into fear, but you have received the spirit of sonship [or, 'adoption']." Calvin sees here clearly a comparison between law and gospel:

> In order to make this more clear, Paul states that there are two spirits. One he calls *the spirit of bondage,* which we are able to derive from the law; and the other, *the spirit of adoption,* which proceeds from the Gospel. The first, he states, was formerly given to produce fear; the other is given now to afford assurance. The certainty of our salvation, which he wishes to confirm, appears, as we see, with greater clarity from such a comparison of opposites.[99]

Calvin sees the same antithesis expressed in Hebrews 12:18 and following. He also notes that this text raises the question whether the Spirit of adoption was completely absent under the old covenant. This he denies. He supports his argument from the fact that Paul makes this deliberate contrast because of the false apostles of the law. He then explains how Paul could make such a sharp contrast:

> Although the covenant of grace is contained in the law, yet Paul removes it from there, for in opposing Gospel to the law he regards only what was peculiar to the law itself, viz., command and prohibition, and the restraining of transgressors by the threat of death. He assigns to the law its own quality, by which it differs from the Gospel.... Finally, the law, considered in itself, can do nothing but bind those who are subject to its wretched bondage by the horror of death as well, for it promises no blessing except on condition, and pronounces death on all transgressors. As, therefore, under the law there was the spirit of bondage which oppressed the conscience with fear, so under the Gospel there is the spirit of adoption, which gladdens our souls with the testimony of our salvation.[100]

Much more could be cited from Calvin's works on the antithesis of law and gospel.[101] Here we must yet raise the question as to what is the crucial distinction between law in the narrower sense and the gospel. What is the focal point of the antithesis that explains how the law becomes the letter that condemns and kills and brings people into the bondage of fear?

99. *Comm.* on Rom. 8:15; cf. *Inst.,* II.xi.9,10.

100. *Comm.* on Rom. 8:15. For further references on the antithesis of "bondage" and "freedom," cf. *Comm.* on Rom. 6:14; *Comm.* on Rom. 7:4-6; and *Comm.* on Gal. 5:1, 18.

101. See the summary in Hesselink, *Calvin's Concept and Use of the Law,* chap. 7, pp. 54 ff. On the idea of the gospel relieving us from the rigor of the law, see John H. Leith, "Creation and Redemption: Law and Gospel in the Theology of John Calvin," *Marburg Revisited,* pp. 149 f.

Calvin's answer is: "*The contradiction between law and faith lies
in the cause of justification. You will more easily unite fire and water
than reconcile the two statements that men are justified by faith and
by the law. The law is not of faith, that is, it has a method of justifying a man which is completely foreign to faith.*"[102] The reference to
the law's "method of justifying" recalls Calvin's distinction between
"legal promises" and "evangelical promises." He says: "I call
'promises of the law' not those sprinkled everywhere in the books
of Moses, since in them many evangelical promises also occur, but
those properly pertaining to the ministry of the law. Promises of this
sort, by whatever name you wish to call them, declare there is recompense ready for you if you do what they enjoin."[103] Since sinful man
cannot do what the law enjoins,[104] this bare law, "considered in
itself, can do nothing but bind those who are subject to its wretched
bondage by the horror of death as well, for it promises no blessing
except on condition, and pronounces death on all transgressors."[105]

So the two contrary ways of achieving righteousness are the central
focus of the antithesis between law and gospel: the one way by works,
the other by faith. This is the same as saying that there are two kinds
of promises, one legal and the other evangelical. At this point the
antithesis is at its sharpest, like that of fire and water.

It must be remembered, of course, that this way of achieving
righteousness is not true of the "whole law" or the "universal office"
of Moses. In his universal office, Moses was also a preacher of the
gospel: "The universal office which Moses had was the instruction
of the people in the true rule of godliness. If this is true, it was his
duty to preach repentance and faith. But faith is not taught without
offering the promises, the free promises of divine mercy."[106] As a
preacher of both repentance and faith, Moses was a preacher of
the gospel according to his universal office. But Moses had also
a "peculiar office" entrusted to him: "The function, therefore,
of teaching the character of true righteousness of works is, with
justification, properly and peculiarly attributed to Moses, as is also
the functioning of showing the nature of the remuneration which
await those who observe it, and what punishment awaits those
who transgress it.... Whenever the word *law* is used in this re-

102. *Comm.* on Gal. 3:12 (italics added).

103. *Inst.,* III.xvii.6.

104. See the extensive argument on man's inability to keep the law, in *Comm.* on
Gal. 3:10.

105. *Comm.* on Rom. 8:15.

106. *Comm.* on Rom. 10:5.

stricted sense, Moses is implicitly contrasted with Christ."[107] Note well that Calvin argues that this peculiar ministry of teaching true righteousness of works is "properly" and "with justification" attributed to Moses by Paul. The teachings of the false apostles were the *occasion* for Paul to contrast so sharply the law and the gospel. But he set up this opposition with justification.

This distinction, on the one hand, of the universal office of Moses and the total law and, on the other, of the peculiar office of Moses and the narrow or bare law, creates sharp tension within the ministry of Moses and, in turn, between law and gospel. Yet, for Calvin, this tension must be seen *within* the context of the unity of the two covenants, with their unity of substance and difference of form.

It is precisely in this tension of continuity between law and gospel and yet the radical newness of the gospel over against law that we find the closest parallel to Paul's teaching. Paul, as we noted earlier, characteristically views law as *demand,* a demand for perfect obedience, which, if given, would issue into life (Rom. 7:10). If, however, the law is not fully obeyed, a person can only experience its wrath and its curse (Rom. 4:15; Gal. 3:10). When Paul sharply contrasts law and promise, as he does especially in Galatians 3 and Romans 3 and 4, he presents them as two "totalities," each with a life of its own. Each operates with a sort of "internal autonomy." Strictly speaking, the "promise" operates according to the principle of free grace, eliciting and calling for the response of faith. Strictly speaking, the law, when considered as *demand,* operates on the principle of rigidly requiring all of that which it demands, calling for the response of works. If a man keeps the demands, he will live; if he fails to keep them, he is under the law's judgment and curse. This is not simply "Jewish perversion of the law," but, as Galatians 3:15-21 shows, this is the very character of law itself, when considered as demand.[108] The antithesis in Paul that is involved in the law-gospel motif centers in this definition of promise and law.[109] Thus when Calvin is seen developing this creative tension between law in the narrower sense and the gospel, yet within the context of the basic unity of law (in the broader sense) and gospel, he may be seen as a faithful interpreter of the Pauline kerygma.

Before leaving this section, we must raise a final question. Has

107. Ibid. For the contrast of the "whole office" of Moses and his "peculiar office," see also *Comm. Harm. Pent.* on Exod. 19:1 and *Comm.* on II Cor. 3:6 f.

108. Cf. A. J. Bandstra, *The Law and the Elements of the World,* pp. 119 f.

109. For a summary of these distinctions in Paul, see E. Schlink, "Gesetz und Paraklese," *Antwort,* in honor of Karl Barth (Zollikon-Zürich: Evangelischer Verlag, 1956), pp. 324 ff.

Calvin integrated this idea of the antithesis of law and gospel in a significant way into his total teaching on the law? This is a perplexing and complex question. It must be admitted, it would seem, that this aspect is not clearly enough represented in his discussion of the law in the *Institutes* II.vii-xi. For what in the commentaries comes out as "antithesis" or as "opposition" of law and gospel, in the *Institutes* II.xi tends to dissolve into a series of "differences" or "distinctions." Therefore if one limited his research simply to the *Institutes*, the idea of the antithesis of law and gospel would not clearly emerge. This lack of clarity can be illustrated from the judgment made by Helmut Thielicke. Limiting his warrant to the *Institutes*, he can, with some justification, say:

> The Law-Gospel antithesis [in Calvin] is thus to be understood as being quite relative, not unconditional. Only "by way of comparison"*[per comparationem]* is it presented in the extreme form of death and life; for only thus can the Gospel's full "plenitude of grace" *[affluentia gratiae]* in "comparison" with the Law be shown. The Law is therefore related to the Gospel as partial grace is related to total grace. What was once a distinction has now become a mere "difference": the contradiction has become a mere dissimilarity *[dissimilitude]*. The qualitative relation is now a quantitative one: perspicuous, calculable, and teleologically determined.[110]

Thus Calvin himself may have to shoulder some of the blame for the fact that his views on law and gospel have often been only partially presented. His position on law and gospel has been presented most frequently only under the two rubrics of unity of substance and difference of form. The rubric of antithesis of letter and Spirit has hardly received a hearing; no doubt this is in part due to the fact that this aspect is not so clearly represented in the *Institutes*.[111]

On the other hand, the *Institutes*, no matter how important, do not represent Calvin's total view. Calvin the exegete is as important as Calvin the theologian. Surely the commentary materials need to be taken seriously in attempting to assess the whole of Calvin's view on the law-gospel motif. When this is done, it is clear that the antithesis of law and gospel, properly defined, is a necessary and important part of his total perspective.

The law-gospel question is a matter of continuing importance for understanding the Christian faith and life. The proper understanding of this question continues to be a source of debate between Calvinists

110. *Theological Ethics*, I, pp. 122 f.

111. The idea is present in *Inst.* II.xi, but in muted form. The sharp distinction between "legal" and "evangelical" promises also appears in *Inst.*, III.xvii.6.

and Lutherans,[112] and even among Lutherans themselves.[113] In the Calvinist-Lutheran debate, Calvin has been represented as not dealing adequately with the Pauline material with its sharp contrast between law and gospel. It is hoped that in some small way this study has shown that Calvin attempted to deal seriously with the Pauline material and has reflected Paul's teaching more clearly and more faithfully than has often been recognized. It should be acknowledged that to speak of Calvin's view on law and gospel only under the two rubrics of unity of substance and difference of form is inadequate. To these a third must be added, with the terms properly defined, namely, the antithesis of law as "letter" and gospel as "Spirit." The recognition of all three aspects of this relationship will tend to enhance Calvin's reputation as a Biblical exegete in general and as a Pauline scholar in particular.[114]

112. Cf. the "Summary Statement" on law and gospel in *Marburg Revisited*, p. 152.

113. Cf. T. H. Rehwaldt, "Is the Law a Guide for Good Works?", *Currents in Theology and Missions* 1 (1974), pp. 3-11.

114. Cf. Hesselink, *Calvin's Concept and Use of the Law*, chap. 3, p. 14, who reminds us that Calvin's "reputation as a biblical exegete resulted first of all from his fame as a Pauline scholar."

*John H. Primus*

CHAPTER **2** CALVIN AND THE

PURITAN SABBATH: A COMPARATIVE STUDY

One of the family quarrels of longest standing within the Reformed tradition involves the fourth commandment in the Decalogue. From Heidelberg and Westminster have come two clearly different understandings of what the Sabbath commandment means for the Christian community today. The Heidelberg Catechism asks in Question 103, "What is God's will for us in the fourth commandment?" The authors give this answer:

> First, that the gospel ministry and education for it be maintained, and that, especially on the festive day of rest, I regularly attend the assembly of God's people to learn what God's Word teaches, to participate in the sacraments, to pray to God publicly, and to bring Christian offerings for the poor. Second, that every day of my life I rest from my evil ways, let the Lord work in me through his Spirit, and so begin already in this life the eternal Sabbath.[1]

Eighty-five years later the Westminster divines spoke about the fourth commandment not only at much greater length, but with much different content.

> As it is the law of nature, that, in general, a due proportion of time be set apart for the worship of God; so, in His Word, by a positive, moral, and perpetual commandment binding all men, in all ages, He hath particularly appointed one day in seven, for a Sabbath, to be kept holy unto Him: which, from the beginning of the world to the resurrection of Christ, was the last day of the week; and, from the resurrection of Christ, was changed into the first day of the week, which, in Scripture, is called the Lord's Day, and is to be continued to the end of the world, as the Christian Sabbath.

---

1. From the new translation adopted by the Synod of the Christian Reformed Church in 1975.

This Sabbath is then kept holy unto the Lord, when men, after a due preparing of their hearts, and ordering of their common affairs beforehand, do not only observe an holy rest, all the day, from their own works, words and thoughts about their worldly employments and recreations, but also are taken up, the whole time, in the public and private exercises of His worship, and in the duties of necessity and mercy.[2]

The quarrel, at least in recent times, has been a relatively friendly one. Rarely has the disagreement broken out into open conflict, but once in a while there is evidence that the old struggle is still there between the continental and English Reformed traditions, just smoldering under the surface, and producing some tension. In fact, because the old dispute continues to smolder there has been a recent call for a "basic rethinking" of the whole matter.[3]

This essay constitutes a response to that call. It arises out of the conviction that the rethinking should include a careful examination of the sources to which the Westminster and Heidelberg views of the Sabbath can be traced: to the Puritans and to John Calvin respectively. On this issue, an excellent representative of the early Puritans is Nicholas Bound,[4] the author of the first extensive Puritan interpretation of the Sabbath commandment. The matter becomes complicated somewhat by the fact that Nicholas Bound was acquainted with the writings of Calvin, surely regarded himself as a follower of Calvin, and even appealed to Calvin for support of some of his views on the Sabbath. Nevertheless, the intent of this essay is to compare the full Sabbath positions of John Calvin and Nicholas Bound, not only for the purpose of discovering whether Bound's appeal to Calvin was justified, but also with the hope that the comparison of these two early sources will add to our understanding of the differences between the Heidelberg and Westminster Sabbath traditions. Perhaps this analysis of the two positions will also correct some misapprehensions of what the Puritans and John Calvin believed concerning the Sabbath commandment.

John Calvin needs no introduction. Nicholas Bound does. Nicholas Bound was born into a physician's family and was educated at Cambridge where he received his B.A. in 1571, his M.A. in 1575, and his D.D. in 1594. He was a Puritan of the nonseparatist variety, and spent most of his professional career as a Church

2. *The Westminster Confession of Faith,* chapter XXI, sections vii and viii.

3. John H. Stek, "The Fourth Commandment: A New Look," *Reformed Journal* 22 (July-Aug. 1972): 26-29; 22 (Nov. 1972): 20-24; 23 (Jan. 1973); 18-22. Cf. Paul Jewett, *The Lord's Day* (Grand Rapids: Eerdmans, 1971).

4. Other common spellings are "Bownd" and "Bownde." For a brief account of Bound's life see the *Dictionary of National Biography.*

of England clergyman in the rectory of Norton in Suffolk where he was installed in 1585. In 1611 he became minister of the church of St. Andrew the Apostle at Norwich, and died there in December of 1613. There was a deep and abiding concern about the Sabbath in his family. His stepfather was Richard Greenham, whose Sabbath position strongly influenced Bound's interpretation.[5] And Bound's brother-in-law was John Dod, who, subsequent to Bound's first book on the Sabbath, published a highly popular (among the Puritans) treatise on the Ten Commandments,[6] and who gained a reputation as an arch-Sabbatarian.

Among Nicholas Bound's several treatises, none became more famous than his two books on the Sabbath, the first written in 1595, with an expanded edition appearing in 1606.[7] The importance of these works has been described in several ways. Thomas Fuller claims with enthusiasm that the revival of a strict keeping of the Sabbath in England traces to Bound's books.[8] The accuracy of that observation is difficult to assess, but it should be noted that Bound was not the first to raise the Sabbath issue. Sabbath theology and Sabbath ethics were subjects of intensive debate at Cambridge throughout the 1580s.[9] It is probably more accurate then to say that Bound's works provided "a focus point at which were concentrated tendencies which had been developing for many years and from which started a very keen controversy."[10]

The importance with which Bound's books were regarded is also evident in the opposition they aroused. None other than Archbishop Whitgift attempted to have Bound's first book suppressed after its publication in 1595.[11] And in his preface to the 1606 edition,

5. In the preface to his first volume on the Sabbath, Bound refers to an earlier attempt by Greenham to publish something on the Sabbath but he died before it was finished.

6. *A Treatise or Exposition upon the Ten Commandments* (s.l., 1603). Nineteen editions of this treatise were published by 1635. Dod coauthored it with Robert Cleaver.

7. *The Doctrine of the Sabbath* (London: Orwin for Porter and Man, 1595). *Sabbathum Veteris et Novi Testamenti* (London: Kyngston for Man and Porter, 1606). Hereafter the two volumes will be identified in the footnotes as *Doctrine* and *Sabbathum* respectively.

8. *The Church History of Britain* (London: Thomas Tegg, 1837), III: 159.

9. W. B. Whitaker, *Sunday in Tudor and Stuart Times* (London: Houghton, 1933), pp. 54 ff. Lancelot Andrewes was lecturing on his Sabbatarian position to large audiences at Cambridge in the early 1580s. Cf. M. M. Knappen, *Tudor Puritanism* (Chicago: University Press, 1939), p. 449.

10. Whitaker, *Sunday... Times*, p. 66.

11. Knappen, *Tudor Puritanism*, p. 450.

Bound refers to his earlier, aborted attempt to prepare an expanded and revised version. He states that he had prepared such an edition in 1597 and sent it to the printer, only to have it confiscated there by the opposition. He does not identify the culprits. Finally after requests from others "both often and many" he wrote the edition of 1606 in spite of the lamentable fact that "all my former papers were lost."[12]

Difference over the Sabbath issue, after the publication of Bound's first work, became the most visible mark of distinction between the two parties in English Protestantism, the Puritans and Anglicans.[13] The Sabbath dispute took the place earlier occupied by the dispute over vestments and other ceremonies, and by the "Presbyterian" issue. By the turn of the century, Sabbatarianism had become the badge of Puritanism. One early Puritan, Edmund Calamy, spoke of a minister who "carry'd Puritanism in his very Name." And who was this minister? Sabbath Clark![14]

Nicholas Bound's claim to fame lies in the publication of his two books on the Sabbath. He was the first to publish the position that has come to be known as Puritan Sabbatarianism. His books stand as a monumental endeavor to provide a theoretical basis on which to build a stricter Sabbath practice. Christopher Hill is probably too cynical when he says that "it was the habit of the age to find Biblical texts to justify men in doing what they would have done even if no texts could be found,"[15] but it is true that Bound struck a highly responsive chord. His works served to crystallize the thought of an expanding group of Sabbatarians. He provided just what they needed: an authoritative statement, based on divine command, for strict Sunday observance. His works offered theological leverage for scrupulous Sabbath keeping. And, astonishingly, Sabbatarianism underwent no further development after Bound completed his prodigious works. It sprang, full-blown, from his pen. Literally dozens of works were written on the Sabbath in the fifty years following the publication of Bound's first book, but they added virtually nothing. Taken together, his books were the classic and original treatment, the Puritan *magnum opus* on the Sabbath. In

12. *Sabbathum*, p. A3.

13. M. M. Knappen calls the Sabbath controversy "the first doctrinal dispute between the Puritans and the high-church party in the English protestant church" (*Tudor Puritanism*, p. 442).

14. Cited by G. Nuttal, *The Beginnings of Non-Conformity* (London: J. Clarke and Co., 1964).

15. *Society and Puritanism in Pre-Revolutionary England* (London: Secker and Warburg, 1964), p. 167.

sheer length of treatment, he overwhelmed all of the competition—
286 pages in the first edition, and a staggering 459 pages on the
fourth commandment in the second! Only a Sabbatarian could write
that much on the Sabbath.

For the purposes of this essay "Sabbatarianism" should be understood as a term with both theological and ethical implications.[16]
Bound fully develops both: a Sabbatarian theology and a Sabbatarian ethics.

## Bound's Sabbatarian theology

Two theological positions relative to the Sabbath commandment are articulated by Bound, and they became from then on
the hallmarks of Sabbatarian theology. First, the Sabbath is rooted
in Creation and therefore antedates both the Fall and the Mosaic
Law. The fourth commandment, no less than the other commandments, is a creation ordinance. It is a natural, perpetual,
moral law binding on all mankind, not a ceremonial law binding
only on Old Testament Israel. This means, furthermore, that the
Christian observance of the Lord's Day is not simply a practical
regulation established by the church, but is an observance that is
based directly and immediately on the fourth commandment in the
Mosaic Law, which traces, in turn, to Creation itself.

The second theological position concerns the shift of the day of
rest and worship from the Jewish seventh day to the Christian first
day. The Sabbatarian view spelled out by Bound is that the substitution of Sunday for the Sabbath is based not simply on an early,
somewhat arbitrary, ecclesiastical decision, but is based on divine
authority which came ultimately from Christ Himself and was
transmitted through His apostles. The first day of the week, moreover, is distinctive from and superior to the other days, and no
other day may be substituted out of convenience for the church.
The Sabbath—first the Jewish and now the Christian Sabbath—
is sanctified by God.

Before explicating these two positions, Bound, by way of introduction, proclaims the fourth commandment as the key commandment in the whole Decalogue, "for in the practice of it, consisteth the
practice of all the other, and in the neglect of it is the neglect of
all religion."[17] The fourth commandment stands out among the com-

---

16. For a working definition of Sabbatarianism see Patrick Collinson, "The Beginnings of English Sabbatarianism," *Studies in Church History* (London: Nelson,
1964), pp. 207-8.

17. *Doctrine*, pp. 1, 2.

mandments in four ways. First, it begins with "remember" or "observe," whereas all the other commandments simply command this or forbid that. Second, in all the other laws God forbids the sins and assumes the virtue. In the fourth commandment He both commands the good and forbids the evil—"in it do no work." Third, the Sabbath commandment has more reasons affixed for keeping it "because our nature is most against the observation of it."[18] In the whole second table of the law no reasons are attached to the commands because in them "our nature is not so corrupt, as having the light of it shining more cleerely within us...." But with regard to the first table of the law we "are as blind as beetles."[19] To commend the excellency of the fourth commandment, three reasons are attached to it: the appeal to the six days of labor, to God's creation example, and to God's sanctification of this day. Bound's Sabbatarianism begins to emerge when he says, "God hath bestowed an especiall blessing upon this day distinct from the rest."[20] The fourth way in which the Sabbath commandment stands out in excellence above the rest of the Decalogue is found in its unique concern with others in our charge—beasts of burden, servants, and strangers.

The first premise of Sabbatarian theology is that the fourth commandment is rooted in Creation. Like the other commandments, therefore, the Sabbath commandment is a natural, universal law. The commandment against desecrating the Sabbath has the same kind of moral significance and is as universally applicable as the commandments against stealing and killing.

With regard to this premise Bound is unequivocally clear. Sabbath keeping is traced to Adam. "Adam and his posteritie, if they had continued in their first righteous estate, should have kept that day holie above the rest."[21] He states it even more boldly in the 1606 edition, where he makes the astonishing claim that the fourth commandment "was first delivered by lively voyce, namely to Adam and Eve in Paradise."[22] The other nine commandments were naturally engraved on the heart of man, but the fourth commandment came by the express word of God. This commandment, therefore, "hath so much antiquitie, as the seventh day hath being: for so soone as the day was, so soone was it sanctified... and as it was in the beginning of the world, so it must continue to the ending of the same."[23] Bound only very reluctantly disagrees with the posi-

18. Ibid., p. 2.
19. Ibid.
20. Ibid., p. 4.
21. Ibid., p. 5.
22. *Sabbathum*, p. 11.
23. *Doctrine*, p. 6.

tion that "this commandment should be placed first in the Decalogue, because it is most ancient, and was first given out in
expresse words."[24] And he quotes Hieronymus Zanchius approvingly who opines that when God created the seventh day, "the
Sonne of God taking upon him the shape of man, was occupied
that whole seventh day in most holy colloquies with Adam . . . instructing our first parents, and in exercising them in the worship
of God . . . ."[25]

In Bound's view, therefore, the fourth commandment is "naturall,
morall, and perpetuall,"[26] and he offers as evidence the fact that
even the Gentiles who were without the law kept some days holy.
The law of the Sabbath is etched on the heart of man, and since
the Sabbath is part of the natural creation order it must be universally
observed. To ensure that it is, Bound demands that this command,
no less than any of the others, must be incorporated into the laws
of the land. Both rulers of commonwealths and heads of households
must make provisions for the "rest" that this commandment requires.

> Therefore it behoveth al Princes and Magistrates, that be in
> highest authoritie, to provide that lawes bee enacted for the
> preservation of this rest, with civill punishments to be inflicted
> upon them that shall break it . . . .[27]

Later he argues that all citizens must be "compelled to sanctifie"[28]
the Lord's Day, a demand that seems quite clearly impossible to
fulfill.

The fourth commandment is so fully moral and perpetual that it
should not be regarded as even partly ceremonial, according to
Bound. Just as man cannot be man and beast at the same time,
so a commandment cannot be both moral and ceremonial at the
same time. Bound is concerned that if the fourth commandment is
regarded as even partly ceremonial, mankind will feel less bound
to it. But we are bound to it today as certainly as ancient Israel
was. Today we "are as precisely to rest as the Jews were."[29]

The second theological pillar of Sabbatarianism concerns the
specific day appointed and sanctified by God to be the day of rest
and worship. In a long and involved discussion of this matter,
Bound begins by stressing the absolute character of the seventh day
in the Old Testament. It was *the seventh day* on which God rested;
it was *the seventh day* which God sanctified. The pope has sancti-

24. *Sabbathum*, pp. 7, 8.

25. Ibid., pp. 19, 20.

26. *Doctrine*, p. 7.

27. Ibid., p. 94.

28. Ibid., p. 260.

29. *Sabbathum*, p. 248.

fied the other "holy days" but God Himself sanctified this one.[30]

Bound's argument about the seventh day is so emphatic that one wonders how he can go on to justify the shift from the seventh to the first day in the Christian tradition. His insistence on the absolute uniqueness of the seventh day very nearly traps him, but that insistence is to be explained by Bound's concern to make Christian Sabbath keeping a direct and immediate response to the fourth commandment. He glorifies the seventh day of the fourth commandment because he believes it comprehends not only the Jewish Sabbath, but also the Christian Lord's Day. He makes this position explicit when he declares that the fourth commandment includes both the Jewish Sabbath and the Lord's Day "as genus comprehendeth both his species."[31]

Bound's explanation of the shift to the first day of the week as the day of rest and worship is not simple. It takes fifteen pages of intricate argument, and the paragraph that opens the discussion reveals the sleight of hand necessary for Bound to make his case.

> But now concerning this very speciall *seventh day,* that now we keepe in the time of the Gospell, that is well knowne, that it is not the same, as it was from the beginning which God himselfe did sanctifie, and whereof hee speaketh in this Commandment, for it was the day going before ours, which in latine retaineth his ancient name, and is called the *Sabbath,* which we also grant, but so that we confesse, it must alwaies remaine, never to be changed anymore, and that all men must keepe holie this seventh day, and none other, which was unto them not *the seventh,* but the first day of the weeke, as it is so called many times in the new testament, and so it still standeth in force, that we are bound unto *the seventh day,* though not unto that very seventh.[32]

Apparently Bound is using "seventh day" in two senses here, first in the sense of the seventh day of the week or Saturday, and second in the sense of "every seventh day" which could be any day of the week but which Bound goes on to tie down specifically to Sunday.

It is the practice of the apostles that provides the foundation for Bound's argument concerning the shift to the first day of the week. Using typical Puritan Biblical methodology, Bound argues that not only the apostolic word, but apostolic practice is normative and binding. For it is practice that resulted either from the direct command of Christ, or from the work of the Holy Spirit within them.

30. *Doctrine,* p. 32.
31. *Sabbathum,* p. 71.
32. *Doctrine,* p. 35.

And as we doe not dispute of the authoritie and credite of their writings, which wee know not to have proceeded from the spirite of man, so wee doe not call into question the lawfulness of this change, which wee see in their writings allowed, and by themselves commended unto us in the same.[33]

Since the apostle John in Revelation 1:10 calls Sunday the Lord's Day, we know with certainty that the day has been authoritatively changed. This change is analogous to several other Old to New Testament shifts: from priest to apostle, sacrifice of animals to sacrifice of self, sacrament of Passover to Lord's Supper, and circumcision to baptism. Similarly, the Sabbath was changed from the last day of the week to the first.

The apostolic choice of the first day was determined by the resurrection event on that day. Because the first day of the week was the day of the Lord's resurrection, the climax and end of the Lord's work of redemption, and the fulfillment of all the ceremonies of the Jews, the apostles "were directed by the ... Spirite advisedly to chuse *this day* (which we now keepe, and must keepe to the end of the world)...."[34] Then still more boldly Bound declares that "not so much the Apostles, as Christ himselfe brought in this chaunge, and was the author of this day."[35] The first day of the week, therefore, must be recognized as "ordained by speciall advice, and none but *this day* could be chosen to be the Sabbath and day of Rest, in which Christ Jesus the Creator of the new world, rested from his work of the new creation...."[36] Consequently, to observe this day becomes a witness to "all Turkes, Infidels, Paynims and Atheists in the world,"[37] that we serve Jesus Christ.

That the church has discretionary power to name some other day as the day of worship is unthinkable for Bound. The day must not be changed "unto the ende of the world," and "it must not so much as enter into men's thoughts to goe about to change it."[38] To change the Christian day of rest and worship and "to keep it upon Munday, Tuesday, or any other day, the Church hath no authoritie; for it is not a matter of indifferencie, but a necessarie prescription of Christ himselfe...."[39]

The name "Lord's Day" must always be used for it gives added stature to the day. It "breeds reverence" for the day and "maketh the day more highly to be esteemed."[40] In fact, the name "Sunday" should be abandoned, for by origin that name is heathenish and

33. Ibid., p. 39.

34. Ibid., p. 42.

35. Ibid., p. 44.

36. Ibid., pp. 45, 46.

37. Ibid., p. 46.

38. Ibid., p. 47.

39. *Sabbathum*, p. 67.

40. *Doctrine*, p. 48.

profane. The name "Sunday" could have been arbitrarily attached to any day of the week, but because of the distinctiveness and uniqueness of the first day of the week, that day alone can be called the Lord's Day, "for as by it can bee ment no other day, but that which wee keepe for our Sabbath, so the name cannot be imparted to any other day without sacriledge."[41] Given this strong emphasis, it is curious that Bound throughout both of his works refers to the Christian day of worship as "the Sabbath" more frequently than as "the Lord's Day."

Bound states unabashedly that the Lord's Day is holy in a way in which the other days are not. He simply takes the literal sense of the fourth commandment and applies it to the Christian Sabbath. In what hardly seems to be consistent with a Puritan-Protestant approach to the sacraments, Bound argues that everything used in the service of God is sanctified and made distinctive—such as the water of baptism and the bread and wine of the Lord's Supper. God has sanctified these elements in such a way that He "made them so wholly to differ from all other, as though they were not of the same nature and kinde, and so, from that they were before, as though they were not the same anymore."[42] Similarly, the Sabbath has been sanctified so that it becomes a unique day among the days. It is a holy day, the one holy day that remains in the Christian era. Bound equivocates on the nature of this holiness, stating in one place that its holiness consists in being set apart for special use rather than in being "indued with any holy qualitie or holines more than the other daies";[43] and in another place quoting Junius with approval, that "besides the common blessing, which it had with the other daies, by the law of nature, it had a speciall blessing of holinesse."[44] The Sabbath comes very close to being a third sacrament in Bound's view:

> Wee should acknowledge it to be the singular mercy of God towards us in Christ Jesus, that hee hath given us his Sabbath, given them to us (I say) who when wee were plunged in the bottomlesse pit of all miserie, and there pressed downe with the weight of our owne sins, had no meanes to be raysed out of it againe (as frome the dead) saving his holy word, and blessed Sacraments . . . hath together with them given us his Sabbaths, that upon them we being so fully and altogether occupied in these meanes as we should be, (and as we cannot bee in the other daies, because of our callings) might through the blessing of God be made partakers of him, who was made of God the father for us wisedome, righteousnes, holines and redemption, and so be saved by him.[45]

41. Ibid., pp. 48, 49.    42. Ibid., p. 151.    43. *Sabbathum*, p. 292.
44. Ibid., p. 16.    45. *Doctrine*, p. 17.

Nicholas Bound, in his Biblical analysis of the Sabbath, clearly enunciates the two central pillars of Sabbatarian theology: the creation origin of the Sabbath, and the divine institution and sanctification of the first day of the week as the Christian Sabbath.

## Bound's Sabbatarian ethics

Sabbatarianism is a term commonly used to designate a certain style of Sabbath observance as well as a certain theory about the Sabbath. In other words, Sabbatarianism denotes an ethic as well as a theology. Sabbatarianism is "an over-scrupulousness and strictness in the observance of the Sabbath," says one dictionary rather judgmentally.[46] Sabbatarians are "those who are rigid in their interpretation of Sunday observance," says another.[47]

Nicholas Bound does not ignore the practical, ethical implications of his Sabbath theology. Nearly one-half of each book is devoted to rather precise and detailed instructions on how to keep the Sabbath. In addition to this material, Bound deals at length, in the first part of each book, with the command to "rest" and gives an elaborate interpretation of the character and purpose of this rest. This discussion also leads quickly to advice on Sabbatarian practice.

The fourth commandment requires *rest*. Bound emphasizes that this is a literal, physical rest, not a spiritual rest connoting eternal life or redemptive rest from sin and evil. It is a rest that entails cessation from ordinary daily work and play. Yet it is a special rest, different from rest taken at other times. It "must be a most carefull, exact and precise rest."[48] For this rest is never an end in itself. It is only a means to the end of worship. Given their spatial limitations, Christians cannot engage in their ordinary daily pursuits and gather with others for worship at the same time. Human nature is such that we allow our daily affairs to "justle out (as it were) the meditation of God's service . . . ."[49]

Since he does not regard the Sabbath rest as an end in itself, Bound does not at first appear to be excessively legalistic about the nature and extent of that rest. Commenting on Mark 2:27, he says that the fourth commandment does not mean

> that *the rest* upon the Sabbath day should bee so severely required, that for want of things necessarie, man should take hurt thereby, seeing that the Sabbath and day of rest was

46. J. S. Purvis, *Dictionary of Ecclesiastical Terms* (London: Nelson, 1962), p. 172.

47. *Corpus Dictionary of Western Churches* (Washington: Corpus, 1970).

48. *Doctrine*, p. 53.     49. Ibid., p. 13.

ordained by God for the profite and commodities of man, and not for his hindrance . . . .[50]

Bound, in fact, pokes fun at excessive legalism by telling this little story.

> Some English histories make mention of a Jew, who about the yeare of our Lord 1257, fell into a privie at Tukesbury upon a Sabbath day, who for the great reverence he had to his holy Sabbath, would not suffer himselfe to be plucked out: and so Lord Richard Earle of Glocester, hearing of it, would not suffer him to be drawn out upon the Sunday, for reverence of the holie day: and thus the wretched superstitious Jew remaining there till munday, was found dead in the dung.[51]

It is clear from Matthew 12, says Bound, that "certaine workes may be done upon the Sabbath," such as the preparation of necessary food "and the ringing of one bell" to call men to worship (but not the disorderly jangling of many bells).[52] Bound finally provides a convenient catchall, advising that such works are permissible that

> the time present doth necessarily require to be done for our own furtherance, the commoditie of our brethren, or the benefite or preservation of any of the creatures, which cannot be deferred unto another day without loss or hindrance, neither could any waies be provided for before.[53]

Examples of such necessities are warfare; care of the sick; fighting floods, fire, and thieves; care of brute beasts; and, above all, works of mercy toward others since the service of God is designed to make us "more fit to helpe our brethren."[54]

Bound refers very infrequently to Sabbath rest as a fulfillment of man's need for physical rest. But he does include it as a kind of fringe benefit. At one point Bound says that God ordained a day of rest for man's sake, "that he being holpen thereby, and his nature refreshed, might bee made more fit to doe the worke of God, and his owne worke in his calling."[55] At one other point he declares that the Sabbath rest enables mankind "even in the strength of their bodies, to do the works of their calling cheerfully."[56] But it is difficult to demonstrate from Bound's writings that he was very sensitive to the social and economic climate of which Christopher Hill writes when he argues that the changing social setting from a rural to

50. Ibid., p. 27.                                    54. Ibid., p. 110.

51. *Sabbathum*, p. 113.                       55. Ibid., p. 28.

52. *Doctrine*, pp. 103-5.                      56. Ibid., p. 58.

53. Ibid., pp. 106-7.

an industrial economy in the 1590s helped to bring about the Puritan Sabbath in England.[57]
Rather than stressing physical rest, Bound emphasizes that the rest required by the fourth commandment must lead to vigorous activity. God is not pleased with idleness. Bound rebukes those who

> know no other thing to do upon the Sabbath but to rest, and to take their ease, and therefore lye many times at home sleeping, most prophanely, and so their oxe and their asse in ceasing from their worke, keepe as good a Sabbath as they....[58]

Obedience to the fourth commandment requires both rest from "ordinarie workes" and from "honest recreation and lawfull delightes." Farmers must rest even in seedtime and harvest seasons, and village dwellers should not frequent fairs and markets. Everyone must rest. There are no exceptions. Schoolmasters and students, lawyers and clients, and even "the Physitian from the studying of the Anatomie." All people "even from him that sitteth upon the throne to the maid servant that is at the Mill, and the captive that is in prison, must rest from their ordinarie workes...."[59]

The commandment requires that even the animals should rest. There are two reasons for giving beasts of burden a day off, according to Bound. Their rest will enable them better to serve man "for the which purpose they were made in the beginning."[60] Furthermore, when the work animals rest, man will be reminded to rest. The commandment that the "stranger within thy gates" should rest is also for the benefit of the Christian, not the stranger. Its purpose is to remove from the Christian another temptation to work.

Nicholas Bound undoubtedly contributed to the climate that eventually produced King James's famous *Book of Sports* in 1618, for Bound plunges headlong into the debate concerning Sabbath recreation.[61] He affirms that recreation is necessary for human exis-

---

57. Hill argues that economic and political developments in England in the late sixteenth century gave rise to the Puritan Sabbath. Laborers tended to be exploited in the emerging industrial economy and sorely needed a weekly day of rest (*Society and Puritanism*, pp. 152, 153, 208, 209; cf. Whitaker, *Sunday... Times*, pp. 205 ff.).

58. *Doctrine*, p. 169.

59. Ibid., pp. 78-79. This is Bound's only reference to the monarch. Queen Elizabeth was known to be cool toward a rigid Sabbath keeping that precluded all work and recreation (cf. Whitaker, *Sunday... Times*, p. 25).

60. Ibid., p. 85.

61. Christopher Hill makes some interesting observations about recreation's debilitating effect on the Sabbath in Tudor England. He calls opposition to Sunday sport a matter of "political order, security, discipline" (*Society and Puritanism*, p. 202). He gives a graphic account of abuses and excesses accompanying Sunday sports on pp. 183 ff. Hill concludes, "We must be very careful not to sentimentalize ye olde morris dances of Merrie England" (p. 191; cf. Whitaker, *Sunday... Times*, p. 59).

tence "to further us in the workes of our calling,"[62] but it is not absolutely necessary in the sense that eating and drinking are necessary. If rest from daily labor is required on the Sabbath, therefore, then surely rest from recreational pursuits is doubly mandatory. For recreation serves "but *for pleasure,* without the which mankind may continue, though not so well continue."[63] The purpose of rest from recreation is to eliminate another distraction from our basic Sabbath duty—the duty to worship. It is clearly impossible for people to "both be at Church serving God" and "in their houses sporting themselves with their companions"[64] at the same time. Shooting, hunting, hawking, tennis, fencing, and bowling are all mentioned—and forbidden—by Bound. The popular sports of bear-baiting, bullbaiting, and cockfighting are also mentioned, but Bound makes it clear that these are off-limit areas for Christian conduct at all times. At this point his Sabbatarianism leads him to a double standard, for he argues that these sports are more scandalous when indulged in on Sunday than at any other time, for "as it is a sinne to be occupied about them at any time, so a double sinne at this time."[65] Cessation of Sunday recreation must extend to the thought and speech as well as actual practice. The commandments are intended "not onely *to restraine* the hand and the foote, but the *lippes and tongue* also.... "[66] For Bound, speaking and talking about recreation is as distracting from "heavenly meditation" as actual participation.

Bound's Sabbatarian ethics become progressively more detailed as he continues, in the second part of both books, to delineate the specific activities in which the Christian should engage on the Sabbath. The Lord's Day, above all, provides opportunity for public worship. Bound states that "the chiefest poynt of hallowing the Sabbath day, consisteth in comming to God's house...."[67] At the heart of this public worship is the reading, preaching, and hearing of God's Word. The preaching of the word "is the greatest part of God's service."[68] Bound laments the state of preaching in the English churches. He complains about preachers who cannot or even will not preach and charges them with prime responsibility for the desecration of the Sabbath day. Many of them "cannot so much as distinctly reade, so that they may profitably be understood."[69] Others can read but cannot preach, and what good does reading

62. *Doctrine,* p. 131.
63. Ibid.
64. Ibid.
65. Ibid., p. 135.
66. Ibid., p. 137.
67. Ibid., p. 172.
68. Ibid., p. 174.
69. Ibid., p. 190.

do compared with "the endlesse profit that commeth by preach-ing?"[70] Others are very poor preachers, some never study, and some preach only to their own honor and glory. As a result, people neglect the worship service, for "many say, what good shall I get by going to the church? what can I heare there, which I may not heare or read at home?"[71]

In other complaints about deficiencies in the worship services, Bound reveals the chaotic conditions that must have prevailed in the English churches in the late sixteenth century. Puritan Sabbatarian-ism was undoubtedly in part a response to a seriously inadequate worship situation.

The first disorder with which Bound deals concerns a conflict between hunting and worshiping. He warns hunters that proper Sabbath keeping means leaving your bows and arrows and falcons at home. Worshipers should not come to church "with their bowes and arrowes in their hands" nor "with their hawkes upon their fists."[72] Those birds in church, after all, are a little distracting. Bound makes his point by arguing that

> a living creature which is stirring... is more able to hinder the minde from being attentive, than a senselesse creature, or a peece of a sticke, which a man may cast behinde him, or throw where he list.[73]

His response to a falconer's potential objection is based on a sound theology of the Word and sacrament.

> If they themselves would be ashamed to holde them upon their fistes when they should receive the sacrament, upon what ground doe they holde them in the ministerie of the word?[74]

Another contributing factor to disorderly worship was apparently the traffic conditions in church. Bound finds it necessary to insist that the people come on time and remain until the end of the service.

> For all the people, nay the severall housholds come not to-gether, but scattered, and one dropping after another in a con-fused manner: First comes the man, then a quarter of an houre after his wife, and after her, I cannot tell how long, especially the maidservants, who must needes bee as long after her, as the menservants are after him: Whereby it cometh to passe that either halfe the service of God is done before all be met, or else if the minister tarrie till there be a sufficient congregation, the first commers may be wearie, and sometimes cold with tarrying, before the other shall bee warme in their seates.[75]

The problem arose in part because people were very selective about

70. Ibid.

71. Ibid., pp. 190-91.

72. Ibid., p. 132.

73. Ibid.

74. Ibid., p. 133.

75. Ibid., p. 268.

the various elements of the worship service, coming and going at will. Some under pretence of comming to the sermon, tarrie at home a great part of the service, and so neither are they at the confession of sinnes with God's people, nor are made partakers of the prayers of the Church for the forgiveness of their sinnes, neither doe ever heare much of the Scripture read: other under colour of being at all these departe away before the blessing is pronounced upon them, and too many times lose the fruite of all (as Judas did) or else tarie not the ministring of the Sacrament, as though it were a thing impertinent unto them.[76]

To enhance the good order of the worship service, Bound urges that the people "bee present at the whole action."[77]

Additional disorder surrounded the mechanics of almsgiving during the worship service. The picture Bound paints is reminiscent of the money changers in the temple. In many churches, during the worship service, Bound claims that

you shall see men go up and down asking, receiving, changing, and bestowing of money, wherein many times you shall have them so disagree, that they are louder than the minister; and the rest stand looking, and listning unto them, leaving the worship of God (as though it did not concerne them) and thus all is confused.[78]

Consequently, he urges that alms be gathered at "some other time of the day... to bestowe at the end of the service upon the needie...."[79]

In the 1606 edition Bound issues one more complaint about disorder. He warns against the danger of transforming the church into a kennel. He is opposed to anyone bringing dogs to church,

for they are as troublesome to the eares with their mouthes... and more offensive to the eye.... And if one man may be permitted to bring his dogge to the Church, why might not another, and why might not all? And then what a thing were this to have in a place an hundred or two hundred dogs together... and that in time of divine service.[80]

Such worship conditions, described so graphically by Nicholas Bound, must have played some role in the development of a stricter and more orderly Sabbath observance. The need for more discipline was apparent. More order had to be introduced. The total discipline which characterized the Puritan Sabbath must have been an attractive option by which to overcome the disorderly abuses common in that day.[81]

76. Ibid., p. 175.

77. Ibid.

78. Ibid., p. 193.

79. Ibid.

80. *Sabbathum,* pp. 264-65.

81. Cf. especially chapter IV in Whitaker, *Sunday... Times.*

The worship of God is the purpose of the Puritan Sabbath; and while communal worship is regarded by Bound as "the chiefest poynt," Christian worship must extend far beyond the hours for public assembly. God, after all, sanctified the whole day, "not a parcell of it onely."[82] More than a "peece of a day"[83] must be devoted to the service of God. Look at how Achan was punished for taking for himself a part of Jericho's spoils which all belonged to God. Holy things are not to be divided "betwixt him and our selves."[84] The whole day is the Lord's. And that day is a full twenty-four hours, extending from morning to morning. Bound declares that "we must spend the morning, evening, and whole day, yea some part of the night, so farre as our necessarie rest and sleepe will permit us in praising and serving the Lord."[85] He expounds at length on the proper observance of the Lord's Day, apart from the time of communal worship.

First, he recommends that there be private reflection at home in preparation for communal worship. This preparation should include self-examination on how the past week was spent, what sins were committed, what blessings received, and what graces are needed. Prayer is also necessary, especially on behalf of the minister of God's Word. Private reading of Scripture is urged, not only in preparation for communal worship but afterward as well, in order to contemplate at greater length what has been commanded in the sermon. Another requirement is meditation on what was heard in the sermon and read in the Scripture. Bound goes on for seven pages describing the need and great profit in the art of meditation. The godliest men, he says, are not necessarily "the greatest hearers and readers of the Word," but are rather "the greatest musers and meditoours thereon."[86] Another important exercise is discussion with others about what was heard or read in the service, for this will help to fix the Word or the sermon in the memory. Such spiritual exercises lead to a greater thankfulness to God that will extend throughout the rest of the week.

Psalm singing is stressed as another important element in Sabbath activity. The Psalms should be sung at home as well as in church. They are a desirable part of worship because they express so well every man's spiritual condition. Furthermore, they are expressions of joy; and the Sabbath, says Bound, should be above all a day of joy. The "fittest time" for Psalm singing is

82. *Sabbathum*, p. 366.
83. Ibid., p. 369.
84. Ibid.
85. Ibid., p. 374.
86. *Doctrine*, p. 208.

the time of joy, and there is no joy comparable to that which we have in Christ Jesus: and we never injoy that so fully, as by the meanes whereby he conveyeth it unto us, and we never have all the meanes so plentifully, and so continually, as upon the Sabbath.[87]

Bound laments that there is a great neglect of Psalm singing in the land. The "singing of ballades" has become popular and is supplanting Psalm singing in Christian homes!

Bound's view of Sabbath keeping also includes a social emphasis. Works of mercy are to be done especially on the Sabbath, for the whole worship of God is ordained to this end—that we be better equipped to show love to others. We must, therefore, feed the hungry, clothe the naked, lodge the harborless, visit the sick and prisoners. The Lord's Day is "the day of shewing mercy."[88] Bound includes among deeds of mercy, spiritual aid designed to pull the needy "out of hell fire" and to "feede their soules."[89] Showing considerable insight into the human condition, Bound stresses the importance of deliberately going out to *see* the miseries of others in order to stimulate greater compassion. Especially those appointed as overseers of the poor should do this, an apparent reference to the deacons of the church.

> It were a worke therefore meete for them above others, after evening prayer so to divide themselves, that they might walke through the townes where they dwell, and to visite the poore houses, to see what is the number and quality of every such familie; what is their charge and expenses weekly; what is their provision for meate and drinke, and lodging, and firing; what is their greatest earning, that thus by their owne eyes taking knowledge both of the one and of the other, they might accordingly bee moved of conscience to discharge their dutie, both in faithfull and speedily distributing that unto them, which is committed unto them of trust . . . .[90]

Bound concludes his Sabbath exposition with still another admonition to all in authority to enact good laws both publicly in the commonwealth and privately in the homes, compelling all people to sanctify the Sabbath. Sabbath desecration, after all, is the underlying cause for all manner of evil, including rebellious children, disobedient servants, and unfaithful wives.[91] And in a closing reminder of the purpose of the Sabbath, Bound for the first time relates the literal Sabbath to the spiritual, eternal Sabbath of Hebrews 4. The principal end of the Sabbath is that "we might be fashioned

87. Ibid., p. 239.

88. Ibid., p. 247.

89. Ibid., p. 256.

90. *Sabbathum*, p. 445.

91. *Doctrine*, p. 271.

unto the image of God, and begin that Sabbath here, that shall bee for ever continued in heaven."[92]

At the heart of Bound's Sabbath ethic is his conviction that the "rest" required by the fourth commandment is not an end in itself but a means to a day filled with spiritual "work" or activity. That spiritual activity is primarily worship, both public and private, to which the entire Sabbath day must be devoted.

## The Calvin references in Bound's works

Nicholas Bound does not claim originality for his Sabbatarian views. He is most eager to show that they have the support of many saints that have gone before in the Christian tradition. His sense of history and community is strong enough to cause him to appeal to an impressive array of ancient, medieval, and Reformation authorities for support—some forty authorities in all. They include Ambrose, Chrysostom, Cyprian, Ireneus, Augustine, and Aquinas, and such Reformation stalwarts as Beza, Bucer, Calvin, Bullinger, and Peter Martyr. Bound is clearly determined to preclude charges of novelty for his Sabbath views.

In the 1595 edition his most numerous citations come from the works of John Calvin. In the 1606 edition the references to Calvin are exceeded only by references to Augustine and to Hieronymus Zanchius. Evidently between 1595 and 1606 Bound acquainted himself with the distinctive Sabbath views of Zanchius, the Italian-born reformer of the German Palatinate.[93] There are no Zanchius quotes in the 1595 edition; in the book of 1606 they exceed all others.

With specific regard to the Calvin references, the commentaries provide the source for some of the citations. The commentaries on Genesis 2:3, Exodus 20:8 and 34:21, Leviticus 25:20, Numbers 15:32, Psalm 32:2, Jeremiah 17:27, John 5:17, and Acts 1:11 are all cited. These references to the commentaries, however, are used in the context of relatively minor points in Bound's Sabbatarian argument.

By far the most numerous of Bound's citations from Calvin come from the Deuteronomy sermons, especially sermons 34 and 35, Calvin's two sermons on the fourth commandment.[94] There are

---

92. Ibid., p. 282.

93. See Collinson, *Studies*.

94. *Ioannis Calvini Opera quae supersunt omnia*, eds. G. Baum, E. Cunitz, E. Reuss (Brunsvigae: C. A. Schwetschke, 1883), XXVI: 284-308. Two English translations of these Deuteronomy sermons had been published by the time Bound wrote his first book on the Sabbath: *Sermons of M. Iohn Caluine, upon the X Com-*

in each of Bound's books sixteen references to these sermons. On the other hand, it is significant that there are no references at all to Calvin's *Institutes* in spite of the fact that they were well known and widely used at Cambridge and must have been well known to Bound. They were also available to Bound in his own language.[95] It is important for the purposes of this essay, nevertheless, to include a careful consideration of the Sabbath material in the *Institutes,* for it is here that Calvin gives his most thorough exposition of his Sabbath theology. A consideration of this material will also make it quite clear why Bound chose to ignore it. On the other hand, a careful consideration of the Deuteronomy sermons will reveal why Bound appeals to them with such regularity.

## Calvin's theology of the Sabbath

The best source for Calvin's theology of the Sabbath is Book II, chapter VIII of the *Institutes,* where Calvin offers his exposition of the Ten Commandments. Most of this material derives from the 1537 edition and it appears that there was very little subsequent development in Calvin's Sabbath theology. There are, moreover, no substantial additions to his Sabbath theology to be found in the numerous references to the Sabbath that are sprinkled throughout the rest of Calvin's works.

In the *Institutes,* Calvin's opening statement on the fourth commandment reveals the fundamental theme of Calvin's Sabbath theology.

> The purpose of this commandment is that, being dead to our own inclinations and works, we should meditate on the Kingdom of God, and that we should practice this meditation in the ways established by him.[96]

In the phrase "being dead to our own inclinations and works" Calvin's fundamental theological keynote is implicit, the keynote of *grace.* His interpretation of the fourth commandment is governed

---

*mandements of the Lawe,* translated out by French by John Harmar (London: T. Woodcodke, 1579); and *The sermons of M. Iohn Caluin upon the fifth booke of Moses called Deuteronomie,* translated out of French by Arthur Golding (London: H. Middleton for G. Bishop, 1583). The quotations from the Deuteronomy sermons that follow in this essay are from the Golding translation but with modernized spelling. They have been checked for accuracy against the French original. The footnote references will be simply to *Deuteronomy sermon* 34 or 35 with page numbers from the Golding translation.

95. The Thomas Norton translation was first published in 1561 with at least five later editions before 1595.

96. This citation and those that follow in this section, unless noted otherwise, are from the *Institutes,* book II, chapter viii, sections 28-34.

and controlled by that theme. Our salvation is by the gracious act
of a sovereign God. The Sabbath is given as a reminder of this
grace, for it calls us to rest from our own works. In Calvin's view,
the call to a Sabbath rest is a call to abandon completely our own
works as a basis for our relationship to God, for that relationship
is grounded in grace.

Calvin immediately goes on to state that "this commandment has
a particular consideration distinct from the others" and he therefore calls for a "different order of exposition." Bound also believed in the uniqueness of the fourth commandment, but Calvin
finds this uniqueness in something that Bound consistently denied:
the ceremonial character of the fourth commandment. Calvin agrees
with the early Fathers who "called this commandment a foreshadowing because it contains the outward keeping of a day, which,
upon Christ's coming, was abolished with the other figures." In
fact, for Calvin, this ceremonial foreshadowing "occupied the chief
place in the Sabbath." Calvin clearly affirms a strong ceremonial
element in the fourth commandment that was fulfilled and abrogated by the coming of Jesus Christ.

There is more to Calvin's view of the Sabbath than the ceremonial dimension, however. In addition to the ceremonial element
that has been abolished, there are two elements that must be continually observed by the Christian community throughout all time:
a provision for communal worship and a command to give a day
of rest to those who are under the authority of others. The paragraph
which outlines his three-dimensional view of the fourth commandment deserves quotation in full.

> First, under the repose of the seventh day the heavenly Law-
> giver meant to represent to the people of Israel spiritual rest,
> in which believers ought to lay aside their own works to
> allow God to work in them. Secondly, he meant that there
> was to be a stated day for them to assemble to hear the law
> and perform the rites, or at least to devote it particularly to
> meditation upon his works, and thus through this remembrance
> to be trained in piety. Thirdly, he resolved to give a day of
> rest to servants and those who are under the authority of others,
> in order that they should have some respite from toil.

Calvin then returns to the first of these three elements, the
foreshadowing of spiritual rest, which is of primary importance in
his Sabbath theology. He cites evidence of the great emphasis on this
commandment and the requirement of absolute obedience to it
throughout the Old Testament era. The implication of Calvin's
stress on the strict Old Testament observance is that in Christ
"the spiritual rest" element of the Sabbath was fulfilled so that

there is, consequently, a diminished emphasis on precise Sabbath observance in the New Testament. Nevertheless, although the outward sign of the strict observance of a particular day has been abolished by Christ, the "inward reality" of the Sabbath remains for the Christian community of the New Testament era and for all time. This "inward reality" is at root the reality of grace.

> We must be wholly at rest that God may work in us; we must yield our will; we must resign our heart; we must give up all our fleshly desires. In short, we must rest from all activities of our own contriving, so that, having God working in us, we may repose in him as the apostle also teaches.

The rest and repose that Calvin speaks of here, however, is a perpetual duty of the Christian, not restricted to one day in seven. It is a redemptive rest, an "eternal cessation," which for the Jews was represented by the observance of the seventh day of rest.

In his Deuteronomy sermon 35, Calvin asserts, in contrast with Bound, that since the Sabbath is in essence a sign of spiritual, redemptive rest for God's people, the commandment is not universally applicable to all mankind.[97] It is a sign for sanctified people, a sign of God's covenant relationship.

> God saith, I have given you the Sabbath day to be as a sign that I make you holy, and that I am your God who reigneth among you. This is not common to all mortal men. For God granteth not such grace and privilege to the paynims and infidels, as to make them holy. He speaks but only to the people whom he adopted and chose to be his heritage.[98]

Calvin underscores this argument by stating that the Sabbath is a "sign of God's separating of his faithful Church from all the rest of the world."[99]

By the "ceremonial" element of the Sabbath Calvin apparently has reference to the strict Jewish observance of a particular day each week as a representation or symbol or type of redemptive, eternal repose in God. Since this redemptive rest, symbolized by the Sabbath day in the history of Israel, finds its fulfillment in Christ, the external observance as a redemptive symbol is in Christ abolished. In the *Institutes* Calvin says emphatically, "He is, I say, the true fulfillment of the Sabbath." What was in the old order represented by the observance of one day in seven, is now in the new order represented by the living Christ, namely, spiritual life and redemp-

---

97. Richard B. Gaffin has written a good survey of Calvin's view of the Sabbath but errs, I believe, on this point ("Calvin and the Sabbath" [Master's thesis, Westminster Seminary, 1962] p. 63 et al).

98. P. 207.

99. Ibid.

tive repose in God. Calvin concludes his interpretation of the first meaning of the Sabbath with this exhortation: "Christians ought therefore to shun completely the superstitious observance of days." By "superstitious observance of days" he apparently means the keeping of holy days as a means of salvation. We now find our eternal rest in Christ, not in a holy day.

The other two elements of the Sabbath commandment, however, are not abrogated but are applicable to all times. The first of these is the cultic element. By setting aside a day from the rest of the week, the fourth commandment conveniently provides time for communal worship. The commandment itself does not explicitly require this, of course, but Calvin argues that God's Word in other places makes it quite clear that God's people are enjoined to assemble regularly for worship.[100] Calvin raises this very practical question, "But how can such meetings be held unless they have been established and have their stated days?" Some order must be established. All things must be done decently and in order; and if there is no "arrangement and regulation" to set aside some specific time for worship, "immediate confusion and ruin threaten the church." The need of the ancient Israelites for such regulation was one of the reasons why God established the Sabbath. And since Christians today are subject to the same necessity as the Jews in ancient times, Christians should continue to observe the Sabbath institution. "For our most provident and merciful Father willed to see to our needs not less than those of the Jews." Calvin develops this second element of the Sabbath commandment, then, in the context of the practical need for good order in the church.

In a perfect world, Calvin goes on to suggest, God's people would meet daily for worship "so as to remove all distinction of days." But we live in an imperfect world, and this second element of the fourth commandment represents God's concession to man's weakness. Calvin makes this remarkable statement about God's concession to human sin and frailty.

> But if the weakness of many made it impossible for daily meetings to be held, and the rule of love does not allow more to be required of them, why should we not obey the order we see laid upon us by God's will?

To set aside a day a week for worship will, of course, involve the risk of appearing to observe a "distinction of days." But that risk must be run. In fact, Calvin's Geneva was criticized for the practice of a Jewish "observance of days," an indication, inci-

---

100. Gaffin puts it too strongly when he states that Calvin "grounds the present obligation for worship in the fourth commandment" ("Calvin," p. 44).

dentally, that a "Lord's Day" was quite strictly observed there. Calvin defends Genevan practice by arguing that although the observance of the Sabbath continues, the reason for and spirit of this observance have radically changed in the New Testament order.

> For we are not celebrating it as a ceremony with the most rigid scrupulousness, supposing a spiritual mystery to be figured thereby. Rather, we are using it as a remedy needed to keep order in the church.

Manual labor is set aside on the day of worship in Geneva, not because of a superstitious "honoring of mysteries" but "because these are a diversion from sacred studies and meditations." Sheer practical necessity requires cessation of labor on the Sabbath, and nothing more. So Calvin distinguishes between a "distinction of days"—which he opposes—and the "lawful selection that serves the peace of the Christian fellowship"—which he supports. The Jewish Sabbath was abandoned by the early Christian community in order to overthrow superstition, but "because it was necessary to maintain decorum, order, and peace in the church" a different day was selected even at the risk of the appearance of a distinction of days.

That "different day" used by the early Christians for the day of worship was Sunday, the first day of the week. Is there something special about that day, something that makes it inherently a better day for worship than the other days, and is it consequently a day established by divine authority? Calvin answers the first part of this question by stating that the first day of the week is peculiarly appropriate for worship because it was the day of the Lord's resurrection, and "the purpose and fulfillment of that true rest" is ultimately to be found in Christ's resurrection. "Hence, by the very day that brought the shadows to an end, Christians are warned not to cling to the shadow rite." In his commentary on Exodus 20:8, Calvin speaks of a "peculiar excellency in the Sabbath." But the context allows for interpreting "the Sabbath" in this quotation as a reference to Sabbath rest rather than to a specific day that is superior to other days. In his Deuteronomy sermon 34, Calvin alludes to the primary reason why the early Christians changed the day, but he does not heavily stress the specific day to which it was changed. He argues that the day was changed after Christ's resurrection to show that we have been freed from the ceremonial bondage to the observance of days in the old order.

> But to the intent to show the liberty of Christians, the day was changed, because Jesus Christ in his resurrection did set us free from the bondage of the law, and cancelled the obligation thereof. That was the cause why the day was shifted.[101]

101. P. 205.

In the *Institutes* Calvin states explicitly that the church is not bound to the first day by divine authority, nor is the church absolutely bound to the rhythm of one day in seven.

> Nor do I cling to the number "seven" so as to bind the church in subjection to it. And I shall not condemn churches that have other solemn days for their meetings, provided there be no superstition.[102]

A bit later he criticizes the legalistic "fixing of one day in seven." In the commentary on Exodus 20:8, Calvin deals further with the question of the one in seven rhythm. Why, he asks, did God assign every seventh day as the Sabbath rather than the sixth or the tenth? In the course of his argument, Calvin links the one in seven rhythm to God's creation-rest pattern in Genesis 1. This does not mean that Calvin thinks of the fourth commandment as a creation ordinance. He seems, rather, to say that when God gave the Israelites the Decalogue, a model for the fourth commandment was available, namely, His own creation activity. So God selected that rhythm and introduced it into the fourth commandment.

> I do not, however, doubt but that God created the world in six days and rested on the seventh, that He might give a manifestation of the perfect excellency of His works, and thus, proposing Himself as the model for our imitation, He signifies that He calls His own people to the true goal of felicity.

A little later on, in his comments on the words "for in six days the Lord made heaven and earth . . . and rested on the seventh day," Calvin notes, "From this passage it may be probably conjectured that the hallowing of the Sabbath was prior to the Law." There is earlier in Exodus, after all, the injunction of Moses prohibiting the gathering of manna on the seventh day. But again, Calvin falls short of supporting the view that the fourth commandment was a creation ordinance. He only says that the observance of the seventh day of rest "seems to have had its origin from a well-known and received custom." When, then, was the Sabbath first instituted? Calvin rather tentatively offers this possibility: it was probably instituted "when God revealed the rite of sacrifice to the Holy Fathers." By "Holy Fathers" Calvin apparently means the Jewish patriarchs. He concludes, "But what in the depravity of human nature was altogether extinct among heathen nations, and almost obsolete with the race of Abraham, God renewed in His Law."

In his commentary on Genesis 3:2, Calvin, at first reading, appears to contradict his insistence in the *Institutes* that the church is not

---

102. John Pocklington in *Sunday no Sabbath* (R. Young, 1636), p. 8, reports that in Calvin's Geneva there was talk of switching the day of worship from Sunday to Thursday.

bound today to the one in seven rhythm.[103] In the Genesis commentary he lays rather heavy stress on God's creation-rest pattern as the foundation for the requirement of "every seventh day" as a day of rest and worship for God's people. The apparent contradiction is easily resolved, however, when account is taken of an additional emphasis of Calvin: that one day in seven for worship is a *minimal* requirement. Several times over, Calvin argues that ideally we should assemble every day for worship, but because of our sloth and weakness we fail to do this. To ensure that some time will be set aside in mankind's busy schedule, God makes this minimal requirement.

> If we were as earnest in serving God as we ought to be, we should not appoint one day in a week only but every man ought to meet both morning and evening without law written, to be edified more and more by God's word.[104]

When Calvin, therefore, states in the *Institutes* that the church is not bound to the number seven and that Christians may have "other solemn days for their meetings" he simply means that he would not object at all if the worship and work pattern were one in six or five or four or three or two. This he makes explicit in his Deuteronomy sermon 34. "But yet must we observe the same order of having some day in the week, be it one or be it two, for that is left to the free choice of Christians."[105] But Calvin is a practical and realistic fellow. Human frailty is such that "men will scarce meet upon the Lord's day, and most of them must be held to it as it were by force."[106] It has already been noted that it is God "in his indulgence" who requires only one day in seven. We should be willing to meet in worship every day; but because of the weakness of the flesh, we do not. God compassionately accepts us in our weakness and realizes that "we cannot lead the life of Angels." Consequently, He "is contented if we allow him one day."[107] This is a most reasonable requirement, for it leaves us six days in which to attend to our own affairs.

Obviously then we are not tied absolutely to this pattern. Simply out of concern for establishing some order for His people, God provided this command. In the setting up of that order He had to

103. Several have commented on and attempted to resolve this seeming contradiction. See A. Kuyper, *Tractaat van den Sabbath* (Amsterdam: J. A. Wormser, 1890), pp. 81 ff.; L. Praamsma, "Calvijn over de Sabbath," *Church and Nation* VI (Nov. 28, 1961): 91-92; and Gaffin, "Calvin," pp. 95 ff. But they all fail to note the significance of Calvin's stress on one day in seven as a minimum frequency of worship.

104. *Deuteronomy sermon* 34, pp. 203-4. 106. Ibid., p. 204.

105. Ibid., p. 205. 107. *Deuteronomy sermon* 35, p. 207.

select some number. One in seven was natural and convenient because it would follow the creation rhythm of God Himself, so God by His own example could allure mankind to keep at least one day in seven. This is not to say that there is anything magical or absolute about the "one in seven" routine. After all, God established this order out of simple concern about a practical need. If His people should choose to worship oftener than this, of course they should do so. It is worth noting, in conclusion, that the Deuteronomy sermons, in which Calvin stresses one day in seven as the minimal requirement, were preached in worship gatherings on Thursday, June 20, and on Friday, June 21, 1555, not on the "seventh day" nor on the "first day of the week."

## Calvin's ethics of the Sabbath

Here and there in his references to the Sabbath in the commentaries and in the *Institutes,* Calvin makes occasional recommendations about how to keep the Sabbath. But by far the best source for Calvin's Sabbath ethics are the two Deuteronomy sermons that he preached from the pulpit of St. Pierre in June of 1555. These are sermons 34 and 35 and, as noted above, Nicholas Bound's most frequent Calvin references are to the Deuteronomy sermons.

Sermon 34 begins with a general statement of the purpose of the Sabbath commandment. It is a commandment concerning the service of God "and of the order which he hath set down for the faithful to exercise themselves in."[108] Obviously, Calvin holds that the fourth commandment has meaning for the Christian community today, as it did for the Jewish community of old.

In this sermon Calvin develops the ethical implications of the first two of his three parts of the fourth commandment. He begins by stressing at length the typological, ceremonial character of the Sabbath. As a foreshadowing of spiritual, eternal rest, the Sabbath has been fulfilled by Christ; and "now that the thing itself is given to us, we must no more stay upon the shadows."[109] And yet there is an internal meaning that remains. The Sabbath rest points to the truth that God's people must separate themselves or rest from their sins. Today we find this separation or holy rest in Christ, but the ancient Israelites needed signs and symbols of the separation. For them the Sabbath was "a warrant of the grace that was purchased us to mortify our thoughts and affections, that God might

108. P. 200.

109. Ibid.

live in us by the power of his holy spirit."[110] It is clear once
again that Calvin's grace theology controls his view of the Sabbath.
And from that grace theology flows Calvin's first point of his Sabbath ethics. To keep the Sabbath means most fundamentally to
depart from the bondage of our works of sin into the freedom of
the gracious work of God. In the new order ushered in by grace,
"keeping the Sabbath" means first of all a constant, daily resting
from sinful deeds. It means the mortification of the old man and
the putting on of the new through the gracious work of God.

Calvin supports this sweeping view of Sabbath keeping by references to Ezekiel 20 and Isaiah 58, where it appears that the
"profaning of my sabbaths" involves the total departure of Israel
from God. This is why punishment for Sabbath breaking was so
severe according to Calvin. Why punish someone with death when
all he did was to "cleave wood"? Surely not because God takes
such great pleasure in idleness, but because under the Sabbath
figure "was comprehended the whole service of God."[111] Calvin
believes that the Jews were required to observe the Sabbath with a
view to this underlying spiritual meaning as certainly as the Christian community should today. For simply to rest from daily work
and assemble in worship "and yet in the meanwhile to nourish their
own wicked affections"[112] would have been a mockery of God and
His law. But the Jews also had to abide by the ceremony of
external observance, for God would not allow them the substance
without the shadows.

Since Christ's coming "we be no more tied to the old bondage
of keeping the Sabbath day."[113] But "in substance" we must continue to observe the commandment by suppressing our own will and
works and by opening ourselves to the will and work of God.
This is the "rest" required by the fourth commandment today.
"And how must we rest? We must stand at a stay, so as our
thoughts run not roving abroad, to invent one thing or other."[114]
Whenever we are full of "envy, rancor, ambition, cruelty or guile"
we break the Sabbath commandment. But when we "refer ourselves
unto God, that he only may work in us, and guide and govern by
his holy spirit,"[115] we are faithfully observing the substance of the
Sabbath command. The Sabbath, therefore, teaches "a perfect doctrine of holiness."[116] The renunciation of self and total dedication

110. Ibid., p. 201.
111. Ibid., p. 202.
112. Ibid., p. 201.
113. Ibid.
114. Ibid.
115. Ibid.
116. Ibid., p. 201.

to God is explicitly called by Calvin the "spiritual keeping of the Sabbath of the Lord."[117] He repeats, "We be no more bound to the ceremony that was kept so straitly under the law."[118]

Christians have much more liberty regarding the use of the particular day than did the Jews of old, a liberty "purchased for us by the death and passion of our Lord Jesus Christ."[119] But that increased liberty does not mean diminished responsibility for Christians. The spiritual keeping of the Sabbath is not only for one day a week but for all time and eternity. In Calvin's words, "the rest that God commandeth us is everlasting, and not by pangs or fits as they say."[120] From that perspective, the spiritual keeping of the Sabbath is far more demanding than the mere external observance of a day. Anyone can perform the requirement of external rest from labor, but only by the grace and Spirit of God can people rest from their sinful works and allow God to work in them redemptively. In fact, in this life it is impossible to "attain to the perfect holiness"[121] which God requires. For this reason God established the one in seven pattern for the Jews. It was a reminder that under the conditions of the flesh no one can keep a perpetual, daily rest from his sinful works. Calvin therefore admonishes that we must not become overconfident in our abilities to "keep the Sabbath rest." Our sinful nature is such that we are "to mislike of ourselves, and to mourn continually."[122]

The first point of Calvin's Sabbath ethics flows clearly and directly from the first point of his three dimensional Sabbath theology. Sabbath rest is essentially redemptive rest in Christ. This implies for Christian life the mortification of the old man of sin and the putting on of the new man in Christ.

The second function of the fourth commandment is to provide a time for communal worship. "For that day was ordained for men to assemble in, to hear the doctrine of the law preached, to communicate together with sacrifices, and to call upon the name of God."[123] In elaboration of this second aspect of Sabbath keeping, John Calvin sounds very much like Nicholas Bound. Most of Bound's references, in fact, are to this portion of sermon 34.

Calvin calls for a literal, physical cessation of daily labor on the Lord's Day, not as an end in itself, but to provide time for worship of God. Recreational activity should also be suspended, for such

117. Ibid.
118. Ibid.
119. Ibid., p. 202.
120. Ibid., p. 203.
121. Ibid.
122. Ibid.
123. Ibid.

activity interferes with worship as certainly as daily labor does.

> If we spend the Lord's day in making good cheer, and in playing
> and gaming, is that a good honouring of God? Nay, is it not
> a mockery, yea and a very unhallowing of his name?[124]

Calvin urges that shop windows be shut on the Lord's Day, that
travel be curtailed and recreation avoided so that there is sufficient
time and freedom to hear from God's Word, to meet together and
make confession of faith, to pray, and to use the sacraments.
Calvin bemoans the neglect of worship in the Geneva of his day.

> And though the bell toll to bring them to the sermon, yet it
> seems to them that they have nothing else to do but to think
> upon their business, and to cast up their accounts concerning
> this and that matter. Other some fall to gluttony, and shut
> themselves in their houses, because they dare not show a mani-
> fest contempt in the open streets.[125]

Calvin takes an additional step in this second part of his Sabbath
ethics. Like Nicholas Bound he argues that the Sabbath should
be used not only for public worship and "hearing of sermons," but
also that "we should apply the rest of the time to the praising of
God."[126] By "the rest of the time" he apparently means the rest
of the day of worship, at least, the remainder of our waking hours. To
use the Lord's Day to full advantage will aid us in the continued
reflection on God's works which is required throughout the week. It
will "fashion and polish" us for the giving of thanks to God "upon
the Monday and all the week after." Conversely, if men desecrate
the Lord's Day they are likely to "play the beasts all the week
after."[127] So we should not only publicly hear the sermon, but privately reflect on it. We must digest it and "bend all our wits to
consider the gracious things that God hath done for us."[128]
Calvin calls on God's people to "dedicate that day wholly unto
him so as we may be utterly withdrawn from the world."[129] Even
though we need not "keep the ceremony so straight as it was
under the bondage of the law," it is important for us to "consider
how our Lord requireth to have this day bestowed in nothing else,
but in hearing of his word, in making common prayer, in making
confession of our faith, and in having the use of the Sacraments."[130]

He concludes the sermon with a brief summary, calling the people
to spiritual rest in Christ, and to the observance of an outward
order for the purpose of worship and reflection on the words and

124. Ibid., p. 204.
125. Ibid.
126. Ibid.
127. Ibid.

128. Ibid.
129. Ibid.
130. Ibid., p. 205.

works and gracious gifts of God. In his closing words, he exhorts, "Let us show all the week after that we have profited in the same."[131]

The second part of Calvin's Sabbath ethics is very similar to the view of Nicholas Bound. Both insist that there be cessation of labor and recreation in order to provide time for day-long worship, both public and private. There is a noticeable difference of course in the measure of detailed instructions each of them gives regarding this aspect of Sabbath observance. Calvin's is a sermon length treatment; Bound goes on for literally a hundred pages. And the greater the measure of specifics, the greater the threat of a new Sabbatarian legalism. Especially in the 1606 edition, Bound enters into some discussion about just what constitutes a Sabbath-day journey, whether the Sabbath is from morning to morning or evening to evening, and whether it is a full twenty-four hours or less. Such concern for minutiae would surely receive Calvin's criticism about "Jewish superstitious observance of days." On the other hand, in his general outline of the use of the day Calvin does not differ from Bound. Surely to some extent the Puritans late in the sixteenth century were still looking at Calvin and Geneva as a representative model of pure Christianity.

The third part of Calvin's Sabbath ethics is developed in his Deuteronomy sermon 35, which covers especially that part of the fourth commandment that reads:

> Six days you shall labor, and do all your work; but the seventh day is a sabbath to the Lord your God; in it you shall not do any work, you, or your son, or your daughter, or your manservant, or your maidservant, or your ox or your ass, or any of your cattle, or the sojourner who is within your gates, that your manservant and your maidservant may rest as well as you.

Calvin first rejects the view that the phrase "six days shalt thou labor" should be regarded as a divine command to work for six full days. God has included those words only as a reminder that He has given His people plenty of time for their own affairs; so it is not unreasonable for Him to require that one day of seven be set aside for worship. Calvin alludes again to the totality of service required on the Lord's Day, at one point speaking of God's requirement of "the seventh part of your time."[132] It is, once again, clear from this passage that while Calvin was not absolutely committed to the one in seven rhythm, he does take it very seriously and assumes it as a normal and typical routine for the Christian community.

131. Ibid.

132. *Deuteronomy sermon* 35, p. 206.

In the remainder of this sermon, Calvin elaborates on the social implications of the fourth commandment's requirement that rest be granted to servants and beasts of burden and "the stranger that is within thy gates." Calvin clearly regards this requirement as applicable to the Christian community as well as to the ancient Jewish people of God. On the day of worship, servants, strangers, and beasts of burden are to be given the opportunity for physical rest; but it is a rest designed primarily for the benefit of God's people and only secondarily for the servants, strangers, and animals themselves. When beasts of burden are released from their labors on this day they serve as a reminder to God's people of the need for rest. With the "stables and stalls shut up" there is a "monument before our eyes" reminding us of the Sabbath. Twice in this context Calvin refers to the Sabbath as a sacrament.[133]

Nowhere in his view of the Sabbath does Calvin suggest that the intent of the Sabbath has anything to do with man's need for physical rest. He therefore has a bit of trouble with the requirement for servant-rest. God's intention, says Calvin, was not to grant to servants a day of rest "so as they should be tired." So the servant's rest is an "overplus" or an "accessory."[134] It is a fringe benefit, not at the heart of the Sabbath's intent. For the primary intent is the service of God and growth in holiness and obedience. And yet, Calvin says that the command to give servants rest has social, not spiritual purpose. "Here it should seem that God ordained not the Sabbath day for a spiritual order only, as is said afore, but also for charity's sake."[135] This part of the commandment, therefore, should remind the "haves" to deal compassionately with the "have-nots," with "the poor . . . all underlings and subjects, and of all such as (to our seeming) are not worthy to be compared or matched with us in respect of the world."[136] We must remember that in spite of differing social and economic stations in life, mankind is "knit together as one flesh."[137] All are created in the image of God. When I meet another, says Calvin, "There ought I to behold myself as in a looking glass."[138]

The Jews were also called on to remember their once desperate condition as slaves in Egypt. Reflecting on this, Calvin says that consideration of our own misery prompts us to discharge more readily our responsibilities toward others. Shared experience with the oppressed makes us more willing to help them. He concludes this

133. Ibid., pp. 207-8.
134. Ibid., p. 208.
135. Ibid.
136. Ibid., p. 209.
137. Ibid., p. 210.
138. Ibid.

passage with an interesting comment about the golden rule as natural law. "We ought at leastwise to do to other folks as we our selves would be done unto. Nature teaches us that, and we need not go to school to learn it."[139]

With regard to "the stranger within thy gates," Calvin again argues that the benefits that result from their rest are primarily for God's people, not for the strangers. They are to rest lest God's people be led astray by evil example. For this reason and apparently this reason only, Calvin defends legislation enforcing this commandment along with others of the first table of the law. Laws against blasphemy are necessary because the God-despisers who blaspheme may lead Christians astray. Similarly, Sabbath rest must be enforced. Only in this sense is it a commandment for all men, with universal applicability.

## Conclusion

It is clear from this survey of the Sabbath positions of John Calvin and Nicholas Bound that there are both significant differences and similarities between them.

They differ most sharply in their respective theological interpretations of the Sabbath commandment. For this reason, it is not at all surprising that Bound never cities the *Institutes* for support, for it is in the *Institutes* that Calvin's Sabbath theology is best summarized. Particularly on the two cardinal principles of Sabbatarian theology, Calvin and Bound do not agree. Bound gives clear expression to these principles when he argues that the Sabbath command is rooted in the creation order and is therefore moral and universal in scope, and when he insists that the first day of the week and no other is specially sanctified by God as the Sabbath, so that it literally becomes the Christian Sabbath.

Calvin does not express these views. He seems at times to flirt with the idea of some abiding, internal connection between the Sabbath and Creation, but he falls short of declaring the fourth commandment a creation ordinance. He only uses God's rest after His creative activity as an alluring example for both Jews and Christians to follow. For Calvin the Sabbath is not, therefore, a universal, moral law binding on all mankind. Calvin, in fact, stresses the ceremonial, typological significance of the Jewish Sabbath much more than its moral significance. And, of course, his treatment is weighted heavily with emphasis on the abolition of this ceremonial meaning of the Sabbath and its fulfillment in Christ. Calvin's stress on the ceremo-

139. Ibid.

nial nature of the commandment leads him to give persistent warnings against reverting to the old Jewish observance of days and clinging to shadow rites. Bound not only fails to warn of this danger but falls into it. Moreover, Calvin does not hold, as Bound does, that the Christian community is absolutely tied to the observance of the first day of the week or even to the rhythm of one day in seven, except as a minimal requirement. He regards the first day of the week as highly appropriate for worship because it is the day of Christ's resurrection, but he rejects as a "superstitious observance of days" any attempt to turn the first day of the week into a Christian Sabbath directly akin to the Jewish Sabbath of the fourth commandment.

While Bound stresses the morally binding principles of the fourth commandment and of the New Testament apostolic practice, Calvin emphasizes—with a greater spirit of flexibility and freedom—the practical need for good order in the church. It is in the interest of good order that Christians today should make use of the pattern provided by the fourth commandment. This is literally *good* order, for no one less than God provided it for the ancient Israelites. Since the Christian community is no less in need of such order than were the Jews of old, Christians should continue to use the fourth commandment for ordering and providing time for both communal and private worship today. It should be emphasized again, however, that "good order" was a very high priority issue for Calvin. Consequently, one should never conclude from his stern warning against Sabbatarian superstition that Calvin wanted to abandon the traditional use of a weekly day of rest and worship. He urges the continued use of the fourth commandment "in order to prevent religion from either perishing or declining among us."

There are both differences and unmistakable similarities between John Calvin and Nicholas Bound in their respective views on the ethical implications of the fourth commandment. The most significant difference arises in connection with Calvin's first of the three purposes of the Sabbath. Since the Sabbath represents spiritual, redemptive rest, keeping the Sabbath means to depart from sinful works so that God may work in us. Nicholas Bound does not develop such a doctrine nor its subsequent ethic.[140]

On the other hand, with regard to what Calvin calls the second reason for the Sabbath, Calvin and Bound spell out remarkably similar recommendations on how to use the Lord's Day. Both call for cessation of daily labor and recreation, not as an end in itself, but

---

140. In fact, he seems to reject this view explicitly in *The Doctrine of the Sabbath* where he criticizes the "Familists" and other "prophane men" for holding this interpretation (p. 23).

to provide opportunity for worship. Both assert that this worship should extend throughout the day and should involve private meditation as well as public assembly. With respect to the "social ethic" arising from the last part of the fourth commandment, there are again marked similarities in Calvin's and Bound's interpretations.

From the foregoing analysis, it is apparent that when Bound quoted Calvin, he did so selectively and opportunistically. At the same time he quotes Calvin accurately; for in spite of fundamental differences in approach, Bound could find in Calvin support especially for his views on how to observe the weekly Lord's Day.

At the beginning of this essay, the Westminster and Heidelberg interpretations of the fourth commandment were quoted as convenient synopses of the two positions that have lived in tension within the Reformed tradition for the past four centuries. Those credal interpretations very clearly reflect the views of Nicholas Bound and John Calvin respectively.

Especially striking is the similarity between the Westminster Confession and Nicholas Bound. The Westminster appeal to the "law of nature" in support of the Sabbath, and its reference to the fourth commandment as a "moral, and perpetual commandment binding all men in all ages," could have been lifted right out of Bound. And when the Confession argues that God has for all time adopted the Sabbath rhythm of one day in seven,

> which, from the beginning of the world to the resurrection of
> Christ, was the last day of the week; and from the resurrection
> of Christ, was changed into the first day of the week . . . and is
> to be continued to the end of the world, as the Christian Sabbath,

it proclaims in phrases very similar to Bound's second theological pillar of Sabbatarianism.

In its exposition of Sabbath practices the Westminster Confession also clearly reflects the thought of Nicholas Bound. Sabbath keeping includes a "due preparing of . . . hearts" for worship, and a "holy rest, all the day, from . . . works, words and thoughts about . . . worldly employments and recreation." Christians are also required to spend "the whole time, in the public and private exercises of . . . worship, and in the duties of necessity and mercy." This is so similar to Bound's exposition that one can easily imagine the Westminster divines working on these Sabbath articles with an open volume of Bound's *Sabbathum Veteris* before them.

The spirit of Calvin, on the other hand, is in the background of the Heidelberg Catechism's brief exposition of the fourth commandment. Reminiscent of Calvin's first element of his three dimensional approach to the Sabbath are the closing words of the Catechism's treatment which state that the Sabbath commandment requires "that every day of my life I rest from my evil ways, let the Lord work in me through his Spirit, and so begin already in this life the eternal Sabbath." And when the Catechism asserts that the fourth commandment leads to diligent church attendance in order "to learn what God's Word teaches, to participate in the sacraments, to pray to God publicly, and to bring Christian offerings for the poor," it likewise reflects Calvin's views.

But it should be observed as a conclusion of this study that the Heidelberg Catechism does not reflect the whole Calvin. A dimension that is especially prominent in the Deuteronomy sermons is missing from the Catechism. It is the material in which Calvin offers his recommendations on how to observe the day of rest and worship. On this issue Calvin, like Bound and the Westminster Confession, urges a full, weekly day of rest from daily labor and recreation, a day that should be used not only for public but also for private worship. With this emphasis Calvin provides at least a partial bridge between the disparate views of Heidelberg and Westminster. This dimension of Calvin's view is typically not recognized, however, because of an almost exclusive dependence on the *Institutes* only for his Sabbath views.[141] For too long the wealth of material in the Deuteronomy sermons has been neglected.

In short, Calvin in his theology is not Sabbatarian, and in his ethics he would be quite comfortable with many of the Puritan emphases. At the same time, it should be recognized that in their overall approaches to Sabbath ethics, Calvin and the Puritans differed. Calvin's approach is strongly colored by his practical concern for good order in the church. The Puritan approach, reflected in Bound and the Westminster Confession, is a more principled one by which the Christian observance of a day of rest and worship is based more directly and immediately on the law of the fourth commandment. Calvin, moreover, adds an extremely important ethical dimension when he draws from the fourth commandment the sweeping, spiritual, redemptive conclusion that we are only keeping the Sabbath when we rest from our evil works and let God work in us by His Spirit all the days of our lives.

141. E.g., in Paul Jewett, *The Lord's Day.*

Louis A. Vos

# CHAPTER 3    CALVIN AND THE CHRISTIAN SELF-IMAGE: GOD'S NOBLE WORKMANSHIP, A WRETCHED WORM, OR A NEW CREATURE?

## Introduction: The problem stated

The old adage "know thyself" is as important today as it was in the days of Socrates and Aristotle. Philosophy, psychology, theology, and education are all particularly—though not exclusively—concerned with man's knowledge and conception of himself. The importance ascribed to this self-knowledge varies within these disciplines, and even more so within the variety of perspectives from which these disciplines are presented.

In the writings of John Calvin much attention is given to the development of self-knowledge. In fact, Calvin highly recommends this area of knowledge when he says, "With good reason the ancient proverb strongly recommended knowledge of self to man. For if it is considered disgraceful for us not to know all that pertains to the business of human life, even more detestable is our ignorance of ourselves, by which, when making decisions in necessary matters, we miserably deceive and even blind ourselves."[1] The purpose of this article is to get to know ourselves better, as this knowledge of ourselves is developed in the writings of Calvin. The focus is the Christian self-concept or self-image as presented in and derived from the works of one of the most important and influential writers of the Reformation period.[2]

1. *Inst.,* II.i.1.

2. The words self-concept, self-image and self-esteem are considered to be virtually synonymous. By them is meant what S. Coopersmith defines as "the evaluation which the individual makes and customarily maintains with regard to himself: it expresses an attitude of approval or disapproval, and indicates the extent to which the individual believes himself to be capable, significant, successful, and worthy" (*The Antecedents*

76

That there is a correlation between religion and the self-image is generally accepted, although the precise nature of that correlation is a matter of debate. Albert Trew says, "It would be agreed by the vast majority of psychologists that religious experience has a determining effect on personality, even though many do not necessarily accept the objectivity of religious beliefs."[3] And H. J. Clinebell states, "The point at which religion influences self-esteem most directly is in the doctrine of man."[4] This is no less true of the Christian religion because "the Christian life involves not just believing something about Christ, but also believing something about ourselves."[5]

However, as was said above, the precise nature of this correlation between religion and one's self-image is a matter of debate. Some authors would maintain a definite cause and effect relationship, as does, for example, W. M. Counts in his article, "The Nature of Man and the Christian's Self-Esteem."[6] On the other hand, G. R. Martindale cautions against drawing the causal relationships too tightly because of the other "personality factors which are prior in origin to any theological awareness or expression,"[7] and in a related manner W. Oates cautions against exaggerating the role of religion in causing mental illness.[8]

Religion can both mold and mirror the self-esteem of the individual. Referring to religion which molds the self-esteem, Clinebell writes about religion which hurts and religion which heals. The former is referred to as "distorted religion" which contributes to immaturity, guilt, isolation, fear, and rage. In such a case, religion is a dark, repressive, life-crippling force.[9] However, religion can also be a con-

*of Self-Esteem* [San Francisco: Freeman, 1967], pp. 4 and 5). In a very real sense the self-image is uniquely personal and nonobjectifiable. Consequently, this essay is concerned with the resources which Calvin offers for the building of a positive Christian self-image.

3. Trew, A., "The Religious Factor in Mental Illness," *Pastoral Psychology* (May 1971), p. 21.

4. Clinebell, H. J., *Mental Health Through Christian Community* (New York: Abingdon, 1965), p. 49.

5. Hoekema, A. A., *The Christian Looks at Himself* (Grand Rapids. Eerdmans, 1975), p. 55.

6. Counts, W. M., "The Nature of Man and the Christian's Self-Esteem," *Journal of Psychology and Theology* I, no. 1 (1973): 38-44.

7. Martindale, G. R., "Worm Theology or Wormhood Feelings—Which?" *Journal of Psychology and Theology* I, no. 1 (1973): 45-49.

8. Oates, W., *Religious Factors in Mental Illness* (New York: Association Press, 1955).

9. Clinebell, *Mental Health*, pp. 26-28.

structive, creative, healing, and life-affirming force. In the first
instance, religion can weaken self-esteem; in the second, religion
can strengthen self-esteem.[10]

From all sides Calvin's theology has been attacked as presenting
a negative picture of man which may and, it is claimed, does have
disastrous effects on the development of a positive and healthy self-
image. Counts begins his article, "John Calvin . . . wrote in his *Institutes*, ' . . . we have sufficiently proved that he [man] can of his own
nature neither aspire to good through resolve nor struggle after it
through effort. . . . ' "[11] Following two quotations from other
sources, Counts summarizes, "The common thread running through
these statements is a negative, pessimistic view of human nature."
And he concludes,

> Calvin . . . was not wrong in asserting that man is fallen, though
> he could have expressed it in a more balanced fashion. But to
> emphasize this negative piece of truth without an offsetting
> and greater emphasis on the positive truths about man can only
> create a neurotic and perverted form of Christian experience.[12]

So, too, Clinebell, reflecting on only a part of Calvin's theology,
bemoans the fact that

> a considerable slice of Christian theology through the centuries
> has pictured man as groveling in depravity, total or partial. The
> Genesis story of the fall of man has been interpreted to mean
> that man's original goodness and the *imago dei* in him were
> completely corrupted by his disobedience to God. According
> to this view, man in his present condition is fundamentally bad
> and lost.[13]

He adds, "Negative theological views of human nature have prolif-
erated, emphasizing man's inner corruption and impotency to do
anything to save himself. . . . "[14] Clinebell is critical of the fact that
"some recent theologians have agreed with Calvin that as Christians
we ought to despise 'everything that may be supposed as excellent
in us,' "[15] and he concludes, "Negative views of man sometimes
produce detrimental effects on self-esteem, particularly in children

10. Ibid., pp. 49 ff.

11. Counts, "Nature of Man," p. 38.

12. Ibid., p. 44. G. R. Martindale has a good corrective response to Counts' article
in this same journal, as does also R. L. Saucy, "Both Depravity and Value," *Journal
of Psychology and Theology* I, No. 1 (1973): 49-50.

13. Clinebell, *Mental Health,* p. 50.

14. Ibid.

15. Ibid., p. 51.

and youth."[16] Furthermore, it is not uncommon to read opinions similar to that expressed by M. Beversluis that the root of Calvinism is the doctrine of man's damnableness.[17]

On the other hand, A. Hoekema claims that a more positive self-image (believers are new creatures in Christ) is found in the Reformed creeds and in the writings of Reformed theologians than is commonly found among Calvinists.[18] Among the latter the self-image is more negative than positive, emphasizing the Christian's continuing sinfulness more than his newness in Christ. Hoekema speaks about the self-image Calvinists seem to grow up with, the kind of self-abasing "climate" in which they commonly live. The plaguing question is, Why is there such a difference between the Reformed writers and creeds and what Hoekema calls "the self-image that is commonly found among . . . the Reformed community"?[19]

T. F. Torrance expresses similar sentiments. He deplores the tendency in later Calvinistic theology which obscures Calvin's fundamental position and has made him out to be the author of a thoroughly pessimistic view of man. "Nothing," says Torrance, "is further from the truth."[20] Thus the question stated above might be rephrased, Why is there a pessimistic view of man in later Calvinistic theology when it is claimed that Calvin himself presented a different picture? Or is Calvin himself responsible for the negative self-image in his followers, as some authors quoted above seem to think? It remains for us to attempt to answer these questions by looking first of all to the picture of man as reflected in Calvin's writings, and then asking whether Calvin's theology contains resources for a positive Christian self-image. If this latter question can be answered affirmatively, we will then attempt to analyze why later Calvinistic tradition seems to differ. Perhaps it should be emphasized that this paper does not simply aim to present Calvin's doctrine of man or Calvin's anthropology. We are interested in the image of the Christian which is portrayed in Calvin's writings. It is recognized that these two facets are certainly and very closely related, but we do not consider them to be identical. The difference may be mainly in perspective and standpoint. However, a proper perspective on the one ought ulti-

16. Ibid., p. 50.

17. *De Dwalingen van het Calvinisme* (Leiden: 1906), pp. 7, 23.

18. "The Christian's Self-Image," *Reformed Journal* (Sept. 1971), pp. 23-24.

19. Hoekema's book *The Christian Looks at Himself* does not attempt to answer this question. His very helpful book is primarily concerned with the Biblical resources for building a positive self-image.

20. *Calvin's Doctrine of Man* (Grand Rapids: Eerdmans, 1957), p. 20.

mately to contribute to a proper perspective on the other. Nor does this paper attempt to analyze or even suggest to what extent the emphasis in Calvin results in negative self-images. We are aware of the limitations of this type of study and also of the fact that religious experience and theological reflection are not the only factors which contribute to the development of a self-image.

There certainly must be a reason why the authors cited above, as well as many others, chide Calvin for his negative perspective on man. Calvin had much to say about man, and from isolated statements we can understand the conclusions of many concerning Calvin's doctrine of man. It is not particularly edifying to read, "There is more worth in all the vermin of the world than there is in man, for he is a creature in whom the image of God has been defaced,"[21] or, "Men can produce nothing of themselves but what is filthy and abominable."[22] A positive perspective certainly does not leap forth from such statements as: "In the whole of our nature there remains not a speck of uprightness,"[23] and "To whatever part of man we turn our eyes, it is impossible to see anything that is not impure, profane, and abominable to God."[24] Lest we think that Calvin does not have us in mind, he reminds us that "even the most perfect... find nothing in their own nature but wretchedness."[25]

Isolated statements of this sort tend to support the position that Calvin had a very pessimistic view of man, and this, then, might contribute to the negative self-image of many Calvinists. But while the above statements are representative of Calvin's thought, they are isolated statements taken out of context. Our contention is that the context and perspective of Calvin's writings—their confessional nature, as well as their expressed purpose and aim—shed a different light on these and similar statements, so that the overall instruction of Calvin contributes to a positive instead of a negative self-image for the Christian.

## Self-image and the knowledge of God

Undoubtedly the most basic question regarding the development of a self-image is that of the point of reference. From what does one start for his materials or from where does one get his criteria for

21. Sermon on Eph. 2:1-5 in *Sermons on the Epistle to the Ephesians* (Edinburgh: Banner of Truth Trust, 1973), p. 133.

22. *Comm.* on Isa. 6:5.

23. *Comm.* on John 3:6.

24. *Instruction in Faith* (Philadelphia: Westminster, 1949), p. 21.

25. *Comm.* on Rom. 7:24.

judgment regarding what gives the self value and meaning? Is the point of reference in man himself or in the culture and world in which he lives? Does the secular world set the standards for self-esteem or is there another source for the Christian which results in a different perspective on the self, apart from which it is impossible to understand, appreciate, or appropriate the Christian self-image?[26]

Calvin understood these questions very well, and very clearly and consistently gave answer to them. Calvin's point of reference for man's self-knowledge is always and most emphatically God, although this is not to say that Calvin's anthropology is simply a logical deduction from his doctrine of God.[27] The familiar opening words of the *Institutes* speak poignantly to this point:

> Nearly all the wisdom we possess, that is to say, true and sound wisdom, consists of two parts: the knowledge of God and of ourselves. But while joined by many bonds, which one precedes and brings forth the other is not easy to discern. In the first place, no one can look upon himself without immediately turning his thoughts to the contemplation of God, in whom he "lives and moves" (Acts 17:28). For, quite clearly, the mighty gifts with which we are endowed are hardly from ourselves; indeed, our very being is nothing but subsistence in the one God.[28]

Further Calvin says, "It is certain that man never achieves a clear knowledge of himself unless he has first looked upon God's face, and then descends from contemplating him to scrutinizing himself."[29] This is true because

> until God reveals himself to us, we do not think we are men, or rather, we think that we are gods; but when we have seen God, then we begin to feel and know what we are. Hence springs true humility, which consists in this, that a man make no claim for himself, and depends wholly on God.[30]

Two things stand out in these quotations. One is that true knowledge of man depends on true knowledge of God, and the other is that man's existence likewise depends wholly on God. Thus the epistemo-

---

26. Cf. F. Wise, "Some Implications of the Self-concept for Christian Education," *Journal of Psychology and Theology* I, no. 1 (1973): 71; and Hoekema, *The Christian Looks at Himself*, pp. 19-21.

27. E. Linwood Brandis states, incorrectly in my opinion, "The doctrine [of man] itself wasn't even a major one for Calvin. It was rather a fact tacked on to his doctrine of God, a logical conclusion, as it were" ("A Study of the Man in Relation to His Doctrine of Man" [Master's thesis, Andover Newton, n.d.], p. 53). This position substitutes the logical dependency of one doctrine on another for the dynamic and integral relationship between God and man in Calvin's theology.

28. *Inst.*, I.i.1.

29. *Inst.*, I.i.2.

30. *Comm.* on Isa. 6:5.

82 *Exploring the Heritage of John Calvin*

logical question is closely related to the question of the very being of man.

Man lives and moves and has his being in God. To consider man and his self-image apart from this central reference point is to consider man in abstraction. The point of departure, then, for our self-knowledge cannot be divorced from our knowledge of God. The knowledge of man in Calvin is not an isolated or disinterested teaching. To develop a self-image concept apart from this central God-relationship is to run into error and ignorance. In fact, so important is this God-relationship for man that if it is broken, man is less than he should be. Calvin says, "It is worship of God alone that renders men higher than the beasts, and through it alone they aspire to immortality."[31] This is so because

> all men are born and live to the end that they may know God, and yet if knowledge of God is unstable and fleeting unless it progress to this degree, it is clear that all those who do not direct every thought and action in their lives to this goal degenerate from the law of their creation.[32]

Only from this theistic reference point are we able to appreciate the perspectives on life which Calvin offers as resources for our self-image. The self-image is certainly very much influenced by the values and standards which one holds to be important and worthwhile. That which contributes to the happy life, the true life, and how one sees himself in relation to these values will have a deciding effect on his perception of himself. Is it wealth, or beauty, or intelligence— some of the prime standards of the secular society? Or is it something else? Concerning the question of the true life of man, Calvin answers,

> It is not that he should be shrewd and quick-witted, and be able to conduct his business well in this world by his own skill and wits, or to purchase great renown for himself, or to be knowledgeable and well advised, able to give counsel to all other men; it is not that he should excel in all human sciences and in all arts; neither is it that he should be esteemed and renowned as a man of noble courage or as one that has other virtues commendable among men. But it is a higher thing that we must begin at, namely, to know that God is our Father, that we are defended and preserved by the light of his Word, and enlightened by faith to know the way of salvation, and to assure ourselves that our whole welfare lies in him, so that we seek it there with all lowliness. It also lies in our knowledge of the means whereby we attain to it, that is to say, by having our Lord Jesus Christ in whom the whole fulness of grace is presented to us.[33]

31. *Inst.*, I.iii.3.

32. *Inst.*, I.iii.3. Cf.: "If once religion is absent from their life, men are in no wise superior to brute beasts, but are in many respects far more miserable" (ibid.).

33. Sermon on Eph. 2:1-5, p. 125.

Consequently "nothing is better than to obey his [God's] commandments and . . . to be loved by him is the consummation of a happy
life."[34] The benevolence of God is the full happiness of man.[35]
Calvin recognized the universal problem concerning self-
knowledge, that is, that there is much disagreement as to how we
are to acquire that knowledge. Certainly Calvin was vehemently
opposed to the idea that true and correct self-knowledge can be
derived through reason and nature. The problem is not only that
man's reason is not reliable and his standards and judgments twisted,
but that this procedure begins with the presupposition that man is an
independent, autonomous creature who can be understood and can
understand himself wholly apart from God. Calvin continually
criticizes this process for self-knowledge.

> According to carnal judgment, man seems to know himself very
> well, when, confident in his understanding and uprightness, he
> becomes bold and urges himself to the duties of virtue and,
> declaring war on vices endeavors to exert himself with all his
> ardor toward the excellent and honorable.[36]

Moreover,

> We always seem to ourselves righteous and upright and wise
> and holy—this pride is innate in all of us. . . . For, because all
> of us are inclined by nature to hypocrisy, a kind of empty image
> of righteousness in place of righteousness itself abundantly
> satisfies us. And because nothing appears within or around us
> that has not been contaminated by great immorality, what is a
> little less vile pleases us as a thing most pure—so long as we
> confine our minds within the limits of human corruption. . . . As
> long as we do not look beyond the earth, being quite content
> with our own righteousness, wisdom, and virtue, we flatter
> ourselves most sweetly, and fancy ourselves all but demi-
> gods.[37]

Hypocrisy, blind self-love, and the desire for flattery produce
ignorance of ourselves rather than knowledge. Accordingly, when we

> become aware that [our] gifts are highly esteemed, [we] tend
> to be unduly credulous about them. . . . since blind self-love
> is innate in all mortals, they are most freely persuaded that noth-
> ing inheres in themselves that deserves to be considered hateful.
> Thus even with no outside support the utterly vain opinion
> generally obtains credence that man is abundantly sufficient
> of himself to lead a good and blessed life.

34. *Comm.* on Gen. 3:6.

35. *Inst.,* III.ii.28.

36. *Inst.,* II.i.3.

37. *Inst.,* I.i.2. Cf. *Comm.* on Isa. 6:5.

> Nothing pleases man more than the sort of alluring talk that
> tickles the pride that itches in his very marrow. Therefore . . .
> when anyone publicly extolled human nature in most favorable
> terms, he was listened to with applause. But however great
> such commendation of human excellence is that teaches man
> to be satisfied with himself, it does nothing but delight in its
> own sweetness; indeed, it so deceives as to drive those who
> assent to it into utter ruin. . . . Whoever, then, heeds such
> teachers as hold us back with thought only of our good traits
> will not advance in self-knowledge, but will be plunged into
> the worst ignorance.[38]

Such self-knowledge which looks only to ourselves and uses reason
as its source and criterion leads not to wisdom but to ignorance, not
to healthy self-concepts but to destruction.

Consequently there is another way for man to obtain true knowledge about himself. The Christian acknowledges that he cannot attain a correct self-concept apart from his knowledge of and relationship with God. This is the positive teaching of Calvin in the opening sections of both Books I and II of the *Institutes*.

> Again it is certain that man never achieves a clear knowledge
> of himself unless he has first looked upon God's face, and then
> descends from contemplating him to scrutinize himself. For we
> always seem to ourselves righteous and upright and wise and
> holy—this pride is innate in all of us—unless by clear proof
> we stand convinced of our own unrighteousness, foulness,
> folly, and impurity. Moreover, we are not thus convinced if we
> look merely to ourselves and not also to the Lord, who is the
> sole standard by which this judgment must be measured. . . .
> Suppose we but once begin to raise our thoughts to God, and
> to ponder his nature, and how completely perfect are his
> righteousness, wisdom and power—the straight edge to which
> we must be shaped.[39]

Moreover, "there is none but he alone who may be a competent
judge to know who we are, or that has authority to say it."[40] And,
"even though we consider ourselves either equal to or superior to
other men, that is nothing to God to whose judgment the decision
of the matter must be brought."[41]

In this connection it is important to understand the centrality of
Christ in Calvin's conception of the knowledge of God. Since for
Calvin the right knowledge of ourselves is embraced in the same way

38. *Inst.*, II.i.2.
39. *Inst.*, I.i.2. Cf. I.i.3; III.xii.5.
40. Sermon on Job 11:7 f. as quoted in Torrance, *Calvin's Doctrine*, p. 15.
41. *Inst.*, III.xii.2.

as the right knowledge of the world, what he says in the introductory "Argument" in his commentary on Genesis concerning the latter is also applicable to the former.

> It is vain for any to reason as philosophers on the workmanship of the world, except those who, having been first humbled by the preaching of the Gospel, have learned to submit the whole of their intellectual wisdom (as Paul expresses it) to the foolishness of the cross (I Cor. 1:21).... As soon as ever we depart from Christ, there is nothing, be it ever so gross or insignificant in itself, respecting which we are not necessarily deceived.[42]

Basically then, it is only the Christian who can have a proper self-knowledge because he has been schooled in the Word; he sees himself correctly through the spectacles of Scripture and is restored to a right relationship with his Creator through Jesus Christ. God's truth, even Jesus Christ, is his light and his standard by which his own self-image is mirrored and molded.[43]

Thus far we have simply tried to set the stage for considering the self-image of the Christian in Calvin's writings. We have purposely avoided any abstract discussion of the sinfulness of man or, for that matter, the knowledge of man as created. The reason for this is that the correct appreciation for these concepts comes only through the Word, whose authority only the Christian accepts and to which only the Christian acknowledges himself to be bound.[44] We will, however, return to these topics in their proper pedagogical place.

### The self as new creature

The heart of the material for the Christian's self-image in Calvin lies in what Calvin says about the believer. It is his positive analysis of the man in Christ and not his negative description of sinful man apart from Christ that provides the resources for Calvin's contributions to the Christian self-image. Perhaps the failure clearly to understand this basic point is one of the chief causes of the negative self-image of many Calvinists. What, then, does Calvin say about the man in Christ? A few basic descriptive titles ought to help paint the picture. Believers are first of all saints: "No man, therefore, is a believer who is not also a saint, and on the other hand, no man is

---

42. *Comm.* on Gen., vol. I, pp. 63-64.

43. Calvin's doctrine of man is thus dependent solely on the Word, and not on his stomach ulcers as the thesis of E. Linwood Brandis ("A Study of the Man") suggests.

44. See the very important instructional statement in the midst of Calvin's discussion of the knowledge of God as Creator: "In this ruin of mankind no one now experiences God either as Father or as Author of salvation, or favorable in any way, until Christ the Mediator comes forward to reconcile him to us" (*Inst.*, I.ii.1).

a saint who is not a believer."[45] This is certainly due to God's gracious act in Jesus Christ and His ingrafting us into the body of Christ. In Christ we are sanctified, and in Him we become new creatures.[46] In this situation, "Let no one doubt that God is favorable to him."[47] The great honor that we have is to possess the "rights of citizens with Abraham, with all the holy patriarchs, and prophets and kings, nay with the angels themselves."[48] Believers are said to be "children of light," enlightened by the Spirit of God,[49] and possessors of a new nature which we have in Christ.[50] So, says Calvin, "our old man is destroyed by the death of Christ, so that his resurrection may restore our righteousness, and make us new creatures."[51] Christ puts to death what is mortal in us. "We are dead to sin by the grace of Christ."[52] This is not exhortation to believers, but the plain teaching about the benefits which we derive from Christ.[53] Romans 6:1-4 teaches believers the facts of the case, that is, that the death of Christ is efficacious to destroy and overthrow the depravity of our flesh, and His resurrection to renew a better nature within us.[54]

> This is the view you are to take of your case—as Christ died once to sin, so you have died once in order that in the future you may cease from sin. Indeed you must make daily progress in the mortification of your flesh which has begun in you, until sin is wholly destroyed. As Christ was raised to an incorruptible life, so you are regenerated by the grace of God, in order that you may lead the whole of your life in holiness and righteousness, since the power of the Holy Spirit, by which you have been renewed is eternal and will flourish forever.[55]

Christians are children of God, knowing that God is their merciful Father, because of reconciliation effected through Christ, and knowing that Christ has been given to them as righteousness, sanctifica-

45. *Comm.* on Eph. 1:1.

46. *Comm.* on I Cor. 1:2.

47. *Comm.* on Eph. 2:14.

48. *Comm.* on Eph. 2:19. Cf. Sermon on Eph. 2:16-19.

49. *Comm.* on Eph. 5:8.

50. *Comm.* on Gal. 5:22.

51. *Comm.* on Rom. 6:4.

52. *Comm.* on Rom. 6:1.

53. *Comm.* on Rom. 6:5.

54. *Comm.* on Rom. 6:4. The exhortation, says Calvin, begins in v. 12.

55. *Comm.* on Rom. 6:11. Cf. *Inst.*, II.xvi.13.

tion, and life.[56] "It is obvious, therefore, that those whom God embraces are made righteous...."[57] Furthermore, we have been "rescued from the pit of perdition," through God's grace adopted and set apart for His own, begotten anew and conformed to a new life, and consequently embraced as new creatures, endowed with the gifts of His Spirit; as approved of God, we are pleasing and lovable to Him, renewed in the divine image, mirroring the marks and features of God's countenance.[58] Moreover, we are the temple of God, in which God dwells by His Spirit, and priests to our God.[59] Believers are confident—not in themselves, but in God.

> Briefly, he alone is truly a believer who, convinced by a firm conviction that God is a kindly and well-disposed Father toward him, promises himself all things on the basis of his generosity; who, relying on the promises of divine benevolence toward him, lays hold on an undoubted expectation of salvation.[60]

According to Calvin, the Christian life derives its motivation not from fear but from the positive perspective of the believer's situation and status in Jesus Christ. The motivations which Calvin lists, therefore, serve to describe what the believer is: he is united to God in the bond of holiness, returned to favor with God through Jesus Christ, adopted as a son by the Lord, having God as Father, cleansed by the blood of Jesus, engrafted into His body, dedicated by the Holy Spirit as a temple of God, and destined for heavenly incorruption.[61]

This brief section sufficiently demonstrates how Calvin viewed the Christian man. It is this positive picture of the position in which the Christian finds himself that offers tremendous resources for a positive Christian self-image. But this is only the beginning of the picture. We will look more closely at some of the details.

First of all, the Christian sustains a positive relationship with God. It is positive because it rests on God's mercy and grace. In fact, the right definition of faith, says Calvin, is "a firm and certain knowledge of God's benevolence toward us, founded upon the truth of the freely given promise in Christ.... "[62] It is God's mercy, not our fear, which is the foundation stone of our relationship with Him.

Now the first thing respecting God is, that we should acknowl-

56. *Inst.*, III.ii.2 and 4.

57. *Inst.*, III.xi.21.

58. *Inst.*, III.xvii.5. Cf. I.xiv.18 and Sermon on Eph. 2:13-15.

59. *Comm.* on I Peter 2:5. Cf. Sermon on Eph. 2:19-22.

60. *Inst.*, III.ii.16.

61. *Inst.*, III.vi.2 and 3.

62. *Inst.*, III.ii.7.

edge him to be beneficent and beautiful, for what would become of us without the mercy of God? Therefore, the true and right knowledge of God begins here, that is, when we know Him to be merciful toward us. For what would it avail us to know that God is just, except we had a previous knowledge of His mercy and gratuitous goodness?[63]

This is a constant emphasis of Calvin. Far from emphasizing a negative and harsh picture of God, Calvin consistently directs the Christian's attention to His love and kindness, which, he says, is the proper object of the Christian's contemplation.[64] In fact, the recognition of God's grace, which is the exercise of faith, must even precede repentance. For serious repentance does not take place without knowing that one belongs to God, and no one is truly persuaded that he belongs to God unless he has first recognized God's grace.[65]

Secondly, the Christian sustains a positive relationship with God because through Christ he is forgiven, cleansed, and made a new creature. Calvin claims that the sum of the gospel consists in repentance and forgiveness of sins, that is, in newness of life and free reconciliation.[66] "These are the benefits of the gospel, a double grace; namely, that being reconciled to God through Christ's blamelessness, we may have in heaven instead of a judge a gracious Father, and secondly, that sanctified by Christ's spirit we may cultivate blamelessness and purity of life."[67] The first of these is wrapped up in what Calvin considers to be justification, which consists of gracious acceptance by God and forgiveness of sins.[68] This is the tremendously positive dimension of the gospel, that is, to be reckoned in the condition not of a sinner, but of a righteous man, having God to witness and affirm his righteousness.[69] God accomplishes this, purging the believer of the guilt of all his sin.[70] Consequently Calvin insists that the believer need not have a troubled conscience, that he need not tremble before God, that he need not be fearful of God's punishment. The forgiveness of sins is accomplished, Jesus Christ has offered full satisfaction for all our sins.[71] And this refers not only

63. *Comm.* on Jer. 9:23. Cf. *Inst.*, III.ii.29.

64. *Inst.*, III.ii.29.

65. *Inst.*, III.iii.2.

66. *Inst.*, III.iii.1.

67. *Inst.*, III.xi.1.

68. *Inst.*, III.xi.4.

69. *Inst.*, III.xi.2.

70. *Inst.*, III.iii.11.

71. Cf. *Inst.*, III.xi.1 and 16; II.xvi.18; III.iv.27; III.ii.27.

to past sins! Calvin interprets Romans 6 to be saying, "Even though they [believers] do not yet clearly feel that sin has been destroyed or that righteousness dwells in them, there is still no reason to be afraid and cast down in mind as if God were continually offended by the remnant of sin, seeing that they have been emancipated from the law by grace, so that their works are not measured according to its rules."[72] This is true because of the wonderful fact that the Judge of all mankind has become their Redeemer, and is now their head, advocate, intercessor, and most merciful ruler. Consequently, believers live not in dreadful fear but in joyful and trusting devotion.

This positive picture of the Christian's self-image in Calvin cannot be overstressed. This is particularly true since guilt is such a devastating ingredient in the production of the self-image, often resulting in a very low self-esteem and negative self-image. So important is the relationship of guilt and self-image that B. Narramore claims that one's self-esteem is one subexperience of the wider emotion of guilt.[73] Calvin clearly and repeatedly emphasizes the one and only effective means for helping people move from a sense of guilt to forgiveness: the full satisfaction of Jesus Christ.

Consequently, confidence and assurance is ours because we know that we are not judged by the law but accepted by God on the basis of Christ's complete sacrifice for us. The law of God now takes on a very positive and constructive function in our life. Whereas Calvin certainly acknowledges that through the law comes the knowledge of sin (Romans 3:20), he notes that this is its first function "which sinners as yet unregenerate experience."[74] And even though for both unbelievers and believers this law of God shows how far we are from conforming to God's will and consequently how unworthy we are before God, that law still has a positive function. The purpose of this function of the law is not "to cause us to fall down in despair or completely discouraged rush headlong over the brink."[75] While it may and should lead us to mistrust ourselves and to break down all our pride and arrogance before God, its goal is to lead us to drink of the mercy of Christ. Consequently, "for the children of God the knowledge of the law ought to have another purpose . . . they come

72. *Inst.*, III.xix.6.

73. See his excellent series of articles in the *Journal of Psychology and Theology* II, no. 1 (1974): 18-25: "Guilt: Where Theology and Psychology Meet"; II, no. 2 (1974): 104-15: "Guilt, Its Universal Hidden Presence"; II, no. 3 (1974): 182-89: "Guilt: Christian Motivation or Neurotic Masochism"; and II, no. 4 (1974): 260-65: "Guilt: Three Models of Therapy."

74. *Inst.*, II.vii.7.

75. *Inst.*, II.vii.8.

to realize that they stand and are upheld by God's hand alone; that naked and empty-handed they flee to his mercy, repose entirely in it, hide deep within it, and seize upon it alone for righteousness and merit."[76] Thus even in Calvin's first function of the law there is a positive perspective. However, that positive ring comes more clearly to expression in his third and principal function of the law, which is as "the best instrument for them [believers] to learn more thoroughly each day the nature of the Lord's will to which they aspire, and to confirm them in the understanding of it."[77] Calvin explicitly says that "the law has a function for Christians different from that for unbelievers." It is now "our wisdom through which we are formed, instructed and encouraged to all integrity; it is our discipline which does not suffer us to be dissolute through evil licentiousness."[78]

The law does not stand over our head as a club which would beat us down, for Christ has fulfilled that law for us and our righteousness is in Him, not in our works.[79] This frees us to obey God's law willingly; for freed from the yoke of the law we hear ourselves called with Fatherly gentleness by God, and we cheerfully and with great eagerness answer and follow His leading. We are no longer slaves to the law under its rigorous demands by which we measure our righteousness and form our all too negative—but in such a case correct—self-image. We are children of God, happy and willing to obey our gracious Father. This gives us a positive approach to our actions, "firmly trusting that our services will be approved by our most merciful Father, however small, rude, and imperfect these may be."[80] Such assurance is necessary for a positive self-image. It is lack of faith which considers our works nonacceptable and in vain. Calvin interprets Peter to be saying that our works are accepted "not for the merit of their own excellency, but through Christ.... God ... in Christ sets a value on our works, which in themselves deserve nothing."[81] This perspective helps us to accept ourselves

76. Ibid. Cf. *Inst.*, II.viii.3.

77. *Inst.*, II.vii.12.

78. *Instruction*, p. 42.

79. *Inst.*, III.xix.2. Cf. "Before God's judgment seat it [the law] has no place in their [believers'] consciences.... But where consciences are worried how to render God favorable, what they will reply, and with what assurance they will stand should they be called to his judgment, there we are not to reckon what the law requires, but Christ alone, who surpasses all perfection of the law, must be set forth as righteousness" (ibid.).

80. *Inst.*, III.xix.5.

81. *Comm.* on I Peter 2:5.

and "self acceptance based on God's acceptance is the starting point of spiritual growth."[82]

Life's direction has for the Christian a very positive dimension. Calvin's concept of repentance, which he equates with regeneration, has as its core a complete reorientation of life. The life of the sinner which was turned to himself and this world is redirected to God and His world. This reorientation is the essence of salvation. Repentance is defined as "the true turning of our life to God, . . . and it consists in the mortification of the flesh and of the old man, and in the vivification of the Spirit."[83] This is not to be considered merely a surface change. It is not just a reupholstery job, for "we require a transformation, not only in outward works, but in the soul itself."[84] Only through this complete reorientation of our life does the meaningless and uncertain existence of the sinner find meaning and certainty. The old sinful self in us must die, that is, be "violently slain by the sword of the Spirit and brought to nought."[85] But that is not the end of the matter! Through the resurrection of Christ we are raised up into a newness of life to correspond with the righteousness of God.[86] "Both things happen to us," says Calvin, "by participation in Christ."[87] This is what Calvin means when he talks about regeneration, "whose sole end is to restore in us the image of God that had been disfigured and all but obliterated through Adam's transgressions."[88]

It is in this connection that we must understand the related concepts of humility and self-denial in Calvin. For sanctification—the equivalent of Calvin's broad concept of regeneration—and humility are organically related.[89] Humility is the attitude of the Christian which makes him rely totally on the grace of God. It is the knowledge that apart from God he is nothing. Humility, far from being the underevaluation of an otherwise good self, is the honest and genuine recognition that we as sinners are totally unworthy of God's gracious and forgiving love. And the more we grow in the knowledge

82. Clinebell, *Mental Health,* p. 36.

83. *Inst.,* III.iii.5.

84. *Inst.,* III.iii.6.

85. *Inst.,* III.iii.8.

86. *Inst.,* III.iii.9.

87. Ibid.

88. Ibid.

89. Cf. G. C. Berkouwer, *Faith and Sanctification* (Grand Rapids: Eerdmans, 1952), p. 128.

of God's grace the more we become aware of our own unworthiness.[90] Humility and gratitude go hand in hand. For if we think that we deserve God's grace, if we think that there is something in us that merits God's attention, we would not be thankful to God but demanding of God.[91] Consequently humility is the only proper response to God's grace! The man who claims his own righteousness before God is only making a false defense. What is needed, rather, is a true confession.[92] Therefore, Calvin approvingly quotes Augustine concerning the three precepts of the Christian religion, "first, second, and third, I would answer 'humility.' "[93] The absence of humility is for Calvin not the sign of a positive self-image, but rather the sign of stupidity.[94] So humility is the recognition of the reality of the situation—that before God we stand naked and totally dependent on His love and grace. The more we know our sinfulness, the more we see the need for humility; and conversely, the less we see need of humility, the less we know of our sinfulness. Therefore, Calvin calls self-assurance before God and false confidence in ourselves pests—in fact, the two worst pests—which must be broken down in our deliverance by God.[95] Only the word of God brings one to the recognition of this fact. For self-love and self-assurance are innate in sinful man. Therefore, the sinful man, "laying aside the disease of self-love and ambition, by which he is blinded and thinks more highly of himself than he ought, rightly recognizes himself in the faithful mirror of Scripture."[96]

Self-denial, then, is that action of heart and hand which is spawned by humility. It is not the denigration of an otherwise independent self; rather it recognizes that we are not our own but that we belong to God. The great thing is this: "we are consecrated and dedicated to God in order that we may thereafter think, speak, meditate, and do nothing except to his glory."[97] The direction of our lives is changed from living for sinful self to living for God and His world. This is the reorientation of ourselves back to our original direction and function. It recognizes that it is with God that we have to do

90. Cf. ibid., p. 129.
91. *Inst.*, III.xii.6.
92. *Inst.*, II.ii.11.
93. Ibid.
94. *Comm.* on Gen. 2:7.
95. *Instruction,* pp. 23f. Cf. *Inst.*, III.vii.4.
96. *Inst.*, II.ii.11. Cf. II.viii.54.
97. *Inst.*, III.vii.1.

throughout all of life.[98] A self-image based on such a concept ever increasingly reflects God, as the Christian sees himself being renewed more and more into the image of God. This is the most positive resource for a healthy self-image that exists. Calvin cautions against building ourselves up by wealth, honor, striving for authority, heaping up riches, or by being fearful of poverty and lowly birth. We see that "all these things are nothing nor will we benefit at all."[99] The Christian self-image is best established by looking to God and His will. "He alone has duly denied himself who has so totally resigned himself to the Lord that he permits every part of his life to be governed by God's will."[100]

All of this does not mean that for Calvin the believer is perfect. Much to the contrary. Yet it ought to be remembered that for a healthy self-image every ingredient need not be positive. If a religion helps its adherents realistically to see themselves as they are and then to accept themselves as such, it can be constructive for one's self-image. So Calvin's view of the Christian as not sinless likewise offers a positive contribution to the Christian's self-image and urges him to continue to grow into Christ.

The Christian is freed through regeneration from the bondage of sin. Nevertheless, "there remains in a regenerate man a smoldering cinder of evil."[101] Sin still dwells in the saint, but it has lost its dominion. Therefore, the picture is not all negative: "For the Spirit dispenses a power whereby God's own people may gain the upper hand and become victors in the struggle."[102] The vestiges of sin which remain are there, says Calvin, not to rule over the Christian, but to humble him by the consciousness of his own weakness.[103] The important thing to remember, however, is that the saints are free from the guilt of sin. This guilt is not imputed to them; on the contrary, Christ's righteousness is! Even when Calvin seems to emphasize the continued evidence of sin in the Christian, the purpose is positive:

> Therefore I think he has profited greatly who has learned to be very much displeased with himself, not so as to stick fast in this mire and progress no farther, but rather to hasten to God and yearn for him in order that, having been engrafted into the life and death of Christ, he may give attention to continued

98. *Inst.*, III.vii.2.

99. *Inst.*, III.vii.8.

100. *Inst.*, III.vii.10.

101. *Inst.*, III.iii.10. Cf. III.iii.11-15.

102. *Inst.*, III.iii.11. Cf. *Comm.* on Rom. 6.

103. *Inst.*, III.iii.11. Cf. III.xiv.9.

repentance.... For no one ever hates sin unless he has previously been seized with a love of righteousness.[104]

So the Christian views his life as one of continual striving and of
progress in the process of regeneration, that is, of mortification and
vivification. The goal is clear: the restoration of the image of God in
us. But

> this restoration does not take place in one moment or one day
> or one year; but through continual and sometimes even slow
> advances God wipes out in his elect the corruptions of the flesh,
> cleanses them of guilt, consecrates them to himself as temples
> renewing all their minds to true piety that they may practice
> repentance throughout their lives and know that this warfare
> will end only at death.... In order that believers may reach
> this goal, God assigns to them a race of repentance which they
> are to run throughout their lives.[105]

We have already seen that Calvin offers many resources for a positive Christian self-image. Yet it may seem to some that the self-image
of man is not Calvin's concern. To a degree this is correct. For even
in the area of the Christian life, the area of sanctification, as well as
in the other facets of his theology, Calvin does not place man and
his change or his works in the foreground, but the grace of God. Calvin's anthropology is not man-centered, but God-centered. When the
Christian looks to his own works, apart from God's grace, he de-
thrones grace by his own self-righteousness.[106] That is why Calvin
is insistent about the centrality of Christ and the bond of the Holy
Spirit in the life of the Christian. But this does not mean that man is
wiped out of the picture. It is for man that Christ died and was raised,
and it is to man that the Holy Spirit effectively applies the benefits of
Christ's work! Calvin simply reflects the absolute terms of the Word,
"Apart from me you can do nothing," when he says, "Now Christ
simply means that we are dry and worthless wood when we are
separated from him, for apart from him we have no ability to do
good."[107] That is why "we always need Christ, so that his perfection may cover our imperfection, his purity may wash our impurity,
his obedience may efface our iniquity, and finally his righteousness
may gratuitously credit us with righteousness."[108] Far from contributing to a perspective of passivity and nonidentity on the part of
the Christian, Calvin insists that the Christian finds his identity in

104. *Inst.*, III.iii.20.

105. *Inst.*, III.iii.9.

106. Cf. Berkouwer, *Faith and Sanctification*, p. 117.

107. *Inst.*, II.iii.9.

108. *Instruction*, p. 45.

Christ. His self-image rightfully reflects the image of Christ, which is the most positive, healthy, and sure self-image in all the world! Calvin approvingly quotes Bernard:

> Accordingly, the Lord's compassion is my merit. Obviously, I am not devoid of merit so long as he is not devoid of compassion. But if the mercies of the Lord abound, then equally do I abound in merits. Shall I sing my own righteous acts? O Lord, I shall remember thy righteousness only for it also is mine.... This is man's whole merit, if he put his whole hope in him who makes safe the whole man.[109]

It is important to remember that the process of regeneration (sanctification) is in no way to be separated from justification. For "Christ justifies no one whom he does not at the same time sanctify.... You cannot possess him [Christ] without being made partaker in his sanctification... since in our sharing in Christ, which justifies us, sanctification is just as much included as righteousness."[110] Therefore even in sanctification we look not to ourselves, as though this is our work apart from God, our independent striving, our self-righteousness. Calvin says that Paul tells us in Galatians 5:22, "That all virtues, all good and well regulated affections proceed from the Spirit, that is, from the grace of God and the renewed nature which we have in Christ."[111] Therefore, we are not to fondly flatter ourselves, nor excuse our evil deeds, but with continuous effort strive toward this end: "That we may surpass ourselves in goodness until we attain to goodness itself."[112]

### The self as God's noble workmanship

We are now at the point where we can briefly consider the knowledge of ourselves as created and as sinner. According to Calvin, "the knowledge of ourselves is twofold: namely to know what we were like when we were first created and what our condition became after the fall of Adam."[113] The first ought to move us to gratitude, the second to humility. The first is instructive for the Christian regarding "how great his natural excellence would be if only it had remained unblemished; yet at the same time to bear in mind that there is in us nothing of our own, but that we hold on sufferance whatever

109. *Inst.*, III.xii.3.

110. *Inst.*, III.xvi.1. Cf. Berkouwer, *Faith and Sanctification*, pp. 35 ff.

111. *Comm.* on Gal. 5:20.

112. *Inst.*, III.vi.5.

113. *Inst.*, I.xv.1. Cf. II.i.1.

God has bestowed upon us."[114] In a sense this is "hypothetical" knowledge of man, since no one is now as he was when God created man. Yet for the Christian it is instructive because it shows him what he regains through Jesus Christ. The great nobility which was ours in the first Adam is now ours in the second Adam. Such knowledge should then lead us to recognize God's grace toward us in creation and the goal of our re-creation.

Scripture rightly instructs us in the knowledge of man as created when we recognize that there is one God and one Lord of us all, to whom each and everyone of us owes his existence and his love. Our understanding of the creation account ought to lead us to contemplate God's Fatherly goodness and love toward mankind, in that He prepared this earth and furnished it with all manner of good things for man.[115] The positive and harmonious relationship between God and His creation, as well as the dependence of all creation upon His Fatherly care and nourishment, is revealed in the creation account.

Such knowledge of God the Creator leads us not only to observe His greatness and power, but also "to feel his power and grace in ourselves and in the great benefits he has conferred upon us, and so bestir ourselves to trust, invoke, praise, and love him."[116] To see that God, before He fashioned man, prepared a place most suitable, useful, and salutary for him, is to see that this most gracious Father had us in His care and concern even before we were born.[117] Moreover, Moses tells us, says Calvin, that through the liberality of this gracious Creator and Father, all things on earth are subject to us. To call God Creator therefore is to bear in mind that we are His children, whom He has received unto His own faithful protection to nourish and educate.[118] Calvin continues his discussion of the creation account in a way that puts us in such a positive relationship with this gracious Creator-Father that it ought certainly to enhance our own awareness and confidence in life:

> We are therefore to await the fullness of all good things from him alone and to trust completely that he will never leave us destitute of what we need for salvation, and to hang our hopes on none but him! We are therefore, also, to petition him for whatever we desire; and we are to recognize as a blessing from him,

114. *Inst.*, II.i.1.
115. *Inst.*, I.xiv.2. Cf. I.xiv.20-22.
116. *Inst.*, I.xiv.22.
117. Ibid.
118. Ibid.

and thankfully to acknowledge every benefit that falls to our share. So, invited by the great sweetness of his beneficence and goodness, let us study to love and serve him with all our hearts.[119]

More specifically concerning man, "we shall learn that in forming man and in adorning him with such goodly beauty, and with such great and numerous gifts, he put him forth as the most excellent example of his works."[120] "Among all God's work, here is the noblest and most remarkable example of his justice, wisdom, and goodness...."[121] In fact, from Psalm 8 we learn that man was "adorned with so many honors as to render his condition not far inferior to divine and celestial glory. And, in the second place, the psalmist mentions the eternal dominion and power which they [men] possess over all creatures, from which it appears how high the degree of dignity to which God hath exalted them."[122] Man, as created, was given the "singular honor and one which cannot be sufficiently estimated, that mortal man, as representative of God, has dominion over the world."[123]

The great nobility of man is nowhere better seen than in the fact that he was created in the image of God: "It is a nobility far more exalted, that he should bear resemblance to his creator, as a son does to his father. It was not indeed possible for God to act more liberally towards man, than by impressing his own glory upon him, thus making him, as it were, a living image of the Divine wisdom and justice."[124] This concept of the image of God involves the perfection of our whole nature, the integrity of our whole being—mind, will, affections, sense—in tune with the divine order and will.[125] This image of God gives man an excellence and places man far above the rest of the living beings.[126] It is that which man expresses rather than possesses. That is to say, the image of God is man's unique reflection of his maker; and this is a dynamic relational concept, not a static abstract concept. This is seen most clearly in the fact that in sinful man that image of God is "all but obliterated, destroyed, corrupted, frightfully deformed,"[127] and in the fact that the goal of

---

119. Ibid.

120. *Inst.*, I.xiv.20.

121. *Inst.*, I.xv.1. Cf. *Comm.* on Gen. 1:26.

122. *Comm.* on Ps. 8:5.

123. *Comm.* on Ps. 8:6.

124. *Comm.* on Gen. 5:1.

125. *Comm.* on Gen. 1:27. Cf. *Inst.*, I.xv.3.

126. *Comm.* on Gen. 9:6.

127. *Inst.*, I.xv.4. Cf. *Comm.* on Gen. 5:1.

regeneration is that Christ should re-form us to God's image, a restoration of true and complete integrity, living in harmony with God and man.[128] With such a picture before us of man as created, we ought to be filled with praise and gratitude to our Creator-Father. Instead man is tempted to turn to pride, and consequently, says Calvin, "Genesis 2:7 reminds us that we are dust, alerting us of our creation-hood and creaturely kinships with the rest of the world, as a curb to his [man's] pride and self-exaltation."[129]

## The self as sinner

Now we are prepared to consider undoubtedly the most well known and at the same time the most maligned dimension of Calvin's theology: his teachings about the sinfulness of man. Calvin spared no harsh words in presenting the picture of man the sinner. "With regard to our corrupt nature and wicked life that follows it, all of us surely displease God, are guilty in his sight, and are born to the damnation of hell."[130] "We are so vitiated and perverted in every part of our nature that by this great corruption we stand justly condemned and convicted before God to whom nothing is acceptable but righteousness, innocence, and purity."[131] "The whole man is overwhelmed... so that no part is immune from sin and all that proceeds from him is to be imputed to sin."[132] "Only damnable things come forth from man's corrupt nature."[133] Such statements as these, taken by themselves and out of context, give occasion for the negative self-image in Calvin. Calvin's picture of the man in sin is total. How then can we speak of a positive self-image in the writings of Calvin?

First of all the knowledge of man in sin is never an end in itself. Its purpose is not to picture how dark and utterly hopeless the condition of man is—and to leave him there. Its purpose is to lead one to grace—God's forgiving grace, grace that moves one from this hopeless state to that happy state of being a forgiven sinner.[134]

128. *Inst.*, I.xv.4. Cf. *Comm.* on Eph. 4:24; *Comm.* on Col. 3:10.

129. *Comm.* on Gen. 2:7.

130. *Inst.*, II.xvi.3.

131. *Inst.*, II.i.8.

132. *Inst.*, II.i.9.

133. *Inst.*, II.iii.1.

134. Cf. J. L. Schmidt, "A Comparative Study of the Doctrine of Man in Sigmund Freud and John Calvin" (Master's thesis, Pittsburgh-Xenia Seminary, 1959), pp. 73-74. This thesis contains a helpful analysis and critique of Freud from the Biblical, Calvinistic perspective. However, the very heavy dependence on T. F. Torrance's *Calvin's Doctrine of Man* without due (or as a matter of fact, without any) recognition is deplorable.

Second, it must be remembered that Calvin's discussion of man in sin is confessional. This confessional perspective is certainly very clearly communicated to us with regard to the *Institutes*.[135] This means that the standpoint of the author is "in Christ." His writings are not detached, speculative, and philosophical theology, but the heartfelt expression of his soul. The warmth of expression and the personal involvement with the content is clearly indicated through the use of the personal pronouns in Calvin's writings. Calvin identifies with sinful and corrupt mankind. He does not merely paint the awful picture of the sinfulness of other men. His description of man in sin is, in a very real sense, a confession of his own sin and guilt. It is reflective of the depth of apostasy to which men apart from God sink, and out of which he was redeemed. It is a pointer to the absolute necessity and superiority of God's grace in life. Where grace abounds, there the knowledge and confession of sin all the more abound. As Berkouwer says, "Litanies of guilt are spoken on the way of salvation, not only during the first stage of conversion, but as Christ becomes more wonderful to us, in crescendo."[136]

Calvin's discussion of man in sin presupposes faith, for the doctrine of sin is not an abstraction but a confession. It presupposes that one is aware of, and a participator in, God's mercy. Faith, which involves a knowledge of God's merciful will toward us, is the prerequisite for repentance; and repentance is the arena in which one becomes more and more aware of his need of God's grace and of his own hopeless condition without it. So the standpoint of Calvin's doctrine of man in sin is that of one in faith, confessing the depth of depravity from which he has been brought. Such a posture and confessional perspective does not then transport the believer back to that former condition. Such a confession does not put the confessor back in the situation in which he stands apart from God, nor does it make him a continual participator in that condition. For if one were still "back there" he would not see himself as such, and consequently would not make that type of confession either concerning his sin and guilt or concerning his dependence on God's grace.

However, though the *Institutes* are the confessional writings of Calvin, that does not make them simply one man's subjective experience. Calvin had no intention simply to bare his soul—a stream-of-consciousness writing, a catharsis for his troubled soul. One of

---

135. Cf. the "Prefatory Address to King Francis I of France," *Inst.*, p. 9, and the preface to the *Comm.* on the Psalms, p. xlii.

136. *Faith and Sanctification*, p. 112.

Calvin's chief aims was to instruct his readers in the teachings of Scripture and he wished for his teachings to be judged by the message of the Word of God. So, when Scripture spoke of men apart from Christ as being "dead in their trespasses and sins," Calvin could do no less. But it must be carefully noted that such a description is of man apart from Christ—and that is not the posture of the Christian!

In this connection it is most important to note the tense of the verbs in Calvin's writings and to pay close attention to the important and pivotal word "UNTIL." The Christian's self-image should not be based on the past tense, prior-to-God's-grace situation. For example, in a sermon on Ephesians 2:13-15 Calvin says, "And let the small ones . . . rejoice in their nobility, because God has exalted them, so much so that whereas they were simply like wretched worms and had nothing but ignominy in them, God has taken them up and made them new creatures."[137] It is obvious that the Christian self-image will be influenced differently if one concentrates on the phrase "were simply like wretched worms" or whether one puts the emphasis on that part of the sentence which reads, "nobility . . . God has exalted them . . . taken them up and made them new creatures." The first is past tense and is no more. The second describes God's work in and for us which gives us a new position and perspective—and, we might add, positive resources for the Christian self-image.

So too with the big "UNTIL." In a sermon on Ephesians 2:1-5, Calvin says: "And now he [Paul] shows us . . . what men are *until* God has gone before them with his grace and called them back to himself. . . . We are only wretched putrefying flesh. There is nothing but rottenness and infection in us. God loathes us; we are damned and lost before him; the angels abhor us; all creatures curse and detest us . . . *until* we are renewed by the gospel and by the faith that proceeds from it . . . ."[138] In the *Institutes* a common thought is that "man is God's enemy *until* he is restored to grace through Christ."[139] It may be rather elementary to point out the importance of this "UNTIL," but that little word makes all the difference in

---

137. Sermon on Eph. 2:13-15, p. 188.

138. Sermon on Eph. 2:1-5, pp. 128-29. See further, "*Until* God has worked in us by his grace, then, whose are we? The devil's!" (ibid., p. 133); and for one example from the commentaries see *Comm.* on Gen. 6:5, "Let men therefore acknowledge that inasmuch as they are born of Adam, they are depraved creatures, and therefore can conceive only sinful thoughts, *until* they become the new workmanship of Christ and are formed by his Spirit to a new life" (italics mine).

139. *Inst.*, III.xi.21.

the world! The big "UNTIL" separates the Christian from the conditions described by Calvin preceding this conjunction. We were damned UNTIL God's grace picked us up. All that precedes this "UNTIL" is then wiped away. Perhaps much of our negative self-image may be due to our failure to note the presence and importance of this pivotal "UNTIL." Not to notice this is to transport ourselves back to the situation apart from Christ, which is then no longer material for the Christian self-image, but for the non-Christian self-image.

The Christian ought to recollect his past condition not for the purpose of collecting material for his present self-image, but rather in order better to appreciate God's grace. Calvin says, "In order that you may better esteem the value of God's grace and what it brings with it, do not think only upon your present state but consider what would have become of you if God had left you such as you were in yourselves."[140]

*Calvin's worm references*

There is, however, an expression which occurs in Calvin's writings which seems to be very depreciatory concerning man. Calvin has the unsettling habit of calling man a worm. For example, in the context of man's ungrateful response to the revelation of God in man and the universe, Calvin says, "Do all the treasures of the heavenly wisdom concur in ruling a five-foot worm while the whole universe lacks this privilege?"[141] And in his commentary on the Psalms Calvin comments, "How is it that God comes forth from so noble and glorious a part of his works, and stoops down to us, poor worms of the earth, if it is not to magnify and to give a more illustrious manifestation of this goodness?"[142] Certainly Calvin's description of man as a worm is not the best resource material for building a positive self-image. However, when we consider the context of such statements we find that even this designation is not entirely negative. The context in which this is done usually speaks of the unique majesty and glory of God, the awesome wonder of the greatness of His power and wisdom in the universe. In such a context and with such a comparison, man is indeed but a worm. This is likewise a confessional statement, balanced to be sure by the many positive comments which Calvin makes in the same contexts

140. Sermon on Eph. 2:1-5, p. 130.
141. *Inst.*, I.v.4.
142. *Comm.* on Ps. 8:4.

about man.[143] Moreover, Calvin writes in the context of man as sinner; and it is especially in the comparison of sinful man with the perfect righteousness and holiness of God, that Calvin's designation of man as a worm seems not too inappropriate.[144] This is a comparison which may not be considered apart from its comparative object and which may not be considered in isolation from Calvin's total perspective on man, especially the renewed man in Jesus Christ.

## Calvin's theology and mental health

From a variety of sources one can derive what makes for a healthy positive self-image. Certainly mental health and a positive self-image go hand in hand. So if we look at Clinebell's tests for a mentally healthy religion and compare them to Calvin's theology, we would then have a standard by which to judge whether Calvin might contribute to a positive or a negative self-image.[145] Clinebell states that a religion which promotes mental health is one which builds bridges, not barriers, between people. Certainly Calvin does this in two ways. First, his concept of the communion of the saints and of the church is of a very warm, interpersonal, helping, sharing type of community.[146] Second, his development of self-denial as it relates to other people is constructive and positive; that is, God's image in others binds you to them so that "whatever man you meet who needs your aid, you have no reason to refuse him."[147]

A religion which promotes mental health is one which strengthens a basic sense of trust and relatedness to the universe. Calvin promotes this in two ways. First, in his doctrine of creation and providence, he places the believer in the special eye of God who provides for and continues to so govern the world that the believer may have

---

143. Cf. *Inst.*, I.v.1: "They [men] have within them a workshop graced with God's unnumbered works and, at the same time, a storehouse overflowing with inestimable riches." Cf. also *Comm.* on Ps. 8:5 where Calvin says that the Psalmist represents men "as adorned with so many honors as to render their condition not far inferior to divine and celestial glory."

144. Cf. *Inst.*, I.i.3, and Sermon on Eph. 2:13-15, p. 188.

145. Clinebell, *Mental Health*, pp. 31-54. Ten of Clinebell's twelve standards will be considered. Two of the standards are omitted simply because they are not applicable to this paper.

146. Cf. *Inst.*, IV.i.3.

147. *Inst.*, III.vii.6.

full confidence, assurance, and trust.[148] Second, Calvin's development of the full satisfaction of Christ's sacrifice and his doctrine of
salvation by grace alone through faith is the *only* and real source of
trust. The Christian's trust is in God, in His promises, and in His
mercy and faithfulness—not in his own fickle, undependable, sinful self.

A religion which promotes mental health is one which stimulates
the growth of inner freedom and personal responsibility. Calvin
recognizes that the Christian is free before God, though not autonomous. The Christian ever remains a God-related and dependent
creature. Growth is the key concept in Calvin's view of regeneration, and his sermons are filled with exhortations to take the responsibility of growth and calling seriously. At the same time, Calvin
never lets the Christian believe that he is God—that, in fact, is the
unhealthy deception of the non-Christian. Rather, Calvin honestly
recognizes that the Christian is very dependent on God and on his
fellow beings for his blessedness and life. Such dependency is not
based on authoritarian power or abstract sovereignty, but on grace,
mercy, and restored community.

Furthermore, a mentally healthy religion provides effective means
of helping persons move from a sense of guilt to forgiveness, and
provides well-defined, significant ethical guidelines instead of
emphasizing ethical trivia. This certainly lies at the heart of Calvin's
theology. Sin is forgiven; and though the Christian remains a sinner,
that guilt is not imputed to him. God looks at him through the spectacles of Christ in whose righteousness the forgiven sinner stands.
Moreover, in the sections of the *Institutes* on the Christian life and
Christian freedom, the trivia of life are not at the focal point; but the
freedom of the believer before God, whose will is now revealed
through His law, is the significant ethical guideline for meaningful
and God-glorifying living.

A religion which promotes a mentally healthy perspective increases rather than lessens the enjoyment of life. In spite of all the
presentations of Calvin as an austere and rigid sort of person, it must
be said that Calvin promoted joyful living. Our happiness, he claims,
is in the Lord. Our joy is to be restored to the right order of things—
that is, living in thankful obedience to our Creator-Redeemer.[149]
With regard to this world and life in it he says, "We have never been
forbidden to laugh or to be filled or to join new possessions to old

148. Cf. *Inst.*, I.xvi.1. and I.xvii.6.
149. Cf. Sermon on Eph. 2:1-5, p. 128.

or ancestral ones, or to delight in musical harmony, or to drink wine."[150] Calvin had a healthy appreciation of things which God gives to man—things not only for his necessity but also for his delight and pleasure.[151]

Such a mentally healthy religion encourages the acceptance of' reality over against the denial of it. Calvin forces us to squarely confront the complexity of life and its problems, including its sinfulness, its doubts, and its sorrows. He does not whitewash the life of the Christian, but faces it realistically and boldly.[152]

Such a mentally healthy religion gives its adherents a frame of orientation and object of devotion that is adequate in handling existential anxiety constructively. Certainly the world-and-life view of Calvinism, with its very meaningful and fulfilling perspective on life, its firm and beautiful and certain object of devotion being the merciful and benevolent Creator-Redeemer of this universe, its sense of transcending the earth-boundness of life with the goal of heavenly immortality, its deep sense of trust in God and purpose in this world—all of this is most applicable here.

Such a mentally healthy religion does not accommodate itself to the neurotic patterns of society but endeavors to change them. Here too Calvin provides the resources, the goal, the motivation, and the perspective for meaningful change and involvement in the kingdom of God in this earthly existence. The resources are the power and presence of the Holy Spirit. The goal is the full expression of the kingdom of God. The motivation is the holiness of God and the work of Jesus Christ. And the involvement is in the change of society to conform to the will of God.[153]

Such a mentally healthy religion strengthens rather than weakens self-esteem. This aspect of Clinebell's standards is in effect the object of this entire article, and it is our contention that the type of mentally healthy religion that Clinebell describes will provide basic resources for such a strengthened self-esteem. Calvin's perspective on man provides a solid sense of worth for the individual before God in Jesus Christ, it strengthens and encourages him to live fully and in a fulfilling way, and it provides a solid religious life with great depth and perspective.

150. *Inst.*, III.xix.9.

151. Cf. *Inst.*, III.x.1-4.

152. Cf. *Inst.*, III.viii.9.

153. Cf. H. Hageman, "Does the Reformed Tradition, in 1975, have anything to offer to American Life?" *Reformed Journal* (March 1975), pp. 10-18.

## The problem analyzed

On all of the points which Clinebell sets as standards for a mentally healthy religion, Calvin provides a positive Christian perspective. Our conclusion, therefore, is that Calvin's theology ought to provide the resources for a most positive—if not the only real and healthy—Christian self-image.[154] We must yet analyze the situation with which we began. It was said that the later Reformed thought seems to produce a rather negative self-image, whereas in the writings of the Reformers themselves, especially in Calvin as was demonstrated by this paper, a much more positive image emerges.

Our suggestion is that the *loci* approach to the study of theology, as was typical in the later Reformed tradition, is at least partly responsible for a negative perspective on man. In contrast to Calvin, who presents a rather complete picture of man in his *Institutes*—that is, man-as-created conformed to the image of God, man-in-sin deformed in the image of God, and man-in-Christ re-formed in that image—the *loci* approach to the study of Reformed theology divorces the doctrine of man from the doctrine of salvation. In a typical case the doctrine of man describes man as created and man as sinner. Following this, one finds the material of Christology, which concentrates on the person and work of Christ, and soteriology, which covers the concepts of the *ordo salutis*, for example, calling, conversion, repentance, faith, justification, sanctification, and so forth. These concepts are treated in a rather abstract and detached manner. They are at the center of attention, not the redeemed man. Thus soteriology is not immediately related to the doctrine of man in the *loci* approach to theology. In the specific doctrine of man, man was left in sin; he remained lost. The picture of man as redeemed and renewed in Christ is not typically part of the doctrine of man in such

---

154. Another approach to this question would be to use the criteria which J. W. Carter mentions in his article, "Maturity: Psychological and Biblical," *Journal of Psychology and Theology* II, no. 2 (1974): 89-96. Carter mentions five basic dimensions of life on which, he says, psychologists, though differing in terminology, focus to describe maturity. These are: "(a) having a realistic view of oneself and others; (b) accepting oneself and others; (c) living in the present but having long range goals; (d) having values; and (e) developing one's abilities and interests and coping with the task of living." Carter finds these aspects or dimensions of maturity to center in the concept of "self-actualization" which, he says, occurs in the Christian as created, fallen, and redeemed. This parallels Calvin's discussion of man in the *Institutes* and each point could be demonstrated as being a very integral part of Calvin's doctrine of man. Although self-actualization and self-image are not identical, they are integrally related and thus this approach would also provide us with abundant resources for a very positive Christian self-image in the writings of John Calvin. Cf. also A. Trew, "The Religious Factor in Mental Illness," *Pastoral Psychology* (May 1971), p. 24.

a theological structure.[155] In contrast to this, Calvin's treatment of man does not stop with man in sin, but continues to the very end of his writings with the unifying theme being "man, the image bearer of God"; and the greater emphasis is on man renewed in that image of God through the grace of God in Jesus Christ.[156]

Second, a negative self-image for the Christian may emerge in the later Reformed tradition due to the abstraction of the doctrine of man from the history of redemption perspective. In such an abstraction, theologizing becomes a-temporal. Then, that which the Bible teaches concerning man in sin is considered to be as equally and eternally applicable to man as is that which the Bible teaches concerning man in Christ. In such a situation the doctrine of total depravity, for example, remains as applicable to the Christian man as does the doctrine of justification. The time sequence is lost sight of; the tense of the verbs is ignored. "You were dead through your trespasses and sins," is read, "You are dead through your trespasses and sins." The history of redemption's sequence, that is, passing from death to life, dying with Christ and rising to newness of life, is not emphasized.[157] This a-historical or a-temporal theologizing fails to view the Christian in his new status and relationship in Christ and continually transports him back to his old status and relationship in sin apart from Christ.

In the reading of Calvin, there is always the danger of selective perception and contextual abstraction.[158] By selective perception we mean reading and emphasizing only such negative statements as those with which this paper began. By contextual abstraction we mean considering the doctrines of man in sin and total depravity apart from their context of "the knowledge of God the Redeemer"

155. See the treatment of Calvin's anthropology in "A Study of the Man in Relation to his Doctrine of Man." Under the theme of Calvin's doctrine of man, Brandis includes the revelation of God in Creation and in the Bible, providence, original sin, sin and freedom of the will, total depravity, and a brief paragraph on God's grace. He concludes, "Calvin has two more sections before he finishes off his treatment of the doctrine of man. In the one he enlarges the claim that the will of man is not free, and in the other that man is unable to keep the moral law," pp. 53-65. This type of analysis of the content of Calvin's doctrine of man seems to be conditioned by a traditional loci type approach to the doctrine of anthropology.

156. Thus the statement of R. N. Plummer that "Calvin in his Institutes dispenses with the teaching of sanctification in few words" is incomprehensible ("The Doctrine of Sanctification as Taught by Martin Luther and John Calvin, the Reformers" [Ph.D. thesis, Central Baptist Theological Seminary, Kansas, 1952], p. 130).

157. See A. Hoekema, *The Christian Looks at Himself,* pp. 47-48, regarding the non-applicability of the term "totally depraved" to the regenerate person.

158. See G. Martindale's critique of Wm. Counts' use of Calvin, "Worm Theology?" p. 48.

and divorced from God's completely sufficient and totally renewing grace in Christ.[159] The result, as Torrance has so aptly pointed out, "can only be pessimistic and black."[160] However, if we put Calvin's statements in context and keep in mind the confessional dimension of his writings, the results are both constructive and positive.

Another reason for the emergence of a negative self-image in later Reformed circles may be related to the Reformed teachings on justification and sanctification. We are referring to the situation in which justification is rightly seen as being "by faith," but then sanctification is separated from justification and considered to be "by man."[161] Sanctification, unfortunately, is thus separated from both faith and Christ, and consequently the focus of the eye in sanctification is not on God's renewing grace but on man's efforts. And apart from grace even our efforts in sanctification are not only very inadequate but repugnant to God. Only as we continually have our eye focused on Christ and only as He is continually being formed in us, and only as God sees our "good works" through His merit do we have any confidence and assurance before God. But if the conscientious Christian takes his eye off Jesus and looks to his own works, he cannot but despair. Then the familiar words haunt him: "Even the best of our works are as filthy rags." And that begins the negative self-image syndrome all over again. The status of being a *forgiven* sinner is twisted into that of being a forgiven *sinner*. Then, too, the familiar words of Paul, "The good that I would I do not, and the evil that I would not, that I do . . . . O wretched man that I am . . ." (Rom. 7:15, 24), speak with particular relevance—sometimes quoted as an excuse for sin, a rationalization that any lapse into sin is the common condition which all men, including even the apostle Paul, share.

159. Cf. G. C. Berkouwer, "First and foremost, the confession of the total depravity *(corruptio totalis)* of man is not a pessimistic confession but rather a confession of guilt in the light of the forgiveness of sins" ("The Reformed Faith and the Modern Concept of Man," *The International Reformed Bulletin* III [April 1959]: 9). See also Torrance, "The very heart of Calvin's doctrine of man . . . [is that] we can formulate [it] only from the standpoint of the grace of God in Jesus Christ," and, "Calvin's doctrine of the fall of man and of sin is a corollary of the doctrine of grace in forgiveness and salvation." This, according to Torrance, provides the only proper context for the doctrine of total depravity—" 'total' because grace 'totally' undercuts all human righteousness and wisdom as based upon independence and self-will . . . . Take away from Calvin his basic position in regard to grace, and his great comprehensive inferences from grace, and then translate his total judgments into merely moralistic terms, and the result can only be called pessimistic and black" (*Calvin's Doctrine of Man*, pp. 18-20). Moreover, contextually it is of interest to note that, according to Calvin, the total inability of man to do good is best seen from the perspective of the work of redemption (*Inst.*, II.iii.6ff.).

160. Torrance, *Calvin's Doctrine*, p. 20.

161. Cf. Berkouwer, *Faith and Sanctification*, pp. 17-44, for a discussion of this problem.

Though Calvin maintains that these verses in Romans 7 apply to the believer, he does not end his description on a note of despair and frustration.[162] He says, "We know how easy it is, even in grief which we deserve, to fall into discontent or impatience.... In examining their defects, the saints should not forget what they have already received from God.... They are never without a reason for joy."[163]

Add to this man-centered view of sanctification a legalistic interpretation of the law and a moralistic view of life, and one may well be on the road to a negative self-image. This might happen especially when Calvin's first use of the law is divorced from his third use, and when the first use is seen to be the principal use in Reformed theology and practice.

We will propose but one more suggestion: the mistaken notion that to belittle ourselves is to give glory to God; or in other words, to think negatively of ourselves is to give greater honor to God. There is a sense in which this is true, particularly in connection with our salvation—where it comes from and for whom we live.[164] But at the same time, Calvin warns us against depreciating our new position in Christ. He rebukes those who "cry aloud that it is also great temerity on our part that we thus dare to glory in the Spirit of Christ."[165] He opposes those who think that it is a matter of modesty and humility not to be sure of the presence of the Spirit in us.[166] Calvin answers, "It is a token of the most miserable blindness to charge with arrogance Christians who dare to glory in the presence of the Holy Spirit, without which glorying Christianity itself does not stand!"[167] Similarly Calvin answers those who think that it is the point of modesty not to be sure of their salvation, and who assert that it is the height of arrogance to claim such certainty and assurance for the future.

> How absurd it is that the certainty of faith be limited to some point of time, when by its very nature it looks to a future immortality after this life is over! Since, therefore, believers ascribe to God's grace the fact that, illumined by his Spirit, they enjoy through faith the contemplation of the heavenly life, such glory-

---

162. Cf. *Comm.* on Rom. 7:15. For a cogent argument that Rom. 7:13-25 is not a description of the regenerate man, but of the unregenerate man who is trying to fight sin through the law alone, apart from the strength of the Holy Spirit, see A. Hoekema, *A Christian Looks at Himself*, pp. 61-67.

163. *Comm.* on Rom. 7:25.

164. Cf. *Inst.*, III.xiii.1 and 2; II.ii.10.

165. *Inst.*, III.ii.39.

166. Ibid.

167. Ibid.

ing is so far from arrogance that if any man is ashamed to confess it, in that very act he betrays his extreme ungratefulness by wickedly suppressing God's goodness, more than he testifies to his modesty or submission.[168]

On the contrary, Calvin approves the fact that "saints quite often strengthen themselves and are comforted by remembering their own innocence and uprightness, and that they do not even refrain at times from proclaiming it."[169] Such is done, according to Calvin, through the presence of "good works," which are testimonies of God dwelling in and ruling over us. "When, therefore, the saints, by innocence of conscience strengthen their faith and take occasion to exult, from the fruits of their calling they merely regard themselves as having been chosen as sons by the Lord."[170] Furthermore, Calvin warns us, particularly with regard to other people, but equally applicable to ourselves, that, "he, then, who truly worships and honors God, will be afraid to speak slanderously of man."[171]

Whatever the causes for the shift from the positive emphasis in Calvin regarding man to a more negative emphasis in the later Reformed tradition, such a shift can only be considered deplorable. It certainly deprives the Reformed Christian of tremendous resources for a positive perspective on himself and on life. Calvin repeatedly emphasizes that the Christian lives now with the reality of the new birth, new life, new relationships with God and with men, renewed image of God, new status of being forgiven before God, new motivations for positive Christian living, new goals, and a new home—all having their focus in God, our Creator-Redeemer through Jesus Christ our Lord. This reality ought to provide the resources for building a very positive self-image in the Reformed Christian.

168. *Inst.*, III.ii.40.
169. *Inst.*, III.xiv.18.
170. *Inst.*, III.xiv.19.
171. *Comm.* on James 3:9 (1948 edition).

*David E. Holwerda*

CHAPTER 4 ESCHATOLOGY AND HISTORY:

A LOOK AT CALVIN'S ESCHATOLOGICAL VISION

Calvin has never been famous for his eschatology. Yet political and economic historians have frequently emphasized Calvin's revolutionary understanding of history. In fact, there are those who believe that the two most influential revolutionaries of the modern world have been John Calvin and Karl Marx.[1] Whether one agrees with that estimation or not, historians do agree that the Protestant Reformation restored a sense of dynamism and purpose in history, and provided its adherents with a fresh interpretation of the past and a vivid sense of historical destiny. The key figure in this development was John Calvin.[2]

However, is it possible to hold a revolutionary view of history without having, implicitly or explicitly, an equally significant eschatology? Of course, one can hold eschatological beliefs concerning life after death and the return of Christ without seeing any significant relationship between history and eschatology. But is it possible for a Christian theologian to advocate a dynamic view of history without seeing a direct and positive relationship between history and eschatology?

In the Middle Ages history was viewed as static, and eschatology was not really concerned with history.[3] Consequently, there was no

1. Cf. R. H. Tawney, *Religion and the Rise of Capitalism* (London: John Murray, 1960), pp. 111 ff.

2. E. H. Harbison, "History and Destiny," *Th. Today* 21 (Jan. 1965): 395. See also his book *Christianity and History* (Princeton: Princeton University Press, 1964), chap. 12.

3. The notable exception was Joachim of Floris (1131-1202), who attempted to revive an eschatological perspective on history, but whose views were considered heretical. Cf. K. Löwith, *Meaning in History* (Chicago: University of Chicago Press, 1949), chap. 8.

sense of dynamic movement in history. There was the passing of time, but no essential change. At best, events were recorded as examples of timeless truths, not as signs of the times. History was static and so was the kingdom of God, for it was embedded in the permanent and unchangeable structure of the church. The Reformation challenged these static views of kingdom and history. The dynamic, active God of the Bible was rediscovered, and from that flowed the vision of history as constant change and meaningful turmoil until the final consummation of the kingdom.[4]

For those acquainted only with the characteristic theological face of Calvin, it must be noted that Calvin's theological thinking was deeply involved with the structures and realities of everyday life. W. F. Graham observes that

> for Calvin the real world was to be taken seriously, and for him the real world involved shoemakers, printers, and clockmakers, as well as farmers, scholars, knights, and clergymen. Calvin's world-affirming theology is quite apparent.[5]

More than any other in his time, Calvin attempted to see the relevance of the gospel for all areas of life. It is precisely here in Calvin's social and economic thought that Graham sees his revolutionary character, rather than in his more strictly theological positions. From this perspective Graham describes Calvin as "an almost thoroughgoing secularist in the sense that he understood the gospel to be irrevocably concerned with the world."[6] The evidence supplied by Graham demonstrates conclusively that Calvin was a constructive revolutionary, but the relationship between Calvin's revolutionary social and economic ideas and his theological perspective is left unanswered.[7]

Traditionally the theological taproot for Calvin's historical dynamism is found either in his doctrine of the sovereignty of God[8] or in his doctrine of predestination.[9] Both of these doctrines are essentially the same. Calvin's God is not the "empty, idle" God of the scholastics, but a "watchful, effective, active sort, engaged in ceaseless activity." He is the omnipotent and sovereign God because "govern-

4. Harbison, "History and Destiny," pp. 396 ff. Cf. also T. F. Torrance, "The Eschatology of the Reformation," *Eschatology* (Edinburgh: Oliver & Boyd, 1957), pp. 37 ff.

5. W. F. Graham, *The Constructive Revolutionary: John Calvin and His Socio-Economic Impact* (Richmond: John Knox, 1971), p. 79.

6. Ibid., p. 160.

7. Cf. also A. Biéler, *The Social Humanism of Calvin* (Richmond: John Knox, 1964).

8. W. S. Reid, "The Genevan Revolutionary," *Evang. Q.* 32 (1960): 75-78.

9. Harbison, "History and Destiny," pp. 402 ff.

ing heaven and earth by his providence, he so regulates all things that nothing takes place without his deliberation."[10] This same sovereign God who determines all things by His will calls men to effective obedience in the world. Thus the life of the elect is created by God's redemptive purpose in the world, and their task becomes one of obediently advancing the kingdom of God in the world. Without a doubt Calvin's view of the sovereignty of God and of His predetermining will gives considerable impetus to his view of history. This is what I call the "push-view" of history. God is pushing history toward its destiny, like the great stone in Daniel cut from the mountain by no human hand, rolling down and crushing the kingdoms of the world until finally there stands the sovereign kingdom of God which will never be destroyed. Calvin was filled with this vision of the sovereign God controlling human history and destiny. But this is not the only source of his historical dynamism.

There is another taproot for Calvin's historical perspective, one generally overlooked in the past but today beginning to receive its due emphasis. Calvin held not only a "push-view" of history, but also a "pull-view" of history. There is a new reality at work drawing and pulling us into the future. Since Christ appeared "there is nothing left for the faithful," says Calvin, "except to look forward to His second coming with minds alert."[11] For Calvin, the predetermining will of God has been revealed and accomplished in the Person and work of Christ. Now after Christ's ascension to heaven, this new reality draws believers upward and forward toward the culmination of human history and the consummation of the kingdom of God.[12] Calvin's eschatological vision is indispensable for a proper understanding of his dynamic view of human history.[13]

10. *Inst.*, I.xvi.3.

11. *Comm.* on I Peter 4:7.

12. Although W. F. Graham makes little reference to Calvin's theological perspective, several of his statements suggest an eschatological source for Calvin's historical perspective. For example, "Luther leaned toward the medieval idea of God present at holy times in holy places. He understood history to be nearing its end, and waited in anticipation for the imminent divine disclosure. Calvin pointed toward the future and had little need for holy times or places. His God was dynamic, futuristic, concerned for human obedience in the present" (*Constructive Revolutionary*, p. 208; cf. also pp. 54-56). If this is so, perhaps it would be fruitful to argue that Calvin's occasional "overuse" of government to achieve the demands of the gospel lay in his failure to consistently distinguish the eschatological reordering of man and society, which occurs in Christ, from the political reordering appropriate to human government. In a chapter on "Success and Failure," Graham argues, however, that this was caused by a failure in Christology. That may be the case, but I am not convinced.

13. Torrance, "Eschatology of the Reformation," pp. 39 ff. Where Calvin's view of the sovereignty of God is separated from eschatology, the possibility arises of transforming that sovereignty into a rigid determinism which destroys all human responsibility for history.

Why was this taproot not stressed in the past? Probably because the positions Calvin adopts on specific eschatological doctrines are quite traditional. Naturally Calvin argued against Roman Catholic speculation about purgatory and the location of paradise, and he vigorously opposed the fanatical belief that the kingdom of God could be established by violence (as attempted in Münster in 1534). Still his eschatology remained a rather moderate, nonspeculative, middle-of-the-road position, containing no creative reformulation of the church's eschatology. At least such is the case when one focuses on *specific* doctrines, such as the intermediate state, resurrection, return of Christ, judgment, and the future kingdom of God.

In addition, there are elements in Calvin's theology that create problems for the thesis that his eschatology contributes significantly to his historical dynamism. One such element is his meditation on the future life coupled with his doctrine of the immortality of the soul. To some interpreters this seems to short-circuit any real concern for historical destiny or for the cosmic sweep of Biblical eschatology.[14] Another problem stems from Calvin's stress on the unity of the Testaments. Some believe that this leads Calvin to a position where there are no longer any real differences created within the history of God's people,[15] and that the only significant moments are eternal and transcendent.[16]

Therefore, in order to establish the thesis that Calvin's eschatological vision contributed significantly to his revolutionary stance, it will be necessary, first of all, to examine the problem areas mentioned above.

## Meditation on the future life and immortality of the soul

Sometimes it seems that for Calvin the death of the individual is the dividing line between time and eternity, the present and the future life. Death appears to be the key eschatological event because through death the immortal soul enters into the perfection of the future kingdom. The entire eschatological perspective seems to be removed from the plane of history and to be exhausted in its application to individual destiny.

14. Cf. H. Quistorp, *Calvin's Doctrine of the Last Things* (London: Lutterworth Press, 1955), pp. 12-13; J. P. Martin, *The Last Judgment: In Protestant Theology from Orthodoxy to Ritschl* (Grand Rapids: Eerdmans, 1963), pp. 4, 12.

15. H. H. Wolf, *Die Einheit des Bundes* (Neukirchen Kreis Moers, 1958), chap. 6.

16. L. G. M. Alting Geusau, quoted in I. J. Hesselink, "Calvin and Heilsgeschichte," *Oikonomia* (Hamburg: Bergstedt, 1967), p. 164.

114    *Exploring the Heritage of John Calvin*

For example, how should the following words of Calvin be understood?

> If heaven is our homeland, what else is the earth but our place of exile? If departure from the world is entry into life, what else is the world but a sepulchre? ... If to be freed from the body is to be released into perfect freedom, what else is the body but a prison? If to enjoy the presence of God is the summit of happiness, is not to be without this, misery? ... Therefore, if the earthly life be compared with the heavenly, it is doubtless to be at once despised and trampled under foot.[17]

Does Calvin advocate a world-flight which seeks the freedom of the soul apart from the body? Does his "contempt for the present life"[18] make death the key eschatological event? Is Calvin's eschatology more Greek than Biblical?

Calvin did hold to what is essentially a philosophical doctrine of the immortality of the soul. But like most of the early Church Fathers, Calvin modified the Platonic doctrine by means of the doctrine of creation.[19] The soul is not immortal in and of itself. Immortality is a gift of God and the life of the soul is continually dependent on the grace and will of God. If God's grace were withdrawn, the soul would be but a passing breath. Nevertheless, the immortality of the soul was very important to Calvin. He found it useful for articulating important perspectives on life and death, and for constructing theological or philosophical refutations of opposing positions.

The doctrine of the immortality of the soul was especially important in Calvin's first theological writing, the *Psychopannychia*. This work was devoted to a refutation of the position of some Anabaptists who held to the doctrine of soul-sleep between death and final resurrection. In this work Calvin expresses himself, as he continues to do later in the *Institutes,* in terms of a dichotomy of body and soul.

> If the body is the prison of the soul, if the earthly habitation is a kind of fetters, what is the state of the soul when set free from this prison, when loosed from these fetters?[20]

Calvin followed the doctrine of creationism, which holds that the soul is a direct creation of God. Consequently, the soul is considered

18. *Inst.*, III.ix.1.

19. Cf. H. A. Wolfson, "Immortality and Resurrection in the Philosophy of the Church Fathers," in *Immortality and Resurrection,* ed. K. Stendahl (New York: Macmillan, 1965), pp. 57-58; and Wm. Niesel, *The Theology of Calvin* (Philadelphia: Westminster, 1956), p. 66.

20. "Psychopannychia," in *Tracts and Treatises in Defense of the Reformed Faith* (Grand Rapids: Eerdmans, 1958), p. 443.

to be a substance independent of the body. And it is primarily in the soul that one finds the image of God.

Calvin's thought on the preeminence of the soul is complex.[21] On the one hand, it is rooted in creation. Calvin can say that without any doubt "man was made for meditation upon the heavenly life."[22] Since the first man had an immortal soul which "was not derived from the earth at all,"[23] it is the chief activity of the soul to aspire to heaven. Nonetheless, under the impact of Paul's teaching in I Corinthians 15, Calvin can still suggest that there was something insufficient about man's created condition. Even though Adam possessed an immortal soul, "he yet smacked of the earth, from which his body had its origin, and on which he had been set to live."[24] In fact, Calvin can go so far as to say that

> the state of man was not perfected in the person of Adam; but it is a peculiar benefit conferred by Christ, that we may be renewed to a life which is *celestial,* whereas before the fall of Adam, man's life was only *earthly,* seeing it had no firm and settled constancy.[25]

Therefore, on the other hand, the preeminence of the soul is ultimately rooted in redemption. For in comparison with the life we have in Adam and the immortality of the soul which we share with him by virtue of our created nature, the life which we receive in Christ is far superior.

> Christ . . . has brought us the life-giving Spirit from heaven, in order that He might regenerate us into a life that is better and higher than that on earth. In short, our life in this world we owe to Adam, as branches to the root; Christ, on the other hand, is the originator and source of the life of heaven.[26]

Calvin believed that the soul can die only a spiritual death, that is, it can be the recipient of the judgment of God with all that that entails for human life. But the believer has been born anew by the Spirit of God, and in his soul is being constantly transformed into the image of Christ. So for reasons of both creation and redemption the teaching of soul-sleep made no sense to Calvin.

> If they (souls) always increase till they see God, and pass from that increase to the vision of God, on what ground do these men bury them in drunken slumber and deep sloth?[27]

One senses that Calvin's anthropology is inclined toward a basic dichotomy between body and soul, earth and heaven. In fact, these

---

21. For an excellent discussion of this issue, see Quistorp, *Calvin's Doctrine,* chap. 2.

22. *Inst.,* I.xv.6.

23. *Comm.* on I Cor. 15:47.

24. Ibid.

25. *Comm.* on Gen. 2:7.

26. *Comm.* on I Cor. 15:47.

27. Calvin, *Psy.,* p. 441.

dichotomies are essentially the same. As far as heaven is from the earth, so far removed is the heavenly soul from the earthly body.[28] Thus part of Calvin's eschatological vision seems to proceed as follows: since the soul is the nobler part of man[29] and eternal life (or the kingdom of God) has already begun in it, the life of the body or earthly life should be despised[30] and death should be desired.[31]

If this were the whole of Calvin's perspective, the thesis that eschatology contributes significantly to his historical dynamism would fall flat on its face. The entire dynamic of the Christian life would then be reduced to the quest of the soul seeking its origin in heaven and in God. It would be exclusively individualistic, ignoring the cosmic sweep of Biblical eschatology. But this is not all that Calvin says. In fact, in his letter to Cardinal Sadolet, Calvin explicitly rejects the view which reduces the Christian life to the quest of the soul seeking its salvation in heaven.[32] Although Calvin's anthropology may create some tensions within his attempt to do justice to history and the cosmos, we will see that Calvin does not allow his anthropology to cancel a genuine appreciation for the eschatological dynamic of human history and of the renewal of the creation.

### Eschatology and meditation on the future life

The doctrine of the immortality of the soul clearly makes an impact upon Calvin's meditation on the future life. But it is not the basis for that meditation, neither does it constitute the central or even one of the most important perspectives. When Calvin's meditation on the future life is carefully read in the context of his entire discussion of the Christian life,[33] the most fundamental and pervasive perspective is clearly eschatological.[34]

For Calvin, the Christian life is a life lived in imitation of Christ. Christ "has been set before us as an example, whose pattern we

28. Ibid., p. 444. "Had they a particle of sense they would not prattle thus absurdly about the soul, but would make all the difference between a celestial soul and an earthly body, that there is between heaven and earth."

29. *Inst.*, I.xv.2.

30. *Inst.*, III.ix.1.

31. *Inst.*, III.ix.5.

32. Reply to Cardinal Sadolet's Letter, *Tracts and Treatises on the Reformation of the Church* (Grand Rapids: Eerdmans, 1958), pp. 33-34.

33. *Inst.*, III.vi-x.

34. Wm. Niesel asserts that "all other points with regard to the origin of Calvin's *meditatio vitae futurae* should be subordinated to this insight," viz., that Calvin gave "his arguments about the imitation of Christ an eschatological bearing" (*Theology of Calvin*, p. 149, fn. 3).

ought to express in our life."[35] The Christian life will be characterized, therefore, by self-denial. We deny ourselves because we belong
to God.

> We are God's: let us therefore live for him and die for him.
> We are God's: let his wisdom and will therefore rule all our
> actions. We are God's: let all the parts of our life accordingly
> strive toward him as our only lawful goal.[36]

But this striving toward God as our goal must be understood in
connection with the eschatological motive of "our blessed hope."

> For, as Christ our Redeemer once appeared, so in his final
> coming he will show the fruit of salvation brought forth by him.
> In this way he scatters all the allurements that becloud us and
> prevent us from aspiring as we ought to heavenly glory. Nay,
> he teaches us to travel as pilgrims in this world that our celestial
> heritage may not perish or pass away.[37]

These comments of Calvin conclude a section devoted to the
exhortation found in Titus 2:11-14, where Christians are urged "to
live sober, upright, and godly lives in this world, awaiting our blessed
hope, the appearing of the glory of our great God and Savior Jesus
Christ."

There is an additional element in Calvin's understanding of self-
denial as imitation of Christ which is extremely important. Self-denial
means bearing the cross. Calvin's description of life under the cross
frequently strikes Christians who live in times of peace and prosperity
as too gloomy, too negative toward the joys of life. Even those who
claim Calvin as a spiritual father feel a bit depressed by this theme
in Calvin, and consequently fail to appreciate its full significance.
But unless the theme of cross-bearing as descriptive of the Christian
life is given its full significance, one cannot understand Calvin's
concept of unworldliness and contempt for this present life. In other
words, one will miss the basic eschatology behind Calvin's vision.

If Christians are to reflect the pattern of Christ in their lives, each
must bear his own cross.

> For whomever the Lord has adopted and deemed worthy of his
> fellowship ought to prepare themselves for a hard, toilsome, and
> unquiet life, crammed with very many and various kinds of
> evil. It is the Heavenly Father's will thus to exercise them so
> as to put his own children to a definite test. Beginning with
> Christ, his first-born, he follows this plan with all his children.[38]

Cross-bearing is absolutely essential to lead the believer to trust
in God's power, to develop patience and obedience, to allow him to
experience the faithfulness of God, and to create within him hope for

35. *Inst.*, III.vi.3.
36. *Inst.*, III.vii.1.
37. *Inst.*, III.vii.3.
38. *Inst.*, III.viii.1.

the future. In addition, to suffer persecution for righteousness'
sake is an "honor God bestows upon us in thus furnishing us with
the special badge of his soldiery."[39] But whatever shape the cross
may take and for whatever reason it is borne, it always entails sorrow, grief, bitterness and pain. Although the bitterness of the cross is
"tempered with spiritual joy," spiritual joy does not cancel sorrow,
grief, and suffering.

This discussion of self-denial and cross-bearing is the immediate
context for Calvin's meditation on the future life. He begins his discussion with this sentence:

> Whatever kind of tribulation presses upon us, we must look to
> this end: to accustom ourselves to contempt for the present
> life and to be aroused thereby to meditate upon the future life.[40]

Because this life is nothing but struggle, the thought of the crown
that awaits the believer causes him to raise his eyes to heaven.

> For this we must believe: that the mind is never seriously
> aroused to desire and ponder the life to come unless it be previ-
> ously imbued with contempt for the present life.[41]

Calvin's reasons for advocating contempt for the present life are
not rooted primarily in a body-soul dichotomy, but are to be found
rather in a contrast between the present life under the cross and the
future life of the heavenly kingdom.

Yet, no matter how often one is reminded that the phrase "contempt for the present life" must be understood as part of an eschatological contrast, the phrase still seems far too negative for Calvin.
If he intended it seriously, how could he ever attempt to participate
meaningfully in this life? Why would Calvin vigorously throw himself
into the struggles and turmoils of his time, if he advocated contempt
for this present life?

We need to be reminded that the phrase did not originate with
Calvin. He borrowed it from the devotional literature of his time,
although he used it in a significantly different way. L. J. Richard,
a Roman Catholic theologian, has compared Calvin's understanding
of "contempt" with that advocated in the devotional literature of the
Middle Ages. The classic example is Thomas à Kempis' *On the
Imitation of Christ and Contempt for the World*. The full title of
that work is important. The imitation of Christ entails contempt
for this world or this present life. Although there are many formal
similarities between Calvin's view of the Christian life and that of
à Kempis—for example, imitation of Christ, self-denial, and cross-

39. *Inst.*, III.viii.7.
40. *Inst.*, III.ix.1.
41. Ibid.

bearing—there is a decisive difference in their understanding of contempt for the world.

Thomas á Kempis' idea of contempt is a very literal one. It means simply to avoid, shun, or reject the world. Richard summarizes this view as follows: "The *Imitatione Christi* projects the image of a pilgrim who pays no heed to the things around him that he may offer his entire attention to the other world, which is eternal."[42] The Christian is preoccupied with his interior life. "There is very little interest in the apostolate of a service of God and the world."[43]

Calvin's view of contempt for the world, however, does not lead to a withdrawal from the world. Immediately after speaking of contempt, Calvin urges gratitude for earthly life. In spite of the fact that it is "crammed with infinite miseries," this life is a blessing of God in which we already begin "to taste the sweetness of the divine generosity in order to whet our hope and desire to seek after the full revelation of this."[44] Although like á Kempis, Calvin uses the Biblical imagery of Christian life as a pilgrimage toward the heavenly kingdom, it is a pilgrimage in which one must use the world as God intends.[45] So Calvin does not advocate a rejection of the present life as such.[46] Contempt means only a rejection of what is evil, and a recognition that true life must be sought in Christ. Since Christ is in heaven, Christians must seek their life in heaven and in the future, not on earth and in the present. Or from another perspective, "believers ought to lead a heavenly life in this world."[47] The Christian pilgrimage has important consequences for the world.[48]

Hence the perspectives that dominate Calvin's meditation on the future life are eschatological in nature. His entire outlook is determined by the believer's relationship to the ascended Lord.

However, since Calvin believes that one enters the peace of the kingdom already at death, his belief in the immortality of the soul plays an important role in his understanding of the future life. Accordingly, Calvin can speak of this future life as "eternity after death,"

42. L. J. Richard, *The Spirituality of John Calvin* (Atlanta: John Knox Press, 1974), p. 176.

43. Ibid., p. 29.

44. *Inst.*, III.ix.3.

45. *Inst.*, III.x.1.

46. Quistorp asserts that Calvin's "aspiration towards heavenly life cannot . . . imply any flight from the world but rather impels us already in this world to live another kind of life" (*Calvin's Doctrine*, p. 43).

47. *Comm.* on Phil. 3:20.

48. Richard, *Spirituality of Calvin*, chap. 6.

"heavenly immortality," "immortality to come," or "heavenly kingdom." Nonetheless, for Calvin this future, immortal, or heavenly life may never be divorced from the final eschatological reality of the return of Christ and the resurrection of the dead.[49]

Even though H. Quistorp believes that Calvin's perspective on the position of the soul after death in its relationship to the final resurrection lands Calvin in a contradiction, he nevertheless stresses that for Calvin the soul "does not perish nor sleep in death but in so far as it is born again in Christ already enjoys heavenly peace in the expectation of the resurrection of the body, which will bring in consummate blessedness."[50]

Calvin did not allow his belief in the immortality of the soul to negate the Biblical eschatological hope.

> We would certainly agree that the correct exposition of Scripture is that the life of the soul without hope of resurrection will be a mere dream. God does not promise souls the survival of death, glory complete and immediate, and enjoyment of blessedness, but delays the fulfillment of their hope to the last day.... Scripture informs us that the life of the spirit depends on the hope of resurrection, and to this souls released from the body look with expectancy. Whoever destroys the resurrection is also depriving souls of immortality.[51]

Earlier it was pointed out that Calvin modified the classic view of the immortality of the soul by means of the Biblical doctrine of creation. In the above quotation it is further modified by the doctrine of the resurrection of the body. Although Calvin advocates the preeminence of the soul over the body, he frequently corrects his own onesidedness by affirming that for man the body is essential in both creation and redemption.

Commenting on Peter's phrase "the salvation of your souls," Calvin finds it necessary to say something about the body. "The body is not excluded from participation in glory in so far as it is connected to the soul." The soul is clearly preeminent, and because it is immortal "salvation is properly ascribed to it."[52] Yet when Calvin addresses himself self-consciously to this matter, he relates immor-

49. *Inst.*, III.ix.5-6

50. Quistorp, *Calvin's Doctrine,* pp. 81-82. Cf. also pp. 87-92.

51. *Comm.* on Matt. 22:23. Cf. also *Comm.* on Isa. 26:19, and *Inst.*, III.vi.3. It is important to note that for Calvin meditation on the future life and meditation on the resurrection are synonymous: "Accordingly, he alone has fully profited in the gospel who has accustomed himself to continual meditation upon the blessed resurrection" (*Inst.*, III.xxv.1).

52. *Comm.* on I Peter 1:9.

tality ultimately to the resurrection of the body. As quoted above, "whoever destroys the resurrection is also depriving souls of immortality." And in more general terms Calvin affirms that

> it is a dangerous piece of scoffing when they cast doubt on the resurrection of the last day, because if this is taken away nothing is left of the Gospel, the power of Christ is drained away, and all religion is destroyed. Satan directly attacks the throat of the Church when he destroys faith in the return of Christ.[53]

Because of his Biblical sensitivities, and because Christian life is life in Christ, Calvin refuses to allow his eschatological vision to be determined simply by the philosophical doctrine of the immortality of the soul. It is one of the factors which may at times loom large (especially in the discussion of the intervening state between death and resurrection), but the most important perspective governing Calvin's vision of the Christian person in life and death continues to be the eschatological one. Life in Christ is for Calvin basically an eschatological reality.[54]

## Eschatology and Jesus Christ

Jesus Christ stands at the center of Calvin's perspective on the Christian life. Everything said about self-denial, cross-bearing, and contempt for this life, as well as everything Calvin says about the history of the world and its future, is determined by the person and work of Jesus Christ. Calvin makes no attempt to speculate directly about world history as such, because its meaning and future are determined by the redemption accomplished by Christ.[55]

The advent of Christ, including His death and resurrection, is for Calvin the decisive point at which the renewal of the world has occurred. Sin brought disorder into the world, but the death of Christ restored all things to order. Listen to Calvin's remarkable comment on John 13:31:

53. *Comm.* on I Peter 3:4.

54. Quistorp describes Calvin's perspective as fully eschatological in the Biblical-Pauline sense, i.e., "a *theologia crucis* demanding sheer faith in the hidden glory of Christ and His kingdom and also at the same time a lively hope of its future manifestation" *(Calvin's Doctrine,* p. 11). And commenting on Calvin's stress on death and immortality, Quistorp argues that "it is the Christological foundation of his eschatology and whole theology which prevented Calvin from lapsing into a certain philosophy of death to which he perhaps was inclined" (ibid., p. 47).

55. Cf. H. Berger, *Calvins Geschichtsauffassung* (Zürich: Zwingli Verlag, 1955), pp. 92 ff. T. F. Torrance asserts that the Reformers "taught that the earthly future is divinely governed through the mission of the Church" ("Eschatology of the Reformation," p. 39).

> For in the cross of Christ, as in a splendid theatre, the incompa-
> rable goodness of God is set before the whole world. The glory of
> God shines, indeed, in all creatures on high and below, but
> never more brightly than in the cross, in which there was a
> wonderful change of things—the condemnation of all men was
> manifested, sin blotted out, salvation restored to men; in short,
> the whole world was renewed and all things restored to order.[56]

A similarly striking comment is found in his interpretation of the
phrase "now is the judgment of the world."

> The word *judgment* is taken as "reformation" by some and
> "condemnation" by others. I agree rather with the former, who
> expound it that the world must be restored to due order. For
> the Hebrew word *mishpat* which is translated as *judgment*
> means a well-ordered constitution. Now we know that outside
> Christ there is nothing but confusion in the world. And although
> Christ had already begun to set up the kingdom of God, it was
> His death that was the true beginning of a properly-ordered
> state and the complete restoration of the world.[57]

The advent of Christ, His death and resurrection, is for Calvin the
eschatological turning point of world history. At that moment the
renovation of the world—all that was necessary for the reordering
of the disordered world—was completed in Jesus Christ. There can
be no other event of such decisive significance for human history
and the life of the cosmos. Every subsequent event can have meaning only in relationship to that "renovation of the world which took
place at the advent of Christ."[58]

To highlight these remarkable statements, it will be useful to introduce briefly the contemporary dispute as to whether or not Calvin's
eschatological perspective fits the history-of-salvation mold. The
central reason for the dispute will be obvious to anyone who has
ever read Calvin's discussion of the similarities and differences
between the Old and New Testaments. His stress on unity is so
emphatic that there seems to be no essential difference between
the two Testaments. "In substance and reality," says Calvin, "the
two are really one and the same."[59]

Consequently, H. H. Wolf, for example, argues correctly that
for Calvin there is only a difference in the administration of the covenants, not in their substance. There is only a difference as to how
we participate in Christ, not as to the content of that participation.
The promise and the salvation enjoyed are the same; only the mode

56. *Comm.* on John 13:31.

57. *Comm.* on John 12:31.

58. *Comm.* on Gen. 17:7.

59. *Inst.*, II.x.2.

of participation differs. The Old Testament saints participated by means of a more obscure and hidden promise; whereas the New Testament saints participate by means of a more clearly revealed promise. But in both cases, what is promised is basically a future reality, even though in both cases there is already a certain distribution of these future gifts. And even though the advent of Christ distinguishes the two Testaments, His Kingdom even now remains basically a future reality for which we still hope. Thus both the Old and New Testament people of God live by promise, both meditate on the future life, and both already share in what is promised because the promises of God are sure. The fact that the New Testament people see the reality more clearly is only a relative difference, not a substantial or essential one.[60]

Therefore, Wolf concludes that there can be no genuine history-of-salvation development in Calvin's eschatological vision. For if such a development actually existed in Calvin's theology, Wolf asserts that the unity and identity of the covenants in their substance and reality would be threatened.[61]

However, does a genuine history-of-salvation development require that there be no unity or identity in the substance of the covenants? Doesn't Wolf confuse participation in the promise (which in substance is always the same for Calvin because there is only one covenant) with the history that actualizes what is promised?

Calvin is fond of the metaphor of the sun and its light, using it to explain various mysteries, including that of the relationship between the Testaments. Concerning the position of the Old Testament saints, Calvin declares:

> Faith was not yet revealed; not that the fathers lacked light altogether but that they had less light than we .... However much darkness there might be under the law, the fathers were not ignorant of the road they had to take. The dawn may not be as bright as noonday, but it is sufficient for making a journey, and travellers do not wait until the sun is up. Their portion of light was like the dawn; it could keep them safe from all error and guide them to everlasting blessedness.[62]

The metaphor of the sun and its rays, of dawn and noonday, is a metaphor stressing unity and continuity. The light of dawn and noonday is in substance the same light. Yet when that metaphor is used to explain the differences in the history of salvation, it is clear that a decisive event in history distinguishes the dawn from the noonday. The two conditions can be neither equated nor reversed. Conse-

60. Wolf, *Die Einheit,* chap. 6.     62. *Comm.* on Gal. 3:23.
61. Ibid., p. 64.

quently, in explaining the meaning of the word *gospel,* Calvin affirms:

> Thus a distinction is set between the promises which held the
> hopes of the faithful in suspense, and this glad news, wherein
> God testifies that He has brought to pass that event which before
> He had made the object of hope.[63]

That "event which before He had made the object of hope" is
for Calvin the advent of Christ in which the whole world was renewed and all things restored to order. Thus within the essential
unity of the covenants Calvin expresses a sensitivity to a history-of-
salvation perspective.[64] A decisively new event has occurred which
establishes all the promises and determines the whole of human
existence. The goal of history and creation, previously announced
by the prophets and participated in by hope, has entered history in
order to move it toward its destiny.

Although the renovation of the whole world has already occurred
in Christ, the world has not yet arrived at that destiny. The actual,
visible renewal of all things is still in the process of completion.[65]
Until Satan's kingdom is wiped out, the right ordering of all things
cannot actually be set up in the world. This tension between the goal
already achieved in Christ and the destiny still to be achieved dominates Calvin's eschatological perspective. As we will see shortly,
this tension provides him with a basic principle for interpreting
prophecy. It leads him to assert again and again that the words of
Scripture which seem to point to a victory that is momentary and
final, actually point to a victory which is not limited to any short
period of time. For example, the casting out of Satan on the cross
continues to be "the remarkable effect of Christ's death which
appears *daily*."[66]

Because of this tension between the goal achieved in the advent
of Christ and the destiny to be achieved at His return, and because
Christ is now in heaven, the ascended Christ dominates Calvin's
thinking about eschatology.

> Ascension goes along with resurrection. Therefore, if we are
> members of Christ, we must ascend into heaven, because when
> He had been raised from the dead, He was received up into
> heaven, that He might draw us up with Him.[67]

Calvin's so-called unworldliness is in actuality a seeking for re-

63. Preface to *Comm.* on the Harmony of the Gospels, vol. I, p. xi.

64. Cf. Berger, *Calvin's Geschichtsauffassung,* pp. 99-103; I. J. Hesselink, "Calvin
and Heilsgeschichte."

65. *Comm.* on Acts 3:21.

66. *Comm.* on John 12:31.

67. *Comm.* on Col. 3:1.

newal and life in Christ who is now in heaven. Meditation on the future life is not a rejection of this created world in favor of another heavenly world unrelated to this one, but it is always a seeking of Christ in whom the renovation of this world has occurred.[68] "We must seek Christ nowhere else but in heaven, while we wait the final restoration of all things."[69]

The ascended Christ holds together Advent and Return. Seeking the ascended Christ in heaven may never be separated, therefore, from an eager anticipation of His return. Since the perfected kingdom is already complete in Him, the Christian is always waiting for the final, visible restoration of all things. And since the present life of the believer is "buried under the ignominy of the cross and various distresses" and "differs nothing from death,"[70] he is always looking for the revelation of the life that is now hidden. For Calvin, the "principle" governing the Christian life is "that from the time when Christ once appeared, there is nothing left for the faithful except to look forward to His second coming with minds alert."[71]

The ascended Christ, who incorporates within Himself both Advent and Return, stands at the center of Calvin's eschatological vision.

## Prophecy and eschatology

Unless one understands how significantly the ascended Christ dominates Calvin's eschatological perspective, his handling of specific prophecies can be rather exasperating. Calvin always seems to know, quite apart from the immediate context, that the particular prophecy in question is not exhausted in a single, momentary fulfillment in time. Almost all prophecies appear to be fulfilled on a continuum. Calvin knows this, of course, because of the Christ who incorporates within Himself both Advent and Return: both the fulfillment already completed and the fulfillment that will one day be fully revealed.

Calvin's characteristic handling of prophecy is seen, for example, in his interpretation of Isaiah 26:19, "thy dead shall live, their bodies shall rise." He faults both rabbinic and Christian interpreters: the rabbis for thinking it would be fulfilled in the Messiah's first coming,

---

68. "*Heaven, heavenly,* refer as a rule in Calvin's thought not to some empyrean realm but to the new or celestial condition of God's creation" (Torrance, "Eschatology of the Reformation," p. 59, fn. 1).

69. *Comm.* on Acts 3:21. Cf. also *Inst.*, III.vi.3.

70. *Comm.* on Col. 3:3.

71. *Comm.* on I Peter 4:7.

and the Christian interpreters for limiting it to the last judgment. Calvin knows that "the Prophet includes the whole reign of Christ from the beginning to the end." In other words, Calvin interprets this prophecy in the light of its fulfillment in Christ. Christ has already made believers alive, and yet they do not "literally" or "fully" live until the resurrection.

> Believers, by fleeing to God, obtain life in the midst of afflictions, and even in death itself; but because they have in prospect that day of the resurrection, they are not said literally to live till that day when they shall be free from all pain and corruption, and shall obtain perfect life; and, indeed, Paul justly argues, that it would be a subversion of order, were they to enjoy life till the appearance of Christ, who is the source of their life.[72]

How does Calvin know that these words in Isaiah are not restricted to a final, single event in history but rather embrace the whole reign of Christ? Calvin replies:

> For, although we begin to receive the fruit of this consolation when we are admitted into the Church, yet we shall not enjoy it fully till that last day of the resurrection is come, when all things shall be most completely restored; and on this account it is called "the day of restitution."[73]

A prophecy can contain only what as a matter of fact has happened and will happen in Christ. Thus every prophecy announcing final victory receives a twofold fulfillment in the Advent and Return of Christ. And the eschatological existence of believers living between these times participates in both the identity and the distinctiveness of these two events; that is, believers share in the already completed, yet hidden, renovation of the world which someday will become fully visible.

The prophecy in Daniel 7:27, concerning the kingdom and the dominion which will be given to the people of God, is handled by Calvin in precisely the same manner. The dominion of the saints under heaven began already "when Christ ushered in his kingdom by the promulgation of his Gospel." The prophet announces the commencement of Christ's kingdom in the first preaching of the gospel, but he also goes further to draw "a magnificent picture of Christ's reign embracing its final completion." Again we meet Calvin's principle for interpreting the prophets:

> I may here remark again, and impress upon the memory what I have frequently touched upon, namely, the custom of the Prophets, in treating of Christ's kingdom, to extend their mean-

72. *Comm.* on Isa. 26:19.

73. Ibid.

ing further than its first beginnings; and they do this while they dwell upon its commencement.[74]

Advent and Return, commencement and completion—both are intended by the prophet. But notice the stress on commencement. For Calvin this is always the starting point in the interpretation of prophecies because already in the Advent of Christ prophecies find their fulfillment. And even when a prophecy points to a final future event in the eyes of most interpreters, Calvin usually insists that it is already being fulfilled.

For example, Matthew 24:27—"For as the lightning comes from the east and shines as far as the west, so will be the coming of the Son of Man"—is interpreted by Calvin as a promise that Jesus will suddenly extend the borders of His kingdom to the farthest ends of the earth. But this is not simply a promise to be fulfilled at a future date; rather it has already been fulfilled in the spread of the gospel.

> The wonderful rapidity with which the Gospel flew out to every region of the globe was a shining testimony to the divine power. It could not be the result of human industry that the light of the Gospel should flash like lightning and reach from one corner of the world to the other extreme: it is sound commendation of the heavenly glory that Christ presents.[75]

Calvin knows that fulfillment has occurred and therefore is occurring and will occur. He knows that Christ has come and therefore is coming and will come. His entire perspective, focused on the ascended and presently reigning Christ, moves between the two poles of Advent and Return.

Calvin's rejection of an earthly millennial kingdom flows naturally from this fundamental perspective. The millennial belief assumes that Christ will reign visibly on the not-yet-renewed earth for a limited period of time. But Calvin believes that the perfected kingdom already exists in Christ, that it is eternal and includes the renovation of the world. Consequently, Christ's visible appearance can mean only the final revelation of the perfected kingdom. A temporally limited messianic kingdom on a nonrenewed earth struck Calvin as a childish fantasy[76] similar to the teaching of the rabbis.[77] Until

74. *Comm.* on Dan. 7:27.

75. *Comm.* on Matt. 24:20.

76. "This fiction is too puerile to need or deserve refutation" (*Inst.,* III.xxv.5).

77. Cf. *Comm.* on Dan. 7:27 for Calvin's dispute with the position of Rabbi Abarbinel. All the Reformers rejected Chiliasm as a kind of Jewish heresy. For example, the Second Helvetic Confession of 1566: "We further condemn Jewish dreams that there will be a golden age on earth before the Day of Judgment, and that the pious, having subdued all their godless enemies, will possess all the kingdoms of the earth" (chap. XI, sec. 14).

Christ's return on the day of the general resurrection, Calvin believed that "God rules in the world only by His Gospel."[78] Between Advent and Return, Christ's kingdom is visible only to the eyes of faith.

From this perspective also one other characteristic of Calvin's interpretation of prophecy becomes intelligible. Since the poles of prophecy are Advent and Return, with fulfillment occurring on a continuum moving from one pole to the other, prophecy cannot be used as the basis for calculating the time of Christ's return. Attempts to predict the time violate not only the express teaching of Jesus but also the very nature of prophecy itself. The time references in prophecy are intended, according to Calvin, to elicit hope and patience, not to give specific dates and time frames.

### The kingdoms of Christ and Antichrist

The various perspectives in Calvin's basic eschatological outlook, which have been discussed above, come together in his discussion of the Antichrist. This discussion reveals Calvin's refusal to calculate or even guess at the time of Christ's return, his basic anti-apocalyptic bias, and his continual weaving together of eschatological themes with the themes of history and Christian existence.

The central text for this discussion is II Thessalonians 2:3, "Let no one deceive you in any way; for that day will not come, unless the rebellion comes first, and the man of lawlessness is revealed." The apostle Paul is correcting the erroneous impression of some early Christians that the Day of the Lord had come.

Because this teaching of Paul "corresponds in every respect" to the words of Jesus in Matthew 24 and 25, Calvin moves back and forth from Paul to Jesus to establish his interpretation. Even though the Day of the Lord is at hand, it is not now. "It is at hand in regard to God," says Calvin, "with whom one day is as a thousand years."[79] In addition, Calvin believed that the sin of man could delay and upset the arrival of the kingdom, even though it could not finally prevent its coming.[80] For these reasons, only false prophets calculate a speedy advent. The Lord Himself wants believers to "keep in constant watch for Him in such a way as not to limit Him in any way to a particular time."[81]

Unlike Luther, Calvin did not speak about the time of Christ's

78. *Comm.* on Rom. 14:11.          80. *Comm.* on Matt. 24:4.

79. *Comm.* on II Thess. 2:2.         81. *Comm.* on II Thess. 2:2.

return.[82] Instead he believed that the eschatological discourses of Jesus and Paul point to a "protracted conflict" for the church on earth. Consequently, the basic thrust of eschatological teaching is not to produce calculation, but patience and hope.

> In short, the preaching of the gospel is like sowing seed. We must patiently wait for the time of harvest. It is wrong to be soft and effeminate, and have our enthusiasm crushed by winter's frost, snow clouds or adverse seasons.[83]

Evils in the world should lead the faithful to "equip themselves with patience for a long stretch."[84]

The perfected kingdom of Christ is in heaven and must be sought there. There is no way of dragging it to earth prematurely, nor of jumping immediately into the rest of the blessed. The perfected kingdom is possessed only in hope. And the promise that it will be fully disclosed one day is given precisely to establish believers in that hope lest they be overwhelmed by the ensuing chaos. The church in history is a suffering church, a church long tested with hard and wearisome temptations.

> Not that the glory and majesty of Christ's Kingdom will only appear at His final coming, but that the completion is delayed till that point—the completion of those things that started at the resurrection, of which God gave His people only a taste, to lead them further along on the road of hope and patience.[85]

The basic intention of the eschatological discourses is to "keep the minds of the faithful in suspense to the last day." Believers may not attempt to hurry on to triumph ahead of time. Instead they should so hope and look for the day of Christ's coming that "yet no one should dare ask when it will come." They must walk by faith without knowing the times with certainty, and they must wait for the final revelation with patience. "Beware then," Calvin warns, "not to worry more than the Lord over details of time."[86]

The kingdom of Christ has a history in time, and so does the kingdom of the Antichrist. Neither kingdom is limited to a single moment

82. Luther cherished several hopes about the return of Christ. He hoped that Christ would come in his own lifetime, that at least it would not be delayed over one hundred years, and he was rather certain that the Day of Judgment would not be absent three hundred years hence. Cf. R. V. Vinglas, "An Investigation into the Eschatological Teaching of Martin Luther and John Calvin" (diss., S.D.A. Theological Seminary, Washington D.C., 1948), pp. 35-40.

83. *Comm.* on Matt. 24:4.

84. *Comm.* on Matt. 24:6.

85. *Comm.* on Matt. 24:29.

86. *Comm.* on Matt. 24:29, 36.

in human history. Both kingdoms in their coming and in their ruling affect human history over a very long period of time.

The coming of these two kingdoms is interrelated. The final coming of Christ cannot occur until there is a general apostasy and the rule of Antichrist in the church. But before there can be apostasy, there must be the universal proclamation of the gospel. The term *apostate* refers only to "those who have previously enlisted in the service of Christ and His Gospel." Therefore, the defection can take place only "when the world has been brought under the rule of Christ."[87]

Calvin's understanding of that "which is restraining" the revelation of the Antichrist corresponds to his interpretation of the "falling away." In distinction from the common medieval belief that the Roman Empire was the restraining force (which Calvin accepted as historical fact but not as Paul's intention), Calvin understands the restraining force to be the necessary spread of the gospel through every part of the world. The general apostasy could not occur until the gospel had been proclaimed to the nations. Therefore, the "gracious invitation to salvation was first in order of precedence." In fact, the one is, at least in part, for the sake of the other. Calvin affirms that God's grace was offered to all "in order that men's impiety might be more fully attested and condemned." The coming of the Antichrist is thus punishment for the rejection of the gospel.[88]

If such is Calvin's understanding of that which restrains, how could he identify the Papacy as the Antichrist? Did Calvin believe that the gospel had already been proclaimed to the nations? Yes, he did. Even though he was aware that in his day some remote nations had "not even the faintest word of Christ," he did not find Jesus' words in Matthew 24:14 to be an insuperable obstacle to his position. When Jesus affirmed that the gospel would be preached throughout the whole world to all nations before the end would come, Calvin believed that Jesus was talking not of "individual tracts of land or fixing any particular time but only affirming that the Gospel . . . would be published to the furtherest ends of the earth before the last day of His coming."[89] For Calvin, that had already happened essentially through the ministry of the first apostles. The gospel had been proclaimed to the nations, the universal church had come into being, and now a general apostasy had occurred in the church. The necessary conditions for the arrival of the Antichrist had made their appearance.

87. *Comm.* on II Thess. 2:3.  89. *Comm.* on Matt. 24:14.

88. *Comm.* on II Thess. 2:5-6, 10.

The Antichrist was not equated with a particular pope, for he was not considered to be a single individual. Instead, the Antichrist was viewed by Calvin as a succession of individuals, or more accurately, as a kingdom controlled by Satan. This kingdom was not limited to the Papacy because anyone who led believers from the truth was a part of that kingdom, including Mohammed. Yet since the Papacy ruled in the church and there usurped powers belonging only to God, the Papacy was in particular the Vicar of Satan.[90]

If then Calvin believed that the gospel had been proclaimed to the nations, the apostasy had occurred, and the Antichrist had come, did he conclude that the end of history was near at hand? No, he did not. Here again Calvin's characteristic eschatological perspective controls his understanding. For example, Calvin interprets Paul's prophecy, that the Lord Jesus will slay the Antichrist "with the breath of his mouth and destroy him by his appearing and his coming," as referring only to the manner of his destruction, not to the time. Calvin admits that it seems that these words of II Thessalonians 2:8 refer to the final appearing of Christ when He will come as Judge from heaven. Yet he holds that it is by no means certain that this reference should be restricted to the final appearance of Christ. For Calvin knows that "Paul does not think that Christ will accomplish this in a single moment."[91]

Calvin discovers two perspectives in this prophecy concerning the slaying of the Antichrist. Obviously, the Antichrist will be "completely and utterly" destroyed when the final day has come. But in addition—and this is the most distinctive element in Calvin's perspective—Paul is also predicting that

> in the meantime Christ will scatter the darkness in which Antichrist will reign by the rays which He will emit before His coming, just as the sun, before becoming visible to us, chases away the darkness of the night with its bright light.[92]

Thus Calvin develops his eschatological vision along historical lines. Since the breath of the Lord's mouth is simply His Word, the victory of Christ over Antichrist is already occurring and can be seen in history. True and sound doctrine is destined "at all times to be victorious over all the devices of Satan." At the same time, the preaching of true and sound doctrine is "Christ's coming to us."[93] Hence through its proclamation of the gospel, the church is already effecting in history the dawning of that future day of the return of Christ. The Reformation itself, with all the turmoil and commotion

90. *Comm.* on II Thess. 2:3-4.        92. Ibid.

91. *Comm.* on II Thess. 2:8.          93. Ibid.

that accompanied it, was seen as a manifestation of the eschatological movement in history through which the kingdom of God comes.

## Life between the times

Life between Advent and Return is thus determined by the ongoing conflict between the kingdom of Christ and the kingdom of Satan or Antichrist. Calvin's interpretation of the eschatological defeat of Antichrist as an ongoing process imparts a vigorous dynamic to his view of the task of the church in the world. Believers may not sit and wait, because the great eschatological events are not limited to the final moment of human history. Eschatological events contain for Calvin both the element of finality and of process. At the end Christ will come and "fully and completely" overthrow evil. But meanwhile through the proclamation of the Word there is an anticipatory, continual defeating of Satan and Antichrist. Consequently, believers are called to "fight hard under Christ, equipped with spiritual armour."[94]

Warfare is the shape of the church's life between the times. Believers must participate in Christ's continual war against His enemies because until the last day Christ "has no peaceful possession of His kingdom."[95] Consequently, Calvin's view of the Christian life is active and dynamic. Believers are soldiers waging active warfare against Christ's enemies in order to establish the reign of God on earth,[96] and the organization of the church is essentially organization for battle.[97] The battle is waged with patience and hope because the outcome is sure. The Word of the gospel contains such "divine and incredible power" that it can and will with violence cast down the prince of the world, for "at the thunder of the gospel Satan fell down like a lightning flash." Characteristically Calvin applies this word of Jesus in Luke 10:18 not only to the final defeat of Satan but

94. *Comm.* on II Thess. 2:8-10. E. C. Rust summarizes the impact of eschatology on Calvin's view of history as follows: "For Calvin, this era is no tension-filled waiting period prior to the final consummation. *Armageddon* is now in process, and, although Calvin emphasized the ultimate triumph, he saw the Church as now actively engaged with the powers of darkness. Here we have a *dynamic approach* which sees the Church waging war to transform the realm of historical existence more into the likeness of the Father's will in Christ. God is building His kingdom in this world, and through the history of this world, and all must not be left to the end" (*Towards a Theological Understanding of History* [New York: Oxford Press, 1963], p. 250).

95. *Comm.* on Heb. 2:8.

96. "It is a work of immense difficulty to establish the heavenly reign of God upon earth because of the obstacles Satan erects." Letter to Nicholas Radziwill, *Letters of John Calvin* (New York: Burt Franklin Reprints, 1972), III:135.

97. "Denn die organisation der calvinischen Gemeinde ist Kampforganisation." Berger, *Calvins Geschichtsauffassung*, p. 166.

to "the whole course of the Gospel." "We cannot doubt," says Calvin, "that whenever He raises up faithful teachers He will give success to their work."[98]

There is nothing speculative about Calvin's eschatology. He was "no conjurer in numerical calculations." Specific numbers in Daniel and Revelation had to be interpreted figuratively. Through them God promises His elect some moderation, some shortening of the days; but the precise point of termination remains hidden in the secret counsel of God.[99] And the signs of the times cannot be added up like dates on a calendar. The point of all such prophecies is patience and persistence. Calvin's eschatological vision is in essence a call for decision and obedient action here and now.[100] Because the final victory is already occurring in the present defeats suffered by the Antichrist, the kingdom of God is already being established in the world. Such present victories anticipate and lead to the final victory of Christ over Antichrist. The church and its activity is an essential part of the eschatological movement of history from Advent to Return.

Is there any real progress in establishing the kingdom between the times? Calvin spoke of progress.[101] He said that "the Kingdom of God increases, stage upon stage, to the end of the world."[102] But this increase or progress of the kingdom was not for Calvin a kind of evolutionary growth by which the kingdom of God gradually and progressively displaces the disordered structures of the world. Calvin was under no delusion concerning the elimination of evil prior to the return of Christ. He never became falsely optimistic about a time in history in which the struggle against evil would be easier than in his own time. For Calvin believed that "the more pressingly God offers Himself to the world in the Gospel, and invites men into His Kingdom, the more boldly will wicked men belch forth the poison of their impiety."[103] Christian existence between the times will always be in the shape of a cross, "for it is in this way that God wills to spread his kingdom."[104]

---

98. *Comm.* on Luke 10:18.

99. *Comm.* on Dan. 7:25.

100. Cf. Berger, *Calvins Geschichtsauffassung*, p. 77.

101. "Zeal for daily progress is not enjoined upon us in vain, for it never goes so well with human affairs that the filthiness of vices is shaken and washed away, and full integrity flowers and grows. But its fullness is delayed to the final coming of Christ" (*Inst.*, III.xx.42).

102. *Comm.* on Matt. 6:10.        104. *Inst.*, III.xx.42.

103. *Comm.* on II Peter 3:3.

Calvin's view of history is hopeful rather than optimistic, because he believed that the power of the kingdom of God would continually defeat the power of evil. But until that final return of Christ when God will be all in all, there will always be constant turmoil, conflict, and suffering. Calvin lived in a time when the church was under the cross. His commentary on Daniel, dedicated to the persecuted church in France, clearly reflects his eschatological outlook. Calvin discovers that Daniel was already warning the people of God that

> the Church's state would not be tranquil even when the Messiah came. The sons of God should be militant to the end, and not hope for any fruit of their victory until the dead should rise again, and Christ himself should collect us into his own Celestial Kingdom.[105]

## An authentic eschatology?

What is an authentic eschatology? In terms of the contemporary discussion, an authentic eschatological vision perceives history and eschatology as one. Eschatology concerns the dynamic of human history, the cosmic sweep of the rule of God involving the judgment and renewal of human life and all its structures. Eschatology is not concerned just with the final momentary events of history, but with the dynamic force moving at the core of human history here and now, giving history its meaning and its destiny.

Does Calvin's eschatological vision qualify? We have seen that Calvin did not allow his belief in the immortality of the soul to short-circuit his eschatological vision. His vision is focused on Christ who is in heaven. Yet this focus on heaven is not world-flight, for the Christ at the center is the One in whom the renovation of the world has occurred. Consequently, Calvin's eschatology leads to obedient action in which, through the promulgation of the gospel, the kingdom of God begins to occur here and now in the history of the world. Such a perspective seems to qualify as an authentic eschatology.

However, before a final answer can be given, there is an additional issue to be discussed. Although Calvin affirms that the kingdom of God manifests itself in history when God forces His enemies "all unwilling—with Satan at their head—to accept His authority, till all become His footstool,"[106] nevertheless, he sees the kingdom of God primarily in the renewal of individuals and the church. The kingdom of God is a spiritual reality manifesting itself at present in the "inward and spiritual renewing of the soul," or in a person being

105. Preface to *Comm.* on Daniel.

106. *Comm.* on Matt. 6:10.

"reformed to the image of God by His Spirit."[107] From this perspective Calvin can say that the kingdom of God or of Christ means the same thing as the church of God.[108] Thus even when he is speaking of the presence of the kingdom of God, Calvin's focus is first of all on the renewal already occurring in the body of Christ.

Does this restrict Calvin's eschatological vision? Is his perspective more a philosophy of church history than an authentic eschatology? It is true that Calvin focuses on the church in history and makes almost all prophecies concerning the future apply to the present life of the church. But Calvin's understanding of the church is not parochial or even merely ecclesiastical. The history of salvation which becomes visible in the church contains within it the meaning of the history of the world. And the renewal manifesting itself in the body of Christ is the renewal that embraces the whole creation. Calvin would not understand the dichotomy expressed in the question above. The history of the church cannot be divorced from the history of the world. The destiny of the church cannot be divorced from the destiny of the world.

The kingdom of God, according to Calvin, is fundamentally the reordering of all things. "The opposite of the kingdom of God is complete disorder and confusion."[109] The mission of Christ is "to gather together out of a state of disorder those things which are in heaven and which are on earth."[110] We have seen that Calvin believed that the reordering of the whole creation has already taken place in the Advent of Christ, especially in His death and resurrection. Following the Biblical principle of the first-fruits, Calvin sees this reordering of all things occurring first of all in individuals and the church. There we can see "the beginnings of God's Kingdom, for we now begin to be reformed to the image of God by His Spirit so that the complete renewal of ourselves and the whole world may follow in its own time."[111]

Thus Calvin's focus on the renewal of the individual and the church imposes no restriction on his eschatological vision. He clearly under-

107. *Comm.* on Luke 17:20; Inst., III.xx.42.

108. *Comm.* on Amos 9:13.

109. *Comm.* on Matt. 6:10.

110. *Comm.* on Isa. 11:6. Cf. also *Comm.* on Eph. 1:10. For the significance of the restoration of order in Calvin's eschatology, cf. R. S. Wallace, *Calvin's Doctrine of the Christian Life* (Grand Rapids: Eerdmans, 1961), pp. 103-11; and B. C. Milner, *Calvin's Doctrine of the Church* (Leiden: Brill, 1970), chap. 2.

111. *Comm.* on Luke 17:20. Calvin also interprets Peter's statement about the elements being dissolved by fire as "renewal" of the elements rather than destruction. Cf. *Comm.* on II Peter 3:10.

stands the Biblical teaching that man and the creation are in essence related to each other not only in origin but also in destiny. In a very remarkable comment Calvin affirms that the whole creation continues to function because of hope.

> From hope comes the swiftness of the sun, the moon, and all the stars in their constant course, the continued obedience of the earth in producing its fruits, the unwearied motion of the air, and the ready power of the water to flow. God has given to each its proper task, and has not simply given a precise command to do His will, but has at the same time inwardly implanted the hope of renewal.[112]

Eschatology makes the world go round! The whole machinery of creation, says Calvin, would have fallen out of gear after the Fall of Adam were it not for this hope of renewal. Ever since that time the creation has been groaning age after age for the perfection that is still to come. Hence the creation should be an example for us who live by hope for only such a short period of time. "If the creatures have continued their groaning for so many ages, our softness or indolence will be inexcusable if we faint in the brief course of our shadowy life."[113] Man and the creation are companions in hope. But the beginnings of hope, or its first-fruits, are seen in believers who have been endowed with the Holy Spirit.[114]

Neither the believer nor the church exists or is saved apart from the world. But the eschatological reordering of the world occurs here and now—at least in its beginnings—in the believer and the church. Hence the destiny of the world becomes visible in the reordering which occurs in the body of Christ. Because that is so, because the restoration of man entails the restoration of order in the world, B. Milner can draw an important conclusion concerning the relationship of Calvin's political activism to his eschatology.

> Calvin's political activism, then, may be traced directly to his conception of the church as that movement which stands at the frontier of history, beckoning the world toward its appointed destiny.[115]

Calvin's eschatological vision is cosmic in scope and contributes significantly to his dynamic view of history. For Calvin, eschatology and history are the same. One may disagree with his exegesis of specific passages, and ask whether his arguments against a millennial reign of Christ on earth are sufficient,[116] because it is the case that at times Calvin's basic perspective seems to override some of the

112. *Comm.* on Rom. 8:20.     114. *Comm.* on Rom. 8:23.

113. *Comm.* on Rom. 8:22.     115. Milner, *Calvin's Doctrine*, p. 195.

116. H. Quistorp, for example, questions both (*Calvin's Doctrine*, pp. 115, 158-62).

exegetical details. Nonetheless, it cannot be disputed that Calvin's basic perspective stems from the core of Biblical eschatology. His eschatology is an authentic eschatology of hope.[117]

## Some concluding remarks

The creative thought of great teachers frequently contains a variety of tensions. Sometimes these tensions exist because such is the nature of truth. Sometimes they exist because of lack of clarity. For whatever reason they may exist in the thought of the teacher, these tensions are usually dissolved by their followers. Disciples find it difficult to keep up with their masters. They become selective and one-sided. Consequently, great traditions become narrow and rich traditions are impoverished.

Traditions developing in the wake of John Calvin have not done justice to his eschatology. Some of the fault lies with Calvin himself. His dynamic eschatological vision is articulated more clearly and forcefully in the appropriate Biblical commentaries than it is in the *Institutes*. Although the positions developed in the *Institutes* are in complete harmony with the commentaries, they need the light of the commentaries to be fully appreciated. But since his followers have usually considered the *Institutes* to be an adequate summary of his thought, the essential nature of Calvin's eschatology has been easily overlooked.

However, it is not just a matter of not reading widely enough in Calvin. The tensions that exist in his thinking have contributed to one-sidedness in his followers. No one would dispute the fact that a kind of pietistic movement arose in the Calvinist tradition, making its appeal to Calvin's doctrine of the immortality of the soul and seeking its life in heaven. The movement became far more individualistic and otherworldly than Calvin ever was. It too focused on the Christ in heaven, but on a Christ divorced from the realities of world and cosmos. No longer was it the cosmic Christ in whom the reordering of the cosmos had already occurred, but rather a Christ who secured the life and destiny of the individual.[118] Calvin's meditation on the

---

117. Calvin's eschatology is thus characterized by H. Quistorp, *Calvin's Doctrine,* chap. 1 on "Hope," and T. F. Torrance, *Kingdom and Church* (Edinburgh: Oliver & Boyd, 1956), chap. 4, "The Eschatology of Hope: John Calvin."

118. Cf. C. R. Andrews, "A Baptist Looks Backward and Forward," *Th. Today* 13 (Jan. 1957): 507-20. Granting that Calvin was able to hold together the doctrine of the immortal soul and the consummation of the universe, Andrews asserts that Calvin's successors could not. "The corporate hope dimmed as the individual hope overspread it. This inner contradiction was to become a source of great weakness in the Reformed tradition, including English Independency" (p. 512).

future life was read as though Calvin were Thomas á Kempis. Perhaps on this score, at least to a limited extent, Calvin can be appealed to against himself; but a close reading of the *Institutes,* in the light of the commentaries, clearly demonstrates that such a reading misses everything Calvin stood for.

Calvin has been called a theologian of the eternal decree, and that description is undoubtedly correct. The significance of the sovereignty of God, predestination, and the eternal decree can hardly be overemphasized; but it can be understood in a one-sided manner. Calvin did not separate the eternal decree from its content or from that which manifests and effectuates it in history. Calvin can say that "the eternal decree of God would be void unless the promised resurrection, which is the effect of that decree, were also certain."[119] Eternal decree and eschatology may not be separated. The eternal decree cannot be understood apart from the history of redemption which manifests and effectuates it.[120] But in parts of the Calvinist tradition the eternal decree has been divorced from eschatology, and the result has been a kind of static, almost fatalistic determinism. History has been viewed as one great big push from behind, and the emphasis has fallen on the necessary action of God to the exclusion of any necessary action of Christians. The dynamic, active pulling into the future stemming from the renewal already possessed in hope has been a negligible ingredient in such traditions. Consequently, history has not been seen as an arena of eschatological happenings involving necessary Christian action; nor has the church been viewed, in Milner's words, as a movement standing "at the frontier of history beckoning the world to its destiny."

The threat of legalism, the nemesis of all Calvinist traditions, also stems from a failure in eschatological perspective. If obedience to the sovereign God, if conformity to the new order of God articulated in the law, is separated from the Christian's present participation in the reordering of all things already accomplished in Christ, the inevitable result is legalism. The law is then imposed only from the outside and obedience is at best external. For Calvin, obedience—even in the creation—is not only obedience to a command, but participation by hope in the new reality of the kingdom of God.

Finally, Calvin has acquired a justly deserved reputation as a social and political revolutionary. His slogan of establishing the kingdom of God on earth has had great appeal, and many of his followers have walked in his footsteps. Yet the use of that slogan in the con-

119. *Comm.* on Rom. 8:23.

120. Note Calvin's assertion that "Christ, then, is the mirror wherein we must, and without self-deception may, contemplate our own election" *(Inst.,* III.xxiv.5).

temporary scene populated by revolutionaries of various stripes can easily imply too much. That slogan can become captive to a kind of social Darwinism, promising a gradual but inexorably progressive development which will bring human society to a state of perfection— provided, of course, that Christians work hard enough and possess sufficient faith. Or that slogan can become captive to a radical revolutionary philosophy promising perfection as the inevitable result of the Marxist revolution—provided, of course, that a little transcendence is thrown in.

For Calvin, however, Christian action in establishing the kingdom may not be viewed apart from a proper eschatological perspective. The perfected kingdom is in Christ who is in heaven. Believers cannot by their actions drag that perfected kingdom to earth prematurely. What is experienced in the present and what is manifested through Christian action are only the beginnings of the kingdom of God. Calvin's eschatological vision tempered his revolutionary action. He was, in Graham's words, a constructive revolutionary.

Eschatology is an indispensable dimension of Christian thought and action. Without it the church becomes static, ineffective, and usually heretical. For eschatology contributes a compelling dynamic to Christian action and obedience. It also sets boundaries and gives direction to Christian thinking about God, salvation, and obedient action in the world. When the basic eschatological perspective of Scripture is minimized or lost, Christian thought becomes heretical and Christian social action merely secular. John Calvin provides a good example of the role Biblical eschatology should play in Christian thought and life.

*Theodore Minnema*

CHAPTER **5** CALVIN'S INTERPRETATION

OF HUMAN SUFFERING

The experience of suffering is universal. The assertion of Romans 8:22 "that the whole creation groaneth and travaileth in pain together until now" is a Biblical teaching so empirically verifiable that it receives consent from non-Christians as well as Christians. The reality of human misery is one of those simple facts for which the common mind asks no proof. It is an assumption on which discussion may begin.

With this assumption Calvin begins his *Institutes*. In the very first paragraph he writes:

> For as a veritable world of miseries is to be found in mankind, and we are thereby despoiled of divine raiment, our shameful nakedness exposes a teeming horde of infamies. Each of us must, then, be so stung by the consciousness of his own unhappiness as to attain at least some knowledge of God.[1]

From this quote an introductory and provisional definition of suffering can be deduced. Suffering is more than just sense experience. It consists not simply of pain and physical discomfort, though these may be included. The essential center of human suffering is human consciousness. Within the dynamics of consciousness, suffering or "unhappiness" arises. These dynamics are extremely complex and involve the interacting relations of mind and body, knowledge and will, reason and emotions. However, for Calvin these relations are never central. Within the dynamics of human consciousness Calvin focuses attention on one major issue, namely, the presence of God. How God is related to and involved in the consciousness of suffering is the fundamental question Calvin asks and answers. The problem of suffering

1. *Inst.*, I.i.1.

arises out of human consciousness, and its interpretation begins with God or "some knowledge of God."

For Calvin personally, misery and unhappiness were not distant and abstract realities, but firsthand experiences. A major motivation for writing the *Institutes* was to make a "Plea for the Persecuted Evangelicals."[2] In his prefatory address to King Francis he describes the collective experience of the Protestant evangelicals:

> What further? Examine briefly, most mighty King, all the parts of our case, and think us the most wicked of wicked men, unless you clearly find that "we toil and suffer reproach because we have our hope set on the living God" (I. Tim. 4:10); because we believe that "this is eternal life: to know the only true God, and Jesus Christ whom he has sent" (John 17:3 p.). For the sake of this hope some of us are shackled with irons, some beaten with rods, some led about as laughingstocks, some proscribed, some most savagely tortured, some forced to flee. All of us are oppressed by poverty, cursed with dire execrations, wounded by slanders, and treated in most shameful ways.[3]

In his private life Calvin also had many experiences of great disappointment and grief. Any number of quotes from his correspondence could be gathered to illustrate his deep sensitivity to suffering. Here is but one of many. This he writes to Farel in reference to the loss of his wife.

> I am trying as much as possible not to be completely overwhelmed by grief.... Besides, my friends surround me and do not fail to bring some comfort to my soul's sadness.... I consume my grief in such a way that I have not interrupted my work.... Farewell, brother and faithful friend.... May the Lord Jesus strengthen your spirit and mine in this great sadness, which would have broken me had He not extended his hand from on high; He whose service includes the relief of the broken, the strengthening of the weak, the renewal of those who are tired.[4]

Calvin in his experience of suffering fought off one of its gravest temptations, the response of nihilism or meaninglessness. Suffering in order to be constructively faced must be meaningfully interpreted. Such an interpretation Calvin begins by claiming that human unhappiness is a source of knowledge. "Each of us must, then, be so stung by the consciousness of his own unhappiness as to attain at least some knowledge of God."[5] Such knowledge of God comes through revelation.

---

2. "Prefatory Address to King Francis," *Inst.*, p. 11.    3. Ibid., pp. 13-14.
4. Richard Stauffer, *The Humaneness of John Calvin* (New York: Abingdon Press, 1971), p. 45.
5. *Inst.*, I.i.1.

## Human suffering and revelation in creation

God surrounds suffering man with revelation. Though suffering attests to and aggravates man's fallen condition, it does not annul revelation. Through all of human suffering God continues to make Himself known. Because of this revelation, suffering for man is not just a reality of the human senses but a fact that makes him conscious of a larger context. Through the awareness of suffering man is driven to look beyond himself as well as at himself. The knowledge of suffering, even as all knowledge for Calvin, stands in the correlation of God and man. The interpretation of suffering assumes the dynamic character of all knowledge as postulated in Calvin's opening sentences of the *Institutes*: "Nearly all the wisdom we possess, that is to say, true and sound wisdom, consists of two parts: the knowledge of God and of ourselves."[6]

What God reveals in human suffering is conditioned by the kind of revelation functioning in it. Calvin distinguishes revelation in relation to God as Creator and Redeemer. God discloses Himself as Creator in both nature and Scripture. The revelation of God as Redeemer comes through Jesus Christ. About the twofold revelation Calvin writes: "First in the fashioning of the universe and in the general teaching of Scripture the Lord shows himself to be the Creator. Then in the face of Christ (cf. II Cor. 4:6) he shows himself to be the Redeemer."[7]

The meaning of suffering that arises in the context of the revelation of God as Creator is our main concern in this first section. The meaning of suffering that arises in the context of the revelation of God as Redeemer will be our main concern in the subsequent two sections.

The counterpart in man of God's revelation as Creator is the *sensus divinitatis*. This natural sense of deity is universally present in mankind. It is an active confrontation between God and man. In this confrontation man gains "an awareness of divinity" and "a certain understanding of his divine majesty."[8] Also a certain conception of God as a unity arises from the *sensus divinitatis*.[9]

The consciousness of divine majesty and unity engraved on the hearts of all people accounts for universal guilt. The knowledge of God through creation, though corrupted through sin, still functions in human consciousness and leaves mankind without excuse before his Creator.

6. Ibid.

7. *Inst.*, I.ii.1.

8. *Inst.*, I.iii.1.

9. *Inst.*, I.x.3.

But all the heathen, to a man, by their own vanity either were
dragged or slipped back into false inventions, and thus their per-
ceptions so vanished that whatever they had naturally sensed
concerning the sole God had no value beyond making them
inexcusable.[10]

Man's inexcusable disobedience is not just a legal or forensic
relationship with God. It reverberates through the whole of human
experience. Signs and symptoms of man being under the judgment of God are manifest in the totality of human life. A major
manifestation of man disobeying the revelation of God is idolatry.
"He prefers to worship wood and stone rather than to be thought
of as having no God, clearly this is a most vivid impression of a
divine being."[11]

Idolatry as a subjective experience consists of two elements, a
religious and a moral one. Calvin interprets man as responding to
God or a god through worship and ethical conduct. This twofold
response may also be expressed by saying that piety for Calvin is
basic to charity, or that obedience to the first table of the Decalogue
is basic to the second.[12]

Human suffering arises in connection with both worship and
ethical conduct. Fallen man exacerbates his inexcusability into an
ever deepening distress through perverted worship and morality.
Each one of these perverse responses to God intensifies in a distinctive way the suffering of mankind.

In order to understand suffering in connection with man's worshiping response to God, the nature of worship itself must be
noted. Worship is man's reaction to the transcendent greatness of
God. It focuses on all those attributes that generate awe, reverence, and the fear of God in man. In the depth of true worship
man apprehends something of God's unapproachable holiness
or what has been described as the "mysterium tremendum."[13]
Through sin man has corrupted his worship, but his religious
sensitivities remain. These sensitivities continue to function but in
an inverted way. Through sin, creaturely awe and reverence are
twisted into dread and terror.

> I confess, indeed, that in order to hold men's minds in greater
> subjection, clever men have devised very many things in religion

10. Ibid.

11. *Inst.*, I.iii.1.

12. Edward A. Dowey, *The Knowledge of God in Calvin's Theology* (New
York: Columbia University Press, 1952), p. 31.

13. Rudolf Otto, *The Idea of the Holy* (New York: Oxford University
Press, 1958), chap. IV.

by which to inspire the common folk with reverence and to strike them with terror. But they would never have achieved this if men's minds had not already been imbued with a firm conviction about God, from which the inclination toward religion springs as from a seed.... One reads of no one who burst forth into bolder or more unbridled contempt of deity than Gaius Caligula; yet not one trembled more miserably when any sign of God's wrath manifested itself; thus—albeit unwillingly—he shuddered at the God whom he professedly sought to despise.[14]

Human suffering has a profound religious dimension. In the situation of sin God continues to actively confront man—and man must respond. In this response the very sensitivities given to man to deepen his relationship of worship aggravate him with immeasurable fears and horrors. Man may attempt to numb his spiritual responses in many ways, but they remain to torment him at any time. If man will not believe in God, eventually he will dread Him.

Idolatry affects not only the worship of man but his moral living. Moral life arises out of the human conscience. The conscience of man responds particularly to the moral factor in the revelation of God. It is a knowledge of what is right and wrong, "the knowledge of the works of righteousness."[15] The total response of man to God includes not only fear and reverence but also moral obedience.

Conscience is part of man's original nature or the image of God. It is the original form in which man knew the moral will of God. Man was created with a morally reliable and completely trustworthy conscience.

A distinction must be maintained between the moral will of God and man's knowledge of it. The moral will of God is objective and universal. Its content remains the same though it may appear in different forms. In the revelation of creation man apprehends the will of God as natural law. "It is a fact that the law of God which we call the moral law is nothing else than a testimony of natural law...."[16] In Scripture the same moral will of God is disclosed in the form of the Decalogue, prophetic comments on the Decalogue, and in the teachings of Jesus and the apostles.

Man's knowledge of the moral will of God has been affected by the fall into sin. God's revelation of what is morally required has not changed, but man's apprehension of it has. All men remain confronted with the demands of moral obedience, but they can no longer with reliability interpret the moral law or obey it. However, moral unreliability does not annul completely the human capacity to distinguish between good and evil, just and unjust. Fallen man can not lay claim to the excuse of ignorance.

14. *Inst.*, I.iii.2.        15. *Inst.*, II.ii.22.        16. *Inst.*, IV.xx.16.

The sinner tries to evade his innate power to judge between good and evil. Still, he is continually drawn back to it and is not so much as permitted to wink at it without being forced, whether he will or not, at times to open his eyes. It is falsely said, therefore, that man sins out of ignorance alone.[17]

The moral dynamics of the human conscience transpire between the moral will of God and man's apprehension of it. These dynamics Calvin instills with sensitivity as he further describes them in terms of personal interaction between God and man. Conscience, from *con-scientia*, etymologically means a knowing-with or -together with someone. It is not a private knowledge that can be isolated within the individual self-consciousness. In the conscience knowledge is not static, but creates an awareness of an other, the other being God. Conscience inherently has a witnessing capacity that speaks out in the presence of God. Knowledge in the conscience, like a sentinel, reports to God its content.

This is what Paul understands when he teaches that conscience also testifies to men, where their thought either accuses or excuses them in God's judgment (Rom. 2:6-16). A simple knowledge could reside, so to speak, closed up in man. Therefore this awareness which hales man before God's judgment is a sort of guardian appointed for man to note and spy out all his secrets that nothing may remain buried in darkness. Whence that ancient proverb, "Conscience is a thousand witnesses."[18]

The conscience, as a sensing of God or a reporting to God, in a fallen world is the source and center of great suffering. Before the Fall one can rightly assume that the conscience was a source and center of human fulfillment. It offered a harmony and fellowship of an ever deepening joint-knowledge *(con-scientia)* between God and man. An increase of knowing together in a situation of perfection would appear to do nothing else but complement the integrity of mutual trust and love between God and man.

But the conscience in Scripture presupposes primarily a fallen world. In such a world conscience continues to function but in an inverted way. It is now a joint-knowledge which, instead of enriching harmony and fellowship between God and man, drives them apart. On the one hand, conscience continues to inform man what he ought to do in relation to the will of God. On the other hand, it witnesses to the fact that man fails to do God's will. This conflicting testimony awakens guilt. It drives man away from God into the experience of alienation. The conscience, with all of its potential for peace, in the situation of sin becomes the origin of fear and loneliness.

17. *Inst.*, II.ii.22  18. *Inst.*, III.xix.15.

"If the conscience reflects on God, it must either enjoy a solid peace with his judgment, or be surrounded with the terrors of hell."[19]

The revelation of God in creation does not have an answer to the problem of human suffering. To the contrary, revelation in creation accentuates suffering by keeping fallen man conscious of his religious and moral turmoil. Suffering only finds an answer in the revelation of God as Redeemer. "Surely, after the fall of the first man no knowledge of God apart from the Mediator has had power unto salvation."[20] In the Mediator, Jesus Christ, suffering itself is a central factor. How Calvin interprets suffering within Christ is the focus of the following section.

## Human suffering and revelation in Christ

In Christ, suffering is a fundamental category of revelation. The cross is the concentration point of His suffering, but "his whole life was nothing but a sort of perpetual cross."[21] The cross stands at the center of the New Testament witness to Christ as the revelation of God's redemptive power (I Cor. 1:17-23). In revealing God's redemptive power, the cross at the same time reveals the true depth of human misery. "For in this exhibition God hath plainly showed to us how wretched our condition would have been if we had not a Redeemer."[22]

How to interpret adequately the reality of the suffering of Christ has challenged the Christian church throughout its history. The reality of the fact itself is beyond dispute, but its conceptual formulation has been discussed and debated throughout church history. At times the discussion and debate generated sharp controversies which the church sought to resolve through ecumenical councils. Against this background of debate and conciliar conclusions Calvin explains the suffering of Christ and makes his own doctrinal conclusions.

In order to keep Calvin's Christological doctrines and formulations in proper perspective, his initial acknowledgement of great mystery must be noted. The suffering of Christ is part of "the unutterable mystery, that the Son of God was clothed with human nature."[23] His concern is not in creedal and doctrinal concepts as such, but in the setting up of boundaries and limits within which the mystery of

19. *Inst.*, III.xii.3.
20. *Inst.*, II.vi.1.
21. *Inst.*, III.viii.1.
22. *Comm.* on Matt. 24:36.
23. *Comm.* on John 1:14.

Christ is maintained. His interest is not refined intellectual abstraction, but a witness that contains the full reality of Christ as disclosed in the New Testament.[24]

The Chalcedonian Council of A.D. 451 is a major watershed in the Christological controversy that flowed through the early church. The Christological concepts and their mutual relations which the Chalcedonian Council ratified have conditioned and influenced all subsequent discussion. For Calvin, the creed sanctioned by this council is the normative framework within which the suffering of Christ should be interpreted. Particularly, the following Chalcedonian affirmations give the doctrinal parameters within which Calvin explains the suffering of Christ. Jesus Christ is

> truly God and truly man ... to be acknowledged in two natures, inconfusedly, unchangeably, indivisibly, inseparably; the distinction of natures being by no means taken away by the union, but rather the property of each nature being preserved and concurring in one Person and one subsistence, not parted or divided into two persons, but one and the same Son, and only begotten God the Word, the Lord Jesus Christ.[25]

Unity and distinction in Jesus Christ must be maintained. In Him the New Testament assumes both divine and human attributes. "Before Abraham was, I am" (John 5:58), Jesus says of Himself; yet He was born and "increased in age and wisdom ... with God and men" (Luke 2:52). Both these divine and human qualities are ascribed to the one individual, Jesus Christ. The problem then is how to preserve the duality of nature without dualism and the unity of the individual without one nature absorbing the other. It is within the content of this problem that Calvin proceeds with the interpretation of the suffering of Christ.

Calvin never leaves the unity of Christ in doubt. The charges of Nestorianism that have been lodged against Calvin's theology[26] seem unfounded in the light of his insistence on the unity of Christ. In the *Institutes* he begins his discussion on the two natures of Christ by first insisting on the unity of His Person. "For we affirm his divinity so joined and united with his humanity that each retains its distinctive nature unimpaired, and yet these two natures constitute one Christ."[27] The unity of Person is the great mystery

24. G. C. Berkouwer, *The Person of Christ* (Grand Rapids: Wm. B. Eerdmans, 1966), pp. 281-87.

25. Philip Schaff, *Creeds of Christendom* (New York: Harper Brothers, 1919), p. 62.

26. Berkouwer, *The Person of Christ*, pp. 283-86.

27. *Inst.*, II.xiv.1.

which he never loses sight of, in spite of firm distinctions in the natures of Christ.

A firm distinction in the natures of Christ is stressed in relation to the suffering of Christ. Christ did not suffer in His divine nature, but only in His human nature.

> Surely, when the Lord of glory is said to be crucified, Paul does not mean that he suffered anything in his divinity, but he says this because the same Christ, who was cast down and despised, and suffered in the flesh, was God and Lord of glory.[28]

Calvin consistently maintains not only that the divine nature in Christ does not suffer, but he also generalizes this in relation to God. His development of this generalization helps clarify in some ways what he means when he excludes suffering from God.

> Surely God does not have blood, does not suffer, cannot be touched with hands. But since Christ, who was true God and also true man, was crucified and shed his blood for us, the things that he carried out in his human nature are transferred improperly, although not without reason, to his divinity.[29]

"To suffer" in this context is a disorder on a continuum with "blood" and "touched with hands." It is rooted in physical and bodily qualities. When suffering is equated with such qualities, it clearly follows that God—who is noncorporeal—cannot suffer, even though Scripture "not without reason" may transfer it to Christ's divinity. For example, as Calvin indicates, God was not crucified, though we read in I Corinthians 2:8, "the Lord of glory was crucified"; and God's blood was not shed, though Paul says, "God purchased the church with his blood" (Acts 20:28). In these passages we have what is called *communicatio idiomatum,* an attributing to one nature something which is only applicable to another. Such communication of properties between the divine and human natures remains meaningful only in the light of the unity of Person in Christ.[30]

Calvin's interpretation of suffering in relation to God becomes more difficult to understand when he assumes that in God there is no reality corresponding to mental and emotional disturbance. On this assumption he concludes that God never suffers anger and that the divine mind and sensitivities are never actually distressed.

> Now the mode of accommodation is for him to represent himself to us not as he is in himself, but as he seems to us. Although he is beyond all disturbance of mind, yet he testifies

28. *Inst.,* IV.xvii.30.

29. *Inst.,* II.xiv.2.

30. Ibid.

that he is angry toward sinners. Therefore whenever we hear that God is angered, we ought not to imagine any emotion in him, but rather to consider that this expression has been taken from our own human experience; because God, whenever he is exercising judgment, exhibits the appearance of one kindled and angered.[31]

The context of this statement is theological. Calvin is explaining Biblical statements about God's "repentance." He contends that God's "repentance" must be qualified and conditioned by His immutability. Divine immutability is identified with a transhistorical and eternal plan. Given this theological point of departure, Calvin concludes: "Meanwhile neither God's plan nor his will is reversed nor his volition altered; but what he had from eternity foreseen, approved, and decreed, he pursues in uninterrupted tenor, however sudden the variation may appear in men's eyes."[32]

In making this conclusion Calvin's logic is clear. Given the premise of an eternal transhistorical decree, then what God says about Himself in history is "appearance," and likewise the anger of God in history can be explained as "the appearance of one kindled and angered." But does such a conclusion do justice to the givens of Scripture? Emotional disturbance is used in Scripture as a category for God's self-disclosure. In Old Testament prophecy God is often portrayed as emotionally upset about Israel's unfaithfulness. Even as a good husband becomes deeply disturbed about the infidelity of his wife, so God becomes disturbed about the infidelities of His people (Hos. 1—3; Isa. 54:4-8). The Old Testament revelation of God in no way hesitates to portray God as grieved and upset. This portrayal stands in sharp contrast to the Greek unmoved mover who remains disinterested and detached from all historical tension and problems. Biblical revelation never assumes—as is done in so much Greek thought—that emotion is incompatible with perfection.[33]

Calvin's one-sided stress on God's transcendent imperturbability can be amended by one of his own theological claims. He maintains the premise that God is truly known only in His special revelation as it culminates in Jesus Christ.

"Blessed be God who is the Father of Jesus Christ." For, as formerly, by calling himself the God of Abraham, he designed to mark the difference between him and all fictitious gods; so after he has manifested himself in his own Son, his will is not to be known otherwise than in him. Hence they who form their

31. *Inst.*, I.xvii.13.

32. Ibid.

33. Abraham J. Heschel, *The Prophets* (New York: Harper & Row, 1962), pp. 247-67, also chap. 14.

ideas of God in his naked majesty apart from Christ, have an idol instead of the true God.[34]

God's self-disclosure in history which climaxed in the coming of Christ means that God Himself is deeply involved in the dynamics of personal relations. How and why a transcendent God condescends to be so intimately involved with His covenant people remains a mystery. But an essential part of this mystery is that this intimacy involves on the part of God profound personal feelings and emotions (Jer. 31:20). Calvin rightly maintains a distinction between the divine and human natures in Christ, but his insistence that God is "beyond all disturbance of mind" and "that we ought not to imagine any emotion in him" is evidently an inference drawn from an abstract presupposition of impassible divinity rather than from the data of Scripture and the history of salvation.

Christ suffers only in His human nature. Before proceeding to a further investigation of Calvin's explanation of this suffering, it should be restated that this human nature must never be separated from the Person of Christ. The assurance that God was involved in the full work of Christ comes not through the direct activity of the divine nature in human experience but through the unity of the two natures in one Person. The unity of Christ as a Person is the point of God's direct identification with the suffering of mankind. To the different natures of Christ different actions may be attributed, but these differences are grounded in one Person.[35]

Calvin explicates the suffering of Christ through certain major soteriological concepts. The most comprehensive one is obedience. Through disobedience the creation fell and it is through the obedience of Christ that it is restored. Obedience is equivalent to the perfect life God requires of men. "But not only faith, perfect in every way complete, but all right knowledge of God is born of obedience."[36]

Obedience is what makes the suffering of Christ fundamentally different from the suffering of the sinner. Fallen man must suffer because of disobedience, but Christ suffers because of obedience. Involuntary suffering is what befalls sinners in this world. Voluntary suffering is what Christ chooses in this world. Christ in no way is the victim of a tragic fate or an inevitable doom. He freely consents to be a servant with all of its suffering consequences. "That he was a servant was a voluntary act, so that we must not think that it detracted anything from his rank."[37] In Christ is revealed the perfection of obedient suffering. Though personally identified with the depths of

34. *Comm.* on I Peter 1:3.                36. *Inst.*, I.vi.2.

35. *Comm.* on Matt. 24:36; *Inst.*, II.xiv.3.    37. *Comm.* on Isa. 12:1.

human weakness, through obedience Christ preserves His perfection. "In Christ [is] a weakness pure and free of all vice and stain because he held himself within the bounds of obedience."[38]

In Christ, obedient suffering begins with the incarnation. "It was necessary that he should assume flesh in order that he might submit to obedience."[39] Obedience in this context underscores Christ's voluntary submission to the troubles of the flesh. With the sinner, Christ experienced the pain and disorder of the body. Scripture gives many evidences that "show him to have been subject to hunger, thirst, cold and other infirmities of our nature and these account for the fact that 'we have not a high priest who is unable to sympathize with our infirmities' (Hebrews 4:15a)."[40]

A special spiritual and moral dimension in the obedient suffering of Christ is accented through His humiliation. He humiliates Himself by "giving up his equality with God and taking on the form of a servant, being made in the likeness of men" (Phil. 2:7). The humiliation is so deep because while Christ "was not only immortal, but the Lord of life and death, he nevertheless became obedient to his Father, even so far as to endure death."[41] The whole life of Christ was a pattern of humility that culminated in an ignominious death as a common criminal.

The preceding quote from Calvin includes something that should be singled out for special attention. "[Christ] became obedient to his Father." The obedience of Christ is obedience not to some impersonal law but to His Father's will. Though for Christ the will of the Father included great suffering, He never contradicted it. Between the Son and the Father there is no conflict of wills, no dualism. This means that when one believes in Christ one need never doubt that God both as Father and Son offer complete salvation. The salvation that Christ gives to the world is fully sanctioned and supported by the will of the Father.[42]

Another soteriological term basic to Calvin's interpretation of the suffering of Christ is substitution. Substitution maintains on the one hand that Christ through all His suffering remains sinless, and on the other hand that He through all His suffering stands in the sinner's place. "Him who knew no sin he made to be sin in our behalf" (II Cor. 5:21). "Thus we shall behold the person of a sinner and evil-doer represented in Christ, yet from his shining innocence it will at the same time be obvious that he was burdened with another's sin rather than his own."[43]

38. *Inst.*, II.xvi.12.  40. *Inst.*, II.xiii.1.  42. *Inst.*, III.xxii.6.

39. *Comm.* on Isa. 42:1.  41. *Comm.* on Phil. 2:8.  43. *Inst.*, II.xvi.5.

The dual foci in Christ—sinlessness and yet taking the place of a sinner—must be kept in mind to understand His substitutionary suffering. Never like the sinner does Christ suffer out of disobedience. He suffers in the place of the sinner, but stands in his place obediently —which means in perfect harmony with His Father's will.

The depth of substitutionary suffering is reached on the cross. The magnitude of this suffering comes to light in relation to both God and man. In relation to God, Christ underwent "the severity of God's vengeance, to appease his wrath and satisfy his just judgment."[44] On the cross a torment transpired that no human eye could see. Christ suffered an "invisible and incomprehensible judgment" in the sight of God.[45] In relation to man, Christ endured not just the curse any individual may face, but the curse that rested on the totality of creation. Christ stood in the place of all sinners and bore their punishment. He wrestled with "the guilt of all iniquities, and also with hell itself."[46]

Substitutionary suffering is further clarified from the point of view of sacrifice. Calvin interprets sacrifice against the background of the Old Testament Levitical system. Sacrifice is required in order to expiate God's wrath toward sin. From Scripture it is clear that the only way of expiation is through the shedding of blood. Calvin sees the shedding of blood as a basic principle running through the Old and New Testaments.

> In short, the old figures well teach us the force and power of Christ's death. And in the Letter to the Hebrews the apostle skillfully using this principle explains this point: "Without the shedding of blood there is no forgiveness of sins."[47]

The acceptable sacrifice to God must be by way of a substitute. This was taught in the Old Testament by substituting animals. Christ fulfilled all the demands of the Levitical system by becoming the once-for-all substitute. He fulfilled what was foreshadowed by the shedding of the blood of sacrificial animals in the Old Testament.

The substitutionary suffering of Christ carries finality. This finality is denoted by Calvin in the term "satisfaction." Satisfaction does not reduce salvation to a commercial affair in which the suffering of Christ becomes a simple equivalent of the sinner's guilt. Rather it means that salvation is complete. The believer with a true sense of liberation can stand in the presence of God.[48] "This is the material,

44. *Inst.*, II.xvi.10.

45. Ibid.

46. *Comm.* on Heb. 5:7.

47. *Inst.*, II.xvii.4.

48. *Inst.*, II.xvi.2.

—Christ by his obedience satisfied the Father's justice, and by undertaking our cause he liberated us from the tyranny of death, by which we were held captive."[49] The suffering of Christ is unique in that it reveals and accomplishes complete salvation. The completeness of salvation is achieved through the perfect obedience of Christ to the will of the Father. The will of the Father is fulfilled by Christ making full satisfaction for sinners as their sacrificial substitute. The fundamental reason behind all the secondary reasons for the suffering of Christ is the will or decree of God. All other factors contributing to the suffering and death of Christ, including the Devil, are but means to carrying out the plan and will of God.[50] Though believers are given complete salvation through the suffering of Christ, yet they themselves continue to suffer. Calvin's interpretation of why Christians continue to suffer is the concern of the following section.

## Human suffering and life in Christ

Through the sending of His Son, God identifies Himself intimately with the total human situation. God's direct and immediate identification centers in the Person of Jesus Christ. In the Person of Jesus Christ, unity is restored between God and man. This unity manifests itself as a body in which there is maintained a dynamic interrelation between Christ and the believers. In Christ believers grow together into a deepening community and harmony of life. "Not only does he cleave to us by an indivisible bond of fellowship, but with a wonderful communion, day by day, he grows more and more into one body with us, until he becomes completely one with us."[51] Basic to Calvin's interpretation of the relation between Christ and the believer is the "mystical union."[52]

Suffering is one of the most significant historical experiences involved in the mystical union. Suffering constitutes a fundamental pattern of life among believers, even as it did in Christ.

> For whomever the Lord has adopted and deemed worthy of his fellowship ought to prepare themselves for a hard, toilsome, and unquiet life, crammed with very many and various kinds of evil. It is the Heavenly Father's will thus to exercise them so as to put his own children to a definite test. Beginning with Christ, his first-born, he follows this plan with all his children.[53]

49. *Comm.* on Rom. 3:24.

50. *Comm.* on John 14:31.

51. *Inst.*, III.ii.24.

52. *Inst.*, III.xi.10.

53. *Inst.*, III.viii.1.

Though for Calvin, suffering is obviously a major historical factor with which the believer must reckon, it must never be interpreted apart from union with Christ. For the believer, suffering is never a prerequisite for salvation. Christ's suffering satisfied for the complete salvation of every believer. The suffering of the believer is always in Christ. Only in that relation and on its basis can the believer's suffering be faced and interpreted. Scripture "adds that Christ, through whom we return into favor with God, has been set before us as an example, whose pattern we ought to express in our life."[54]

The pattern of suffering in the life of Christ issues in His death on the cross. The cross is a summation of the pattern of suffering in Christ. To this pattern of suffering the Christian must conform his life. Living in Christ means bearing of the cross. The suffering that the cross entailed for Christ must be reflected and imitated in the believer's life.[55] "The afflictions, which conform us to Christ, have been appointed; and he did this for the purpose of connecting, as by a kind of necessary chain, our salvation with the bearing of the cross."[56]

The pattern of suffering in Christ must never be separated from His resurrection. His suffering was never an end in itself. He suffered in order to be victorious over it. In Christ, suffering is the means to the new life of redemption achieved and disclosed through His resurrection. Likewise in the believer, suffering must never be isolated from its purpose and end. Its reality is never final, but is a way and means to newness of life. "He allots to us the same course of life with himself, that he might lead us with himself to a blessed participation of heavenly glory."[57]

The final goal of the Christian as participation in "heavenly glory" does not lead Calvin to a simplistic interpretation of suffering. The road to the Christian's final destiny winds through a complexity of human affliction. This complexity Calvin seeks to further explain by means of various Biblical concepts and categories.

In the Christian's life there is a being crucified as a counterpart to the crucifixion of Christ. Suffering in the believer terminates in a certain kind of a dying even as it did in Christ. Through Christ, the believer must undergo mortification. This process of mortification has two distinguishable dimensions: an outward and an inward one. Mortification must take place in relation to the external attachments of the Christian to his physical circumstances and in relation to his old nature as expressed in mind and will.

54. *Inst.*, III.vi.3.
55. *Comm.* on Isa. 53:7.
56. *Comm.* on Rom. 8:28.
57. *Comm.* on I Peter 4:12.

That this may be better understood let us take notice that there is a twofold mortification. The former relates to those things that are around us . . . . The other [is] inward—that of the understanding and will, and of the whole of our corrupt nature.[58]

Inward mortification occurs through self-denial.[59] Self-denial is an intense inner struggle in which the redemptive resources of Christ subdue and conquer the fallen nature of man. This fallen nature is not a static corruption, but actively perverse. Calvin characterizes its depravity as "concupiscence." "For our nature is not only destitute and empty of good, but so fertile and fruitful of every evil that it cannot be idle . . . the whole man is of himself nothing but concupiscence."[60]

Because the surging depth of evil in man is so violent, it needs a violent response in order to be overcome. The dominance of concupiscence in the old nature can only be vanquished by a greater counter force. Such a counter force cannot arise out of man's own capacity of self-discipline. The "flesh" is not equal to the battle of self-denial. Christian self-denial and the mortification of the fallen human nature is possible only through the death of Christ. "We are really and effectually supplied with invincible weapons to subdue the flesh, if we partake as we ought of the efficacy of Christ's death."[61] In the death of Christ the old human nature is also put to death. The self that experiences self-denial faces a radical renewal. It must be purged of all self-centeredness, and the "deadly pestilence" of love of self must be torn out.[62] Complete and total surrender to God are the only conditions that meet self-denial and inward mortification.

Inward mortification is a direct means for making the believer conform to the pattern of the life of Christ. It concentrates on making the human will and disposition controlled exclusively by the will of God, even as this perfect control is found in Christ. Outward mortification, like inward mortification, contributes to the purpose of making the believer conform to the pattern of the life of Christ. But conformity in the context of outward mortification centers on the external situations of pain and suffering. The believer, similar to Christ, must face not just an inward development of self-negation but a life that outwardly is shaped and molded by adversity and troubles. How to have one's life properly influenced and affected by observable suffering is the concern of outward mortification. This outward mortification Calvin subsumes under the subject of "bearing of the cross."[63]

58. *Comm.* on Col. 3:5.

59. *Inst.*, III.iii.8.

60. *Inst.*, II.i.8.

61. *Comm.* on I Peter 4:1.

62. *Inst.*, III.vii.4.

63. *Comm.* on Phil. 3:10.

The bearing of the cross enriches the unity of life between Christ and the believer. Suffering is not destructive of Christian living but is instrumental in establishing its reality. "The more we are afflicted with adversities, the more surely our fellowship with Christ is confirmed."[64]

The bearing of the cross not only confirms but further develops fellowship with Christ. In Christ, suffering contributes to positive moral and spiritual benefits. It occasions deeper self-knowledge by awakening human dependence on God's power. "It teaches us, thus humbled, to rest upon God alone, with the result that we do not faint or yield."[65] A further purpose in the bearing of the cross is to train believers in the virtues of "patience and obedience."[66] Included in the training of these virtues may be God's chastisement and discipline. Suffering in the form of persecution is also part of cross-bearing. The very greatness of the Christian's spiritual and moral life may provoke in a sinful society intense hostility and opposition. As Christ taught, one may suffer persecution for righteousness' sake.[67]

The varieties of suffering in the bearing of the cross and outward mortification all eventually aid and foster the goal of inward mortification and self-denial. Self-denial and bearing the cross—though distinguished from each other—do form for Calvin an ethical unity. Together they seek to foster and accomplish a life in Christ of complete obedience to the will of God.[68]

Suffering in Christ is not equated with evil but interpreted as an instrument of good in the hand of God. Suffering in itself is not incompatible with sinlessness. It is not, as in Stoicism, logically inconsistent with the principle of human perfection. For the Stoics, human perfection is a state of rational superiority in which one is unaffected and indifferent to suffering. Calvin soundly rejects this rational transcendence over human troubles and misery.

> It is not as the Stoics of old foolishly described "the great-souled man": one who, having cast off all human qualities was affected equally by adversity and prosperity, by sad times and happy ones—nay, who like a stone was not affected at all.[69]

Throughout his ministry Christ taught in both word and deed that emotional suffering was in keeping with moral perfection. He, as true and perfect man, wept over human misfortune and sorrow. He also taught His disciples that in this world they would weep and have distress (John 16:20). "And that no one might turn it into a vice

64. *Inst.*, III.viii.1.         67. *Inst.*, III.viii.7.

65. *Inst.*, III.viii.3.         68. *Inst.*, III.viii.4.

66. *Inst.*, III.viii.4.         69. *Inst.*, III.viii.9.

he openly proclaimed, 'Blessed are those that mourn'."[70]

The suffering of the believer is interpreted by Calvin against the background of the suffering of Christ. The suffering of Christ is a pattern to which the life of the believer must conform. Conformity to Christ consists of the dual sanctifying processes of inward and outward mortification, or self-denial and bearing of the cross. The suffering of Christ and of the believer have the common goal of obedience. Even as suffering in Christ led to His perfect obedience to the will of the Father, so the suffering of the Christian has as its final goal perfect obedience to the will of the same Father. Within the Christian experience there is a wide diversity and variety of suffering. "But the conclusion will always be: the Lord so willed, therefore let us follow his will."[71]

## Summary and appraisal

Human suffering is centered in the human consciousness. Within the human consciousness certain distinctions may be made between different types of suffering. Suffering may vary from physical, emotional, and mental forms to deep-seated moral and spiritual forms. For Calvin, all these various forms are involved in man's relation to God. Man's relation to God affects the totality of suffering. The many types of human distress can only be adequately interpreted in the larger context of religion. Man's response to God is where the interpretation of human suffering must fundamentally begin.

The response of man to the revelation of the will of God has two distinguishable aspects. These aspects never exist in isolation from each other, but indicate man's twofold responsibility in relation to the revelation and presence of God. The will of God requires of man a worshiping and a moral response. Both responses have been corrupted through sin, and as a consequence are sources and centers of profound human misery.

Man's worshiping response arises out of his *sensus divinitatis*. This *sensus divinitatis* is a created capacity to sense the reality of the presence of God. It is a human ability to know God in His mysterious transcendence. The human responses of awe and reverence are expressive of the *sensus divinitatis*. But because the relation between God and man is broken by sin, the *sensus divinitatis* is the source of great suffering. Because of sin God discloses His presence and will in the form of judgment and wrath. This judgment and wrath the *sensus divinitatis* registers by manifesting fear and dread. Through

70. Ibid.                    71. *Inst.*, III.viii.10.

the *sensus divinitatis* man experiences a frightful mystery in which his suffering goes far beyond the demonstrable sensations of pain and discomfort.

Man's moral response arises out of the human conscience. The conscience apprehends the righteous and moral demands of the revelation of God. The response of the human conscience does not focus on the mystery of God but on what is known of His law. Because of sin, the conscience apprehends the law as an unfulfilled moral obligation. In the situation of sin the conscience registers the verdict of guilt before God's moral will. Guilt is the moral aspect of human suffering. Moral suffering constitutes the experience of alienation through disloyalty and unfaithfulness to the will of God as summarized in the Ten Commandments.

Though suffering in relation to the *sensus divinitatis* and the conscience are distinguishable, they form an organic unity in human consciousness. In human consciousness the relation to God is determinative of all other relations. Disorder in the relation to God will record disorder throughout the whole of human consciousness.

The origin of all human suffering is the conflict of wills between God and man. Man's disobedience has brought on the avalanche of suffering that overwhelms human history. The deepest forms of suffering remain where this conflict of wills remains. But in Christ, suffering is basically different because it does not arise out of a conflict with the will of God but out of obedience to the will of God. Christ demonstrates that suffering can be made consistent with moral perfection.

The suffering of Christ is unique in that He obediently stood in the place of disobedient man. He bore the wrath and judgment of suffering that the sinner provoked in God through disobedience. The suffering of Christ is morally perfect because He submits to it obediently and voluntarily. He is obeying the Father's will while at the same time He endures the opposition of God's will in the form of wrath, judgment, and curse. How God can will Christ to suffer for sinners and at the same time execute His opposing will on Christ in the form of wrath is answered in the doctrine of substitutionary atonement. What needs special notice in this context is that Calvin preserves the perfection of Christ in the midst of suffering by stressing obedience. Suffering is sanctified through voluntary submission to God's will.

The perfection of obedience in the suffering of Christ is the norm according to which the believer should suffer. The believer's life must conform to the pattern of the life of Christ. The believer sanctifies his suffering through submission to the will of God. When the conflict between God's will and man's will is removed, suffering is perfected. Suffering is Christian when it reveals and is received as the will of God. Making the will of God and man a dynamic unity is the answer to suffering.

Calvin's answer rightly rules out the element of tragedy in human suffering. Tragedy arises when human existence is interpreted as consisting of an irreconcilable moral dualism over which man has no control. This tragic view gives no priority to the moral over the immoral or to the good over evil. It affirms that moral opposites have equal status and validity. Between these opposites man suffers with no hope of a meaningful resolution. Man's fate is to exist in the tension of opposite and contradictory wills.[72]

Calvin gives obvious priority to the will of God as a righteous and moral will. He leaves no doubt that the righteous and moral will of God will triumph over all opposition. This triumph is already disclosed in the resurrection of Christ. History is not fated by some irresolvable conflict, but stands open to the transforming power of God as proclaimed in the crucifixion and resurrection of Christ. In Christ the conflict between the will of God and the sinner is resolved.

Through Christ, evil is taken out of suffering. Suffering in Christ is no longer a conflict of wills. The believer in Christ may and will continue to suffer but must do so in obedience. Here is the point where Christian and non-Christian suffering have their fundamental difference. Christian suffering has within it reconciliation and unity with the will of God. This means that the dread and guilt of the fallen *sensus divinitatis* and conscience are removed. The curse is taken out of suffering. Suffering for the believer in Christ, instead of intensifying conflict with God, intensifies fellowship with Him. Through Christ, suffering is transformed from a revelation of wrath and judgment to the revelation of love and grace. Christ makes the will of God even in suffering a mysterious joy and source of communion. Human pain in the life of the Christian is regarded not as an obstacle to the perfect life but an opportunity and means to its fulfillment.

Calvin's interpretation of suffering contains much apologetical and pastoral significance. He takes the obvious fact of human solidarity in suffering and meaningfully relates it to Christian theology. A theology that speaks relevantly to the common problem of suffering has a good possibility of receiving a hearing in any culture. From a pastoral point of view the distinction between disobedient and obedient suffering is readily applicable. It makes clear how the suffering of Christ is different and unique, and yet how the Christian ought to make his sufferings conform to Christ.

72. Nathan A. Scott, Jr., *The Tragic Vision and the Christian Faith* (New York: Association Press, 1957), pp. 26-27.

The pastoral strength and advantage of Calvin's interpretation also contains a danger. Obedience in suffering must not become simple resignation to the status quo. What must not be overlooked is that in some circumstances submission to suffering would be disobedience to the will of God. When there are legitimate resources available to alleviate human misery, they should be utilized. Calvin certainly agrees with such alleviation as demonstrated in his impatience with people indifferent to human need and in his own tireless efforts to help people in hardship. One area, however, in which his emphasis on obedience in the midst of suffering tended toward volitional passivity and acceptance of the status quo was in the authority structure of society.

> But if you conclude from this that service ought to be rendered only to just governors, you are reasoning foolishly. For husbands are also bound to their wives, and parents to their children, by mutual responsibilities. Suppose parents and husbands depart from their duty. Suppose parents show themselves so hard and intractable to their children, whom they are forbidden to provoke to anger (Eph. 6:4), that by their rigor they tire them beyond measure. Suppose husbands most despitefully use their wives, whom they are commanded to love (Eph. 5:25) and to spare as weaker vessels (I Peter 3:7). Shall either children be less obedient to their parents or wives to their husbands? They are still subject even to those who are wicked and undutiful.[73]

Calvin's interpretation of suffering has a certain incompleteness in it. This was already noted in how Calvin denies any emotion in God. With consistency he denies in God not only suffering, but all disturbance of mind and anger itself. Logically he is correct in that when one excludes suffering from God, then he must exclude all forms of emotional agitation.

That this logic does not do justice to the givens of Scripture has already been discussed. What can further be raised against this logic is that it does not do full justice to the reality of Christian suffering. For Calvin, Christian suffering is interpreted exclusively in terms of moral teleology. It is an instrumental means to the perfecting of obedience. In both Christ and the believer, suffering promotes and establishes obedience. Christ suffered only in His human nature, and through this suffering perfected human nature unto perfect obedience. This consistent teleological approach accounts for Calvin's insistence on the nonsuffering nature of God. Certainly in God there is nothing to be completed unto perfection.

But can Christian suffering have other than a teleological meaning and function? This is possible if one assumes that suffering has a

73. *Inst.*, IV.xx.29.

source not only in a situation of moral incompleteness, but also in one of completeness. Suffering not only leads to perfection but arises out of perfection itself. Such an assumption means that moral completeness and perfection must not—as in Calvin—be stressed only as obedience but also as love. Christian love in this context is more than just a unity of wills. It is a completeness and a perfection that may endure even a disunity of wills and the pain of being disobeyed. Love is a fullness that opens itself to the possibility of being disturbed, rejected, and susceptible to emotional stress.

In order to maintain the clear Biblical affirmation that God is love, one must also (even as Scripture does) allow for the dynamics and emotional sensitivities of love. Calvin is correct in denying that God or Christ in His divine nature is in any way subject to creaturely limitations. From this, however, it does not follow that God is incapable of real anger and emotion. Certainly God never experiences anger and emotion in a *creaturely* way, but this does not rule out possible forms of anger and emotion compatible with divinity.

To assert that love in God is a perfection that opens God to a sensitive participation in the suffering of history adds a dimension to suffering that does not come to clear expression in Calvin. Because of love, suffering may arise out of perfection as well as imperfection. This places in Christian suffering a mysterious paradox. Suffering may arise out of a situation of both weakness and power. This paradox is evident in trying to understand the suffering of Christ. Did Christ suffer out of weakness or power? Scripture passages can be quoted to affirm both elements. Weakness is the focus in such texts as, "He made him to be sin" (II Cor. 5:21), He became "a curse for us" (Gal. 3:13), and "God, sending his own Son in the likeness of sinful flesh" (Rom. 8:3). The power of Christ is affirmed when Christ crucified is characterized as "the power of God" (I Cor. 2:5) and as "the Lord of glory" (I Cor. 2:8). This paradoxical combination has a certain theoretical mystery in it, and one is closer to Biblical reality by emphasizing the redemptive love of God instead of this paradox. In Christ, the love of God is a power that makes itself vulnerable to the depths of suffering. This vulnerability in no way carries the despair of tragedy, but through the real struggles of history gains the victory.

The dimension of suffering that arises out of the fullness and perfection of Christian love throws added light on the suffering of the believer in Christ. The Christian's suffering may not be simply moralized into the purpose of increasing obedience. True Christian love makes the believer vulnerable. It opens his life to the undeserved and added burdens of others. It may make him the victim of unwarranted hostilities from enemies. The intensity of Christian love may mean in a sinful world the intensification of suffering. Of course God through all this may also perfect obedience, but when one has the love of Christ in his life there may be more involved in suffering than the demand for obedience.

The combination of love and suffering brings out the aggressive force of evil. Suffering in history is not just an instrument for perfecting man's obedience, but exhibits the demonic and fiendish character of evil. In Scripture, suffering is not just a process of chastisement and sanctification, but a consequence of a wrestling and struggling against titanic forces of destruction (Eph. 6:12). In order to say something about social calamities and holocausts that have erupted and threaten to erupt in history, the apocalyptic factor of evil must be duly recognized. The suffering portrayed in the Book of Revelation is not just a means for perfecting the saints but represents a cosmic struggle in which evil is out to destroy the source of all perfection (Rev. 12). The magnitude of some suffering remains frighteningly mysterious; and the only hope on which one can finally rest is that Christ, the source and center of all love and perfection, will triumph (Rev. 21:4-5). But while awaiting the final triumph, the Christian faces suffering not only to perfect his obedience but because the very Christ whom he follows is also under constant attack from the forces of Antichrist.

Gordon J. Spykman

CHAPTER **6** SPHERE-SOVEREIGNTY

IN CALVIN AND THE CALVINIST TRADITION


## Introduction

One of the boldest conclusions J. T. McNeill draws from his study of the history and character of Calvinism is this: "All modern Western history would have been unrecognizably different without the perpetual play of Calvin's influence."[1]

Granting this conclusion, the underlying thesis of this chapter is that the greatest influence of Calvin and the Calvinist tradition upon, and its most uniquely significant contribution to, Western Christianity lies in its development of a Biblically Reformed world-and-life-view structured along the lines of the principle of sphere-sovereignty.

The central purpose of this chapter is to explore how much support such a life-philosophy finds in the thought and practice of Calvin himself. Is it a product of later reflection by nineteenth and twentieth century Neo-Calvinists? Or is it traceable to the work of Calvin himself in the sixteenth century? Is such a life-perspective an integral feature of classic Calvinism, or a distortion of it, or an accretion to it, or a departure from it? Just how much can be claimed for Calvin, historically and theologically, on the question of sphere-sovereignty?

Looking ahead for a moment, anticipating in a preliminary way the direction this study will take, three general observations should be kept in mind. In researching Calvin on sphere-sovereignty, it is possible, on the one hand, to claim too much. On the other hand, one can also claim too little. Seeking to avoid these two extreme approaches, I believe something substantial can indeed be said on the issue at hand. To this task I address myself in this chapter.

1. J. T. McNeill, *The History and Character of Calvinism* (New York: Oxford, 1962), p. 234.

But if we are to study Calvin from this point of view, it is important at the outset to assure ourselves of at least a working understanding of this issue. In the interest of greater clarity I will therefore set forth the more basic contours of a Calvinist world-and-life-view structured along the lines of the principle of sphere-sovereignty.

## Statement on sphere-sovereignty

Restating the initial thesis: The most uniquely significant contribution of the Calvinist tradition to Christian life in our Western world has been its development of a Biblically Reformed world-and-life-view. Other Christian traditions have made their own distinctive and important contributions—for example, in developing creeds, liturgies, church music, art and architecture, church polities, doctrines, theologies, morals, piety, public policies, and other aspects of Christian living. Many Calvinists have had a hand in such things too. But the hallmark of the Calvinist tradition is its development of a Biblically Reformed world-and-life-view. In no other Western Christian tradition do we find leaders and people together wrestling as seriously with an impelling sense of cultural urgency to develop a principled and structured *Weltanschauung* as in the Calvinist tradition, recognizing as a major God-given calling the task of delineating a comprehensive life-philosophy as a framework of reference for seeking to account for the fullness of our day by day life-experience in God's world from a Biblical perspective.

This cosmic vision, so characteristic of historic Calvinism, is anchored in certain fundamental faith commitments. Its epistemological key is Scripture, viewed as the drama of salvation, unfolding act by act as the history of redemption centered in Jesus Christ. The writings of the Old and New Testament are the "spectacles"[2] through which we seek to discern the meaning of our lives within God's creation. As our window on God's world, the Bible calls us to bow obediently to the full authority of God's Word for all of life. It leads us to recognize the normativity of God's revelation in creation, the creation ordinances by which God from the beginning structured the life of His creation. For creation is a cosmos (a richly diversified, yet coherently unified whole), not a chaos. Though the structures of creation have fallen under sin, God still upholds them by His Word and redeems them in Jesus Christ. Scripture, serving as a pair of glasses, opens our eyes to the norms of these creation-redemption ordinances as they hold continuously for the full range of our societal life. Fundamental to the Calvinist world-and-life-view is,

2. *Inst.*, I.ii.1.

therefore, an integrally unified understanding of the interrelatedness of creation and redemption. Redemption is the restoration of creation.

Out of this commitment is born the conviction that life as a whole is religion; that life in its total extent and in all its parts is a coherent complex of ongoing responses, obedient and disobedient, to God's sovereign claim on the whole man in all his life-relationships. This all-embracing outlook on life is sustained by the Biblical teaching on the covenant as a way of life encompassing every walk of life as service rendered either faithfully or unfaithfully before the face of the Lord. It is rooted in the Biblical view of the kingdom—past, present, future—within which every earthly task is transformed into a calling to erect signposts along the way of the coming kingdom. It is motivated by the central law of love—love for God above all and for our neighbors as ourselves, which gives renewed Biblical direction to life and must come to concrete expression in every sphere of personal and communal enterprise. Thus, as a Biblically Reformed world-and-life-view, Calvinism seeks to do justice to the three fundamental relationships which undergird all of life: our relationship to God, to the cosmos, and to man himself, including our own inner and outer lives.[3]

The basic working principle of such a Calvinist *Weltanschauung,* which highlights concretely Calvinism's influence on Western Christianity, is the structuring principle of sphere-sovereignty. In articulating this principle, Calvinist thinkers sought to delineate the contours of God's sovereign rule of His creation and His norms for man's cultural activities. By way of contrast, other Christian traditions have been shaped by other structuring principles. The structuring principle operative in Roman Catholicism is that of sphere-subsidiarity. On this view the various spheres of life within the Roman Catholic community and society at large are regarded as subsidiaries of and subservient to the institutional church.[4] Typical of the Lutheran tradition is its two-kingdom idea as embodied in the Lutheran political principle of the Reformation, the principle of "princely favor" *(cuius regio, eius religio),* whereby regional rulers were granted decisive power in establishing official church bodies *(Landeskirchen).* This Erastian view of church government placed the so-called spiritual aspects of life in the hands of church assemblies while delegating the so-called secular tasks to the state, thus positing a dialectical relationship between the church, on the one hand,

3. A. Kuyper, *Calvinism* (Stone Lectures), (Grand Rapids: Eerdmans, 1934), pp. 19 ff.

4. H. Denzinger, *Enchiridion Symbolorum* (Freiburg: Herder, 1953), No. 1866-1870, 1936a, 1936b, 1995, 2253.

and the state and other societal institutions, on the other hand.[5] Historically a similar pattern prevailed in traditional Anglicanism in which a certain sovereignty was conferred on the crown over both church and state.[6] The Anabaptist tradition was governed by a purist-spiritualist concept of the church in which all non-church spheres in societal life were viewed as belonging to the kingdom of darkness.[7]

Taking its place amid these conflicting traditions in Western Christianity, classic Calvinism worked out its own Biblically Reformed world-and-life-view. Confessing redemption as the restoration of creation, it stood for the sovereignty of God over all, and held that the saving work of Jesus Christ liberates the Christian community for obedient discipleship and responsible stewardship in every sphere of life. There are no alien terrains. Scripture reopens the doors to every corner of God's creation. Christian liberty is a gift of God in Jesus Christ, a freedom which is to be exercised in holiness.[8] Such holy freedom impels Christians to reclaim every sphere of life for the King—home, school, church, state, college, university, labor, commerce, politics, science, art, journalism, and all the rest.

No limitations may be placed on the sovereignty of God or the kingship of Christ or the renewing power of the Holy Spirit (these three are one and may not be played off against each other). Supreme sovereignty is God's alone, allowing for no competition. Everything creaturely has a dependent existence. This is its glory. It is what it is by a grant from God. Therefore the sovereignty which holds for the various spheres in life should never be understood as preempting the sovereignty of God. That would be an idolatrous caricature. God alone is sovereign in the absolute, supreme, ultimate sense of the word. The sovereignty of each sphere is a God-given sovereignty—a dependent, derived, delegated, and therefore limited sovereignty. It is limited by the supreme, overall sovereignty of God and by the coexisting and proexisting sovereignty of other spheres in life. Sphere-sovereignty (its equivalents are sphere-authority, sphere-responsibility, sphere-stewardship) is always a subservient sovereignty, subservient to the sovereign rule of God. It is the creaturely means by which God makes His sovereign rule

---

5. H. R. Niebuhr, *Christ and Culture* (New York: Harper's, 1951), pp. 170-85.

6. W. Walker, *A History of the Christian Church* (New York: Scribner's, 1949), pp. 403-4.

7. Walker, *History of the Church*, p. 368.

8. H. Ridderbos, "The Church and the Kingdom of God," "The Kingdom of God and our Life in the World," *International Reformed Bulletin* (No. 27: October, 1966; No. 27: January, 1967), pp. 3-10.

concrete in the affairs of men and by which He exercises His sovereign authority over the whole cosmos. His sovereignty comes into sharp focus and is given specific expression in the various differentiated spheres of our life-relationships: parental authority in the home, kerygmatic authority in the church, pedagogical authority in the classroom, governing authority in the state's administration of public justice, and so on.

The various spheres in society are, therefore, not sovereign, but subservient in their relationships to God. They do, however, possess a certain sovereignty in their mutual relationships and interrelationships with each other. Each sphere has its own identity, its own unique task, its own God-given prerogatives. On each God has conferred its own peculiar right of existence and reason for existence. In each sphere man is called to exercise his threefold office as prophet, priest, and king; but that office is differently focalized from sphere to sphere. Office, in whatever sphere of activity, involves a delegated sovereignty, for the exercise of which man as steward is called to give an account, and which must be made serviceable to God and fellow men. But the nature and extent of such sovereignty is defined by that sphere in life in which we are called to exercise it. Being a husband or father does not exhaust a man's life-relationships, nor does being a teacher or a preacher or a citizen. Biblical norms for living vary from sphere to sphere.[9] God's Word lays its claim on our life as a whole. But obedience to that Word calls for a differentiated response in keeping with the nature of each sphere, since the various spheres bring with them varying sets of life-relationships.

In a highly differentiated society such as ours, sphere-sovereignty offers safeguards against the many forms of worldly authoritarianism and totalitarianism which beset us. For with it comes a recognition of proper limitations on the power of all earthly institutions. It honors a rightful distribution of authority-centers in life. When its religious base is undermined or its unifying vision is lost, this view of things can degenerate into the fragmentation of life and the polarization of society. But as long as these underlying Biblical principles are kept alive and these Biblical perspectives kept in clear focus, such a view of differentiated kingdom service can help the Christian community grow to greater maturity in exercising the many gifts of the Spirit.

This view of life helps to create a true sense of communality not only by fostering a rich diversity of tasks, but also by engendering unity of purpose. As the many members constitute the one body, so the many spheres are integrated into the unified life of the com-

9. Ephesians 5—6.

munity. For the corollary to the principle of sphere-sovereignty is the complementary principle of sphere-universality. When kept together, this twofold principle preserves communal life against both monotonous uniformity and tyranny, on the one hand, and fragmentation and polarization, on the other. Sphere-sovereignty (diversity of tasks) may not be sacrificed to sphere-universality (unity of life), nor vice versa. When both sides of this principle are honored in their integral coherence and in their mutual and reciprocal interactions, then a view of community emerges in which various coordinate spheres of activity stand in all kinds of partnership arrangements with each other.

For purposes of illustration, take as a mini-model an academic community such as Calvin College. Communal Christian scholarship depends on the living, dynamic presence of a common core of faith commitments—in this case, commitment to the sovereignty of God; the lordship of Jesus Christ in the entire academic enterprise; and an openness to the moving, leading power of the Spirit. In all kinds of concrete ways this undergirding and overarching commitment must come to differentiated expression from one area of study, one discipline, one branch of learning, one academic sphere to another. As the college represents one sphere within the larger life of the Christian community, so on a smaller scale each of the roughly twenty disciplines, each lodged in a department, represents an academic subsphere within the college as a whole. Each has a sovereignty (task, authority, responsibility) of its own kind, a sovereignty subservient to the overall religious commitment of the college. Each has its own identity, integrity, its own right of existence and reason for existence, its own central function. Each deals with its own specific aspect of created reality, which serves to define its nature as a discipline and to circumscribe the extent of its explorations.[10] Academically speaking, sphere-sovereignty is real. But sphere-universality is also real. For just as there is a meaningful unity binding together the various aspects of created reality, so also the various disciplines which study them are interrelated in many ways, making possible all kinds of interdisciplinary studies. The sovereignty of each discipline is limited by the coexisting and proexisting sover-

10. "A discipline is the scientific (theoretical) study of some aspect or segment of reality.... Two disciplines may be distinct either because they deal with different aspects of entities, or with different sorts of entities, or both.... The disciplines, then, differ from each other in being concerned with different aspects or segments of reality.... Further, the Biblical revelation speaks to our view of the place of each discipline in the scheme of the disciplines, or the limits of a particular discipline, and of its bearing on other disciplines" (*Christian Liberal Arts Education* [Grand Rapids: Calvin College and Eerdmans, 1970], pp. 47, 48, 49, 50, 60).

eignty of other disciplines. Academic sovereignty is then properly distributed over several departments. This view of things eliminates the need for a "queen of the sciences," allows no room for academic "stepchildren," and puts an end to collegiate "empire-building." Now to put things back into larger perspective: just as each department in the college is defined by its discipline, which in turn is defined by that aspect of created reality which it studies, so too each societal sphere is defined by its own central task. From the beginning God assigned man the cultural mandate. This great commission embraces in a sweeping way a diversity of tasks (marriage, tilling the soil, guarding the garden, worship, naming the animals, etc.). As history moves along, creating an ever widening arena for cultural differentiation, these nuclear tasks take on more sharply delineated institutional forms, commonly called the structures of society. Through history, therefore, which is the record of man's obedient and disobedient responses to God's Word, which is at the same time God's way of unfolding the potentials of His creation on the way to the coming kingdom, these core tasks, given to man in the beginning, open up into increasingly more structured spheres of life-relationships and communal activity, each sphere normed by a certain irreducible and nontransferable character in keeping with its mandate as we learn to know it from the Word of God.

These then are some of the basic contours of a Biblically Reformed world-and-life-view structured along the lines of the principle of sphere-sovereignty. The ultimate intent of this chapter, once again, is to seek to determine in how far Calvin's thought and practice contributed to the development of these perspectives.

It can hardly be questioned that many Reformed thinkers from Calvin's time to the present made their contribution to an increasingly clearer understanding of the principle of sphere-sovereignty, and in doing so believed that their thinking was in line with Calvin's.[11] Some made a direct appeal to Calvin's theology. Others wrote in explication of Calvin's views, samplings of which will be given later in this chapter when we examine the writings of Calvin himself. Before turning to Calvin, however, let us listen to some of these

11. "Everything we cited gives evidence of Calvin's intense involvement in all of life; not as a result of a certain clericalism, nor as a temperamental tendency toward a dictatorial desire for power; but as the fruit of a conviction, rooted deeply in the heart, that the Lord rules all things through his Son, Jesus Christ, and that he must be obeyed everywhere; a conviction which was once expressed by one of his great spiritual descendants (Kuyper) in these words, that 'Er geen duimbreed grond is, waarop de Christus, die aller Souverein is, de hand niet legt, en roept: Mijn!' " (L. Praamsma, *Calvijn* [Wageningen, Neth.: Zomer & Keuning, n.d.], p. 141).

voices from the past. I will quote them in roughly reverse order, moving from the present back through modern history toward Calvin, and with a minimum of comment.[12]

## Sphere-sovereignty in the Calvinist tradition

As a way of getting into this brief historical survey in retrospect, I call attention to the following excerpts from recent and contemporary Calvinist writers.

H. Henry Meeter, "the dean of the Bible Department" at Calvin College, made the principle of sphere-sovereignty a major theme in his teachings on Calvinism.

A third boundary limiting the State's authority lies in such natural spheres in society as the home, the school, the church, economic and social organizations, which do not owe their origin or mode of existence to the State, and have their own task entrusted to them by God. These are sovereign within their own boundaries. Only insofar as any of these should overstep its limits, or endanger the welfare of other spheres, or of individuals, or of the State, or insofar as by neglect of its duty it should endanger the well-being of the State, has the State here a duty to perform. A case in point would occur when parents neglect the proper training of their children, or when a husband tyrannizes over his wife, or one group in society tyrannizes over another group.

The Calvinist would not credit the government with the right to step into the separate sphere of economic or social organizations, and adopt as a policy the notion that it has the right to own and manage these. Nevertheless, he does believe it to be the duty of the government to administer justice by enacting such regulations as will prohibit any individuals or groups in society from overstepping their proper boundaries, and thereby encroaching in any way on the rights of others or of the State as a whole. And, positively, he believes it to be the duty of the government to provide such regulation of business and other economic and social forces as will bring about better living conditions for all.

The Calvinist found in his Bible proof in abundance for adopting this position. The divine ordinances for the civil administration of the Jewish nation determined not only the procedures of justice in the punishment of crimes as murder and theft, but also the regulations concerning the taking of interest; proper working conditions and wages of laborers; the rights of the poor to the leavings of the grain and vintage harvest; provisions against the exploitation of the poor by means of the return of the land to the original owners in the year of Jubilee; and other important regulations.

12. Cf. L. Lindeboom, "Souverein," and K. Dijk, "Souvereiniteit Gods," *Christelijke Encyclopaedie* (Kampen: Kok, 1929), V:230-231.

While the Calvinist maintains that these divine regulations for the Jewish nation were not intended for and are not applicable to present-day conditions, yet he does maintain that they embody principles of government which are eternal and should hold everywhere under all conditions, and in all ages. Today, too, the government must consider it to be its duty by proper regulation of the economic and social conditions, not alone to counteract existing evils, but positively to promote the most equitable conditions and relations for all concerned. . . . And the various spheres of society, such as the school, the church, the economic, social, and intellectual organizations in society have their own God-given circle in which they are individually sovereign. To bring all under the dominance of the State would lead to the suppression of these spheres.

It is of importance to have clearly in mind the exact nature of the authority which God delegates to government officials and the method whereby these receive it. The authority which God delegates is never an unlimited one, as State-absolutists would claim. Rulers never have a right of absolute and final authority over the entire life of citizens. Their right of rulership is always restricted to their own governmental precincts. The Creator has also delegated a measure of authority to other groups in human society, to parents in the home, to officials in schools and churches, and to heads of corporations in society. Upon this authority, which is likewise delegated by God, the State's officials may not infringe. Their authority is always limited to the dispatch of their own proper functions.

From this brief historical reference we glean the following facts regarding the Calvinistic view of the authority of rulers. This authority is received from God. It always remains the authority of God. It is never relinquished by Him to the rulers. They remain His ministers. Their authority is restricted to their own domain of government and does not extend to the entire life of the citizens. The home, the church, the school, and other spheres of society have each their own province given them by God to which the authority of the government does not extend, and upon which it may not encroach.[13]

H. Dooyeweerd of the Free Reformed University of Amsterdam, together with his colleague, D. Vollenhoven, has worked for nearly half a century in developing a more penetrating philosophical analysis of the idea of sphere-sovereignty.

The situation is consequently as follows: the model law-spheres themselves are specific aspects of human experience, founded in the order of cosmic time. They are experienced though not explicitly, in the naive, pre-theoretical attitude of mind. Their diversity of meaning is based on the law of refrac-

13. H. Meeter, *The Basic Ideas of Calvinism* (Grand Rapids: Kregel, 1960), pp. 129, 130, 131, 135, 141, 146, 147.

tion of cosmic time . . . . The functional structures of meaning, guaranteeing to the law-sphere its specific internal sovereignty, are indeed nothing but a modal splitting up of the totality of meaning in time.[14]

Since the process of cultural differentiation leads to an increasing typical diversity of cultural spheres, there is a constant danger that one of these spheres may try to expand its formative power in an excessive manner at the expense of the others. Indeed, since the dissolution of the ecclesiastically unified culture which prevailed in medieval European civilization, there has been a running battle between the emancipated cultural spheres of the state, of natural science, of industry and commerce, and so forth, to acquire the supremacy one over the other.

In the progressive unfolding process of history, therefore, the preservation of a harmonious relationship between the differentiated cultural spheres becomes a vital interest of the entire human society. But this cultural harmony can be guaranteed only if the process of historical development complies with the normative principle of cultural economy. This principle forbids any excessive expansion of the formative power of a particular cultural sphere at the expense of the others. Here the aesthetic and economic anticipations in the historical mode of experience reveal themselves in their unbreakable mutual coherence. Both principles, that of cultural economy and that of cultural harmony, appeal to the inner nature of the differentiated cultural spheres as determined by the typical structures of individuality of the spheres of society to which they belong. Thus, they too, are well founded in the divine world-order. In the unfolding (opening-up) process of human culture, as soon as the natural bounds of the different cultural spheres are ignored through an excessive expansion of one of them, disastrous tensions and conflicts arise in human society. This may evoke convulsive reactions on the part of those cultural spheres which are threatened, or it may even lead to the complete ruin of a civilization, unless countertendencies in the process of development manifest themselves before it is too late and acquire sufficient cultural power to check the excessive expansion of power of a particular cultural factor.[15]

In developing a Reformed view of the church, R. B. Kuiper includes the following thoughts on the sovereignty of the church.

God alone is sovereign in the absolute sense, for His authority is truly supreme. He holds unlimited sway over the whole of the universe . . . .

However, the term *sovereignty* has also come to be used in a relative sense. The sovereign God has seen fit to lend authority

14. H. Dooyeweerd, *A New Critique of Theoretical Thought* (Philadelphia: Presbyterian and Reformed, 1957), II: 6-7.

15. H. Dooyeweerd, *In the Twilight of Western Thought* (Philadelphia: Presbyterian and Reformed, 1960), pp. 108-10.

to some of His creatures over others. In consequence, while no creature has an iota of sovereignty in relation to the Creator, certain creatures do possess a measure of sovereignty in relation to other creatures. Therefore it is proper to ascribe sovereignty, for example, to the state, and that is commonly done. Much less frequently are men wont to ascribe sovereignty to the Christian church, and yet to do that is not a whit less proper. Its sovereignty is a significant aspect of its glory....

How clear that the church's sovereignty is severely restricted! With reference to God and Christ it is simply non-existent.

God has, however, given a measure of authority to the church with reference to men, and that authority may somewhat loosely be denominated sovereignty. The question whether this sovereignty is restricted or unrestricted has been the subject of much contention throughout the church's history. While Protestantism insists that it is restricted, the Church of Rome teaches that it is unrestricted. The authority which Rome claims for itself is truly totalitarian. But that claim cannot be substantiated.... Beyond all doubt, the church's sovereignty with reference to the individual is restricted.

So is the sovereignty of the church with reference to the family restricted.... Significantly, God, not the church, brought the family into being, and it antedates the founding of the church. It follows undeniably that the family, like the individual, has certain rights on which the church may not encroach. It is not the church's business to stipulate the precise percentage of the family budget that is to be given to the church, nor to prescribe a menu for the family dinner, nor yet to dictate to a bereaved family where it is to bury its dead.

More instances of restrictions on the church's sovereignty might be named, but in this context the relation of the church to the state deserves special attention....

Today a large part of Protestantism, American Protestantism in particular, is convinced that the Bible teaches what is commonly—and rather loosely—called the separation of church and state. On this score some Anabaptists of the Reformation period and that famous American Baptist, Roger Williams, must be credited with having been ahead of their contemporaries. What is meant by the separation of church and state is that the church may not seek to govern a commonwealth nor interfere with the purely political affairs of the state, and that the state may not seek to govern the church nor interfere with its spiritual affairs. In short, both the church and the state are sovereign, each in its own sphere; and each must recognize the other's sovereignty....

And is it not obvious that neither did the state create the church nor did the church create the state, but God originated both and endowed each with its own specific authority?

The conclusion is inescapable that, while the sovereignty of the state with reference to the church is restricted, the sovereignty of the church with reference to the state is also restricted. The church is sovereign only in its own sphere. Its authority is not totalitarian.... 

The church is in sacred duty bound to rise up in majesty and proclaim to the world that it enjoys freedom of worship, not by the grace of the state, but as a God-given right and that it preaches the Word of God, not by the grace of human governments, but solely at the command of the sovereign God and its sovereign King, seated at God's right hand.

In another respect, too, the sovereignty of the church is positive indeed. It must sovereignly lay down the law of God to the individual, the family, society and the state.

No individual has the right to say that his private life is his own to lead and is none of the church's business. That would be far too sweeping an assertion. The law of God concerns every aspect of human life, and the church has been charged with the proclamation of that law in all its Scriptural fullness....

With reference to the family, too, the church must sovereignly proclaim the whole law of God.

Let the church speak sovereignly for the sovereign God and "the blessed and only Potentate, the King of kings and Lord of lords" (I Timothy 6:15).[16]

In probing various problems with which "the society of the future" confronts us, H. van Riessen relates his discussion to two major issues, the norms of authority and freedom and the principle of sphere-sovereignty.

Man shapes abiding relationships in society, and they are certainly not capricious relationships in which he lives and works: associations, state, school, church, family, business, etc.

Now the Biblical principles by which those life-relationships must be tested are those of authority-and-freedom and sphere-sovereignty.

The Bible surely teaches such diversity in so far as it then manifested itself in practical living. In it societal relationships show up in a natural way, sometimes one after another, as in the epistles to the Ephesians, Colossians, and Titus. In such cases office-bearers as well as subjects are addressed in keeping with the nature of the context in which the relationship exists: parents and children, masters and servants, magistrates and subjects, elders and members of the congregation. And the most striking thing is this, that there is no hint of a hierarchical relationship among those in authority in the various spheres. The independence of each form of authority, their being directly instituted by Christ, and the obligation to obedience for Christ's sake—these ideas form the background for addressing people in their communal relationships.

16. R. B. Kuiper, *The Glorious Body of Christ* (Grand Rapids: Eerdmans, 1958), pp. 313-19, 321.

Naturally the Bible does not give us a theory of sphere-sovereignty. It would be folly to expect that. One cannot even find the term itself there. But what we do meet, once we are attentive to the creational principles for the organization of society, is a harmony with that principle which is everywhere taken for granted, though always in keeping with the historical development of life-practice on a given point. For the Bible addresses us in terms of its own time. Differentiation of life as we know it was not yet evident at that time. Sphere-sovereignty then is a principle, a signpost at the beginning of human history. If current exegesis is correct, then the text in Genesis, "In the days of Enosh men began to call upon the name of the Lord," means that at that time independent worship, that is, an original kind of church fellowship, emerges out of the previously undifferentiated sphere of the family. Thus in the course of history one sees various societal relationships splitting off and taking on an independence in keeping with their own nature.[17]

In his introduction to a symposium on Calvinism, C. Bouma writes on "the relevance of Calvinism for today," discussing a number of key principles, including sphere-sovereignty.

The third principle, that of sphere-sovereignty, lies in a slightly different plane. It may be stated thus. Every sphere of human society has its own principles of life and action, its own type of authority. The Church, the industrial realm, and the state—to use three examples—are three different spheres of human life and action in which the principles that determine the authority obtaining in them differ. Practically this means that those who have authority in the one sphere should not assume to have authority in other social spheres. Each sphere, in this sense, is autonomous. Kuyper coined the term "souvereiniteit in eigen kring," i.e., the principle of sphere-sovereignty. In a sense it is the application of the principle of democracy, if not equality, to the various spheres of human life and action. The church has no right to tyrannize the other spheres, nor has the state. The type of authority which, under the sovereignty of God, who has the ultimate authority, obtains in each one of the social spheres will vary according to the nature of that sphere, and the one sphere has no right to usurp the authority of the other. This, of course, does not mean that in a certain sense the one sphere does not have authority over the other. Everything in human society is interrelated. The authority of the state in a sense is universal in human society. It must be, because it is the business of the state to maintain public order. But—and that is the point—each one of the other spheres, over which the state has in a sense political control as magistrate, also has a type of authority that is distinctive of itself, and that distinctive authority of each sphere must be recognized and honored by the state and by every other sphere. The ultimate reason for

17. H. van Riessen, *De Maatschappij der Toekomst* (Franeker, Neth.: Wever, 1953), pp. 78, 86-87 (translation, GJS).

this is that under the sovereignty of God each one of these spheres has been endowed with its own type of authority, for which those who bear that authority are responsible to God. This means, as far as the Church is concerned, that, however unique its authority and its scope may be, it should honor and respect the God-imposed authority of the other realms (state, school, industry, etc.) and not, like Roman Catholicism, assume that it is supreme over the whole of life.[18]

As a Biblical theologian, G. Vos discusses the New Testament teaching concerning the coming of the kingdom, and, along the way, defines the place and role of the church and other societal spheres within the kingdom.

From this, however, it does not necessarily follow that the visible church is the only outward expression of the invisible kingdom. Undoubtedly the kingship of God, as his recognized and applied supremacy, is intended to pervade and control the whole of human life in all its forms of existence. This the parable of the leaven plainly teaches. These various forms of human life have each their own sphere in which they work and embody themselves. There is a sphere of science, a sphere of art, a sphere of family life and of the state, a sphere of commerce and industry. Whenever one of these spheres comes under the controlling influence of the principle of divine supremacy and glory, and this outwardly reveals itself, there we can truly say that the kingdom of God has become manifest. Now the Lord in his teaching seldom makes explicit reference to these things. He contented himself with laying down the great religious and moral principles which ought to govern the life of man in every sphere. Their detailed application it was not his work to show. But we may safely affirm two things. On the one hand, his doctrine of the kingdom was founded on such a profound and broad conviction of the absolute supremacy of God in all things, that he could not but look upon every normal and legitimate province of human life as intended to form part of God's kingdom. On the other hand, it was not his intention that this result should be reached by making human life in all its spheres subject to the visible church. It is true that under the Old Covenant something of this nature had existed. In the theocracy the church had dominated the life of the people of God in all its extent. State and church were in it most intimately united. Jesus on more than one occasion gave us to understand that in this respect at least the conditions of the Old Covenant were not to be perpetuated, cf. Matt. 22:21; John 18:36; 19:11. And what is true of the relation between church and state, may also be applied to the relation between the visible church and the various other branches into which the organic life of humanity divides itself. It is entirely in accordance with the spirit of Jesus'

18. C. Bouma, *God-Centered Living* (Grand Rapids: Baker, 1951), pp. 27-28.

teaching to subsume these under the kingdom of God and to co-ordinate them with the visible church as true manifestations of this kingdom, in so far as the divine sovereignty and glory have become in them the controlling principle. But it must always be remembered, that the latter can only happen, when all these, no less than the visible church, stand in living contact with the forces of regeneration supernaturally introduced into the world by the Spirit of God. While it is proper to separate between the visible church and such things as the Christian state, Christian art, Christian science, etc., these things, if they truly belong to the kingdom of God, grow up out of the regenerated life of the invisible church.[19]

C. Veenhof's work on sphere-sovereignty takes on added urgency when we remember that it was written in 1939, at a moment when his own Netherlands and the rest of Western Europe were threatened with cruel subjugation under the heel of a totalitarian and tyrannical power.

The pluriformity which marks the undivided oneness of human life, in particular human societal life, Kuyper identified by the concept "sphere-sovereignty." This expression pointed to the principle by which human communal life must be organized. Governed by this principle, Kuyper cast himself with impetuous power into the spiritual struggles of his age. Over against the individualism which was pulverizing societal life in his days and destroying the life-relationships ordained by God and trampling upon authority as instituted by the Creator, he fought passionately for a recognition of the divine order in the organization of human life. Recognition of the creational will of God and reverence for God's law of life with respect to the organic life-relationships into which the Creator has integrated the life of man is the condition of true freedom and the full blossoming of our creaturely human life.

The complete acceptance and consistent application of the principle of "sphere-sovereignty" will prove to be the only adequate defense against the totalitarian insanity of our times, by which the rich, multi-colored life of man is being melted down into the drab, monotonous manifestations of an idolatrous state which levels everything down and devours it.[20]

For decades L. Berkhof has been the most influential theologian within that community which surrounds Calvin College and Seminary. In both his theological and more broadly cultural writings he speaks clearly on the idea of sphere-sovereignty.

The ecclesiastical character of these (church) assemblies

19. G. Vos, *The Kingdom and the Church* (Grand Rapids: Eerdmans, 1951), pp. 87-89.

20. C. Veenhof, *Souvereiniteit in Eigen Kring* (Goes, Neth.: Oosterbaan & Le-Cointre, 1939), pp. 91-92 (translation, GJS).

should always be borne in mind. It is because they are church assemblies that purely scientific, social, industrial, or political matters do not, as such, fall under their jurisdiction. Only ecclesiastical matters belong to their province, matters of doctrine and morals, of church government and discipline, and whatever pertains to the preservation of unity and good order in the Church of Jesus Christ.[21]

The Church should encourage the organization of her members on a distinctly and positively Christian basis for social and philanthropic purposes. They only have within their hearts the forces of a higher life; they only have burning within their souls the love that is willing to spend itself in ministering service; they only are possessed of the spirit of true philanthropy. Hence they must be the leaven permeating the lump, God's spiritual force for the regeneration of the world, His chosen agents to influence every sphere of life, and to bring science and art, commerce and industry in subjection to God.[22]

The following statement, being a synodical pronouncement, falls into a slightly different category. Synods of the Christian Reformed Church have made regular appeals to the principle of sphere-sovereignty in settling issues pertaining to the family, Christian schools, Reformed higher education, labor, politics, the film arts, the redistribution of wealth and goods, and so forth. The line of reasoning embodied in the following report, appealing directly to the principle of sphere-sovereignty, was employed by the Synods of 1910 and 1938 in arriving at the decision to revise Article 36 of the Belgic Confession on the relationship of the state to the church.

This phrase concerning the office of civil government in relationship to the church arises out of the idea of a state-church, implemented first by Constantine and later in many Protestant countries. History argues, however, not in favor of the principle of state domination over the church, but rather for a certain separation of church and state. It is also in conflict with the New Testament dispensation to grant to the state the right to reform the church according to its will and to deny the church the right to take its stand as an independent sphere alongside the state. The New Testament does not place the Christian Church under the authority of civil magistrates to be controlled and extended by the power of the state, but places it solely under the Lord and King as an independent sphere alongside of and wholly free from the state, to be ruled and built up only by its own spiritual powers. Therefore nearly all Reformed churches have already rejected the idea of a state-church as contrary to the New Testa-

21. L. Berkhof, *Systematic Theology* (Grand Rapids: Eerdmans, 1949), p. 591.

22. L. Berkhof, *The Church and Social Problems* (Grand Rapids: Eerdmans-Sevensma, 1913), pp. 18, 20.

ment and have come to defend the autonomy of the churches and personal freedom of conscience in the service of God.

In accord herewith the Christian Reformed Church in America senses the need of declaring that it does not understand the office of civil government to entail the exercise of governmental power in the sphere of religion by introducing a state-church and maintaining and promoting it as the only true church, nor to resist, eradicate or destroy by the power of the sword all other churches as false religions. Rather we firmly believe that within its own worldly sphere civil government has a divine calling to fulfill with respect to both the first and second tables of the divine law. We hold moreover that both state and church mutually, as institutions of God and Christ, have received rights and duties from above and are thus bound to fulfill a very holy calling in relationship to each other through the Holy Spirit who proceeds from the Father and the Son. But they may not intrude upon each other's sphere. The church as well as the state has a claim to sphere sovereignty.[23]

After nearly two centuries of decline, Calvinism experienced a dramatic renewal in the Netherlands during the nineteenth century and at the beginning of the twentieth. Out of these reformations came a recovery of the principle of sphere-sovereignty, some of the earliest impulses in this direction coming from the historian and statesman G. Groen-van Prinsterer, with his idea of "sphere-independence."

Man, in every station and position in life, has received a talent to be freely used. God shall call him to account for the way he uses it.... Thus, whether one thinks of the calling of the state or the purpose of the church, let there be unity between church and state.... But unity bought at the price of independence, this I detest.... I do not know to what extent the Swiss cantons dishonored the memory of Calvin, who did not misunderstand or abandon the independence of the state, nor especially of the church, by their cowardly surrender of what belongs to the church.[24]

The seasoned theologian of the Neo-Calvinist movement, H. Bavinck, expresses himself brilliantly and beautifully on the idea of sphere-sovereignty in the following passages.

Everything was created with its own nature and is based upon ordinances appointed by God for it. Sun and moon and stars have their own peculiar tasks; plants and animals and man

23. *Acts of Synod* (CRC), 1910, pp. 104-5 (translation, GJS).

24. G. Groen-van Prinsterer, *Ongeloof en Revolutie* (Franeker, Neth.: Wever, 1951), pp. 53, 56, 58, 60 (translation). Cf. J. Dengerink, *Critisch-Historisch Onderzoek naar de Sociologische Ontwikkeling van het Beginsel der "Souvereiniteit in Eigen Kring" in de 19ᵉ en 20ᵉ Eeuw* (Kampen: Kok, 1948), pp. 69-94.

have their own distinct natures. There is a rich diversity. But in this diversity there is also a supreme unity. The ground of both lies in God. It is He who created all things according to his incomparable wisdom, who continually sustains them in their distinct natures, who guides and governs them according to the potentials and laws created in them, and as the highest good and goal is desired and emulated by all things in keeping with their measure and manners. Here is a unity which does not destroy, but maintains diversity, and a diversity which does not depreciate unity, but unfolds it in its richness. By virtue of this unity the world can metaphorically be called an organism in which all the parts are related to the other parts and mutually influence each other. Heaven and earth, man and animals, soul and body, doctrine and life, art and science, religion and morality, state and church, family and society, etc.—they are distinct but not divided. There are all kinds of connections among them; an organic, or, if you will, a moral bond holds them together.[25]

Creation bestows upon all creatures a nature which can be unfolded in the process of providence. After all, the world was not created in a state of pure potentiality, as a chaos or fluid mass, but as a cosmos. And man was placed in it not as a helpless child, but as husband and wife. Progress could take place only in such a well-prepared world. And so creation presented the world to providence. The world was, moreover, an organic whole, in which unity was accompanied by the richest sort of diversity. Every creature received its own nature and its own existence, its own life and its own law of life. As the moral law was created into Adam's heart as the rule of his life, so all creatures carried in their own nature the principles and laws of their own development. All things were created by the Word. Everything rests upon divine thought. The whole creation is a system of divine ordinances.... God gave to all creatures a certain order, a law which they do not violate, Psalm 148:6. In all their parts they depend upon the decree of God which is revealed in things small and great. It all comes forth from the Lord of hosts. He is wonderful in counsel, great in deed.... At creation God laid his ordinances in the things He made, an order of reality in which things are made to stand in reciprocal relationships to each other.... As creatures were given their own peculiar natures along with differences among them, so there are also differences in the laws by which they act and in the relationships which they sustain to each other. They differ in the area of both physical things and psychic things, in the intellectual and ethical realms, in the family and in society, in science and in art, in the domain of earth and in the domain of heaven. It is the providence of God coupled with creation which sustains these diverse structures and leads them to full development. In his providence God does not negate, but respects and

25. H. Bavinck, *Gereformeerde Dogmatiek* (Kampen: Kok, 1928), II: 399-400 (translation, GJS).

unfolds everything which He called into being through creation. Thus He maintains and rules all creatures in harmony with their natures.[26]

Thus the church, with its own origin, essence, task, and purpose, stands in the midst of the world. . . . The relationship which must obtain between church and world is therefore primarily organic, moral, spiritual in nature. Christ is still prophet, priest, and king, and He influences the whole world by his Word and Spirit. Through him a renewing, sanctifying influence goes forth from every believer into the family, society, the state, the professions, business, art, science, etc. Spiritual life is intended to make our natural and moral life in its full depth and scope answer once again to the law of God. In this organic way Christian truth and Christian life are carried out into all spheres of our natural life, so that the family and family living are restored to honor, the wife is viewed once again as the equal of her husband, science and art are Christianized, the level of moral living is elevated, society and the state are reformed, and laws, ordinances, morals, and customs are marked by a Christian character.[27]

The gospel always works reformationally; indeed it brings about the greatest possible reformation; for it liberates from guilt and renews the heart, and thus restores in principle the right relationship of man to God. Moving out from this central point it then informs all earthly relationships in a reforming and renewing way. The various spheres of human life, family, society, state, commerce, occupation, business, farming, industry, science, art, etc., have a certain measure of peculiar independence, which must be ascribed to the will of God as revealed in their very nature. These spheres develop and change in the course of time, each one according to its own nature, under the direction of God's providence. The authority of government over its subject, of the husband over the wife, of the father over his children, of the master over his servants differs markedly today from such authority as exercised in Paul's day. The gospel honors fully this development, today as well as in the days of the apostles. It allows freedom and places no obstacles in the path of such development. For the gospel is the Evangel, a happy message for all creatures. It is not a proclamation of death and destruction, but of resurrection and life.[28]

The Christian world-view opposes autonomy and anarchy with all its power. It holds that man is not autonomous, but is always and everywhere bound by laws not invented by man, but set forth by God as the rule for life. In religion and morality, in the family, society, and the state, everywhere there are ideas,

---

26. Bavinck, *Geref. Dogmatiek,* II: 569-571 (translation, GJS).

27. Bavinck, *Geref. Dogmatiek,* IV: 416, 418 (translation, GJS).

28. H. Bavinck, *Christelijke Beginselen en Maatschappelijke Verhoudingen* (Utrecht, Neth.: Ruys, 1908), pp. 43-44 (translation, GJS).

norms which stand above man. They form a unity among themselves and find their origin and continuation in the Creator and
Lawgiver of the universe. These norms are the most precious
treasures entrusted to mankind, the basis for all societal institutions. They are not only the foundation of our perception and
knowledge, but also our willing and doing; they carry authority
in academics, but also in life; they are authoritative for the
head and the heart, for thinking and acting. While human autonomy destroys the relationship between subject and object, and
thus in principle reduces everything to chaos, theonomy as
taught in Scripture grants to every creature its rightful place
and its true meaning. Then no one and nothing exists by itself.
No creature is independent and may do as he pleases, neither
husband nor wife, neither parents nor children, neither government nor citizens, neither master nor servants. They are all
bound to God's law, each one in his own way and in his own
place. That is so not by reason of some contract or arbitrary
choice, not by force or necessity. Rather it is by God's decree
that they live and work together, that they are made for each
other and are bound to each other. These divine ideas and laws
are foundations and norms, the goods and treasures, the inter-
connections and patterns for all creatures. To live in conformity
to those norms in mind and heart, in thought and action, this
is what it means most basically to become conformed to the
image of God's Son. And this is the ideal and goal of man.[29]

No one is more closely associated with the idea of sphere-
sovereignty than A. Kuyper, who gave it definitive formulation as
a working principle pervasively structuring all his works. We find a
classic expression of it in his memorable inaugural address at the
founding of the Free Reformed University of Amsterdam in 1880.

Whenever God invests human office with sovereignty this
very important question arises: how does such a conferral take
place? That is, is the all-embracing sovereignty of God conferred
indivisibly upon a single person? Or does one who on earth is
called a sovereign possess the power to compel obedience only
in a limited sphere, a sphere bounded by other spheres in which
someone else, and not he is sovereign? The answer to that question varies, depending on whether one stands inside or outside
of the arena of revelation....

But, behold this wonderful perspective on freedom! The absolute sovereignty of the sinless Messiah involves rejection of
and opposition to the earthly sovereignty of any sinful man, and
that by the division of life into identifiable spheres, each with
its own sovereignty.

Human life, with its material foreground, which is visible,
and its spiritual background, which is invisible, appears to be
neither simple nor uniform, but represents an infinitely com-

29. H. Bavinck, *Christelijke Wereldbeschouwing* (Kampen: Kok, 1904), pp. 90-91
(translation, GJS).

posite organism. It is so constituted that the individual can exist only within the group and can come to full expression only in community. Call the parts of this great instrument cog-wheels, each driven around its own axle by its own power; or call them spheres. each filled with its own exciting life-spirit—the concept or imagery does not matter—as long as you acknowledge that there are all kinds of spheres in life, as many as the starry hosts in the firmament, whose boundaries are drawn with firm lines, each having its own principle as a focal point. Just as we usually speak of "the world of morality," "the world of science," "the world of commerce," "the world of art," so we may speak more precisely of "the sphere of morality," "the sphere of home life," "the sphere of societal life," each with its own domain. And because each has its own domain, within the boundaries of that domain each has its own sovereignty.

Accordingly there is a domain of nature within which its sovereign exerts power upon material things according to established laws. So there is also a domain of personal, family, scientific, societal and ecclesiastical life, all acting in obedience to their own peculiar laws of life and all subject to their own peculiar authority. There is, for example, a domain of theoretical thought, within which no other law may hold control than the law of logic; and a domain of conscience, within which no one may issue commands sovereignly but the Holy One himself; and finally a domain of faith, within whose boundaries the only sovereign is the person himself, who by that faith commits himself to something in the depth of his being . . . .

He who lives by the light of revelation, and lives within it consistently, confesses quite naturally that all sovereignty rests in God and therefore can only flow forth from Him; that this sovereignty of God has been granted in an absolute and undivided way to just one Man, the Messiah; and that human freedom is safe under this Son of Man who was anointed Sovereign, because every domain of life, including the state, receives from him its own delegated authority, that is, it possesses sovereignty in its own sphere . . . .

Sphere-sovereignty defending itself against state-sovereignty —that is in summary form a description of world history, even before the Messianic sovereignty was proclaimed. For while that royal Child of Bethlehem protected sphere-sovereignty with his shield, He did not create it. It was there from of old. It was embedded in the creation order, in the plan for human life. It was there before state-sovereignty emerged, which sensed in the peculiar sovereignty of the various spheres of life its ongoing opponent. And within these spheres themselves people have weakened sphere-sovereignty's power of resistance by violation of this law of life, that is, by sin. Thus the ancient history of every nation confronts us with the bitter drama of how, after persistent and sometimes heroic struggles, freedom within each sphere died out and the power of the state, transformed into Caesarism, triumphed. Socrates, who drank the poisonous cup, and Brutus, who thrust the dagger into Caesar's heart, and the Galileans, whose blood Pilate mingled with the sacrifices, all these are the desperately heroic convulsions of a free organic life which finally collapsed under the iron hand of Caesarism....

Science too constitutes a peculiar sphere in life in which the truth is sovereign. It may under no circumstances tolerate an infringement upon or violation of its law of life. To do so would not only dishonor science, but would also be sinful before God....

In this address, in accordance with Scripture and the example of Calvin, I have placed the sovereignty of God in the foreground, because this principle alone stimulates life at its root and overcomes all fear of men and even the fear of Satan himself. And if anyone should ask whether the principle of sphere-sovereignty has really been seized from the very heart of Scripture and from the treasury of Reformed life, I would beg him first of all to plumb the depths of the comprehensive faith-principle of Scripture, and then to take note of the Hebronic tribal edict for crowning David as king, and Elijah's resistance to Ahab's tyranny, and the disciples' refusal to back down before the prohibition by the Jerusalem police, and last but not least to listen to the proverb of the coin from the lips of the Lord concerning what is God's and what is Caesar's. Turning to the Reformed tradition, are you not familiar with Calvin's concept of the "minor magistrates"? Does sphere-sovereignty not lie embedded in the very foundations of the whole Presbyterian church order? Were not nearly all Reformed countries inclined toward a confederate form of life? Did not civil liberties flourish most profusely precisely among Reformed peoples? And can one contradict the fact that peaceful home life, decentralization, and the independence of civil communities are even now best guaranteed within the heritage of Calvin's posterity?

It is therefore wholly in a Reformed spirit that we now request sovereignty in our own scientific sphere in keeping with our own principle....[30]

The earliest theoretical formulation of the principle of sphere-sovereignty is traceable to Johannes Althusius (1557-1638), a German churchman and civil official in Emden, whose thinking was shaped in part by Calvin's Geneva.

It is evident from selected passages of Scripture that the care and administration of ecclesiastical things and functions belong not to the secular magistrates, but to the collegium of these presbyters. To this administration even the magistrate is subject with respect to warnings, censures, and other things necessary for the welfare of the soul. Therefore, the guidance of the ministerium, and obedience to it, are commended to each and every person. Sacred and secular duties are distinct, and ought not to be confused. For each demands the whole man.... As the ecclesiastical order of the province will bring forth pious,

---

30. A. Kuyper, *Souvereiniteit in Eigen Kring* (Kampen: Kok, 1930), pp. 9-14, 20, 25-26 (translation, GJS). Cf. Dengerink, *Critisch-Historisch*, pp. 95-161.

learned, wise, and good men, so the political and secular order of the nobility will be concerned to bring forth for the province strong, militant, and brave men who are ready with arms and counsel, and are experienced in military matters.... Administrators are not permitted to overstep these limits. Those who exceed the boundaries of administration entrusted to them cease being ministers of God and of the universal association, and become private persons to whom obedience is not owed in those things in which they exceed the limits of their power.... The wickedness of administrators cannot abolish or diminish the imperium and might of God, nor release the administrators from the same. For the power and jurisdiction of God are infinite. He created heaven and earth, and is rightly lord and proprietor of them. All who inhabit the earth are truly tenants, vassals, lessees, clients, and beneficiaries of his.[31]

Is Christ the Lord of the world? Why would you exclude from his rule one of the foremost powers in the world? The sword of government is God's sword. There is a distinction between the functions of the church and the state, but they are not therefore opposed to each other.... These two swords always continue, each having its own nature, and the one does not negate the other.[32]

## John Calvin on sphere-sovereignty

This series of quotations represents a formidable tradition in the history of Calvinism, a tradition, moreover, which reflects a striking measure of unanimity on matters pertaining to a Biblically Reformed world-and-life-view structured along the lines of the principle of sphere-sovereignty. Through the centuries, however, Calvinism internationally has demonstrated a very cosmopolitan character, adjusting itself to differing situations in various countries and among various peoples and cultures. It has therefore manifested a great diversity in outlooks. During this modern period it also fell repeatedly under the influence of many alien perspectives arising both within and outside of Christian circles. This makes it possible to also cite Calvinists who structured their world-and-life-views along quite different lines. The above voices from the past, however, and others too, clearly made sphere-sovereignty a working principle in their thought and practice, though with some variations in emphasis due to differences in insight, historical-cultural setting, and the problems they encountered.

31. J. Althusius, *Politics,* trans. F. S. Carney (London: Eyre & Spottiswoode, 1964), pp. 54, 56, 93, 110.

32. A. Polman, *Onze Nederlandsche Geloofsbelijdenis* (Franeker, Neth.: Wever, n.d.), IV: 279-80 (translation, GJS).

All these spokesmen for the Calvinist tradition looked back to Calvin in support of their views, either explicitly claiming his support or at least assuming their agreement with his views. Is their appeal to Calvin justifiable? That is the question which must now be faced. On the issue at hand, were they right in thinking that they shared in Calvin's heritage? How much continuity is there on this point between Calvin and the Calvinist tradition? To answer these questions we turn now to a review of Calvin's teachings and practices as they bear upon the salient features of this life-perspective.

### The supreme sovereignty of God

No extensive argumentation is needed to establish Calvin's commitment to the overarching, all-pervading sovereignty of God. This is a central, unifying theme which runs through all his writings. It is not just one idea among others, which Calvin develops in a chapter here or there, but a sustaining conviction which permeates all his teachings. B. B. Warfield captures something of the thrust of this control belief in Calvin as it served to shape the Calvinist tradition in these words:

> He who believes in God without reserve, and is determined that God shall be God to him in all his thinking, feeling, willing— in the entire compass of his life-activities, intellectual, moral, spiritual—throughout his individual, social, religious relations— is by the force of the strictest logic which presides over the outworking of principles into thought and life, by the very necessity of the case, a Calvinist.[33]

This summary statement is true to the best in Calvin. There are numerous concentrated statements in Calvin which highlight his profound and sweeping commitment to the sovereignty of God. I shall cite a single passage. Notice the totalitarian terms which Calvin employs ("every," "all," "everything," "no," "none," "complete"), universal terms which are reminiscent of Paul's words in Ephesians 1 and Colossians 1. In discussing the knowledge of God as Creator, Calvin says that we must be persuaded that

> God is the fountain of every good, and that we must seek nothing elsewhere than in him. This I take to mean that not only does he sustain this universe (as he once founded it) by his boundless might, regulate it by his wisdom, preserve it by his goodness, and especially rule mankind by his righteousness and judgment, bear with it in his mercy, watch over it by his protection; but also that no drop will be found of either wisdom or light, or of righteousness or power or rectitude, or of genuine truth, which does not flow from him, and of which he is not the cause. Thus

33. B. B. Warfield, *Calvin and Calvinism Today* (Philadelphia: Presbyterian & Reformed, 1909), p. 23.

we may learn to await and seek all these things from him, and thankfully ascribe them, once received, to him. For this sense of the powers of God is for us a fit teacher of piety, from which religion is born. I call "piety" that reverence joined with love of God which the knowledge of his benefits induces. For until men recognize that they owe everything to God, that they are nourished by his fatherly care, that he is the Author of their every good, that they should seek nothing beyond him—they will never yield him willing service. Nay, unless they establish their complete happiness in him, they will never give themselves truly and sincerely to him.[34]

A similar emphasis on the supreme sovereignty of God, though stated apologetically, comes to expression in Calvin's commentaries, especially on Biblical passages which depict confrontations between people of God seeking to uphold the sovereignty of God over against earthly authorities who stand opposed to it. In discussing Nebuchadnezzar's infamous claim to absolute sovereignty, Calvin says:

> We know how earthly empires are constituted by God only on the condition that He deprives himself of nothing, but shines forth alone, and all magistrates must be set in regular order, and every authority in existence must be subject to his glory . . . . For earthly princes lay aside all their power when they rise up against God, and are unworthy of being reckoned in the number of mankind. We ought rather utterly to defy them than to obey them whenever they are so restive and wish to spoil God of his rights, and, as it were, to seize his throne and draw him down from heaven.[35]

Calvin reiterates this point in discussing the resolute stand of the apostles in the face of the Sanhedrin's prohibition against proclaiming the gospel of Jesus Christ.

> This is the main point of the defense, that men must, indeed are bound to put God before men. "God commands us to bear witness to Christ, therefore it is in vain for you to order us to be silent." . . . God sets men over us with power in such a way that He keeps his own authority unimpaired. Therefore, we must do the will of those who rule over us to the extent that the authority of God is not violated . . . . Therefore, if a father, who is not content with his own station, tries to take from God the highest honor as Father, then he is a man and nothing else. If a king or a prince or a magistrate extols himself so much that he minimizes

34. *Inst.*, I.ii.1. Cf. A. Biéler, *The Social Humanism of John Calvin* (Richmond: Knox, 1964), p. 24: "At all times and in all circumstances the Christian has only one Lord and Master, and he is Jesus Christ. The partial obedience which the Christian owes to his human masters, to his parents, to his teachers, to his wife or husband, to his employers, to his military superiors, and to state officials is only a derived and conditional obedience which is at all times subordinated to the only absolute authority, that of Jesus Christ."

35. *Comm.* on Dan. 6:21-22.

the honor and authority of God, he is nothing but a man. The same must also hold true of pastors. For anyone who goes beyond his function, because he sets himself against God, must be stripped of his office.[36]

In seeking to honor this Biblical witness, the Calvinist tradition, in line with Calvin himself, defined the Christian heart commitment as allegiance to the sovereign God on the authority of His Word. It laid this at the bottom as its confessional starting point, the anchor point for its entire world-and-life-view. At its best, the Calvinist tradition viewed this presuppositional point of departure not as commitment to the sovereignty of God as though to some abstract principle about God, but as personal and communal commitment to the sovereign God Himself. In this Calvin himself led the way. Recall how he denounced Scholastic inquiries into the essence, the nature, the being of God. Instead he restated the basic religious issues in these words: Who is God *for you?* For a meaningful affirmation of the sovereignty of God is rooted in a deeply spiritual commitment to the sovereign God Himself, His presence having been personally and communally experienced. As Kuyper puts it somewhere in his writings: One cannot speak in a meaningful way about the sovereignty of God over the whole cosmos until he has first experienced the sovereign grace of God in his own heart and life.

God's sovereignty is not one among several attributes of God which man may decide to emphasize more strongly or more weakly. It is a divine prerogative which permeates everything God is and does for His creation. He *is* the Sovereign, always and everywhere—sovereign in creation, sovereign even in our fall into sin, sovereign in the history of redemption, sovereign in the eschatological issues of history and in the coming of the kingdom. He is therefore sovereign in every aspect of His total relationship to us: in His justice, His power, His grace, His mercy, all epitomized in His central and comprehensive relationship of love to His creation. God's sovereignty must therefore be acknowledged and the implications of it worked out concretely in every sphere of life: home, school, church, state, university, industry, business, politics, science, art, journalism, and in every other societal relationship.

Standing firmly on this confession, the Calvinist tradition, taking its cue from Calvin himself, registered its protest against the professed autonomy of human reason in modern thought. In opposition to revolutionary ideologies based on the dogma of popular sovereignty, the Calvinist tradition affirmed its faith in the sovereignty of God in the affairs of men and nations. This was the genius of Kuyper's political vision in establishing the Anti-Revolutionary

36. *Comm.* on Acts 5:27-33.

Party in the Netherlands. Though negatively stated (*versus* the French Revolution), this party banner carried with it a positive intent, namely, to declare the sovereignty of God in political life over against the alleged autonomy of man.

In its confession of the absolute sovereignty of God the Calvinist tradition, again in step with Calvin, discovered the spiritual strength and undergirding reason for its repudiation of the various ancient and modern dualisms which divide life into sacred and secular compartments. If God is sovereign over all of life in its total extent and in all its parts, then Christians must reject every pernicious dichotomy between personal religion and public life, between neutral facts and moral values, between pure reason and practical reason, between church and world, between body and soul, between faith and science, between this-worldly and other-worldly affairs, between a realm of nature and a realm of grace. For if God is God, then His presence is decisively important in the full range of our life-activities. God-centered and God-controlled living is the confession which lay at the heart of this Calvinist view of life. Governed by this transcendent norm, the Calvinist tradition developed its Biblically Reformed world-and-life-view structured by the principle of sphere-sovereignty.

*"Two jurisdictions"*

This confessional stance brought with it a recognition of the limited, subservient sovereignty of the several spheres in life. Armed with this conviction, Calvinists combated, though often inconsistently, every form of worldly totalitarianism. For only God's regime is total. Every form of societal tyranny and monopoly must therefore be resisted, whether governmental, ecclesiastical, commercial, or scientific. Accordingly the Calvinist tradition opposed both the church absolutism of medievalists and the state absolutism of modern secularists as forms of idolatry which dishonor God's exclusive right to absolute sovereignty. Every form of societal planning based on "social contract" theories rather than creation ordinances must be seen as an affront to the sovereign God.[37]

37. "In his ideas about the political order Calvin's basic principle of the sovereignty of God is determinative. For he was strongly opposed to every form of state absolutism, autocracy, and absolute monarchy. Kings and presidents ought to have their power limited by legislators and constitutional law. Calvin cites the concrete case from Scripture of Samuel recording the rights of the people in a book for future reference between them and the king. This differs *in toto* from the social contract idea of Rousseau, in which the collective will of the people is the highest norm. For Calvin, the sovereign God is the Lawgiver of the nations today as well as in the days of Samuel, and popular sovereignty is a figment of the deluded imagination of fallen men" (H. Van Til, *The Calvinistic Concept of Culture* [Grand Rapids: Baker, 1959], p. 96).

These are some of the implications which later Calvinists found embedded in their confession of the sovereignty of God and the corollary to it, the subservient sovereignty of the various spheres in life. It was their contention that Calvin's heart commitment had laid the groundwork for these views. We must now test this claim.

Calvin concludes his discussion of Christian freedom by speaking of "two kingdoms" which are present in human society. As he puts it in his own words:

> There is a twofold government in man: One aspect is spiritual, whereby the conscience is instructed in piety and in reverencing God; the second is political, whereby man is educated for duties of humanity and citizenship which must be maintained among men. These are usually called the "spiritual" and the "temporal" jurisdiction (not improper terms), by which is meant that the former sort of government pertains to the life of the soul, while the latter has to do with the concerns of the present life— not only with food and clothing but with laying down laws whereby a man may live his life among other men holily, honorably, and temperately. For the former resides in the inner mind, while the latter regulates only outward behavior. The one we may call the spiritual kingdom, the other the political kingdom. Now these two, as we have divided them, must always be examined separately; and while one is being considered, we must call away and turn aside the mind from thinking about the other. There are in man, so to speak, two worlds, over which different kings and different laws have authority.[38]

In this same context Calvin further distinguishes these two "kingdoms," "jurisdictions," "orders," "governments," "laws" as pertaining to "civil government" and "church law," the "outer forum" and the "inner forum" of the conscience. Always observant of "right order of teaching," he then postpones further treatment of both "jurisdictions" until he comes later to a separate treatment of each. But he never retreats from this distinction, clinging to it throughout the *Institutes.* When he comes to this later discussion of church government[39] and civil government,[40] Calvin holds that he has established that "man is under a twofold government." The one "resides in the soul or inner man and pertains to eternal life," the other "pertains only to the establishment of civil justice and outward morality."[41]

Also in his commentaries Calvin allows this long-standing distinction to structure his Biblical view of societal relationships, though he qualifies it in one passage as Christ's way of accommodating His teaching to a then popular outlook on life. Reflecting on Christ's words, "Give unto Caesar what is Caesar's, and unto God what is God's," he says:

38. *Inst.,* III.xix.15.          40. *Inst.,* IV.xx.1.

39. *Inst.,* IV.viii.1; IV.x.1.   41. Ibid.

Christ's answer does not stop halfway, but provides full instruction on the question which has been raised. A clear distinction has been set out here between spiritual and civil government.... Perhaps that distinction hardly seems to apply, because properly speaking when we do our duty towards men we thereby fulfill our obedience to God. But to get this message across to the man in the street, Christ is content to distinguish the spiritual kingdom of God from the political order and round of current affairs. Keep this distinction firm: The Lord wishes to be the sole Lawgiver for the government of souls, with no rule of worship to be sought from any other source than his Word, and our adherence is to the only pure service there enjoined. Yet the power of the sword, the laws of the land, and the decisions of the courts in no way prevent the perfect service of God from flourishing in our midst.[42]

What shall we say of Calvin on this point? Is he advocating some sort of Scholastic or Lutheran dichotomy after all? These passages from Calvin do indeed leave a number of questions unanswered. But to push Calvin into the camp of the dualists is also an unwarranted conclusion. It must be admitted that his position does not come through with great clarity here. This twofold treatment of church and state tends to obscure his general emphasis on the religious unity of life and to bifurcate God's sovereign claim on society.

Calvin's way of distinguishing between these two "governments" is analogous to his questionable way of distinguishing between body and soul in man, dividing them so sharply as to obscure the unity and wholeness of man, even describing the body as "the prison-house" of the soul.[43] He wants indeed to maintain that in a certain sense the whole man is image of God, that the whole man is overturned by sin, and that the whole man is transformed by God's redeeming grace. At the same time, within this religiously whole view of man, Calvin compromises his position by working structurally with remnants of a medieval distinction between body and soul. He was not fully successful in shaking off past categories of thought. Thus he failed in consistently reforming his view of man. Yet he did break with the nature/grace scheme of the Scholastics, introducing a breakthrough to a radically new position in holding that the whole man, body and soul, comes under divine judgment and divine redemption.

Similarly here, in dealing with the inner structural relationships of society, Calvin perpetuates distinctions which on the surface are reminiscent of the older Scholastic dichotomies. Fundamentally,

42. *Comm.* on Matt. 22:15-22.

43. Cf. *Inst.*, I.xv.2.

however, he has broken with the past, and broken through to a new position, even though he failed to follow through on it consistently. Religiously he sees both church and state under the sovereign judgment and redemption of God. Structurally, however, the wedges which he drives between church and state are ambiguous and inept, leaving them as rather loosely defined areas of life rather than clearly defined societal institutions. But he no longer identifies the state with nature and the church with grace.

Calvin's move in the direction of a religiously unified view of church and state is clear from his discussion of the topic: "The two 'governments' are not antithetical." He argues there that "this distinction does not lead us to consider the whole nature of (civil) government as a thing polluted, which has nothing to do with the Christian man."[44] He contends vigorously for the office of magistrate as an institution ordained by God and against any derogation of it as though it were disreputable.[45] He even employs overstatement to drive home his point as forcefully as possible: "No one ought to doubt that civil authority is a calling, not only holy and lawful before God, but also the most sacred and by far the most honorable of all callings in the whole life of mortal man."[46]

Calvin's distinction between these two forms of "government" should therefore not be construed as an updated version of the Scholastic dichotomy between the church as the realm of grace and the state as the realm of nature, nor as a variation on the Lutheran dichotomy between a Christianly committed ecclesiastical arena viewed as the "kingdom of God" and a religiously neutral governmental sector viewed rather negatively as a stopgap measure made necessary by the reality of sin within the "kingdom of the world." In His sovereign grace God claims our wholehearted allegiance in both church and state. In both, the norms of God's Word are to be implemented. Both constitute legitimate, God-ordained spheres of Christian service in contrast to Anabaptist negation of governmental authority. Calvin's way of structuring these "two kingdoms" leaves us with a number of unsettled problems. Yet there is also a newly emerging clarity regarding these two spheres in life. He certainly did not give us the last word on the subject. But he did issue a refreshingly new first word, signaling a new direction. Calvin began, in his own somewhat halting way, to see each of these two spheres as exercising in its own unique way a divinely delegated subservient sovereignty under the supremely sovereign rule of God.

Rather than seeing Calvin's position as a reversion to that of the

44. *Inst.*, IV.xx.2.

45. *Inst.*, IV.xx.4, 5.				46. *Inst.*, IV.xx.4.

Constantinian-medieval period or a diversion into Lutheran prob-
lematics, it would be truer to Calvin's intent to interpret his strong
emphasis on the distinctive roles of these "two jurisdictions" as an
initial attempt to introduce the idea which later came to be known as
the "separation" of church and state.[47] This interpretation lends
credence to the appeal to Calvin by later Calvinists in support of
their views on the unique and distinctive identity of the church over
against the state, and vice versa, based on the principle of sphere-
sovereignty. There is indeed evidence in Calvin that he sowed the
seeds which, gradually germinating and ripening, eventually bore
this fruit. In his lectures on Amos 7, Calvin expresses his deep concern over the pattern of church-state relations in both Anglican
England and Lutheran Germany. In both countries a coalition had
been forged between church and state. Calvin expressly repudiates
both patterns, and in doing so implicitly opens the door to the development of the principle of sphere-sovereignty. Calvin comments on
the hostile response by the false prophet Amaziah to Amos's prophecy of judgment against the house of Israel, in which Amaziah asserts
that Bethel, Israel's cultic center, is "the king's sanctuary" and "the
house of the kingdom."

> Hence he ascribes to the king a twofold office,—that it was in
> his power to change religion in any way he pleased,—and then,
> that Amos disturbed the peace of the community, and thus did
> wrong to the king by derogating from his authority. With regard
> to the first clause, it is indeed certain that kings, when they
> rightly discharge their duty, become patrons of religion and
> supporters (*nutricios*—nurses) of the Church, as Isaiah calls
> them (Isa. xlix. 23). What then is chiefly required of kings is
> this—to use the sword, with which they are invested, to render
> free (*asserendum*) the worship of God. But still they are incon-
> siderate men, who give them too much power in spiritual things,
> (*qui faciunt illos nimis spirituales*—who make them too spiritual)
> and this evil is everywhere dominant in Germany; and in these
> regions it prevails too much. And we now find what fruit is
> produced by this root, which is this,—that princes, and those

47. A highly ambiguous notion. In modern parlance the idea of "separation" of
church and state has been so thoroughly secularized as to mean either the divorce
of religion from public life, or the reduction of all matters of religion to the sphere
of the institutional church, or the erection of a so-called insuperable wall between
church and state has been so thoroughly secularized as to mean the divorce of
religion from public life, or the reduction of all matters of religion to the sphere
of sphere-sovereignty, although sphere-sovereignty does allow for a proper understanding of the "separation" (as well as "partnership") between church and state
as societal structures. Cf. Praamsma, *Calvijn*, p. 83: "In principle the separation of church and state flows from Calvin's standpoint" (translation, GJS). Cf. also
W. Niesel, *The Theology of Calvin* (Philadelphia: Westminster, 1956), p. 230:
"[For Calvin] there can be no decisive separation of state and church because the
state has the same Lord as the church."

who are in power, think themselves so spiritual, that there is
no longer any church discipline; and this sacrilege greatly prevails among us; for they limit not their office by fixed and legitimate boundaries, but think that they cannot rule, except they
abolish every authority in the Church, and become chief judges
as well in doctrine as in all spiritual government.... Amaziah
wished here to prove by the king's authority that the received
worship at Bethel was legitimate. How so? "The king has
established it; it is not then lawful for anyone to say a word to
the contrary; the king could do this by his own right; for his
majesty is sacred." We see the object in view. And how many
are there at this day under the Papacy, who accumulate on kings
all the authority and power they can, in order that no dispute
may be made about religion; but power is to be vested in one
king to determine according to his own will whatever he pleases,
and this is to remain fixed without any dispute. They who at
first extolled Henry, King of England, were certainly inconsiderate men; they gave him the supreme power in all things:
and this vexed me grievously; for they were guilty of blasphemy
*(erant blasphemi)* when they called him the chief Head of the
Church under Christ. This was certainly too much: but it ought
however to remain buried, as they sinned through inconsiderate
zeal.[48]

Historically it is understandable that for Calvin the issue of the
sovereignty of the spheres in life should revolve about those two
formidable institutions in life which by this time had come to a loosely
differentiated prominence in society and which perennially demonstrated an inordinate tendency to expand their powers, namely,
church and state. It seems that he viewed the other institutions in
Genevan society as satellites clustered closely around these two
major areas of authority. What was left to later Calvinists was to take
the germinal principle of sphere-sovereignty in Calvin, delineate it
more clearly with respect to church and state, and then extend it to
other spheres in society as one by one they came to the fore in more
clearly differentiated ways: commerce, for example, arising from
modern capitalism; labor unions, emerging from the Industrial Revolution; modern universities, resulting largely from the scientific ex-
plosion.[49]

48. *Comm.* on Amos 7:10-13. Cf. J. Bohatec, *Calvins Lehr von Staat und
Kirche* (Breslau: Marcus, 1937), pp. 615-19, especially p. 614: "He [Calvin] intends
rather to express pointedly that they [church and state] should each lay claim to
independence within their own distinct domain of activity, since by divine ordinance
they are to be coordinate. Both are alike eyes and arms in the same organism. Their
independence and coordinate status do not allow for one agency to trespass arbitrarily
upon the area of others" (translation, GJS).

49. Cf. H. E. Runner, "Sphere Sovereignty," *Christian Perspectives 1961* (Hamil-
ton: Guardian, 1961), pp. 78-79. "If I may be permitted just one more step back into
history, I should like to suggest that Calvin himself had, from his recovered knowl-

*Revelational norms*

These beginnings of the idea of sphere-sovereignty in Calvin were not born out of pragmatic reactions to the pressing needs of Genevan society, though their implementation does reflect the exigencies of this beleaguered city. They were grounded basically in Calvin's understanding of revelation. Calvin was not the kind of man to hold views unless he believed they were rooted in God's Word. The central unifying theme which runs throughout the *Institutes* is Calvin's conception of the "twofold knowledge of God." God reveals Himself fundamentally as Creator "in the fashioning of the universe and the continuing government of it."[50] Due to the curse of sin, however, this original knowledge of God is now "smothered" and "corrupted."[51] To meet man in his need, God renewed His revelation in Scripture so that he might understand anew how he is to serve God obediently in his world. For

> just as old or bleary-eyed men and those with weak vision, if you thrust before them a most beautiful volume, even if they recognize it to be some sort of writing, yet can scarcely construe two words, but with the aid of spectacles will begin to read distinctly; so Scripture, gathering up the otherwise confused knowledge of God in our minds, having dispersed our dullness, clearly shows us the true God.[52]

So that we "might pass from death to life, it was necessary to recognize God not only as Creator but also as Redeemer."[53] In both creation and Scripture God reveals Himself as the sovereign Lord, both revelations finding their unifying focal point in Jesus Christ.

*Creation Ordinances*

Based on this view of revelation, Calvin's writings everywhere breathe the settled conviction that there is a creation order which is normative for man's life in the world. Despite sin, God still upholds the structures of His creation, which give meaning and direction to our lives. In Scripture He redirects us into an understanding of

edge of the centrality and totality of the Christian religion, come to grasp sphere-sovereignty as the basic principle of cosmic order. The important passage here is *Institutes* IV, xi, 1: 'For as no city or town can exist without a magistry and civil polity, so the Church of God stands in need of a certain spiritual polity.' It is true that Calvin seems generally to have had an eye only for the two magnitudes of church and state, so that we can scarcely speak here of sphere-sovereignty in the more elaborated sense in which we have come to think of it since Kuyper. Nevertheless, this passage contains the scriptural idea that the church-institute does not at all exhaust the richness of the Kingdom of God among men, and that in essence the church does not occupy a place *above* all other societal relationships."

50. *Inst.*, I.v.1.                         52. *Inst.*, I.vi.1.

51. *Inst.*, I.iv.1.                         53. Ibid.

and obedience to these creation ordinances. In Christ He redeems our life-relationships within the various structures of society. That there are such "laws of nature" woven into the very fabric of creation, "ordinances" which are normative for an orderly human society, is for Calvin a hermeneutic pre-understanding which pervasively shapes his interpretation of Scripture.

One such creation ordinance is marriage. Calvin calls it variously "a sacred institution of the Lord," "a divine institution," "a perpetual rule of conduct," "a lawful and pure ordinance of God."[54] In discussing sexual immoralities Calvin says:

> I answer, this is a corruption of the Divine institution; and whereas God produces offspring from this muddy pool, as well as from the pure fountain of marriage, this will tend to their greater destruction. Still that pure and lawful method of increase, which God ordained from the beginning, remains firm; this is the law of nature which even common sense declares to be inviolable.[55]

Marriage for Calvin is not a product of cultural evolution. Its author is God. It is built into the very structure of a divinely patterned lifestyle. Marriage is also interwoven into the fabric of other God-given orders of creation. Therefore the norms of marriage created by God cannot be broken with impunity. And what holds for marriage also holds in its own way for the other creation ordinances. For marriage is a crucial index to a well-patterned life in the creation order as a whole.

> The sum of the whole is this, that among the offices pertaining to human society, this is the principal and, as it were, the most sacred, that a man should cleave to his wife.... Now when Christ, in censuring the voluntary divorces of the Jews, adduces as his reason for doing so that "it was not so in the beginning" (Matthew 19:5), he certainly commands this institution to be observed as a perpetual rule of conduct.[56]

Setting marriage in the fuller context of the other creation ordinances, Calvin adds "that the order of creation should be a law, so that a man should be faithful to his wife all his life.... Therefore, the order of creation is proved in the indivisible society of one man with one woman."[57] These passages reflect the strong theology of creation which undergirds Calvin's theology of redemption.

While marriage is therefore a divinely ordained sphere of life founded on the order of creation with a sovereignty of its own, Calvin also recognizes that it is closely interrelated with the spheres of

54. *Comm.* on Gen. 2:22; Matt. 19:7; I Cor. 7:1-7.

55. *Comm.* on Gen. 1:28.

56. *Comm.* on Gen. 2:24.          57. *Comm.* on Matt. 19:3-4.

the church and the state. For there are all kinds of intimate connections and partnership relationships (sphere-universality) among the structures of society. The central meaning of marriage is indeed based on a creation ordinance, not on some grace conferred by the church, nor on some beneficent grant of the state. Yet for Calvin there is both an ecclesiastical and a civil aspect to marriage. In the *Ecclesiastical Ordinances of 1541* Calvin helped in formulating the following guidelines for dealing with marriage problems:

> Touching the legal aspects of marriage problems, since these do not involve spiritual issues [i.e., the church—GJS], but are part and parcel of the civil jurisdiction, the matter rests with the magistrates. Them, however, we advise [since the church cannot legislate for the state—GJS] to leave the problem of investigation [i.e., church discipline—GJS] to the Consistory, which will report their findings to the Council.[58]

Being careful not to read too much of later Calvinist thought back into Calvin, one can nevertheless hardly avoid recognizing in his treatment of marriage at least an intuitive grasp of what later came to be called sphere-sovereignty and sphere-universality.

What is true of marriage is also, according to Calvin, true of the other societal structures. All together they are grounded in the order of creation, which, though fallen under sin, is now called to renewal in Jesus Christ. Let Calvin once again speak for himself as he lectures on Moses' willing acceptance of his father-in-law's advice to decentralize his ruling office.

> In order, therefore, that everyone should confine himself within his own bounds, let us learn that in the human race God has arranged our condition so that individuals are only endued with a certain measure of gifts, on which the distribution of offices depends. For as one ray of the sun does not illumine the whole world, but all combine their operations as it were in one; so God, so that he may retain men by a sacred and indissoluble bond in mutual society and good will, unites one to another by variously dispensing his gifts, and not raising any one up out of measure by his entire perfection.[59]

In Ephesians 5 and 6 Paul addresses the gospel to Christians in various life-relationships. Calvin comments on this passage:

> Paul comes now to the various groups; for, besides the universal bond of subjection, some are more closely bound to each other, according to their respective callings. Society consists of groups, which are like yokes, in which there is a mutual obli-

---

58. G. Aiken Taylor, *John Calvin's Ecclesiastical Ordinances of 1541* (Durham, N.C.: 1952), p. 25.

59. *Comm.* on Exod. 18:13-27.

gation of parties . . . . So in society there are six different classes, for each of which Paul lays down its peculiar duties.[60]

Taking Calvin's concepts "groups," "classes," "parties," "gifts," "callings," "yokes," and "offices," each with its own "bounds," "operations," "mutual obligations," and "peculiar duties," and encapsulating them in the later concept "sphere," once again one can readily understand how the later Calvinist tradition felt justified in appealing to Calvin in support of the correlative principles of sphere-sovereignty and sphere-universality.

The same idea is expressed clearly in Calvin's lecture on the passage, "Be ye subject for the Lord's sake to every ordinance of men."

> The verb *ktizein* in Greek, from which *ktisis* comes, means to form or construct a building. It corresponds to the word "ordinance," by which Peter reminds us that God the Maker of the world has not left the human race in a state of confusion, so that we live after the manner of beasts, but has given them, as it were, a building regularly formed, and divided into several compartments. It is called a human ordinance, not because it has been invented by man, but because it is a mode of living well-arranged and clearly ordered, appropriate to man.[61]

## State sovereignty

According to Calvin each of these "rooms" (spheres) in our "earthly house" (society) has its own identity, right of existence, reason for existence, its own God-given sovereignty, which is inviolable, but limited—limited in one way by the overall supreme sovereignty of God, which must always be upheld, and in another way by the coexisting and proexisting coordinate sovereignties of other spheres of life-activity.[62] Therefore neither church nor state may trespass the limits of its proper authority. If one or the other oversteps its bounds, people suffer either spiritual harassment or political tyranny. Calvin takes this position with respect to the state in his lecture on the classic passage concerning governmental authority, Romans 13:

> Magistrates may learn from this the nature of their calling.

60. *Comm.* on Eph. 5:21—6:9.

61. *Comm.* on I Peter 1:12-17. Cf. R. Wallace, *Calvin's Doctrine of the Christian Life* (Grand Rapids: Eerdmans, 1959), p. 158: "Such order in society has been established by God as the only possible way in which a full and healthy life can be lived by all men."

62. Cf. Van Til, *Calvinistic Concept*, p. 95: "Calvin saw the church and the state as two interdependent entities each having received its authority from the sovereign God. In this conception the state is never secular, nor are state and church separated in the modern sense of the word. Atheistic democracy and popular sovereignty cannot claim Calvin as their father. According to Calvin, church and state must live in peace and must cooperate together in subjection to the Word of God. Each is to have its own jurisdiction. The state has authority in purely civil and temporal matters; the

They are not to rule on their own authority, but for the public
good. Nor do they have unbridled power, but power which is
restricted to the welfare of their subjects. In short, they are
responsible to God and to man in the exercise of their rule . . . .
The whole of this discussion concerns civil government. Those,
therefore, who bear rule over man's conscience [i.e., the
church—GJS] attempt to establish their blasphemous tyranny
from this passage in vain.[63]

The respective sovereignties of church and state (the Consistory
and the Council in Geneva) are likewise honored in the *Ecclesiastical
Ordinances,* even though the job description for each and the lines
of demarcation and interaction between them called for further refine-
ment in the life of later Calvinist communities. On the subject of
criminal justice these are the regulations:

> With respect to crimes that can never be tolerated, if they
> are civil offenses, that is to say, those which should be punished

church in spiritual matters." McNeill, *History of Calvinism,* p. 185: "Certainly the system was a theocracy in the sense that it assumed responsibility to God on
the part of secular and ecclesiastical authority alike, and proposed as its end the
effectual operation of the will of God in the life of the people. In principle, at least,
it was not hierocratic. Calvin wished the magistrates, as agents of God, to have their
own due sphere of action." Niesel, *Theology of Calvin,* pp. 235-36: "That is the
position with regard to the law of secular governments as distinct from the divine law.
Still less, of course, has it the duty itself of preaching the gospel. That is the
business of the church alone. Christ wills that his ministers should openly preach
the gospel even though the power of the whole world be against them, and for this purpose He equips them alone with the inspiration of the Word. But this does not prevent
him from leading earthly rulers into the way of obedience to Him and causing them to
fulfill their duties toward the church. Only it must be strictly noted that they fulfill
their good offices toward the church precisely as holders of civil authority. Calvin
strongly criticized the fact that in the Germany of his day the princes encroached too
much on the spiritual sphere. If the magistrates do not keep within their proper limits,
but try to usurp ecclesiastical control and constitute themselves judges both in
matters of doctrine and in those of spiritual government, their service of the church
becomes disservice." W. S. Reid, "Calvin and the Political Order," *John
Calvin–Contemporary Prophet,* ed. J. T. Hoogstra (Grand Rapids: Baker, 1959),
pp. 251-52: "While Calvin is anxious to preserve the church from political
interference, he is at the same time equally convinced that the church should not intrude
into the state's peculiar area of authority. Christ being both head of the church
and king of kings, the spheres of both are subject to him directly. On the other
hands, since rulers and subjects alike in a 'Christian' state are both citizens and
church members, there is no possibility of really separating church and state. But
they do differ in their functions. Calvin lays no little emphasis in his *Ecclesiastical
Ordinances* on the fact that ministers have no right to interfere with the magistrate's
performance of his duties. Rather the relation of church and state is to be that of
mutual independence, but also of mutual helpfulness and support. Any influence
of the church on the state is to be limited to moral suasion." C. Miller, "The
Spread of Calvinism," *The Rise and Development of Calvinism,* ed. J. Bratt (Grand
Rapids: Eerdmans, 1959), p. 31: "In his view the Church and the State are
both subject to a single common authority, the Holy Scriptures, and hence neither is
subject to the other."

63. *Comm.* on Rom. 13:1-7.

*Exploring the Heritage of John Calvin*

by law, and a minister should fall therein, let the magistrates
lay hand on him, and besides the common punishment meted out
to others, let them punish him by deposing him from his office.

As for other offenses concerning which the first investigation
belongs to the Consistory, let the elders together with the ministers attend to it. And if anyone be convicted, let them make
their report to the Council, together with their recommendations
and judgments, so that final judgment and punishment shall
always be reserved for the magistrates.[64]

In his efforts to eliminate the practice of begging Calvin recognizes
the legal priority of the magistrates in enforcing the law, even against
beggars plying their trade on church premises. For church life too
has its legal aspect. This approach to the problem is codified in the
*Ecclesiastical Ordinances* as follows:

To prevent begging, which is contrary to good order, it will
be necessary that the magistrates delegate certain of their of-
ficers, and thus we have ordered, to be stationed at the doors of
the churches to drive away any who try to resist, and, if they act
impudently, or answer insolently, to take them to one of the
Syndics. In like manner the heads of the boroughs should always
be on guard to see to it that the law against begging is well observed.[65]

In a summarizing statement the *Ecclesiastical Ordinances* lay
down the following general policy, which contains in it an implicit
endorsement of the principle of sphere-sovereignty:

Let all be done in such a manner as to keep from the ministers
any civil jurisdiction whatever, so that they use only the spiritual
sword of the Word of God as Paul ordered them, and that thus
the Consistory may in no wise derogate from the authority of
the magistrates or of civil justice, but rather that the civil power
be kept intact.[66]

The following passage from the *Institutes* is perhaps the most
classic statement on the principle of sphere-sovereignty in Calvin.
In it he affirms not only the unique identity of both church and state,
their mutual independence, and their limited areas of respective jurisdiction, but he also affirms implicitly the corollary principle of
sphere-universality, recognizing that church and state are to interact
with each other in a partnership arrangement to the benefit of society.

For as no city or township can function without magistrate
and polity, so the Church of God needs a spiritual polity. This
is, however, quite distinct from civil polity, yet does not hinder
or threaten it, but rather greatly helps and furthers it. There-

64. Taylor, *Calvin's Ordinances,* p. 11.

65. Ibid., p. 22.

66. Ibid., p. 34.

fore this power of jurisdiction will be nothing, in short, but an order framed for the preservation of spiritual polity.[67]

## Violations

Basically Calvin sought to propound and implement the core ideas involved in the principle of sphere-sovereignty. This is clear from the well-known accounts of his valiant struggle to preserve church discipline from undue encroachments on it by the magistrates. In defense of this principle Calvin suffered great hardship, opposition, and even banishment from Geneva. But the ambiguities of the situation are also apparent, not only in certain of Calvin's practices, but also in some statements of position. A case in point is the following passage from the *Ecclesiastical Ordinances:*

> And likewise, when it shall be necessary to exercise punishment or restraint against any party, the ministers, with the Consistory, shall hear the parties concerned, remonstrate and admonish them as it may seem good, reporting all to the Council which, for its part, shall deliberate and then order and pass judgment according to the merits of the case.[68]

From this passage and others it appears that Calvin's view often led him to overextend the jurisdiction of the civil authorities in such a way as to ascribe to the magistrates considerable responsibility for the discipline and well-being of the church. As he saw it, the state is called not only to protect the church, together with other societal institutions, which is in keeping with the principle of sphere-sovereignty, but also actively to promote the cause of the church by uprooting false religions and reinforcing true religion. It was these ideas of Calvin, incorporated into Article 36 of the Belgic Confession, which later Calvinists, living in a religiously more pluralistic society were called on to revise as a further step in continuing reformation. Calvin's efforts in 1538 to impose a confession of faith on the entire citizenry of Geneva also reflect a still rather fluid understanding of the principle of sphere-sovereignty. Moreover, his position in the Servetus affair of 1555, endorsing the *Corpus Christianum* theory that heresies are to be removed by killing heretics, only adds to the ambiguities. Calvin was still too much a child of his times.[69] This is also evident from both his commentaries and the

67. *Inst.,* IV.xi.1. Cf. *Inst.,* IV.ii.1., where Calvin speaks once again of "the basic distinction." Cf. Bohatec, *Calvins Lehr,* pp. 417-44, 569-71, 611-14.

68. Taylor, *Calvin's Ordinances,* pp. 34-35.

69. Cf. Praamsma, *Calvijn,* p. 85: "The need of the times required a unified citizenry" (translation, GJS). L. Berkhof, *The Church and Social Problems,* p. 17: "Yes, the church as we conceive of her, at once a spiritual fellowship of believers

*Institutes.* Lecturing on Isaiah, he speaks of rulers as "nursing fathers" and "guardians" of the church, and goes on to say:

> Kings and queens shall supply everything that is necessary for nourishing the offspring of the church ... for the Lord has bestowed on them authority and power to defend the church and to protect the glory of God. This is indeed the duty of all; but kings, in proportion as their power is greater, ought to devote themselves to it more earnestly, and to labor in it more diligently.[70]

In commenting on the meaning of Nebuchadnezzar's dream, Calvin says:

> Kings are bound to defend the worship of God, and to execute vengeance upon those who flagrantly despise it, and on those who endeavor to reduce it to nothing, or to adulterate true doctrine with errors, and so to dissipate the unity of the faith and disturb the church's peace.[71]

Calvin's incomplete insights into the meaning of sphere-sovereignty, the unfinished business which he left on the agenda for later Calvinists to deal with, is also evident in his more systematic treatment of the task of government in the *Institutes.*

> Civil government has as its appointed end, so long as we live among men, to cherish and protect the outward worship of God, to defend sound doctrine and piety and the position of the church [this in addition to its more proper task, which Calvin describes as follows], to adjust our life to the society of men, to form our social behavior to civil righteousness, to reconcile us with one another, and to promote general peace and tranquillity.[72]

and an organization, has a task in the movement for social reform. We know that Calvin himself attempted a little more in this respect at Geneva than was consistent with his theory of the church, as we best know it." H. Bavinck, *Gereformeerde Dogmatiek,* IV:20: "Calvin drew the boundary lines between church and state clearly and sharply, but he drew them differently than we do; the domain within which they had their say was much larger than we would define it today.... Nevertheless, the relationship between church and state was contractual and free. The church could do nothing else than proclaim the Word of God and, in His name, witness to his commandments; but if the government or anyone else refused to listen, then neither the church, nor Calvin, nor any other Christian had any power or authority of enforcement.... Calvin's error was not that Christian government was charged with promoting the honor and service of God, but that the lines of demarcation between church and state were mistakenly drawn, and that therefore unbelief, heresy, etc., were regarded as civil offenses. But in the century of the reformation things could hardly have been otherwise" (translation, GJS).

70. *Comm.* on Isa. 49:23.

71. *Comm.* on Dan. 4:1-3.

72. *Inst.,* IV.xx.2. Cf. W. F. Graham, *The Constructive Revolutionary: John Calvin and His Socio-Economic Impact* (Richmond: Knox, 1971): "For Calvin there was an undeniable separation between the two powers. But since both were under the lordship of Christ, the church's task was always an active one toward the state.

## *Church sovereignty*

Calvin maintains the idea of limited sovereignty more consistently with respect to the church than the state. Lecturing on the trial of Peter and John before the Sanhedrin, which was composed of the "churchmen" of the Jewish community, its pastors and spiritual leaders, Calvin says:

> But if it happens that they abuse their office, the Spirit makes plain there as in a mirror that whatever they order and decree ought to be regarded as void. The authority of pastors in particular has fixed bounds which they are not to overstep. If they venture to do so, we may lawfully refuse to obey them; for to obey them would then be the height of wickedness.... We must obey princes and others who are in authority, but only in so far as they do not deny to God his rightful authority as the supreme King, Father, and Lord. If such limits are to be observed in civil government, they ought to be of still greater importance in the spiritual government of the church.[73]

Such teachings tend to confirm Gerstner's judgment that "Calvinism was as useful in producing revolution where it was needed as it was in preventing it where it was not."[74] For as the Calvinist tradition understood Calvin and Scripture, both obedience and disobedience, whether civil or ecclesiastical, must be determined by reference to a transcendent norm, the sovereignty of God in every sphere of life. We are to obey for God's sake; and sometimes, also for God's sake, we are to disobey.

In affirming the limited sovereignty of the church, Calvin takes this position not on the basis of pragmatic considerations, which, as he argues, can lead only to chaos and tyranny, but on the basis of a comprehensive view of Scripture.

... The fact that Calvin was knowledgeable in law makes the problem of the separation of these two realms even stickier than had he been merely a pastor with a passion for social righteousness. But here Calvin the lawyer and pastor showed that he distinguished the two areas—the concern of the church and the concern of the state. That one advised and influenced the other is undeniable. Calvin would not have considered this wrong.... We have argued elsewhere that the theoretical separation of church and state existed for Calvin more in theory than in practice. By his words Calvin expressed an ideal of separation; by his practice it is quite clear that separation for Calvin did not mean what it does for most Americans today." A. Biéler, *Social Humanism of Calvin*, p. 26: "We can rightly censure Calvin with having solicited the intervention of the secular power in sanctioning disciplinary measures in the church. The drama of Michel Servetus illustrates Calvin's error. Yet this excess can be explained by the exceptionally and now easily overlooked hard times in which our reformer lived. Moreover, in all truth, his error can be corrected on the basis of the very teaching of Calvin himself. This shows that his error is accidental rather than fundamental."

73. *Comm.* on Acts 4:13-24.

74. J. W. Gerstner, "Calvin's Political Influence on the United States," *Calvin Anniversary Lectures at Calvin College*, 1959, p. 7.

The power of the church is therefore not to be grudgingly manifested, but yet kept within definite limits, that it may not be drawn hither and thither according to men's whims. For this reason it will be of especial benefit to observe how it is described by the prophets and apostles. For if we simply grant to men such power as they are disposed to take, it is plain to all how abrupt is the fall into tyranny, which ought to be far from Christ's church.[75]

It is also very instructive to hear what Calvin says—and leaves unsaid—about the situation in Corinth where Christians were bringing lawsuits against fellow believers before pagan judges. In principle Calvin holds that courts of justice too are a "divine ordinance," for "retribution belongs to the magistrate by God's appointment." Therefore "the impression may not be given that God was wasting his time in establishing law courts." But what if these halls of justice become so thoroughly apostate and unjust that Christians can no longer expect to get a fair hearing? Such was apparently the situation to which Paul was addressing himself in Corinth. Are Christians then to keep on dragging each other before such pagan judges out of some distorted sense of equity, pleading their cases against each other before magistrates ignorant of or even hostile to the standards of God's Word? Surely there must be a better way. Such is in effect Calvin's argumentation. "As if there were no suitable judges in the church!"

> It is as if Paul were saying, "Even the humblest and least significant among you will carry out this task better than the unbelieving judges to whom you are running, when there is absolutely no need to do so." . . . I think that I myself have faithfully expressed what the apostle had in mind: That he preferred the meanest among believers to unbelievers, when it was a question of ability to judge. . . . "How disgraceful it is that there is not even one of your number who can in a friendly way settle some matter that has arisen between brothers, for you to concede this honor to unbelievers."

Important in Calvin's lengthy discussion of this matter is not only his (and Paul's) strong emphasis on the reality of the religious antithesis in administering public justice, but also the fact that both Paul and Calvin seem completely to overlook what might strike many

---

75. *Inst.*, IV.viii.1. Cf. R. Caswell, "Calvin's View of Ecclesiastical Discipline," *John Calvin* (Grand Rapids: Eerdmans, 1966), p. 223: "The power of the church, said Calvin, is limited to excommunication. No civil penalty is to be inflicted by the church, for the spiritual kingdom of Christ and civil government are things very different and remote from each other (*Inst.*, IV.xx.1). Yet the two powers are not so separate as might appear from that quotation . . . . The church can be subject to the state and, inversely, the state to the church to a certain extent, without either losing their original independence and authority."

today as the obvious answer to such problems within the Christian community, namely, take it to the consistory. Neither Paul nor Calvin even suggest this as a viable option or a possible solution. Silence on this point suggests an implicit recognition by them that matters of civil justice lie outside the proper jurisdiction of church councils. There is here, obliquely at least, a Biblically (via Paul) Reformed (via Calvin) endorsement of the principle of sphere-sovereignty. Both indeed insist that among Christians a Christian solution must be found to such knotty problems. Hence, Paul, it seems, is calling for the appointment of a Christian ombudsman, a Christian court of appeals for arbitrating such issues, thus honoring a proper differentiation of tasks and offices within the Christian community.

In this same context Calvin comments on Augustine's book *On the Work of Monks*. In it monks and bishops are enjoined to obey Paul's instructions to the Corinthian Christians by accepting as part of their calling an involvement in societal life in the form of judging common and civil disputes, including contentions over money and property. This is Calvin's reaction to Augustine's interpretation of this Pauline passage:

> In that ancient custom there are two things with which fault should be found: (1) That the bishops were involved in affairs that had nothing to do with their office, and (2) that they were doing God an injustice in pretending that they were thus departing from their proper calling by his authority and command.[76]

76. *Comm.* on I Cor. 6:1-8. Cf. Warfield, *Calvin and Calvinism* (London: Oxford, 1931), pp. 16-19: "The application of this principle [i.e., church discipline as a criterion of the church— GJS] carried Calvin very far, and, indeed, in its outworking gave the world through him the principle of a free Church in a free State. It is ultimately to him, therefore, that the church owes its emancipation from the State, and to him goes back the great battle-cry which has since fired the hearts of many saints in many crises in many lands: 'The Crown Rights of King Jesus in His Church' . . . By this programme Calvin became nothing less than the creator of the Protestant Church. The particular points to be emphasized in it are two. It is purely Church discipline which is contemplated, with none other but spiritual penalties. And the church is for this purpose especially discriminated from the body of the people—the State—and a wedge is thus driven in between Church and State which was bound to separate the one from the other . . . . In claiming for the Church this discipline, Calvin, naturally, had no wish in any way to infringe upon the police regulations of the civil authorities. They continued, in their own sphere, to command his approval and cooperation. He has the clearest conception of the limits within which the discipline of the Church must keep itself, and expressly declares that it is confined absolutely to the spiritual penalty of excommunication. But he just as expressly suggests that the State, in its own part, might well take cognizance of spiritual offenses; and even invokes the aid of the civil magistrate in support of the authority of the church . . . . Calvin has not risen to the conception of the complete mutual independence of Church and State; his view still includes the conception of an 'established church.' But the 'established Church' which he pleads for is a Church absolutely autonomous in its own spiritual sphere. In asking this he was asking for something new in the Protestant world, and something in which lay the promise and potency of all the freedom which has come to the Reformed Churches since."

*Academic sovereignty*

By 1555 Calvin had attained a position of almost undisputed leadership in Geneva. The power of opposing parties had either been broken or banished. He was then able to implement his programs of reformation with greater consistency in every sphere in Genevan society—in the church, in civil government, in industry, in family life, in the schools. The year 1559 was a climactic point in Calvin's career as reformer. In that year he completed his definitive edition of the *Institutes*. He then for the first time took the official step of becoming a citizen of Geneva, having put it off for some twenty years in order to avoid any appearance of political ambition. For Calvin was primarily minister of the Word and teacher of theology. This vocational concentration too reflects Calvin's way of honoring the idea of sphere-sovereignty. As theologian his crowning achievement was the founding of the Geneva Academy that same year, 1559. In keeping with the idea of sphere-universality, the life of the Academy was interrelated in various ways with the life of the church and the state. But it was also granted a certain sovereignty within its own sphere of operations, as is evident from the following passage:

It is clear that Calvin was impelled to claim a place for science in society.... According to Calvin, the various sciences must keep themselves within their boundaries, conducting themselves as handmaidens, not mistresses. This takes place when they are completely subject to God's Word and Spirit. Piety and faith must be recognized as the foundation of science.... In the light of these and similar utterances it is not difficult to understand Calvin's outlook. As he saw it, both church and state had to carry out a peculiar responsibility with respect to the Academy. Naturally church and state must be understood here in keeping with Calvin's unique vision. This explains why at the founding of the Academy the absence of a papal bull and an imperial certificate was not even noticed. Geneva itself justified the right to establish the Academy.... With respect to the Academy the major emphasis fell upon the church, or rather the office of preaching. For the ministers cooperated in the appointment of teachers and professors. The government was granted the right of confirmation. All instructors were also subject to ecclesiastical discipline. It would be inaccurate, however, to interpret this relationship as placing the Academy, and thereby science, under the church. Church and school were meant to be two institutions in society standing side by side. The Academy possessed, to use this Germanism, *eigenstandigheid* [independence—GJS]. But the Academy was in no way to be estranged from commitment to God's Word. In Calvin's view God's

Word was to be the foundation for the exercise of every science.[77]

## Conclusion

Having traced the historical-theological development of a Biblically Reformed world-and-life-view structured along the lines of sphere-sovereignty, we see that one can claim too much for Calvin. But it is also clear that one can claim too little. Calvin certainly did not speak the last word on this issue. Seen in the context of his times, he did, however, speak a first and, in some senses, a new and liberating word. We find in Calvin a decisive departure from earlier Constantinian-medieval views of society, based upon the nature-grace dichotomy, and structured along the lines of the principle of sphere-subsidiarity with church and state alternatingly pressing their sovereign claims on other institutions in society.

But the clock did not stop with Calvin in the sixteenth century. Calvin helped to write a new agenda. But he also left behind some unfinished business. He introduced some new insights into the idea of sphere-sovereignty. But a number of ambiguities are there too. Though his thinking on the issue at hand is confined largely to those two societal magnitudes, church and state; and though he viewed them more loosely than we would today, regarding them as two rather sprawling sectors of society, with other institutions clustered like satellites about them; and though we may question his way of delineating their tasks and drawing the lines of demarcation between them and patterning their interrelationships; nevertheless, the rough contours of a Biblically Reformed view of communal life emerge in Calvin with unmistakable clarity. Calvin sowed some seeds which already during his lifetime began to germinate and bear their firstfruits, making it possible for his heirs to enter more fully into the harvest of Calvin's pioneering labors.

Calvin's beginnings both called for and helped to create a Calvinist tradition which took hold on his ideas, gradually opened them up, and worked them out more clearly. Therefore we cannot simply identify Calvinism with Calvin. But we cannot disassociate the later Calvinist tradition from Calvin either. He laid foundations, opened the door, and gave fresh impetus to a reforming movement which sent his followers out into new directions. Thus the Calvinist tradition honored Calvin's own commitment to the need for ongoing reformation.

77. D. Nauta, "Calvijn en zijn Academie in 1559," *Vier Redevoeringen over Calvijn* (Kampen: Kok, 1959), pp. 18-21 (translation, GJS).

Calvin gave us a breakaway from the Scholastic principle of sphere-subsidiarity and a breakthrough toward the Reformed principle of sphere-sovereignty. All that remained was to develop a more consistent follow-through. We may conclude, therefore, that the later Calvinist tradition was indeed justified in appealing to Calvin in support of its more fully developed formulation and implementation of the principle of sphere-sovereignty.

*Figure 1*

*Figure 2*

*Figure 3*

*Figure 4*

*Clarence J. Vos*

# CHAPTER 7 HUMAN AUTHORITY: A BIBLICAL STUDY WITH A COMPARISON OF CALVIN'S VIEW

John Calvin, that dour despot from Geneva,[1] what shall he say to our times about authority? The answers to this question will be poles apart. Many, in harmony with the permissive tendencies within Western culture, will say that Calvin is so much the child of medieval thinking that there is nothing we can learn from him, except possibly how not to use authority. After all, he was involved in the burning of Servetus. Whatever is to be learned from Calvin, say these critics of his, will not be found in the area of the nature and proper exercise of human authority. Calvin's own banishment from Geneva would indicate that he apparently had not understood what makes for happy human relationships and a positive use of human authority.

1. Stefan Zweig, *The Right to Heresy* (New York: Viking Press, 1936), p. 4: "His doctrine had become law, and anyone who ventured to question it was soon taught— by arguments that burked discussion, by arguments of every spiritual tyranny, by jail, exile, or burning at the stake—how in Geneva only one truth was valid, the truth of which Calvin was the prophet."
    Calvin's image has suffered not only from such comments, but there is good reason to believe that the visual representations of Calvin—and particularly those most widely circulated—do not do Calvin justice. For example, the most common portrait (see fig. 1) seems to receive its inspiration from the caricature (see fig. 2) rather than from portraits by other artists (see figs. 3 and 4). If one scans the rare volume, E. Doumergue, *Iconographie Calvinienne* (Lausanne: George Bridel & Cie , 1909), it is clear that some artists were more favorably disposed to Calvin than others. That artists could sometimes make unflattering representations of scholars is obvious in such paintings as Frans Hals' portrait of Descartes. Calvin's sketchy—if not negative—treatment of art in the *Institutes* (I.xi.12) would be no basis for making him a favorite of the artists. (Figs. 2 and 3 are from Doumergue's book.)

On the other hand there may be many who would feel that our contemporary world sorely needs the firm hand of authority; and however wrong Calvin may have been in other matters, our society could well use some of the rigidities for which Calvin apparently is famous—or infamous. Advocates of the "law and order" movement might feel that in Calvin they have an ally; his writings might offer valuable grist for their mills.

It is the purpose of this essay to determine whether Calvin's friends (if the advocates of "law and order" may be considered such) and enemies (if the advocates of a permissive society may be considered such) have correctly assessed his view on the nature and proper exercise of human authority. The approach will be to set forth a statement on the Biblical teaching concerning authority and then to see whether Calvin advocated or disagreed with this view.

Some leniency and charity will need to be exercised by both writer and reader. Every person, no matter how great, is a product of his age, seeking to give answers to the problems of his own time. Calvin was no exception. The main question that had to be answered in his day was not so much the nature of human authority, but who or what was the final authority on this earth—the pope, the king, a council, the people, or Scripture? But in discussing the question of *who* has the authority, Calvin did say some significant things about the nature and source of authority. One should also remember that Biblical studies have made considerable advancement since Calvin's time. He obviously did not have access to the archaeological finds which were to come some three to four centuries later. Nevertheless, Calvin's stature as a Biblical scholar hardly needs defense. I am impressed with the frequency with which Calvin's interpretations are referred to in the journals of Biblical studies. Therefore, regardless whether he is "friend" or "foe," anyone wishing to make a serious study of the Biblical data concerning human authority can hardly ignore Calvin's reflections on these data.

### An interpretation of the Biblical data on authority

With the dawning of the "ecological consciousness" my complacency was jolted more than once by the charge of enthusiastic ecologists that one of the main causes of our ecological crisis is to be found in the Judeo-Christian emphasis of man's dominance over nature.[2] This charge seems tantamount to saying that Christianity

2. Cf. Paul R. and Anne H. Ehrlich, *Population, Resources, Environment* (San Francisco: W. H. Freeman, 1970). The Ehrlichs quote Lynn White, Jr., with apparent approval when he says, "By destroying pagan animism, Christianity made it possible to exploit nature in a mood of indifference to the feelings of natural objects."

does not have the answer to the problems of the day, but, in fact, is a contributor to them. It has been affirmed that if our society had been influenced by another religious tradition there would have been no ecological crisis.

Such charges can hardly be ignored. They forced me to reexamine the Genesis material which speaks so forcefully of man's dominion over all things.

*Genesis 1 on man's authority*

An examination of the first chapter of Genesis can lead to no other conclusion than that it was the writer's intent to teach in an unequivocal way that man is to have dominion over nature. Man, we are told, was created in God's image. In the Semitic world, images were used to represent something or someone. The images or idols of the heathen were not the gods themselves but representatives of the gods. This is, no doubt, the meaning of Genesis 1. God made man in His image; man therefore is a representative of God. Since God as Creator has complete and ultimate authority over His works, man as God's representative has a derived but nonetheless real authority. And lest there be any doubt about this matter, the narrator continues that man must "subdue it [the earth]; and have dominion over the fish of the sea and over the birds of the air and over everything that moveth upon the earth." One of the most important teachings of this chapter is that man is an authority-bearing creature.[3] It may be a bit difficult for us who live in the twentieth century to realize how revolutionary this teaching was centuries ago; but if we remember that, in the main, pagan worship is correctly described as nature worship, we will appreciate something of the antithetic disposition of this emphasis. Paul reminds us that the pattern of the pagans was that they "served the creature rather than the Creator" (Rom. 1:25).

The Ehrlichs then go on to posit that "the 'frontier' or 'cowboy' economy which has characterized the United States seems to be a natural extension of the Christian world view" (p. 191). They see little chance for correcting the situation unless there is a change in religious attitudes; again White is quoted: "Both our present science and our present technology are so tinctured with orthodox Christian arrogance toward nature that no solution for our ecologic crises can be expected from them alone. Since the roots of our trouble are so largely religious, the remedy must also be essentially religious, whether we call it that or not" (p. 263).

3. Edmund Jacob, *Theology of the Old Testament* (London: Hodder and Stoughton, 1958), pp. 166-72. Cf. also Hans Walter Wolff, *Anthropology of the Old Testament* (Philadelphia: Fortress Press, 1974), pp. 160 ff. The idea that images were used in the Ancient Near East as representatives is further underscored by the discovery of vast numbers of votive images. These small images were representatives of the worshiper and were placed in the temple to remain in the presence of the god.

In view of the pagan milieu it is understandable that a very force-ful statement is made that man is to rule the things of this crea-tion, rather than that he should serve them. The words used to express this idea are dynamic indeed. The Hebrew word *kabash,* translated "subdue," is one of the few Hebrew words that has crept into our parlance, particularly in the prizefighter's ring. In Hebrew it expresses the idea of treading down, and is even used for rape in Esther 7:8. The Hebrew word *radah,* translated "have dominion," is only slightly less forceful in that it is sometimes used to express the idea of driving the flock, of bringing them to water or pasture; but it is also used to express the idea of treading down or out (cf. Joel 4:13, where it is used to describe the treading of the grapes in the winepress). The conclusion is inevitable: Genesis 1 teaches that man is to be master of his environment. He rules nature; he treads on it; he may change its form. He may make grapes into wine. A more modern version might indicate that he beats wood *(kabash)* into pulp so that he may make paper or rayon of it. One can hardly say, then, that the charge of the ecologists is completely without basis.

### Genesis 2 on man's authority

I am not aware of anyone who disagrees in a substantial way with the interpretation of Genesis 1 presented above. Calvin's emphasis, as we will see in a later section, differed from it in that he was more impressed by the kind providence of God in giving mankind all these things, rather than by the authority invested in man. He does, however, affirm the authority of man. With respect to Genesis 2 there may not be such general agreement with my approach, and this is so for two reasons. First, my interpretation of verses 5 and 15 is not a common one, and, second, if this interpretation is correct, then Genesis 2 offers another dimension to the Bible's teaching con-cerning the authority of man over nature. This latter emphasis may not be congenial to everyone's thinking. It may, moreover, seem initially to be contradictory to the emphasis of Genesis 1, but I believe it is better described as a constructive tension.

Most translations agree substantially with the Revised Standard Version in translating Genesis 2:5b, "and there was no man to till the ground." Similarly, Genesis 2:15 is translated, "The Lord God took the man and put him in the garden of Eden to till it and keep it." In this chapter these two verses are undoubtedly the important ones expressing man's relationship to the earth. A rather careful scrutiny of the Hebrew gives one insight into the phrase "and keep it." The Hebrew word used here is *shamar,* which is commonly used to express the idea of actively preserving in a thoughtful, purposeful way. In this way one keeps *(shamar)* the commandments. The good shepherd solicitously keeps *(shamar)* his flock. It is the Lord who keeps *(shamar)* Israel. This word alone forces us to entertain the idea that Genesis 2 may offer us a different emphasis or perspective on human authority than Genesis 1.

Further examination of these two verses discloses that the Hebrew verb translated "to till" is *'abad*; this verb is nearly always translated "to serve."[4] If one followed the more common way of translating *'abad* it would suggest that man was to serve the ground or the garden. Few translators have been able to bring themselves to the point where they translate *'abad* in Genesis 2:5 and 15 as "serve,"[5] but some deserve to be mentioned. *Young's Literal Translation of the Holy Bible*[6] is true to its "literal" purpose and translates *'abad* in both verses as "serve." J. Sperna Weiland in his *Genesis*,[7] which is a Dutch translation and commentary, also translates *'abad* in verse 15 literally as *dienen*; and his commentary adds the constructive insight that when man exercises his authority in this fashion all tensions and conflicts between man and his environment will be removed and harmony will prevail.

The conclusion seems inescapable: there are two distinct em-

4. In the KJV the verb *'abad* is translated as "serve" 214 times. It is translated "till" ten times (Gen. 2:5, 15; 3:23; 4:12; II Sam. 9:10; Prov. 12:11; 28:19; Jer. 27:11; Ezek. 36:9, 34); but in many cases—except perhaps Ezek. 36:9—the translation "to serve" would be meaningful and probably fit the context better. For example, in Prov. 12:11 the translation "to serve his land" would seem more appropriate than "to till" since verse 10 had indicated that the righteous man had a concern for his beast.

5. B. Jacob, *The First Book of the Bible, GENESIS* (New York: KTAV Publishing House Inc., 1974), p. 16: "Man's relation to the soil has two aspects: he may rule it (1, 26-28), but he must also serve it in order to gain his living." U. Cassuto, *A Commentary on the Book of Genesis* (Jerusalem: The Magnes Press, The Hebrew University, 1961), I:122. He indicates that the rabbinic interpretation understood the term to mean that man was to serve God. That, however, seems a strained way to avoid the simpler reading, namely, that man was called to serve the garden.

6. Robert Young, *Literal Translation of the Holy Bible* (Grand Rapids: Baker Book House, 1953). The third edition appeared in 1898.

7. J. Sperna Weiland, *Genesis* (Amsterdam: De Bezige Bij, 1964), pp. 62, 92. "There is no contradiction between ruling... and serving.... To the contrary, only he who serves, serves the earth, can reflect (image) the ruling 'elohim. The moment he no longer serves, but in his own power takes the earth into his own service he is estranged from God and from himself; he then is no longer the image of God, but its caricature. This expression [to serve the earth] is of great significance for not only the anthropology of the Old Testament, but also for the manner in which God is introduced." (Trans. CJV.)

phases in these two chapters. Genesis 1 stresses the dominance of man over the rest of creation. This emphasis was very important to resist the universal tendency toward nature worship. On the other hand, Genesis 2 stresses the manner in which this authority is to be exercised. It is to be exercised in a most benevolent and constructive manner. The terminology in Genesis 2 is also forceful—so forceful in fact that most translators "boggled" at the plain and literal meaning of the words. There is, however, no reason why the most common meaning of *'abad* should not be given full force. It would mean then that the proper exercise of authority demands that one "lay himself upon the block" and become a servant. It means that authority is exercised correctly only when there is genuine concern for that over which one exercises authority.

These two emphases may seem to be contradictory or even mutually exclusive. But this objection tends to disappear as we carefully scan other areas of Scripture. Scripture repeatedly confronts us with emphases that seem to conflict with one another. Paul stresses salvation by grace; James emphasizes the importance of works.[8] It would be heresy, however, to embrace James and repudiate Paul, or vice versa. Instead it should be recognized that these tensions supply the constructive dynamics of life. They are like the opposing rafters in a building; if one is removed, the opposing rafter not only loses its function, but the entire structure is in jeopardy. Heretical positions often originate from the desire to remove tensions—tensions which were intended to give balance, mobility, and life. Therefore, the tension between Genesis 1 and Genesis 2 must also be maintained and allowed to operate. Human authority is not truly human authority if it does not willingly take its responsibility as controller of the rest of creation (Genesis 1); but neither is it human authority in the divinely intended sense if it is not willing to give itself and serve creation by seeking to develop it to its fullest potential (Genesis 2).

It is my contention that the emphasis as found in the more literal translation of Genesis 2:5 and 15 has been ignored and neglected. The idea of serving is as unattractive to us as it was to Jesus' disciples (Luke 22:24 ff.). Even Biblical scholars who undertook the responsibility of translating Scripture were so under the influence of a warped sense of authority that they could hardly believe that God intended man to serve the ground or the garden. "Common sense" dictates that it is just the other way. The garden, the inferior, is to

8. Other examples may be mentioned: The "oneness" of God versus the "threeness" of God; or the tension between the sovereignty of God and the responsibility of man. Any "solution" to remove these tensions is certain to bring distortion.

serve man, the superior. It is always thus, at least in the world we observe. Authority as we understand it is the power of the strong over the weak. True, the Christian theologian (and, I hope, the politician) is aware that the Bible sets up certain restrictions for those who are in authority. We do indeed make a distinction between authority and tyranny; but often it is more a matter of degree than of kind. This warped sense of authority has had its blighting influence on every sphere of life: political, ecclesiastical, domestic, educational, and so on.[9] This essay, however, centers on the effect such an attitude has had on thinking in matters of faith and practice (theology and ethics, if you like). It is my contention that how one views authority will make a marked difference on how he views God (theology), man (anthropology),[10] Christ (Christology), salvation (soteriology), the church (ecclesiology), and the meaning of his existence (eschatology). I will try to demonstrate this by briefly discussing each of these areas.

## Theology

The question must be asked whether it is necessary to infer that if the authority which man exercises is a serving authority, and man as made in the image of God represents or "mirrors" God, does God then also exercise His authority in a serving manner? Good theological procedure dictates caution here. It is not necessary nor proper to assume that everything apparent or required of man is apparent or required of God. Calvin's criticism of the Anthropomorphites is still relevant. For example, man must be obedient; but I do not see how God can be obedient.

If the material we have in Genesis 1 and 2 were all we had, it would be hazardous to assert that God exercises His authority in a serving capacity. But this material has served as a stimulus for me to review some of what the Bible says about God and His dealings with us. In doing so I will try to heed what I consider Calvin's excellent advice when he says that we ought "not . . . to attempt with bold curiosity to penetrate to the investigation of his essence . . . , but . . . to contemplate him in his works whereby he renders himself near and familiar to us . . . . "[11]

9. Obviously within the limits of this essay we cannot develop this thesis in these areas. But I believe that the dictatorial tendencies in government (whether it is under the label of fascism or democracy), the church (whether episcopal or presbyterial), the home (parental authority can be despotic), and the school (the curriculum and the administration can be autocratically determined) are frequently observed.

10. Cf. J. Sperna Weiland's comments in fn. 7.

11. *Inst.*, I.v.9. Cf. I.x.2; III.ii.6.

As one surveys the story of the Old Testament he must be struck by the divine restraint in response to man's sin. Although sin is not without punishment, man is preserved. Adam and Eve are discovered in their sin, but not deserted. A curse is pronounced, but a promise is welded to it. The more one reflects on the curse, the more one sees that there are even salutary aspects involved in it. The thorns and thistles which humble a man break the *hubris* which plagues him. Cain is admonished and rebuked, but the mark placed on him is as protective as punitive. The Flood is indeed a punitive response to the sin of man, but it is also a washing of the earth to remove its violence. The tower is another act of *hubris*, but, by scattering mankind, God mitigates the evil that they would normally impose on themselves and each other. God's works portray Him as a shepherd who has a real concern for His creatures; He does not delight in the death of the wicked, but that he should turn from his ways (Ezek. 18:23).

The Psalms and the prophetic books also speak of the benevolent rule of God. Repeatedly the Psalms extol God as King because He is the helper of the fatherless and widow,[12] and one who has a special concern for the poor.[13] God rules that He may help. He exacts tribute, but it is impossible to see how the sacrifices and offerings brought are to satisfy any need of His. The highest tribute is the praise of a happy, thankful heart.[14] Even the beasts of the field and the birds of the air know His tender rule.[15] The prophets speak of God's solicitous concern over His people and how He is willing to sacrifice for them (Isa. 43:3 ff.). Israel is called to rejoice, for her King is coming. He is a very different King for He rides, not on a horse—the symbol of despoliation, but He comes on a donkey—the symbol of service (Zech. 9:9).

This Biblical picture of a God who moves so benevolently among His creatures forms a sharp contrast to the mythologies of the Ancient Near East. The Babylonian Creation Epic portrays Marduk as the one who emerges as the "strong man" among the gods, and by his violent victory over Tiamat destroys chaos, and therefore has the right to exact tribute and praise from the other gods. It is fitting for

12. "Fatherless and widow" is the *terminus technicus* in the Old Testament for the poor and underprivileged. Note the following: Ps. 10:14, 18; 68:5; 82:3; 146:9.

13. Cf. Ps. 35:10; 40:17; 113:7. This list, as well as those in the next two fn., is by no means exhaustive.

14. Ps. 27:6; 116:17.

15. Ps. 147:8 ff.

the gods and men to build a house for him.[16] The Bible on the other hand portrays a God who is so gracious to His "subjects" that He is willing to give Himself—or, more significantly, His Son— for His people. His Son assures us that the Father has "mansions" waiting for us (John 14:2 KJV).

I conclude then that as the Lord calls on us to exercise authority in a serving manner, He has not left us without an example—His own. We are indeed made in His image, after His likeness. His Word and His law are not a burden, but they give light and life. Both the proclamation and the program of the church should be patterned after that likeness.

*Anthropology*

If the view we have espoused thus far is valid, it will have far-reaching implications for a correct view of man. Man, made in the image of God, is the representative of God.

The fact that man is a representative suggests on the one hand that he is of little or no value in himself. Just as paper and ink have little value until they combine to form the portrait or representation of an object, so man is of value only as he represents God. This consideration should be enough to humble us.

On the other hand, it is impossible to conceive of anything that could give man more importance than being a representative *of God*. Man represents none other than the Almighty Creator of heaven and earth. Reflection on this should deal the death blow to any inferiority complex.

This perspective opens up the enormity of sin. Sin at heart is wanting to be one's own representative rather than a representative of God. Sin is wanting to exercise authority in an unrestricted way, being answerable to no one. The situation is further complicated by the fact that this man who wants to represent himself is not dismissed from the role of representing God. He continues to represent Him only to *mis*represent Him. The result of all this is that whoever comes into contact with this *mis*representation of God will be prone—wittingly or unwittingly—to curse God rather than to bless

16. *Ancient Near Eastern Texts*[2] (hereafter *ANET*[2]), ed. J. Pritchard, (Princeton: Princeton University Press, 1955), pp. 60-72. I am attracted to the interpretation of this myth given by D. Winton Thomas, *Documents from Old Testament Times* (New York: Harper and Row, 1958), pp. 3 ff., namely, that this story was told to propagate the idea that a centralized or monarchical form of government is better than a council or democratic form of government. If one notes the resistance to the monarchy in the Old Testament it will become clear that there is one type of government (or authority) espoused in the Babylonian myth and quite a different type in the Old Testament. The Babylonian story teaches that authority comes from the superiority of power; the Biblical view of authority is that one is appointed to serve.

Him. This is particularly relevant with respect to the exercise of authority. As man misuses authority, he is misrepresenting God. Such misrepresentation is the stimulus for those who are the victims of such misuse to blaspheme God.[17]

As indicated above, man as made in the image of God is by definition an authority-bearing creature. In the portrayal of man in the "pre-sin" state as we find it in the first two chapters of Genesis, there is no reason to doubt that the male and female were equally called on to exercise authority over creation and over one another. After sin entered the world, the male (at least as husband) exercised rule over the female (at least as wife). As the words "and he shall rule over you" appear in the account, they may be understood predictively as well as prescriptively. Male rule is the result of sin, not the Creator's intent. In any event it seems clear that for one human being to rule over another in a unilateral way was not the original design of the Creator; rather it is the result of sin. The divine intent is that authority and submission must be mutual and reciprocal. This is foolishness to sinful man, but when authority is seen in its twofold dimension of right to command and duty to serve, the exercise of authority does not divide but rather unites persons into a meaningful bond.

It may be objected that if each human being is an authority-bearing creature, that may well be the demise of authority in much the same way that emphasizing every word in a paragraph results in no emphasis at all. Accenting every syllable in the line results in loss of accent. Marking every tree in the forest results in no marked trees at all. Is then the thesis that each has authority doomed to self-contradiction? If there are to be chiefs there must be braves; if there are to be generals there must be privates. Indeed the popular notion of authority and governments is that there are those who rule and there are those who are ruled. It is a simple "one way" process. The superior imposes his rule on the inferior.

This may be a simple and clearly defined view of authority, but in my judgment it is not the Biblical teaching on authority. It is the view that the Babylonian myth of creation espouses.[18] The Bible, however, has a very different model of authority, at least in the "pre-sin" stage. And if I correctly understand the role of the first two chapters of Genesis, they give us a portrait of the goal toward which the kingdom of heaven proceeds by means of the preaching of the gospel. The Biblical model assumes a basic equality among man-

---

17. This perspective cannot be developed further here, but the Biblical basis for it can be found in Rom. 2:24.

18. See fn. 16.

kind. The male represents God to the female and hence has an authority over her. The converse, however, is no less true: the female represents God to the male and has authority over him. Paul is no doubt seeking to reestablish this equality within the sanctity of the home when he says, "The wife does not rule over her own body, but the husband does; likewise the husband does not rule over his own body, but the wife does" (I Cor. 7:4). This mutual, reciprocal authority makes no sense to those whose thinking is determined by the Babylonian motif. But when one begins to see that true authority is a serving exercise, authority becomes the gift of life for both the one who rules and the one who is ruled.

A consistently Biblical anthropology must come to grips seriously with the matter of equality among human beings. This equality is not lost due to misfortune or poverty. When this equality is recognized, it is not difficult to see that the poor represent Christ in a very significant way: "Truly, I say to you, as you did it to one of the least of these my brethren, you did it to me" (Matt. 25:40). No doubt this explains why the poor in Israel had a *right* to such things as gleaning.[19] Their economic status was not to decrease their value as human beings and members of the covenant community. The poor become a significant channel by which the power and beauty of the life of Christ within the church can come to visible expression.

This Biblical teaching of the basic equality among men (obviously this does not mean that the same gifts are given to all men) gives a profound significance to the exodus from Egypt. Human bondage, the exploitation of one man or class of men over another, is an abomination in the eyes of God. As God rescues His people from one bondage He does not deliver them to another. Moses is leader, but he is not king. Joshua at the most may be described as commander-in-chief of the army, but when he dies there is no successor appointed, and I doubt that this should be considered an oversight, any more than that there was no successor appointed for Christ. Israel is to be organized around the ark—the ark which contained the book of the covenant, the words of life. Israel by divine design is to be a people enjoying liberty and equality under God and His law. Yahweh is their King. The throne and the palace which came later introduced a foreign element—a human intrusion. If it be objected that the premonarchical form of government in Israel was

19. Such texts as Lev. 19:10, "And you shall not strip your vineyard bare, neither shall you gather the fallen grapes of your vineyard; you shall leave them for the poor and for the sojourner: I am the Lord your God," indicate that Israel was expected to show concern for the underprivileged simply because of God's attributes of benevolence and mercy. Israel betrays His cause if they do not show mercy.

a failure, such failure must be attributed to the faithlessness of Israel and their idolatrous desire to have a visible king with well-armored chariots and horses. That God yielded to their way is an example of His patience, not His approval. Furthermore, a brief survey of Israel's history is enough to convince us that the monarchy in Israel was no unmixed blessing.

Early Israel had been warned repeatedly about the disadvantages of a monarchy. Jotham's fable in Judges 9 is one of the most intriguing pieces of ancient literature. The fable points out the inherent exploitative dynamics in the monarchical system. As the trees—so goes the fable—seek to make a king, they elect the olive tree; but the olive tree objects that since it is so busy providing fatness it has no time to be king. Likewise the fig tree declines the appointment, for it is simply too busy providing sweetness. Next the vine is approached, but it is too busy providing wine; it has no time to be king. Finally they turn to the bramble, and, of course, the bramble with all its thorns is well equipped to be an effective administrator of power. Furthermore, it shows its true despotic nature by demanding total submission. For if they fail to take refuge in its shade— a highly ridiculous scene which is intended to spoof the bramble's (and by implication a monarch's) malady of megalomania—then a fire will break out to devour the cedars of Lebanon. In other words, the promotion of the bramble's absolute authority is more important to it than the existence and service of the noble trees that live to serve. A finer diagnosis of the sickness often present in the monarchical structures can hardly be found.

Unfortunately Jotham's masterpiece was not enough to prevent the adoption of the monarchy in Israel. She apparently was unwilling to trust the Lord to protect her from the enemy. A king, well equipped with infantry and cavalry as "all the nations" had (I Sam. 8:5), was much more appealing than the simple trust that the Lord would repeatedly frighten away the Philistines (I Sam. 7). Finally the warning against monarchism comes in simple prose: "He will take your sons and appoint them to his chariots and to be his horsemen, and to run before his chariots; . . . he will take your daughters to be perfumers and cooks and bakers. He will take the best of your fields and vineyards and olive orchards and give them to his servants . . . . He will take a tenth of your flocks and you shall be his slaves" (I Sam. 8:11-17).

The history of Israel's monarchy is an eloquent fulfilment of this prophecy. Solomon and Rehoboam were not the only culprits. Even David, the man after God's own heart, did not escape the sin of exploiting fellow human beings for selfish reasons. The ultimate irony is that Israel's royal armies did not prevent the final defeat and banishment from the land of promise in 586 B.C. I can only conclude that monarchism (this means a centralized, "one way" form of government) does not have Biblical sanction.

The Babylonian view of authority was pointed out above, and in harmony with it is the view of man as we reconstruct it from their creation epic. Marduk creates man and explicitly states his reason: "He shall be charged with the service of the gods that they may be at ease."[20] Then of Marduk and Ea we read that they took the blood of Tiamat the rebel: "Out of his blood they fashioned mankind. He [Ea] imposed the service and let free the gods."[21] In such a system, men are quite properly exploited by the gods, for we read: "May the subjects ever bear in mind their god, And may they at his word pay heed to the goddess. May food-offerings be borne for their gods and goddesses."[22] All this to the effect that there may be "A likeness on earth of what he has wrought in heaven."[23] The gods hereby put their stamp of approval on the structure by which the strong make use of the weak for their own advantage. The subjects of the king therefore exist for his "ease." The epic, of course, fails to perceive that this structure is the result of sin and perversion. It is the depraved mind of man that so arranges the affairs of life that the weak serve the strong and the poor enrich the rich.

There is a close parallel between the Bible's revelation of God and its revelation of man. As was pointed out in the previous section, God is not to be viewed only as the one on top of the hierarchical structure, but rather as a kind Father who undergirds His creatures and deals with them in a self-giving way. Man, as God's representative, is called on to reflect this magnanimous stance of God. This stance is seen most clearly in Him who is God's incarnate Son.

### Christology

Many of the Christologies that I have read discuss in a very satisfying way the theme that Christ came into this world because God loved the world. It is clearly pointed out that this is a self-giving love. Many in dealing with Christ's kingship let the reader feel that the kingship of Christ is, indeed, of a very different nature and conducted in a very different manner than the kingships of this earth. These themes are a confirmation of what has been said above.

I do feel, however, that there are lacunae in the writings on

20. *ANET²*, p. 68.            22. Ibid.
21. Ibid.                      23. Ibid.

Christology, and I would like to discuss two areas in which I think I detect these lacunae. The first concerns the "servanthood" of Christ, the second the "kingship" of Christ and how it bears on the correct exercise of authority among human beings.

Christologies rarely omit the theme of the suffering servant. In fact numerous volumes can be found in our libraries whose titles state or imply the theme of the suffering servant. Invariably, however, the servanthood of Christ is discussed only in conjunction with the suffering of Christ. This leaves the impression that the servanthood of Christ is a temporary phase of Christ's ministry through which He had to pass. It was a servanthood of suffering so that He might make expiation for the sins of the people. I have, of course, no quarrel with the thesis that Christ suffered as a servant and that His sacrifice is the atonement for sin. My misgiving arises at these points: Is it correct to view the servanthood of Christ as exclusively one of suffering? And is the servanthood temporary, ceasing at the crucifixion and replaced at the resurrection by the kingship? Admittedly I have found no Christology which states it so crassly, but I do believe that this view of the servanthood of Christ prevails in the church. This view which sees the servanthood and the kingship of Christ as mutually exclusive is enhanced by the older Christologies in which sharp disjunction was made between Christ's states of humiliation and exaltation.[24]

The servanthood of Christ, in my judgment, must be viewed as permanent, not temporary. This in no sense detracts from His lordship; instead His lordship becomes unspeakably glorious because of the servant stance. As the psalmist says, "Though the Lord is high, he regards the lowly" (Ps. 138:6).

Therefore, as Christ stood among His disciples, girded with the towel, holding the basin in His hand, He was not simply giving a model of how things ought to be in the church (and the world, too), but in this stance Christ is also the revelation of the Father. I know of no Biblical data that would preclude us from accepting the thesis that as a servant "He reflects the glory of God and bears the very stamp of his nature, upholding the universe by his power" (Heb. 1:3). As servant Christ plays the dual role of reflecting what God is and what man should be. For therein lies the glory of man. In service man is the healer, coordinator, and harmonizer of creation. The ancient sage had an appreciation of this when he said,

24. For a discussion of the "two states" theology, see G. C. Berkouwer, *The Work of Christ* (Grand Rapids: Eerdmans, 1965), p. 37: "The doctrine of the two states did not in the least proceed from a schematic attempt to divide Christ's life into two distinct phases...."

"A righteous man has regard for the life of his beast but the mercy of the wicked is cruel" (Prov. 12:10).

The salvation which Christ came to bring involves a renewal of man that is so radical that it will affect him even in his relationship to his beast. All of life will be graced by the touch of Him who stooped to seek the lost and wayward. In His role as servant, Christ reveals God.

The second lacuna that I frequently sense is in the area of applying Christ's kingship to our lives. It is frequently pointed out that the kingship of Christ is unique. He rules by His Word and Spirit; He seeks to persuade and teach rather than to coerce; He rules for the sake of the church and He continues to nourish the church (Eph. 5:29). The impression seems to prevail, however, that this kingship is so unique that it really belongs to another world—or at least to a very narrow sphere of our lives (the church perhaps). It is designed for heaven (after all, Christ Himself called it the kingdom of heaven), not for this earth. It is indeed a beautiful kingship, but it is not usable in the present order.

How the kingship of Christ is to be applied to our lives personally, communally, and nationally is an extremely difficult question; and the scope of this essay does not allow for a general discussion of it. Our interest concerns the extent to which the Christian can exercise authority in this semi- or post-Christian world as a servant to that world. (I recall a parishioner asking whether I thought Christ would make out well as mayor of Chicago.) No doubt every Christian will have to "play it by ear." But if the Christian is not aware of this challenge, and if the church is not preaching this challenge, then we may be certain that the witness of the church will be greatly paralyzed. One of the points that must be emphasized when the gospel is preached is this: if human authority is to be exercised as God would have it exercised, it must be done for the welfare of those over whom this authority is exercised. Where tyranny is found, the Holy Spirit is grieved; for He is the Spirit of liberty. Where Christians condone or wink at tyranny "they crucify the Son of God on their own account and hold him up to contempt" (Heb. 6:6). Magistrates are servants of God, but that in no way excludes the fact that they also serve the people.[25] In fact the church, to be true to her Lord, must positively say that if a government facilitates the rich in oppressing the poor it is *mis*representing God and can only expect the judgment of God. All human institutions and establishments must function for the service of mankind (within the guidelines of the law of God); failing in this, they lose their right to existence.

25. This is not the same as saying that they rule by consent of the people.

## Soteriology

It has been said often and well that the salvation which Christ gives to His people is more than escape from eternal punishment; it also includes the renewal of the believer. One way in which renewal comes to expression is in the believer's use of authority. The husband who is tyrannical, the father who is despotic, the teacher who is authoritarian, the factory owner who oppresses his employees, the boy who mistreats his dog, and the magistrate who lusts for power are all defective in the manner in which they are remade in Christ. The implication of this for the leaven of Christianity in society is obvious. Every Christian is a light in the world. But insofar as a Christian espouses the Babylonian (i.e., the worldly) sense of authority[26] and is willing to join any law and order movement for the sake of his own convenience in order that he may escape the chaos brought on by the riots of the oppressed minorities, his light has been dimmed and distorted. A clear witness to society is possible only when the Christian is willing to use whatever authority is granted him (whether it is civil, economic, or influential) for the service of God and man. He does not thereby lose authority; instead, he gives proper expression to it.

God demands that those in authority (e.g., the judges) should execute justice as he does: "Give justice to the weak and fatherless; maintain the right of the afflicted and the destitute. Rescue the weak and the needy; deliver them from the hand of the wicked" (Ps. 82:3, 4). These words, though originally directed to the official judges, can legitimately be applied to all men. For is there anyone who in some sense does not make judgment or dispositions of time and material things? The needs of our fellow men, particularly of the suffering, must always receive our consideration. The believer's use of authority in a sincerely benevolent way becomes one of the most effective ways for the new life in Christ to come to visible expression. Salvation and service are inseparable.

## Ecclesiology

A discussion of the authority exercised within and by the church could become very voluminous if for no other reason than that it was an important point during and after the Reformation. Much of the discussion centered on the question of whether it was the pope, the councils, the king, or Christ who was in authority. The interest of this essay, however, lies in the area of the proper exercise of authority, rather than in who administers it.

26. Cf. fn. 16.

Our knowledge of the history of the development of church organization during its first few centuries is limited, but I cannot escape the feeling of dismay that during this time the church chose a centralized, hierarchical pattern of organization. By doing so it chose the model of Babylon (it literally took the Roman empire as its model), rather than the Biblical pattern. I will not attempt to give an adequate description of how much harm, I think, the hierarchical form of government has done in the church, nor how deeply it has undercut the witness of the church. I simply make two observations.

First of all, Calvin's preference for a plurality of authority (which will be discussed later) is surely a step in the right direction.[27] I believe it to be much closer to the Biblical pattern of authority. The Old Testament, for example, resists the monarchical form of government, but it does not resist the patriarchal form. The latter is no doubt a situation in which the patriarch received "input" from the members of the clan and then tried to make a decision according to the will of God and acceptable to the clan. It must be said, however, that plurality of authority does not per se ensure a proper use of authority. Groups, councils, and majorities can be just as tyrannical as a monarch. Indeed, there probably are monarchs who have truly tried to be properly benevolent. Democracy can easily degenerate into a "demonocracy" if each person casts his vote according to selfish interests.

The second observation is that proper use of authority in the church is important not only for the welfare of the church itself, but also that the church may serve as a model to society by demonstrating good structures and benevolent use of authority. Israel as a nation without a king was no doubt to function as a model that would arouse the curiosity and even amazement of the nations around her. Is it not reasonable to believe that the church which is in contact with society more intimately than Israel was with her neighbors is also to serve as a model for all social living? It would appear that this is true for the church not only as institute, but also as church in the widest sense. In other words, all organizations which claim to be Christian in purpose (schools, hospitals, etc.) should be very sensitive to the matter of proper use of authority with respect to their employees and others whom they seek to serve. Such proper use of authority in a communal and organized way is a particularly effective way to show the renewing effect of the gospel.

*Eschatology*

The view of authority advocated in this essay will probably find

27. *Inst.*, IV.iii.15 (note 13); IV.iv.10-11; IV.xx.8.

support among those who feel that it describes the manner in which authority will be exercised in the future kingdom of Christ (i.e., the millennium). According to this view, Christ will then be visibly present and His rule uncontested. The redeemed will fully trust one another because every contact of theirs will be controlled by the genuine desire to serve each other.

However, as a committed a-millenarian[28] I would insist that the Christian cannot be content to push the rule of Christ to some distant date. It is the goal of the Christian to see the kingdom of God realized in whatever way possible even now. We do indeed live in a world of sin, a world which often seems to respond only to the language of coercion and violence, while the manner in which Christ exercised authority seems pitifully ineffectual. The Babylonian model can boast of great achievements. The Christian, however, is challenged to live in hope that all is not in vain by following this seemingly weak and impractical example of Christ, but that even for this life it has its own rewards in the harmony and love which it brings between persons. It is in that strength that the believer can look to the future with optimism and can meaningfully pray, "Thy kingdom come."

## Calvin on human authority

What, then, is Calvin's view with respect to all of this? It will not be possible to give a complete description of Calvin's view of authority in this section, but an attempt will be made to consult Calvin on much of the Scriptural data alluded to in the former section to see if Calvin shares the view of authority presented in that section. We need not accept Calvin's verdict as final, but Calvin's insights are as valuable and respected as ever.

In his commentary on Genesis 1 Calvin is particularly absorbed with the idea that God is gracious and generous in giving to man a world so fully furnished with that which makes life rich and enjoyable. Calvin's discussion of man's relationship to the rest of creation is dominated by the idea of stewardship.[29] Calvin is impressed by the manner in which the story of man's creation is told. He

28. Possibly the words *pan-millenarian* or *omni-millenarian* are preferable because they not only are more positive, but they suggest the idea that we are in the millennium now.

29. *Comm.* on Gen. 1:28. Calvin's sense of stewardship is not built on an austere framework of fear nor on a barren "reward and punishment" scheme. Stewardship was important for enjoyment: "For it is of great importance that we touch nothing of God's bounty but what we know he has permitted us to do; since we cannot enjoy anything with a good conscience, except we receive it as from the hand of God."

points out that with respect to other creatures, God simply commands and they come into existence. But

> when he approaches the most excellent of all his works, he enters into consultation. God certainly might have commanded by his bare word what he wished to be done: but he chose to give this tribute to the excellency of man, that he would in a manner enter into consultation concerning his creation. This is the highest honour with which he has dignified us.[30]

Calvin's understanding of the term "image of God," however, does not fully harmonize with what was offered in the previous section. Calvin mentions Chrysostom's view, which was that the image "refers to the dominion which was given to man in order that he might, in a certain sense act as God's vicegerent in the government of the world."[31] But Calvin indicates that this is only a very small portion of the meaning of this term. Calvin posits that the image "has been destroyed in us by the fall, [and] we may judge from its restoration what it originally had been."[32] He then offers a discussion of the passages (Eph. 4:23; Col. 3:10) which he understands as speaking of the restoration of the image of God.

Subsequently, however, he does recognize that man is lord of creation, and what he says about the existence of other created things almost reminds one of the scheme of things in the Babylonian myth: "And hence we infer what was the end for which all things were created; namely, that none of the conveniences and necessaries of life might be wanting to men."[33] One can hardly take issue with this, for Genesis 2 explicitly states that the fruit of the trees was given for food. That man was to have a solicitous concern for creation does not escape Calvin's notice. He says

> that the custody of the garden was given in charge to Adam, to show that we possess the things which God has committed to our hands, on the condition, that being content with a frugal and moderate use of them, we should take care of what shall remain. Let him who possesses a field, so partake of its yearly fruits, that he may not suffer the ground to be injured by his negligence; but let him endeavor to hand it down to posterity as he received it, or even better cultivated.[34]

Thus Calvin's view of stewardship forbids exploitation and abuse of creation; instead man's management of the things of this world becomes a holy exercise for God.

Calvin's view of the authority exercised among and over men is also dominated by a sense of stewardship. He is deeply aware of

30. *Comm.* on Gen. 1:26.　　33. Ibid.
31. Ibid.　　34. *Comm.* on Gen. 2:15.
32. Ibid.

the need for government among men. He echoes and reechoes the words from Romans 13 that "the authorities are ministers of God." He renounces the position of the Anabaptists that the Christian must not be involved in civil government. He is equally aware, however, of instances in which there may be a conflict between the command of the magistrate and the command of God. Never wont to indulge in ambiguities, he is particularly clear in his position on this point. Repeatedly he calls Peter "the heavenly herald"[35] who said, "We must obey God rather than men." Calvin's view on stewardship comes full circle on this point. The magistrates are accountable to God; the subjects are accountable to the magistrates, but have a prior accountability to God. The magistrates have an accountability to God, to be sure, but also to their subjects.

In his "Prefatory Address to King Francis I of France," Calvin employs the common decorous language of the day (and I am not suggesting that he was insincere in his use of it), but he does not hesitate to say:

> Even though I regard my country with as much natural affection as becomes me, as things now stand I do not much regret being excluded. Rather, I embrace the common cause of all believers, that of Christ himself—a cause completely torn and trampled in your realm today, lying, as it were, utterly forlorn, more through the tyranny of certain Pharisees than with your approval.[36]

When there is a conflict between the king's command and the command of the Lord, Calvin clearly advocates resistance to the king. But such resistance always stops just short of organized rebellion and revolution.[37]

Some aspects of Calvin's treatment of human governments, however, leave me with questions and misgivings. My questions can be condensed to these two. First, does Calvin mean to teach that there is a legitimate difference (i.e., a God-ordained difference from the beginning) between the manner in which authority is exercised by the state and the manner in which it is to be exercised in the church? Second, does Calvin do justice to the idea that human

35. *Inst.*, "Prefatory Address"; IV.xx.32.

36. *Inst.*, "Prefatory Address"; p. 11.

37. J. T. McNeill in his fn. 54 on IV.xx.31 points out that "Calvin carefully guards against any endorsement of popular revolutionary action, but in some instances his language is less guarded. See, for example his *Comm.* Daniel (1561), lecture xxx on Dan. 6:22, where he says: 'For earthly princes lay aside their power when they rise up against God, and are unworthy to be reckoned among the number of mankind. We ought, rather utterly to defy them [*conspuere in ipsorum capita*, lit., "to spit on their heads"] than to obey them' (CR XLI. 25)."

authority is exercised correctly only when there is a sense of service toward those over whom one rules?

The first question, then, is this. Is the exercise of authority in the state inherently different from the authority exercised within and by the church? I will focus my discussion of it on Calvin's comments on Luke 22:24-30,[38] and Romans 13.

From the Gospels we learn that there was a contention among the disciples concerning the question of rank and primacy in the anticipated kingdom. Jesus' response is that "the kings of the Gentiles exercise lordship over them . . . . But not so with you; rather let the greatest among you become as the youngest, and the leader as the one who serves." Calvin sees in the words of Jesus a sharp disjunction between the function of the apostles from that of kings. For the apostles there can be no consideration of rank or order, but for kings it is natural if not essential. To the disciples Christ is making it clear "that the primacy which was the cause of their quarrel is nothing in His Kingdom."[39] Calvin anticipates that there will be those, no doubt wishing to defend the hierarchical government of the church, who will object and say that Christ did institute orders in the church and made the "dignity of the apostolate superior to the office of pastors . . . ."[40] Calvin's reply to this is most noteworthy: "I reply, if we carefully examine the details, even kings do not rightly rule unless they serve."[41] I regret that Calvin does not stop there, but he goes on to say: "The apostolic office differs from earthly principalities in that their being servants does not prevent kings and magistrates from bearing sway and indeed, rising above their subjects in magnificent splendor and pomp."[42] He reiterates that "the government of the church permits nothing of this sort. Christ gives to pastors nothing more than that they shall be servants and completely abstain from domination."[43]

This seems to suggest that while the ascendance of one man over another has no place among the disciples (i.e., the church), it is inevitable and even proper among rulers of state. This conclusion seems to be borne out by Calvin's comments on Romans 13:1, where he explains that the magistrates are called "*higher powers* because they excel other men . . . ."[44] He, however, does not explain in which way they excel. He simply says:

38. Calvin discusses Luke 22:24 ff. in conjunction with Matt. 20:24-28 and Mark 10:41-45.

39. *Comm.* on Matt. 20:25.     42. Ibid.

40. Ibid.     43. Ibid.

41. Ibid.     44. *Comm.* on Rom. 13:1.

> Paul intended . . . to remove the empty curiosity of those who
> often ask by what right those who are in authority came by
> their power. It ought really to be sufficient for us that they
> rule. They have not attained to this high position by their own
> strength, but have been placed there by the hand of the Lord.[45]

This suggests that in Calvin's thinking the magistrates excel only
in that they in God's providence have been appointed to this function.

Calvin certainly is close to expressing the view of authority which
I have sought to formulate in the first part of this essay when he
comments on the words "for he is God's servant for your good"
(Rom. 13:4):

> Magistrates may learn from this the nature of their calling. They
> are not to rule on their own account, but for the public good.
> Nor do they have unbridled power, but power that is re-
> stricted to the welfare of their subjects. In short, they are
> responsible to God and to men in the exercise of their rule.[46]

On the one hand, Calvin clearly advocates obeying the established government as long as its demands do not conflict with the
law of God. "The Prefatory Address to King Francis I of France"
is sufficient evidence to establish that emphasis of Calvin. On the
other hand, Calvin was no advocate of the so-called divine right of
kings. In his sermon on Deuteronomy 17:14-18 Calvin makes it
clear that in his view the monarch in Israel was a concession by the
Lord and not the ideal. In his exposition on Matthew 1:6 he says
that Israel's request for a king was "wicked." Calvin sees the government by the law and the judges as the ideal: "In respect of worldly
government, he has chosen the best state that could be; namely that
the Law should reign over the people, and therewithal that there
should be Judges in every city . . . ."[47] He repeats this theme a number of times in the sermon and clearly indicates that monarchism
does not have the sanction of Scripture nor of good sense.

> For it is a far more tolerable thing for us to have governors
> that go[vern] by choice and election, who in executing their
> office shall know themselves to be subject to the Law; than
> to have a Prince whose words must stand for reason, and
> whose child must inherit, though he be never so very a babe,

45. Ibid.

46. *Comm.* on Rom. 13:4.

47. *The Sermons of M. Iohn Caluin upon the Fifth Book of Moses Called Deuteronomie*, trans. Arthur Goldring (London: H. Middleton for G. Bishop, 1583),
p. 645b.

48. Ibid. Cf. *Inst.*, IV.xx.8. There Calvin's willingness to blend democracy with
aristocracy is interesting; his judgment that the government must fit the needs or conditions of the people is sound advice for nations which want to force their way of govern-

and consequently obeyed; though he be the wilfullest fool or the cruelest person in the world.[48]

The area in which Calvin leaves me uneasy is in the matter of the pomp and splendor he is willing to let the magistrates enjoy at public expense. In his chapter on "Civil Government" we read,

> I pass over such statements as these: that kings should not multiply horses for themselves; nor set their mind upon avarice; nor be lifted up above their brethren; that they should be constant in meditating upon the law of the Lord all the days of their life (Deut. 17:16-19).[49]

Admittedly Calvin does defend his "passing over such statements" on the consideration that it is not his intent to "instruct the magistrates," but rather "to teach others what magistrates are...." In spite of such explanation I consider Calvin's position on the pomp of the magistrates as less than acceptable. Does such pomp lead to any good? I think not. The position set forth in the first part of this essay—namely, that to be truly human one can exercise authority only in a serving way—applies to rulers as much as to anyone, if not more. The ideal would be that a magistrate could say with Samuel, "Whose ox have I taken? Or whose ass have I taken? Or whom have I defrauded, Whom have I oppressed?" (I Sam. 12:3).

My uneasiness increases as Calvin goes on:

> Lastly, I also wish to add this, that tribute and taxes are the lawful revenue of princes, which they may chiefly use to meet the public expenses of their office; yet they may similarly use them for the magnificence of their household, which is joined, so to speak, with the dignity of the authority they exercise. As we see, David, Hezekiah, Josiah, Jehoshaphat, and other holy kings, also Joseph and Daniel (according to the dignity of their office) were, without offending piety, lavish at public expense, and we read in Ezekiel that a very large portion of land was assigned to the kings [Ezek. 48:21]. There although

ment on other nations. Calvin must surely have known of the Greek "solution" to the problems of power in government, but apparently he deems it unworthy of mention or refutation. In the *Dialogues* of Plato, "Laws" III, 690 f., the Athenian stranger and Cleinias agree that it is part of nature that "the stronger shall rule, and the weaker be ruled." But even more important that "the wise should lead and command and the ignorant follow and obey." The ideal, of course, is that there be a "rule of law over willing subjects, and not a rule of compulsion." The reason why so many governments fail is lack of moderation on the part of rulers. For "if any one give too much power to anything, too large a sail to a vessel ... and does not observe the mean, everything is overthrown...." Obviously moderation in a wrong sense of authority is hardly the answer. Tyranny in moderation can hardly be the solution. The Bible's message of a positive, benevolent use of authority is indispensable. The king who no longer loves his subjects is not a king but a despot. A father who no longer serves his children is not a father but a liability to the family.

49. *Inst.*, IV.xx.9.

the prophet portrays the spiritual Kingdom of Christ, he seeks the pattern for his picture from a lawful human kingdom.[50]

In fairness to Calvin it must be observed that he immediately tempers his statement by saying that these "revenues are not so much their private chests as the treasuries of the entire people (for so Paul testifies [Rom. 13:6])," and that "tributes are nothing but supports of public necessity." Furthermore, "to impose them upon the common folk without cause is tyrannical extortion."[51] Nevertheless, I find Calvin's examples from Scripture in this matter highly selective; and with respect to Ezekiel 48:21, his use of this passage hardly reflects the intent of the author.

Calvin cites the examples of David and the others, but does not mention Solomon and Rehoboam. It is rather amazing that Calvin, though he warns against oppressiveness, does not mention these latter examples. Surely it is clear that the Bible censures the luxury of Solomon and Rehoboam much more strongly than it approves the luxury of David and the others. It would seem proper to view such lavishness as one of those things God "overlooked in times of ignorance" (Acts 17:30), as He did slavery, polygamy, and other weaknesses of human society.

Calvin's use of Ezekiel 48:21 is hardly justified in view of the narrow context of this passage and the broad context of Scripture. In the narrow context we note the boundaries of the princes' domain, after which we read, "And my princes shall no more oppress my people; but they shall let the house of Israel have the land according to their tribe" (Ezek. 45:8). This makes it abundantly clear that the apportionment of the land to the princes had a curbing or restrictive intent. With respect to the broad context of Scripture it would hardly seem necessary to argue the case since in the course of this discussion numerous passages (Deut. 17:14-20; Judg. 9:7-15; I Sam. 8; etc.) have been touched on which indicate the tendency of the monarchy to become oppressive. Even more important is the general theme of Scripture that men are not to exploit one another, but instead are to aid and support each other.

After making a case for the magistrate's lavishness at public expense Calvin attempts a tempering effect: "These considerations do not encourage princes to waste and expensive luxury, as there is surely no need to add fuel to their cupidity, already too much kindled of itself."[52] This cupidity might well have been expanded

50. *Inst.*, IV.xx.13.

51. Ibid.

52. Ibid.

on, since this cupidity was fed by rivalry among the princes. In Calvin's time there was fierce competition among Francis I of France, Charles V of Spain, and Henry VII of England to gain primacy. This rivalry had a draining effect on all three of the nations, but France was particularly crushed. The abuse brought on by rivalry warrants the attention of the people of God so that they may speak in a prophetic way as did Jeremiah to Shallum: "Do you think you are a king because you compete in cedar? Did not your father eat and drink and do justice and righteousness? Then it was well with him. He judged the cause of the poor and needy; then it was well. Is not this to know me? says the Lord" (Jer. 22:15 ff.).

Calvin is probably correct when he says that private individuals should not "shamelessly decry any expenses of princes, even if these exceed the common expenditures of the citizens";[53] yet it is also proper to point out that the careful and even frugal use of this world's goods is recommended for all, prince and subject alike. One of the ways by which the people of God can help to promote loyalty and morale within a nation is to respectfully remind magistrates of the need for moderation in their demands on the people and indicate further that they should abstain from opulence in their personal lives.

The second area in which Calvin leaves me uneasy is his lack of emphasis on the servitude that the ruler should sense toward his subjects. Does Calvin clearly express the idea that rulers must serve those over whom they rule? Some of Calvin's discussions leave me with the impression that he does not sense this dimension of a ruler's authority. He speaks of a primacy of earthly rulers which makes their function totally different from that of the disciples. He uses such language as the rulers "holding sway" over their people. But there are times when he clearly senses the dimension of service, as when he says of the magistrates that "they are not to rule on their own account, but for the public good . . ., they have power . . . restricted to the welfare of their subjects. In short, they are responsible to God and to men in the exercise of their rule."[54] Or again, "even kings do not rightly and truly rule unless they serve."[55] Such comments give me encouragement to say that the view of authority as presented in the first part of this essay is shared by Calvin. Yet it seems to be one of the lesser-developed themes in his writings.

The church must preach the theme that authority is exercised

53. Ibid.

54. *Comm.* on Rom. 13:4.

55. *Comm.* on Matt. 20:24.

correctly only when he who exercises authority has a deep respect for his domain, and a genuine desire to serve, so that whatever he rules may develop to the fullest potential. One of the most exciting ways of preaching the gospel is to point out the joy and power which comes into the life of the believer when he exercises authority in this benevolent and Christ-like way. Such use of authority promotes trust rather than resentment; it produces allegiance rather than alienation; it makes for a cohesive society rather than a fragmented one.

To preach this view of authority the church must present the life and sacrifice of Christ as the first great model. Furthermore, the church must seek to organize itself in such a way that all despotic, centralized forms of government are avoided within the church. Her goal in this is not to be something the world can never become. Rather the church's organization and procedure must be a model of what the world ought to be. Calvin's writings are replete with rejection and condemnation of papal tyranny, and he opts for a plurality of authority. In his discussion on vocation he says that "no deed is considered more noble ... than to free one's country from tyranny."[56] That statement is not passé in the "free world" of the twentieth century. Our culture is infested with economic tyrannies, political monarchies (despite electoral landslides), tyrannical majorities, despotic bureaucracies, all of which have little heart for their realm of authority. Most of them can be moved only by legal, punitive threat. The church must speak dynamically in precept and by example of a happier way.

In making this witness to society, the church must not despair of the ability of all men to grasp and appreciate this message. All mankind has an innate sense of justice and a natural aversion to tyranny. It is doubtful that many are so perverse that they do not recognize inequities when they are pointed out to them. Even in Babylon Hammurabi felt called on by the gods

to destroy the wicked and evil,
that the strong might not oppress the weak.[57]

From this statement in Hammurabi's code we can deduce that when the church is willing to remain silent in the presence of injustice and oppression it not only is disloyal to the gospel but has not even caught up with the nobler sentiments of pagan thought. Hammurabi seemed to sense the debilitating effect that oppression and

56. *Inst.*, III.xi.6.

57. *ANET*², p. 164. The Egyptian wisdom expresses the same sentiments; cf. *ANET*², pp. 422 ff.

injustice by the strong on the weak had on society. Can the Christian message say any less when Christ Himself has demonstrated that the way of life and love and happiness is to give oneself to those who belong to Him?

A more careful reading of the Judeo-Christian heritage will indicate that the message of the Bible is not a basis for exploitation, whether it is political, sociological, economic, or geologic. Quite the opposite is the case. Sensitivity to proper use of authority, whether it is in the governor's chair, in the factory, at the ballot box, or in cultivating the ground, is becoming to the follower of Christ.

*Willis P. DeBoer*

CHAPTER **8** CALVIN ON

THE ROLE OF WOMEN

The resurrected Lord made His first appearance to women. At the empty tomb it was women who were commissioned by the angel to announce the resurrection to Jesus' disciples. Why such prominence for women, a male-dominated church leadership has sometimes asked. John Calvin had an answer:

> It may seem strange that he does not produce more important witnesses; for he starts with a woman. . . . I consider it was done as a reproach, since [the disciples] had been so slow and sluggish to believe. Indeed, those whom the Son of God had so long and laboriously taught with little or no success, deserve to have as their teachers, not only women, but even oxen and asses.[1]

Calvin was not an avant-garde spokesman for the cause of women's liberation!

Calvin's views on women were very traditional. To some modern ears they sound outrageous, even despicable. Calvin knew where he stood on the matter and he stood his ground. In writing his commentaries and in preaching his sermons he was rigorously consistent: women are subject to men by virtue of their created place in this world and by virtue of the curse of sin that is on them. Women may neither rule nor teach men.

It is not as though Calvin had never heard of any alternatives. There were other ideas on this subject being propounded in his day, sometimes even by his associates and friends. Marguerite de Valois, one of Calvin's correspondents among the French royalty and a protector of many with views of reform, proposed in her *Discours docte et subtil* that woman is now nearer to God than man. This

1. *Comm.* on John 20:1, 17.

comes from her having been created later than the man. For God arranged His works in an ascending order of perfection: the last, the best. Hence a woman's perfection should resemble that of her Maker most closely:

> Clearly we see that this is so. The woman does have the advantage over the man. In regard to the body, it is commonly recognized that a woman is more beautiful and more tender, more carefully worked out than a man. In regard to the soul, God takes pleasure in the tranquil, quiet, devout spirit of a woman, rather than in the tumultuous bloodthirsty spirit of a man. For this reason God did not want David, the man of war, to build his temple. Rather he chose Solomon, a man of peace, whose gentle spirit was much more feminine in nature.[2]

Cornelius Agrippa, a German physician-philosopher of the early sixteenth century, had somewhat similar thoughts. He took a clue from the names *Adam* and *Eve, Adam* meaning "ground" or "earth," and *Eve* meaning "life." See the advanced status of Eve, he proposed. She was made of living human flesh, whereas Adam was made of plain old dirt. A woman's body is so pure and exquisite that she can bathe and leave the water clean, whereas a man always soils it. She carries her offspring in her own body, is able to nourish it when born, and can even give birth to a child without recourse to the help of a male (an allusion to the virgin birth). As to that forbidden fruit incident in the garden, notice that it was Adam who received the prohibition before the woman had even come into the world. True, a curse was placed on her, but hasn't someone come to redeem us from the curse? Such was Agrippa's line of reasoning.[3]

Katherine Zell was the wife of the Strasbourg reformer Matthew Zell. During Calvin's exile from Geneva in Strasbourg he was entertained on occasion by the Zells. Frau Zell could express herself powerfully with tongue and pen. In 1524 when her husband, a priest, was under excommunication by the bishop for having married her, Katherine wrote a letter to the bishop and published it as an open letter, in which she made a vigorous defense of clerical marriage and denounced the "celibate" priest who gets seven women pregnant at the same time. Then she turned to the matter of a woman being so immodest as to address her bishop:

> You remind me that the Apostle Paul told women to be silent in church. I would remind you of the word of the same apostle that in Christ there is no longer male nor female and of the

2. Cited in Gonzague Truc, *Histoire illustrée de la femme* (Paris: Plon, 1940-41), I:199.

3. Ibid., p. 200.

prophecy of Joel: "I will pour forth my spirit upon all flesh and your sons and your *daughters* will prophesy." I do not pretend to be John the Baptist rebuking the Pharisees. I do not claim to be Nathan upbraiding David. I aspire only to be Balaam's ass, castigating his master.[4]

Reformation times were in ferment on many issues. The place and role of woman was one of them. This matter got very scant attention in comparison to the large Reformation issues of faith-works, Scripture-tradition, Lord's Supper-mass. Faced with these larger issues, Calvin took a very traditional and conservative stance in the matter of women. For his day, his stance was noncontroversial, and he undoubtedly served the overall cause of the Reformation well by not getting embroiled in further controversy over some disturbing proposals concerning women.

However, some of the lesser issues of Reformation times have not gone away. Or, if they seemed to go away, they have returned. The question of women's place and role in society is again with us, and it is here in revolutionary proportions. The church of today is hardly in the front ranks of the women's movement. Rather it very often throws up stiff resistance. Many find in Calvin an arsenal of weapons which they are happy to use to stem the tide of the new role for women. Hence Calvin's position on this subject bears review and examination once again. It was a well worked out position seeking to take the Biblical materials seriously. It set the pattern for several centuries of Protestant Biblical exposition of these matters. Is the church well advised to continue with this understanding and way of putting together all the Biblical materials?

In this paper we shall proceed as follows: review Calvin's basic stance; notice some open doors Calvin detected for modification and further development of the basic position; point out some troublesome areas in Calvin's overall scheme on women; and finally, attempt to focus the remaining problem toward current Biblical discussions.

## Calvin's basic stance on women

In a sermon Calvin tried one time to speak as a pious woman would view her lot in life:

> I am not one of those who wanders so far off as to know neither my end nor my present lot; rather God has placed an obligation upon me. As married, I am to serve my husband and show him honor and reverence. As unmarried, I am to walk in

4. Roland H. Bainton, *Women of the Reformation in Germany and Italy* (Minneapolis: Augsburg, 1971), p. 55.

the way of complete sobriety and modesty, acknowledging that men hold a superior station and that they must be the rulers. Any woman who desires to exempt herself from this role forgets the very law of nature and perverts what God commands as necessary to observe.[5]

The pious woman recognizes that the very laws of nature have established her place. There need be no argument over woman's role. There is a kind of self-evidence about this which even the heathen intuitively sense and follow.

> It were a great shame for us [in the church] not to have that honesty at least which nature teaches the very heathen. And if it be so that they which know not either what God is, or what true religion means, have yet notwithstanding some kind of governance amongst them, how much more ought it to be amongst us? Now it is certain that women were never received to any public office. And who has hindered it or placed a restraint upon it, other than that God only has imprinted such a knowledge in nature, that although it be not otherwise taught, yet we know that it were an unseemly thing to have women govern men?[6]

Nature, thus, is the most basic and universal witness to the place of women. But for Calvin, nature is never an abstract or self-contained entity. Nature only reflects the structuring mind and hand of the Creator. What can be learned from the creation account about basic relationships between man and woman? For Calvin, this will surely be a more clear and a more authoritative voice on the matter than nature.

The first we hear of man and woman in connection with God's creative activities is in His creation of humankind on the sixth day: "So God created man in his own image, in the image of God he created him; male and female he created them" (Gen. 1:27). There is no hint of what kind of relationship they have to each other at this point. Calvin notes that this manner of speaking suggests "that the man himself was incomplete. Under these circumstances, the woman was added to him as a companion that they both might be one, as he more clearly expresses in the second chapter."[7] Here we get no

5. Sermon on I Cor. 11:4-10 (*Calvini Opera*, ed. Wm. Baum, Edw. Cunitz, Edw. Reuss [Brunswick: Schwetschke, 1863-1900], 49:730-31. Quotations from this edition are my own translation. The work is henceforth referred to as *C.O.*).

6. Sermon on I Tim. 2:12-14 (*Sermons of M. John Calvin on the Epistles of S. Paule to Timothie and Titus: Translated out of French into English by L. T.* [London: Bishop and Woodcoke, 1579], p. 212. In quoting this translation of Calvin's work, I have modernized the spelling and made a few substitutions of more modern wording for very archaic expressions. Henceforth this translation is referred to as *Trans. L.T.*).

7. *Comm.* on Gen. 1:27.

hints on any kind of ranking or order within the couple. They are made to be together—but there are no suggestions of superiority or subjection whatsoever.

As Calvin noted, we must proceed to the second chapter for a fuller account of these things. Here again Calvin finds mutuality to be the prominent thought. The Lord had observed, "It is not good that the man should be alone" (Gen. 2:18). Calvin comments:

> Moses now explains the design of God in creating the woman; namely, that there should be human beings on the earth who cultivate mutual society between themselves.... The commencement, therefore, involves a general principle, that man was formed to be a social animal.[8]

Again there are no hints of any superiority versus inferiority, or ruling versus subjection in Calvin.

We proceed with Calvin to the exposition of the next statement of the Lord: "I will make him a helper" (Gen. 2:18). Someone in Calvin's day had proposed that you can detect man's excellence over woman in the fact that the plural is used regarding man's creation—"Let *us* make man" (Gen. 1:26), whereas regarding woman it is only the singular—"*I* will make him a helper" (Gen. 2:18). Calvin rejects this proposal outright by pointing out that what is said about man in Genesis 1:26 is said about male and female and need not be repeated in the account of woman's creation.[9]

Calvin then goes on to note that by assigning woman the role of helper, God is prescribing her vocation and instructing her in her duty. Again there is no specific allusion to superiority or inferiority, and Calvin notes that "woman is given as a companion and associate to the man, to assist him to live well." Later on he comments that "women, being instructed in their duty of helping their husbands, should study to keep this divinely appointed order." What does Calvin mean by the term "order"? Does it mean here anything more than role, function, or vocation? Does it imply some kind of a ranking between the two? Calvin apparently thinks so, for he soon adds, "The obligation of both sexes is mutual, and on this condition is the woman assigned as a help to the man, that he may fill the place of her head and leader."[10] Notice what Calvin has done. The terms to express man's role and position in relationship to the woman were not derived from something in the Genesis account. Neither were they deduced from the woman's assignment, as though they formed some kind of obvious counterpart to the woman's role. The

8. *Comm.* on Gen. 2:18.          10. Ibid.

9. Ibid.

counterpart to being the helper would be the one who needs some help, or maybe, in light of the context of the man's solitude, the lonely one who needs some companionship. In finding man's role to be the head, Calvin has imported a thought from elsewhere. Paul in Ephesians 5:23 calls the man the head of the woman. But the idea of headship is not specific in the Genesis materials. Neither is the idea of leader. To be created for the role of a help does not thereby constitute the one who is helped as the leader—at least not in the Biblical use of terms. The Lord made Eve to be an '*ezer* (Hebrew) to Adam. In Psalms it is very often the Lord who is called man's '*ezer*.[11] Man does not suddenly become the Lord's leader when the Lord becomes his help.

Where is Calvin getting the ideas of headship and leadership from? Is he not reading the account in terms of what Paul saw woman's role to be, or else in terms of what the woman's role would become as a curse for her sin? Then her husband would rule over her (Gen. 3:16). Calvin has not shown that there is some kind of order of rank or position intrinsic in their very creation that constitutes the man as leader, governor, or ruler. Thus, it becomes a bit difficult to understand Calvin's earlier statements that nature so clearly teaches this.

Calvin undoubtedly has read this creation account much influenced by the allusions Paul makes to it in discussing woman's role in the church. Paul alludes in three ways to the relationships between man and woman that can be detected from their creation. Two ways are in Paul's statement to the Corinthians: "Man was not made from woman, but woman from man. Neither was man created for woman, but woman for man" (I Cor. 11:8, 9). The other allusion is in his letter to Timothy: "Adam was formed first, then Eve" (I Tim. 2:13). Paul introduced each of these statements with the conjunction "for." In each case they enter Paul's line of argumentation as a means of substantiating the advice or instruction he had just given about what is proper for woman. Let us notice how Calvin learns things about woman's created role by way of these Pauline passages.

In I Timothy 2:13 Paul says, "For Adam was formed first, then Eve." It is a simple statement about temporal sequence, made to substantiate certain prohibitions regarding women's activities. Calvin affirms confidently by way of commentary: "Thus he teaches that, even if the human race had remained in its original integrity, the true order of nature prescribed by God lays it down that woman should be subject to man." This is rather bold in view of the fact that Paul simply made reference to the man preceding the woman in

11. E.g., Ps. 33:20; 70:5; 115:9, 10, 11; 121:2; 124:8; 146:6.

time. Calvin wavers for a moment: "Still, Paul's argument, that woman is subject because she was created second, does not seem to be very strong, for John the Baptist went before Christ in time and yet was far inferior to Him." However, Calvin immediately regains his confidence:

> But Paul, although he does not explain all the circumstances related by Moses in Genesis, nevertheless intended that his readers should take them into account. The teaching of Moses is that woman was created later to be a kind of appendage to the man on the express condition that she should be ready to obey him.[12]

One wishes at this point he could cross-examine Calvin to find out what those "circumstances related by Moses in Genesis" were which would make clear Eve's position of obedience to Adam already at her creation. Calvin has not supplied us this information. As we just noticed, it is not there in Genesis, even though Calvin thought he found it there. When Calvin goes on to refer to Eve as "a lesser helpmeet *(adiumentum inferius)*,"[13] he is really coloring the Biblical materials with his own interpretation. Where did he learn that the help was "lesser" *(inferius)*? He would not find it necessary to speak that way about the Lord being man's help. Calvin's preconceived notions about woman's status and role are showing through.

Calvin clearly does not help us understand why or how the statement in I Timothy 2:13 about the temporal sequence of creation serves as substantiation for certain prohibitions placed on women. The Genesis materials simply do not imply such prohibitions. Paul, however, appears to understand the Genesis material as though it did offer the needed substantiation. He certainly is using his reference here to the Genesis account in that way. How does Paul come to use Genesis in a way which goes beyond Genesis? How regulatory for the church of all ages is this way of using Scripture and the interpretations it reflects? These are the kinds of hermeneutical questions which modern interpreters wrestle with. Such questions had not occurred to Calvin—at least not at this spot. Calvin was willing to read Genesis importing Pauline terms into it, and then use the Genesis so read to show that Paul's allusions to Genesis were indeed valid and do substantiate Paul's prohibitions to women. The reasoning is a bit circular. There is a problem in Paul which Calvin has not confronted.

In I Corinthians 11:8, 9 we again find Paul appealing to the creation situation to substantiate his counsel on women's behavior: "For man was not made from woman, but woman from man. Neither was

12. *Comm.* on I Tim. 2:13.  13. Ibid.

man created for woman but woman for man." Here it is not simply the matter of temporal sequence as in I Timothy 2:13. Now it is the matter of origination—from the man; and of purpose—for the man. Calvin finds the matter of origination indicative of women's role of subjection:

> Since the man preceded, and the woman came from him, is it not reasonable that she be thought of as a part and an accessory, and that she not push herself into first place? Does a branch seek to have greater prominence than the root or the trunk of the tree? A branch has emerged from the trunk. Does the branch vaunt itself as if the opposite were the case? And what is all this saying? The woman is like a branch which came from the man, for she was taken from his substance, as we know. It is true that God did this in order to recommend to us the union which we ought to have with one another, for He could easily have created Eve from the dust of the ground, as He did Adam. Instead he decided to take a rib from the man in order that the man might never be able to consider the woman as something wholly different. Rather we must recognize that this has united us as if we were one body, and that we can not be separated, except by a division contrary to God's will. This was God's concern here. But, be that as it may, he forever established the man above the woman.[14]

Interestingly, Calvin notes that the main point in connection with the woman's being taken from the man is the point of their close union to each other. Adam remarks immediately, "This at last is bone of my bone and flesh of my flesh" (Gen. 2:23), and the Genesis account comments on a man and his wife becoming one flesh (v. 24). Calvin had caught the point of the Genesis account. But this was not the point he needed at the moment. With a "be that as it may (*quoi qu'il en soit*)," he goes on simply to assert that such an origination for the woman forever establishes her in the position of subjection to the man. This is a conclusion which does not seem inevitably to follow. Is a king always subject to the queen-mother who bore him, or Jesus of Nazareth forever subject to His mother? Is Adam inferior or somehow subject to the dust of the ground from which he was made? Once again, Calvin is trying to explain Paul, without making it clear that Paul's point is simply not clear from the Genesis materials. It again raises the question of whether Paul is reading Genesis in a certain way not directly derived from Genesis itself.

In the same Corinthian passage Paul points out that the woman was made *for* the man, and not vice versa. The allusion is clearly to the Genesis statement, "It is not good that the man should be alone;

14. Sermon on I Cor. 11:4-10 (*C.O.*, 49:728-29).

I will make him a helper" (Gen. 2:18). The reason or design of the woman's creation was to overcome the loneliness of the man. Once again Calvin finds woman's subjection to man confirmed: "The woman has been created for the sake of the man, and therefore she is subject to him, as a finished article depends on what goes to its making."[15] In this case perhaps the idea of subjection lies a bit nearer the surface than in the previous references to temporal sequence and origination of substance. Calvin reasons that if woman is to fulfill some lack in man and was created specifically with an eye to functioning as his complement and helper, this indicates her role of subjection to him. This does seem to follow, but one must be careful indeed as to the conclusions one draws from this. Subjection need carry no overtones of inferiority whatever. Remember Paul's statement about Jesus Christ in II Corinthians 8:9: "Though he was rich, yet for your sake he became poor." Christ entered earthly life for our sake *(di' humas)*; the woman was brought into earthly life for the man's sake *(dia ton andra)*. The expressions are exactly parallel, but who would dare to conclude there is inferiority in both instances? Biblical subjection after the pattern of Christ is precisely that subjection which carries no notions of inferiority. In fact, Biblical rulership after the pattern of Christ is precisely the subjection unto service: "Whoever would be great among you must be your servant, and whoever would be first among you must be slave of all" (Mark 10:43, 44).

Hence, whatever is meant by the woman's being "for the man" would have to refer to her peculiar form of service or subjection, and not to the fact that she alone, as distinct from the man, has the role of service or subjection. Calvin does not seem to be reading this passage in this way, when in his sermon on it he says that women, both married and unmarried, are to acknowledge "that men hold a superior station and that they must be the rulers."[16] It sounds very much as if Calvin is giving to men the role about which Jesus said, "It shall not be so among you," namely, the Gentile way of lording it over others and exercising authority over them (cf. Mark 10:42, 43). At least we must conclude that Calvin has not made it clear why woman's being made for the man somehow substantiates Paul's point that women ought to wear a head covering as a sign of man's authority over them. Calvin sees something in Paul's

15. *Comm.* on I Cor. 11:8, 9. (The latter part of the sentence here is none too clear. Calvin himself stated the thought more fully in his French version of the commentary, which would translate thus: "as a work fitted for some design is inferior to its cause and the design for which it is made.")

16. Sermon on I Cor. 11:4-10 (*C.O.*, 49:730).

allusion to Genesis that isn't in Genesis. Whether Paul saw it there also is difficult to determine with certainty; but in light of his other allusions to the Genesis situation, one might suspect that he did.

We have now reviewed Calvin's exposition of the Genesis account of woman's creation and of the three ways Paul made allusion to this creation of woman in his writings. Calvin already in Genesis was reading it through the eyes of what he learned from the Pauline material. At each juncture Calvin was finding clear evidence for a unique subjection of the woman to the man—not the general Christian command of "Be subject one to another" (Eph. 5:21) but a subjection which is the woman's place and role, and not the man's. For Calvin the man is not subject to the woman—such would be an upsetting of the created order. The man is head, leader, ruler; he holds a superior station. The woman is to serve him, obey him, and be his lesser help. Calvin is confident that this is the very order of creation. He hasn't noted how little the creation account itself supports him in this. Nor has he asked whether Paul's allusions really interpret and derive from the creation materials or whether Paul's view represents some kind of an elaboration beyond the creation account itself. In short, it is not clear that Calvin's confidence about having information on the creation order regarding woman's station is well founded.

We must note one more thing before leaving Calvin's views on woman's created status. Calvin is sure that woman's subjection applies more broadly than just within marriage. These created relationships apply to men as males and to women as females. He makes this abundantly clear in his sermon on I Corinthians 11:4-10:

> Paul is not speaking here of individual persons, nor of an individual household. Rather he divides the human race into two parts.... Thus there is the male and the female. I say this for the benefit of any unmarried man, lest he at any time abandon his privilege by nature, namely, that he is the head. Of whom? Of women, for we must not pay attention to this only within a household, but within the whole order that God has established in this world. By the same token, a widow or a young girl who is not yet married must not abandon that position of subjection of which St. Paul speaks. Why? Because the subjection applies to the whole feminine sex, as I have said. And so we see the absurdity of those who explain this passage from St. Paul as if it made mention only of married women. For as I have already said, this passage is not speaking of the individual person in particular, but of the whole sex inclusively.[17]

Calvin states the matter just as clearly and just as forcefully in his commentary:

17. Ibid., p. 724.

Someone asks if Paul is speaking of married women only. It
is true that some restrict what Paul teaches here to married
women, because subjection to the authority of a husband does
not apply in the case of virgins. But these people are only showing their ignorance; for Paul looks higher, viz. to the eternal
law of God, which has made the female sex subject to the authority of men. Therefore all women are born to submit to the pre-
eminence of the male sex.[18]

Calvin recognizes that such teaching may not be too pleasing to
the ears of some women. He finds that he can do little more by way
of answer than point out that this is simply the good will and pleasure
of God for women:

Surely we can not be, but too too rude and savage, if we can
not receive that, as good and reasonable, which we know pleases
God. Can the woman have occasion here to be resentful and
complain, seeing that she sees that her Creator has made her in
subjection under the power of her husband? Shall the pot complain against the potter? What is it that either man or woman
has? Is it for them to come and lift up themselves against God,
as though he has not treated them well? So then, there is no
better reason than that which St. Paul brings to make women to
be subject, namely, that they have to mark that their condition
can not be other, neither ought to be, than that which God has
given them. Wherefore? For seeing they hold their life from him,
it is good reason that he have all power to rule them as he wills.
And as God made man of his free goodness, so has he given him
the superiority which he has above the woman: and on the contrary side, it pleased him that the woman should be in subjection:
therefore they must be content with it. If the woman ask, "Why
should men have such pre-eminence?" It pleased God that it
should be so: and we can allege no desert, why God preferred
us before women.[19]

The words sound harsh to our modern ears. But Calvin goes on in
the same sermon to remind his hearers that the situation he has been
talking about is still Paradise:

Yet notwithstanding we must often remember this, and women
must know this, that of a truth, if man and woman had remained
in their first uprightness, man would have had this pre-eminence
even to the end, namely, that women would have been subject
to men: not to serve them as by constraint and force, but they
would have been so established, that they would have been very
well content and glad of their state.[20]

It is surprising to find Calvin so confident of the fact that subjection applies to the woman as female, not just to the woman as wife.

18. *Comm.* on I Cor. 11:10.

19. Sermon on I Tim. 2:12-14 (*Trans. L.T.,* pp. 214-15).

20. Ibid., p. 219.

The Genesis account surely gives him no clues here. The relationship which is there pictured is entirely in the context of Adam and Eve as husband and wife. Calvin himself points out how central to the whole account of the woman's creation was the thought of the unity within the marriage relationship. It is quite beyond the purview of the Genesis account what a woman's relationship to a man other than her husband might be. Could Calvin ever agree that she was appointed helper to that man in the same way as to her husband? Yet Calvin is sure that he has knowledge of the eternal law of God that all women are subject to all men. Calvin learned this from the way he found Paul making references to the creation of women. The passage in I Timothy 2 does seem clearly to speak of women in general. The I Corinthians 11 and 14 passages are less clear, and may indeed refer either to the husband-wife relationship or the man-woman relationship. Calvin's very dogmatic statements on this score are hardly appropriate. Here is another facet of Calvin's clear views about the creation order, which is by no means as clear as Calvin thought it was.

This brings us to the second feature of the early Genesis situation which determined woman's place of subjection to man. Calvin, following Paul, has been at pains to root the whole matter in the created structure. Paul at one place adds a further reason for his prohibitions placed upon women: "And Adam was not deceived, but the woman was deceived and became the transgressor" (I Tim. 2:14). Calvin immediately faces the seeming contradiction here, that to root woman's subjection in the Fall implies that she was not subject before the Fall. Calvin explains:

> My answer is that there is no reason why obedience should not have been her natural condition from the beginning, while servitude was a later consequence resulting from her sin, so that the subjection became less voluntary than it had been before.[21]

Paul's reference to woman's subjection being related to the Fall immediately brings to mind part of the curse placed on the woman after the Fall: "Your desire shall be for your husband and he shall rule over you" (Gen. 3:16). But Paul chose a strange way to bring this Genesis thought to our minds. Paul said, "Adam was not deceived, but the woman was deceived and became a transgressor" (I Tim. 2:14). Calvin is not pleased to stick literally with Paul here. Calvin notes that some make a point of this:

21. *Comm.* on I Tim. 2:14. Cf. the explanations along the same lines in *Comm.* on Gen. 3:16, and Sermon on Eph. 5:22-26 (John Calvin, *Sermons on the Epistle to the Ephesians* [Edinburgh: Banner of Truth Trust, 1973], p. 567. Henceforth this latter translation is referred to as *Banner of Truth Ed.*).

Some have found in this passage justification for the view that
Adam did not fall by his own error, but was only overcome by
the allurements of his wife. They think that only the woman was
deceived by the craftiness of the serpent into believing that she
and her husband would be as gods.[22]

One must agree that Paul certainly does seem to say that. But Calvin
is able to find an explanation for Paul's strange words. He goes to
the Genesis account and shows that it will not support what Paul's
words literally seem to imply. Calvin says, "It is easy to refute this
view, for, if Adam had not believed Satan's lie, God would not have
reproached him by saying, 'Behold, Adam is like one of us' (Gen.
3:22)."[23]

To make his point Calvin might also have appealed to the fact that
the temptation story in Genesis says explicitly that Adam was there
during Eve's temptation: "She took of its fruit and ate; and she gave
some to her husband *with her* [Hebrew *'immah*], and he ate" (Gen.
3:6).[24] At any rate, Calvin is here interpreting Paul's words not for
what Paul literally said, but by way of what we learn from the Genesis
accounts. This is an interesting switch on Calvin's part, for we noted
in his interpretation of the previous phrase about Adam being formed
first and then Eve, that Calvin was working in just the opposite direction—interpreting Genesis not for what is literally there but through
the eyes of Paul.[25] Again the questions are appropriate as to what
view of the Genesis materials Paul is reflecting here in the Timothy
epistle. But again we note that Calvin was not struggling with such
hermeneutical questions. He was busy harmonizing Paul and Genesis by affirming one to the silencing of the other and switching directions to suit his convenience. Calvin ended up with a very clear-cut
position on woman's subjection to man by both creation and the Fall.
But later the hermeneutical questions would arise to haunt his clear-
cut position.

Women are subject to men by creation. But sin has now aggravated
that relationship. Sin has also had its peculiar ways of affecting
women. Calvin does not tire of lowering his sermonic guns against
the specific vices of women when Paul gives him an occasion to do

22. *Comm.* on I Tim. 2:14.

23. Ibid.

24. The RSV and the NEB strangely leave out "with her." The New Jerusalem Bible
says it fully: "her husband, who was with her."

25. One can appreciate why Calvin hastened to go in this direction and to affirm
Adam's full and immediate responsibility at the time of the Fall. The whole doctrine
of Adam as the source of original sin is threatened by allowing very much substance
to Paul's words, "Adam was not deceived, but the woman was deceived and became
a transgressor."

so. There is the problem of clothes. Vanity and wantonness readily raise their ugly heads in the excessive concern and eagerness about dress—"a fault to which women are almost always prone."[26] He finds women more prone to hypocrisy in their religious devotions than men.[27] He sees talkativeness to be a peculiar plague of women:

> Talkativeness is a disease among woman and old age usually makes it worse. In addition to this, women are never satisfied with their talking till they become prattlers and scandalmongers attacking everybody's reputation. The result is that older women by their slanderous garrulity, as by a lighted torch, often set many homes on fire. Many are also given to drinking and with all modesty and gravity forgotten they display a quite indecent wantonness.[28]

Such a sad state of affairs is promoted by women leaving their natural domain, the home. When not busy in the home, they begin to run from one place to another; and this only develops the vices of idleness, curiosity, and talkativeness.[29] And during his day it seemed to Calvin that society was ready to come apart at the seams through women's provocative behavior:

> Now therefore let us note well what St. Paul tells us here. For women have been allowed for a long time to become increasingly audacious. And besides, speech apart, there are very provocative clothes, so that it is very hard to discern whether they are men or women. They appear in new dresses and trinkets, so that every day some new disguise is seen. They are decked in peacock-tail fashion, so that a man cannot pass within three feet of them without feeling, as it were, a windmill sail swirling by him. Then too ribald songs are a part of their behavior.[30]

Women however are not as blamable as men. In his sermonizing on good deeds as "befitting women who profess religion" (I Tim. 2:10), Calvin proposes:

> True it is, that this belongs both to men and women: but let us mark, that when St. Paul speaks here of women, he binds men much more to make such declaration of their faith: for if there were any excuse to be had, no doubt it belongs to women rather than to men, because of their infirmity. And indeed, these poor creatures are to be borne withal.
> But if the case stand so, that women, if they show not indeed that they are duly instructed in the word of God, and their life

26. *Comm.* on I Tim. 2:9.

27. Sermon on II Tim. 3:6, 7 (*Trans. L.T.*, p. 886).

28. *Comm.* on Titus 2:3.

29. *Comm.* on I Tim. 5:13.

30. Sermon on Eph. 5:3-5 (*Banner of Truth Ed.*, p. 497).

be not answerable to it, cannot excuse themselves, and the Holy
Ghost condemns them here, what shall men do? Do they not
deserve to be doubly condemned?[31]

The words which we have been quoting from Calvin have been
rather harsh and demeaning toward women. But Calvin had more
kindly and more hopeful words about them also. His discussions of
the relationships within marriage sometimes bring this out. Marriage
will always be the chief way in which the headship of man and the
subjection of woman come to expression. However, there is no reason for this to be a harsh or demeaning role for the woman, at least not
for the Christians. In marriage the two very truly become one. The
Paradise situation proclaimed it (Gen. 2:24). Long after Paradise
Calvin finds the prophet Malachi still thinking the same way in his
rhetorical question, "Has not God made one?" (Mal. 2:15).

> [In Genesis] after having said that man was created, [Moses]
> adds by way of explanation, that man, both male and female,
> was created. Hence when he speaks of man, the male makes as
> it were one-half and the female the other.... As men were
> created that everyone should have his own wife, I say, that
> husband and wife make but one whole man. This then is the
> reason why the Prophet [Malachi] says, that one man was made
> by God; for he united the man to the woman, and intended that
> they be partners, so to speak, under one yoke.[32]

The marriage union as it existed in creation was beautiful.

> If the integrity of man had remained to this day, ... the sweetest
> harmony would reign in marriage; because the husband would
> look up with reverence to God; the woman in this would be a
> faithful assistant to him; and both, with one consent, would cul-
> tivate a holy as well as a friendly and peaceful intercourse.[33]

The wife is not the only one who must assume obligations. "It is
also the part of men to consider what they owe in return to the other
half of their kind, for the obligation of both sexes is mutual."[34] Or
again:

> The male sex has a superiority over the female, but on this con-
> dition, that they ought to be bound together in mutual good will;
> for the one cannot get on without the other.... Let them then
> be tied to each other by this bond of mutual service.[35]

Calvin never relents on asserting the man's right and duty to take
first place in the control of the household and its affairs. "For in

31. Sermon on I Tim. 2:9-11 (*Trans. L.T.,* p. 200).

32. *Comm.* on Mal. 2:15.

33. *Comm.* on Gen. 2:18.

34. Ibid.

35. *Comm.* on I Cor. 11:11.

his own home the father of the family is like a king. Therefore he reflects the glory of God, because of the control which is in his hands."[36] But there is no room for despotic kingship:

> Let the husbands think on their duty.... They are advanced to that honour of superiority on a certain condition, namely, that they should not be cruel towards their wives, or think all things that they please to be permissible and lawful, for their authority should rather be a companionship than a kingship. For there is no question that the husband is not the wife's head to oppress her or to make no account of her. But let him understand that the authority he has puts him so much the more under obligation to her. For seeing he is the head, he must needs have discretion in himself to guide his wife and his household. And what is the way to bring that to pass but to use kindness and mildness, and discreetly to support his wife in respect of the frailty which he knows to be in her, even as St. Peter warns us (I Pet. 3:7). You see then that husbands must require obedience from their wives while at the same time they themselves must also do their own duty; and let them consider that they will not be upheld before God, if they give occasion to their wives to rise against them.[37]

However, when all does not go well in marriage, the role of subjection remains the wife's duty. The Register of the Company of Pastors of Geneva contains some heart-rending letters from women who were being cruelly mistreated by their husbands. Calvin shows true sympathy in his answers, but his counsel is that they must remain faithful to their husbands. Only when their lives are in danger may they take escape.[38] A sermon one time became very gloomy over the matter of woman's lot: "Let women on their part willingly submit themselves to the pains they have in housewifery, and let them think thus: See, God is chastizing me for the pride that was in the first woman."[39] The thought is neither very comforting nor very helpful. The role of subjection can be a very painful one in a world fallen into sin.

We have now heard Calvin speaking from quite a few angles on woman's role of subjection. But this is not Calvin's only theme on the subject of women. He is free and open to proclaim their equality also. The equality of woman with man shows itself at several points. Most basic is that of humanness. The woman is as much a human being as the man. This was clear even from God's first decision to bring her into being. Calvin finds considerable significance in the fact that God decided to make the man "a help *meet for him*" (Gen.

---

36. *Comm.* on I Cor. 11:4.

37. Sermon on Eph. 5:22-26 (*Banner of Truth Ed.*, pp. 569-70).

38. *The Register of the Company of Pastors of Geneva in the Time of Calvin*, ed. Philip E. Hughes (Grand Rapids: Eerdmans, 1966), pp. 193-98, 344-45.

39. Sermon on I Tim. 2:12-14 (*Trans. L.T.*, pp. 218-19).

2:18). He notes that the Hebrew language here used the particle *caph,* and points out that this particle expresses the note of similitude. He compliments some Greek translators who in his estimation rendered the thought faithfully in Greek, adding, "For Moses intended to note some equality."[40] This small point looms large in Calvin's attention because it gives a clue to the true nature of human marriage. The woman is not a sex object: she was not provided for Adam because he had sexual lusts. She is "the inseparable associate of his life," and not merely "the companion of his bedroom."[41] When it is said that God created man male and female (Gen. 1:28), "in this manner Adam was taught to recognize himself in his wife, as in a mirror."[42] In humanity the man and the woman are equal.

Calvin underlines this point of basic equality in his discussions of man being made in the image of God. He insists that not only the male, but also the female, is the image of God: "Certainly it cannot be denied, that the woman also, though in a second degree, was created in the image of God; whence it follows, that what was said in the creation of the man belongs to the female sex."[43]

Paul in I Corinthians 11 seems to say the contrary. He proposed, "The head of every man is Christ, the head of every woman is her husband" (v. 3), and "[man] is the image and glory of God; but woman is the glory of man" (v. 7). Calvin is not the least bit shaken. He affirms Christ's headship of both men and women:

> To be a child of God, ruled by his Holy Spirit and a participant in inheriting the Kingdom of Heaven, to pray to God, to be baptized, to come to the Lord's Supper—in none of these things are we permitted to distinguish between males and females . . . . This is what we must note concerning Paul's words that the head of the man is Jesus Christ. He is very much the head of men and women in those things I have just mentioned.[44]

Calvin builds a more extensive case for women being the image of God than he does for them being under Christ's headship. Regarding the image, he appeals not only to the statement at creation (Gen. 1:27) but also to the fact that women are included in the renewal of the image in Christ. In his sermon on Paul's statement on man being the image and glory of God, he explains:

> This also certainly has to apply to all women. If they are not in the church, they have no hope of the promised salvation. But

40. *Comm.* on Gen. 2:18.
41. Ibid.
42. *Comm.* on Gen. 2:21.
43. *Comm.* on Gen. 2:18.
44. Sermon on I Cor. 11:2, 3 (*C.O.,* 49:718-19).

we know that there is this sure foundation: God has sent Jesus Christ, who has gathered us to himself in such a way that the image of God which had been destroyed through Adam's sin is restored. Certainly this image belongs to women just as much as to men. Therefore, St. Paul, when he writes to the Ephesians about the hope of salvation, does not speak exclusively to the men. He does not select one sex to the exclusion of the other. Rather he calls without distinction, the men as much as the women, to become involved in becoming like him who created them, even (to use Paul's words) in all holiness. Now can it be required only of men that they develop this holiness, while women live any way they please? Obviously, the opposite is the case.[45]

Calvin does not deny, however, that Paul in I Corinthians 11 was making a distinction between men and women as to headship and as to being an image-bearer. "The statement in which man alone is called by Paul 'the image and glory of God' (I Cor. 11:7, Vg.) and the woman excluded from this place of honor is clearly restricted, as the context shows, to the political order."[46] Men and women are equally image-bearers and both have Christ as their head with regard to the kingdom of God or the spiritual order of things. But there is another order in which we human beings presently live: "the government and order of the present life,"[47] or "the conjugal order *(ad ordinem coniugalem)* . . . [which] has to do with this present life, and, on the other hand has nothing to do with conscience,"[48] or "the external government."[49] Women thus are the image of God spiritually, but not as to their role in this present earthly order. In the present earthly order and its relationships they do not have the man's prerogatives of being God's image-bearer. This situation for women is not the result of the Fall. It is woman's created place, for the external order of this present life was established at creation. Thus, when Genesis tells us that God created man in His image, the image applying to both male and female (Gen. 1:27), Calvin according to his explanation must be diligent always to remind himself that for the woman this image of God is only regarding the spiritual realm, whereas for the man it is something more. Also when Christians are being restored through Christ to God's image, Calvin must propose that this restored image applies to more areas for the man than it does for the

45. Sermon on I Cor. 11:4-10 *(C.O.,* 49:726).

46. *Inst.,* I.xv.4.

47. Sermon on I. Cor. 11:2, 3 *(C.O.,* 49:720): "la police et l'ordre qui y est de la vie présente."

48. *Comm.* on I Cor. 11:7.

49. Sermon on I Cor. 11:4-10 *(C.O.,* 49:727): "la police extérieure."

woman. One has the uneasy feeling that in trying to do justice to Paul, Calvin is willing to give up quite a bit of the meaning of his earlier affirmation that the woman is created in God's image and restored to it through Christ. When woman at her very creation is not the image of God in the same full sense as the man is, we may question whether Calvin has really been fair to the Genesis account. He affirmed in straightforward terms the equality of man and woman as image-bearers; but when he removes this equality entirely from the earthly realm and its relationships, he is calling us to introduce a distinction into Genesis which simply is not there.

The distinction between the spiritual realm and the present earthly realm was introduced to try to do justice to Paul. But it is questionable whether Paul himself could have lived with it very well in regard to the restoration of the image through Christ. What is this growth in holiness which for the man constitutes a being restored to the image of God both spiritually and here in his earthly role, but for the woman means being restored only in spiritual things? Here is a discrepancy not easy to resolve, and it once again raises the question of whether there are not other ways than Calvin has found of accounting for why Paul expresses himself the way he does about man being God's image.

We have noted Calvin's affirmations of a basic equality between man and woman in the realms of their humanness and of bearing the image of God (at least in the spiritual sense). In some more practical areas of everyday life he also affirmed women's equality. Marriage for Calvin, as for the other Reformers, becomes again an honorable estate, no longer inferior to celibacy. This immediately works toward elevating woman's place and role. Although Calvin will insist on her being subject to her husband, there is a role within the family in which she approaches equal stature. Calvin says, "Authority is attributed as much to one parent as to the other . . . . God does not wish the father alone to rule the child but that the mother also have a share in the honor and preeminence."[50] The mother of the family became a very important person in the Reformation struggles, for through her role of spiritual leadership in the family and of instruction of her children, including the sons, she was setting the pattern for future generations. Calvin recognized the powerful role of mothers and urged their honor.

Also on the matter of divorce Calvin took a more egalitarian approach than was customary for his day. In commenting on Jesus' statements about husbands who divorce their wives (Matt. 19:9), Calvin is willing to make the same rule apply for wives:

50. Sermon on Deut. 21:18-21 (*C.O.*, 27:677).

But we must note that each party has a common and mutual right, just as their obligation of loyalty is mutual and equal. A man may hold the primacy in other things, but in bed he and his wife are equal, for he is not lord of his body. Therefore, if he commits adultery, he has defected from marriage and the wife is given freedom.[51]

Calvin sought to incorporate this outlook into the marriage legislation in Geneva. In the Marriage Ordinances of 1547, produced by the Geneva pastors with Calvin at their head, it is stated:

Although in ancient times the right of the wife was not equal with that of the husband where divorce was concerned, yet since, as the Apostle says, the obligation is mutual and reciprocal regarding the intercourse of the bed, and since in this the wife is no more subject to the husband than the husband to the wife, if a man is convicted of adultery and his wife demands to be separated from him, this shall be granted to her also, provided it proves impossible by good counsel to reconcile them to each other.[52]

It was not until 1561 that these ordinances were finally accepted by the City Council and incorporated in the Ecclesiastical Ordinances of 1561. Biéler finds this fairer divorce legislation promulgated by Calvin a prime example of how the spiritual liberty of the gospel can gradually affect the political structures, and can do so without imposing a moral tyranny on society.[53] There were at least some small steps being taken under Calvin's leadership to acknowledge new rights for women.

We have now listened to Calvin on the subject of the equality of men and women. He acknowledged it in a few limited areas: basic humanness, image of God (in the spiritual sense), authority and honor in the home, the right to divorce an adulterous mate. But when it comes to church affairs, either the worship service or the offices, Calvin finds no warrant for any kind of equal status. In Calvin's reading of Scripture Paul had been too clear on these things. Admonitions directed toward women might easily be enlarged to include men, but men's prerogatives are not for a moment to be accorded to women. Listen to Calvin preach on "Let women learn in silence with all subjection":

True it is, that men also, to speak generally, must receive this lesson as well as women: that is to say, to learn with all sub-

51. *Comm.* on Matt. 19:9.

52. Hughes, *Register,* pp. 77, 78.

53. André Biéler, *L'homme et la femme dans la morale calviniste* (Geneva: Labor et Fides, 1963), p. 73.

jection and quietness: for we are all God's scholars.... So then let us mark well, that if we wish to profit in God's school, men as well as women, we must have this subjection and peaceable spirit which we have spoken of. But... women must know that God puts them under yet another subjection, namely, that they are not to exercise the office of teaching, and it belongs not to them to meddle with it. And why so?... Let it be sufficient for them that it is the Holy Ghost that speaks here.[54]

The teaching office of the church is forbidden to women. Calvin finds Paul forbidding it in I Timothy 2:12, and he explains the rationale:

Paul is not taking from women their duty to instruct their family, but is only excluding them from the office of teaching *(a munere docendi)* which God has committed exclusively to men.... The reason that women are prevented from teaching is that it is not compatible with their status, which is to be subject to men, whereas to teach implies superior authority and status.... Women... by nature, (that is, by the ordinary law of God) are born to obey, for all wise men have always rejected *gunaikokratia,* the government of women, as an unnatural monstrosity. Thus for a woman to usurp the right to teach would be a sort of mingling of earth and heaven. Thus he bids them be silent and abide within the limits of their sex.[55]

If teaching is forbidden, so is baptizing. Calvin recognizes that the church had sometimes permitted women to baptize. But this was simply a departure from Christ's clear instruction: "Go, teach all nations, and baptize" (Matt. 28:19). Christ "ordained the same men as heralds of the gospel and ministers of baptism."[56]

In the whole of his writing, Calvin is marvelously consistent in his teaching on women and their role in society. Starting from the premise that women were created subject to men, he explains the various Biblical passages and preaches his sermons with full confidence that he represents the God-ordained and God-revealed order for life in this world. As Biéler observes, Calvin was *très conservateur* on these matters of women's emancipation. However, Biéler immediately adds, "although in principle he did not exclude the changes which a new age would be able to effect in the status of women."[57] Where is there a "principle" in Calvin's teaching which could lead to any changes away from the very rigid position he so consistently held? Let us turn now to this investigation.

54. Sermon on I Tim. 2:9-11 *(Trans L.T.,* pp. 210-11).

55. *Comm.* on I Tim. 2:12.

56. *Inst.,* IV.xv.22.

57. Biéler, *L'homme,* p. 80.

## Some open doors for modification

When Calvin turns to Paul's earliest discussion of the place and role of women in the church in I Corinthians 11, he notes that Paul praised the Corinthians for maintaining the traditions even as he had delivered them to Corinth. As Calvin understands Paul, the traditions here referred to are not the doctrinal matters, which are God-given, and to be neither added to nor changed.

> What then had [the traditions] to do with? The answer is, matters affecting order and polity. We know that each church is free to set up the form of polity that suits its circumstances, and is to its advantage, because the Lord has not given any specific directions about this. So it was that Paul, the first to lay the foundations of the church at Corinth, had given shape to it by means of good, sound directions *(institutis quoque piis et honestis)* so that everything might be done there decently and in order, as he enjoins in chapter 14.40.[58]

Calvin emphasizes the liberty which is applicable in this area of church practices:

> It is not that [Paul] has mixed anything of his own with the design of Christ. It is not that he takes upon himself the imposition of certain laws, and puts souls in bondage. It is not that he has set up a way of serving God as one sees in the Papacy. Nothing of all that. But he has given them some regulations which serve to maintain propriety, peace and concord among them.... Thus it is necessary... that from time to time one establishes various ordinances which are seen to be appropriate and which each one makes use of in his freedom. But in all this, there is no question of adding something to the doctrine of the faith nor of making some laws which put our souls in bondage.[59]

This was Calvin's introduction to Paul's chapter about women's role in the Corinthian church. The constantly recurring theme in Calvin here is *propriety, decorum, good order*.

After beginning with such a straightforward admission of freedom in the area of church government, Calvin is soon speaking in firmer tones:

> In order to prove that it is unbecoming for women to appear in a public gathering for worship with their heads uncovered, and, on the other hand, for men to pray or prophesy with their heads covered, Paul starts off with the arrangements which God has appointed [about Christ being the head of the man, and the man the head of the woman].[60]

58. *Comm.* on I Cor. 11:2.

59. Sermon on I Cor. 11:2, 3 (*C.O.*, 49:712).

60. *Comm.* on I Cor. 11:3.

Since Paul derives the rationale for his regulation about head covering in worship services from the divine mandate that the man is the head of the woman, Calvin finds the regulation to be not just in the realm of the appropriate but rather in the realm of the mandatory. Thus Calvin remarks, "We see that the order of nature is changed and perverted when someone does not govern himself as [Paul] has here shown."[61] If it is the very order of nature itself that underlies the propriety of this regulation about head covering, then this sounds like a very permanent regulation, not open to easy modification. It makes the regulation appear very much like a new law for all ages.

However, Calvin cannot maintain such a firm stance. In fact, before Calvin has completed his exposition of this Pauline passage, he will have come to an insight about Paul's regulations here which once again heavily underlines the church's freedom in these matters.

Paul's line of reasoning in this I Corinthians 11 passage about women is extraordinarily complex. His point is to insist that when women pray or prophesy, they should wear a covering on their heads as a symbol of their subjection to men. By the same token men ought not to cover their heads. The idea of a head covering suggests to Paul the idea that hair itself is a kind of head covering. Hence the idea of the appropriateness of men and women having a covering of hair also intrudes itself into this passage. As to men having their head covered with hair, Paul rhetorically asks: "Does not nature itself teach you that for a man to wear long hair is degrading to him?" (I Cor. 11:14). The thought of men wearing a covering of hair is as atrocious for Paul as if they were to wear a kerchief or veil.

Calvin sees something happening here in Paul's line of argumentation.

> Paul again sets *nature* before them as the teacher of what is proper. Now, he means by "natural" what was accepted by common consent and usage at that time, certainly as far as the Greeks were concerned. For long hair was not always regarded as a disgraceful thing in men. Historical works relate that long ago, i.e. in the earliest times, men wore long hair in every country.... But since the Greeks did not consider it very manly to have long hair, branding those who had it as effeminate, Paul considers that their custom, accepted in his own day, was in conformity with nature.[62]

Here is an open recognition by Calvin that our sensitivities to what is proper and what is shameful can be very much conditioned by the culture in which we have lived and the customs with which we have

61. Sermon on I Cor. 11:2, 3 (*C.O.*, 49:716).

62. *Comm.* on I Cor. 11:14.

become familiar. Paul's use of "nature" here, as Calvin finds he must interpret Paul, cannot refer to some divinely established structuration by God in His original creative activity. It rather must refer to God's providential leading as the thinking of various peoples is formed in various ways. In short, "nature" here means "custom" or "culture." But to appeal to custom immediately relativizes Paul's argument. Propriety and impropriety are sensitivities developed within a cultural setting. They are neither constant from place to place nor do they remain constant in the same place from time to time. Calvin explained this in both his commentary and sermon on this passage, reviewing some of the differing attitudes throughout history toward men wearing their hair long. It was clear to him that the shame of which Paul here spoke could not be felt universally. In fact, he pointed out to his audience how long hair for men was now customary in that day in both France and Germany.[63] Thus by Calvin's own admission the customs of Paul's day were affecting the way Paul argued his case with the Corinthians. Here is a most important insight on Calvin's part, one with far-reaching consequences in the interpretation of this and other passages.

In the verse prior to the appeal against men's long hair Paul had called the Corinthians to judge on another matter: "Judge for yourselves; is it proper for a woman to pray to God with her head uncovered?" (I Cor. 11:13). The appeal is to propriety *(prepon)* regarding women's conduct. But there is a propriety also for men in this matter of head covering: "A man ought not to cover his head" (v. 7). Calvin comments:

> We should not be so hide-bound by conscientious principles as to think that a teacher is doing anything wrong in wearing a skull-cap on his head, when he is speaking to the people from the pulpit. But all that Paul is after is that it may be made clear that the man is in authority, and that the woman is in subjection to him, and that is done when the man uncovers his head in the sight of the congregation, even if he puts his skull-cap on again afterwards so as not to catch cold. To sum up, the one guiding principle is *to prepon,* propriety; if that is preserved, Paul asks for no more.[64]

For Calvin the propriety of head covering and bareheadedness also is not universally applicable. The climate in which one lives may have something to do with what is appropriate. Calvin was not going to risk catching cold in the drafty northern European churches by sticking pedantically to Paul's expressed proprieties. Again he is relativizing the literal point, arguing in effect that propriety in this matter can be maintained in various ways.

63. Cf. Sermon on I Cor. 11:11-16 (*C.O.,* 49:743).    64. *Comm.* on I Cor. 11:4.

Calvin made the same kind of concessions for women regarding their head covering:

> These are no fixed and permanent sanctions by which we are bound, but outward rudiments for human weakness. Although not all of us need them, we all use them, for we are mutually bound, one to another, to nourish mutual love.... What? Does religion consist in a woman's shawl, so that it is unlawful for her to go out with a bare head? Is that decree of Paul's concerning silence so holy that it cannot be broken without great offense?... Nevertheless, the established custom of the region, or humanity itself and the rule of modesty, dictate what is to be done or avoided in these matters.[65]

Apparently there could be situations in society where it would be permitted for women to speak in the churches. Regarding Paul's judgment that it is shameful for a woman to speak in church (I Cor. 14:35), Calvin explains:

> But as he is discussing the external organization *(externa politia)* here, it is enough for his purpose to point out what is unseemly, so that the Corinthians might avoid it. However, the discerning reader should come to the decision, that the things which Paul is dealing with here, are indifferent, neither good nor bad; and that they are forbidden only because they work against seemliness and edification.[66]

Furthermore, Calvin acknowledged that the prohibitions of I Corinthians 14 against women speaking in church arise out of a particular problem in Corinth:

> It appears that the Corinthian church was also spoiled by this fault, that when they met together, there was a place for the chattering of women, or rather it was allowed great liberty. Paul accordingly *(ergo)* forbids them to speak in public, either by way of teaching or prophesying.[67]

The prohibitions arose out of the situation: "Paul accordingly *(ergo)* forbids." We must remember that Paul's prohibition of women speaking comes toward the end of his long discussion of the disorderliness in Corinth arising from the rivalry over spiritual gifts. Especially the gifts of tongue-speaking and prophesying had been occasions of contention. Calvin sees the prohibition as arising particularly from this situation. Calvin further suspected that it was a similar situation in Ephesus that brought forth Paul's prohibitions on women in I Timothy 2:11, 12.[68] Special problems occasioned the prohibitions.

65. *Inst.*, IV.x.31.

66. *Comm.* on I Cor. 14:34.

67. Ibid.

68. Sermon on I Tim. 2:9-11 (*Trans. L.T.,* p. 209).

The prohibition of women speaking is no universal injunction. Calvin maintains this even though Paul very shortly says: "What I am writing to you is a command of the Lord" (I Cor. 14:37). Calvin explains:

> If they are commandments of the Lord, then they are bound to be observed, and bind men's consciences; and yet they are administrative arrangements, and there is not the same compulsion for us to observe them. But all that Paul is saying is that he is laying down nothing but what is agreeable to the will of God. Further, God informed him of His counsel so that he might recommend that way of ordering outward things *(ordinem istum in rebus externis)* at Corinth and elsewhere, not that it might be an inviolable law, like those which deal with the spiritual worship of God, but a useful form for all the children of God, and one not at all to be ignored.[69]

The prohibitions are useful, not to be lightly dismissed, but as administrative arrangements not mandatory in all situations and times.

If rules on head coverings and on women keeping silence can be adjusted to fit the times and current notions of modesty, what about the matter of women showing leadership and taking the rule over men? Calvin used some of his customary strong language for what to him seemed absurd: "There is no doubt that wherever natural propriety itself has had its effect, women in all ages have been excluded from the control of public affairs. And common sense tells us that the rule of women is improper and defective."[70]

However, during Calvin's lifetime this "common sense" and "natural propriety" apparently were either being examined anew or wholly disregarded. In 1553 Mary Tudor became queen of England. Five years later Elizabeth I followed her to the throne. The next year the English parliament passed The Act of Supremacy, making the crown the "supreme governor" of the church. England was developing some new ideas of what could be tolerated in the name of propriety.

Calvin seemed to feel no embarrassment over Elizabeth's ascendance to the throne. Rather he took the occasion to dedicate to her the revised edition of his commentary on Isaiah, which had originally been dedicated to her half-brother Edward VI. In fact, Calvin wrote the dedication the very day of Elizabeth's coronation, seeing in her the hope of restoring Protestantism's fortunes in England. He expressed great hope for her reign. The queen at first rejected this homage from Calvin, associating him as the real source of the ideas expressed in the pamphlet published in Geneva by John Knox: *First*

69. *Comm.* on I Cor. 14:37.

70. *Comm.* on I Cor. 14:34.

*Blast Against the Monstrous Regiment [Rule] of Women.* In a letter to Elizabeth's secretary, William Cecil, Calvin sought to defend himself and set the record straight on his relationship to Knox's ideas:

> Two years ago, John Knox in a private conversation, asked my opinion respecting female government. I frankly answered that because it was a deviation from the primitive and established order of nature, it ought to be held as a judgment on man for his dereliction of his rights just like slavery—that nevertheless certain women had sometimes been so gifted that the singular blessing of God was conspicuous in them, and made it manifest that they had been raised up by the providence of God, either because he willed by such examples to condemn the supineness of men, or thus show more distinctly his own glory. I here instanced Huldah and Deborah. I added to the same effect that God promised by the mouth of Isaiah that queens should be the nursing mothers of the church, which clearly distinguished such persons from private women. Finally I added in conclusion, that since by custom, common consent, and long established usage, it had been admitted that kingdoms and principalities might be by hereditary right transmitted to women, it did not seem proper to me that this question should be mooted, not only because the thing was odious in itself, but because in my judgment it is not permitted to unsettle governments that have been set up by the peculiar providence of God.[71]

Calvin is once again acknowledging that Paul's prohibitions regarding women need not always be followed. "Custom, common consent, and long established usage" may point to another way; and Christians may feel comfortable honoring that other way. Women may sometimes have authority over men.

In view of the strong stance which Calvin took regarding women's subjection to men, there is little reason to expect any flexibility on his part in regard to women teaching in the church. However, even in this regard there are a couple of remarkable statements by Calvin. He judged that the prohibition of women speaking in the church applied to the regular and well-established church. "For a situation can arise where there is a need of such a kind as calls for a woman to speak. But Paul is confining himself to what is fitting in a properly organized congregation."[72] This is an interesting concession, and one wonders what such a concession does to the general principle. But there is another place where Calvin sees even wider possibilities that this prohibition of women speaking in the church may not always apply.

71. *Letters of John Calvin,* ed. Jules Bonnet (New York: Burt Franklin, 1972 [reprint of 1858 ed.]), IV:47.

72. *Comm.* on I Cor. 14:34.

Of the other kind [of ecclesiastical rules] are the hours set for
public prayers, sermons, and sacraments. At sermons there are
quiet and silence, appointed places, the singing together of
hymns, fixed days for the celebration of the Lord's Supper,
the fact that Paul forbids women to teach in the church (I Cor.
14:34), and the like....

But because [the Lord] did not will in outward discipline and
ceremonies to prescribe in detail what we ought to do (because
he foresaw that this depended upon the state of the times, and
he did not deem one form suitable for all ages), here we must
take refuge in those general rules which he has given, that whatever the necessity of the church will require for order and decorum should be tested against these. Lastly, because he has
taught nothing specifically, and because these things are not
necessary to salvation, and for the upbuilding of the church
ought to be variously accommodated to the customs of each
nation and age, it will be fitting (as the advantage of the church
will require) to change and abrogate traditional practices and to
establish new ones. Indeed, I admit that we ought not to charge
into innovation rashly, suddenly, for insufficient cause. But
love will best judge what may hurt or edify; and if we let love
be our guide, all will be safe.[73]

If love leads the way, and order and decorum are maintained, then
apparently women may teach in the church in the appropriate cultural settings. Calvin again shows his awareness that not all Biblical
commands or Biblical prohibitions were applicable across the board
at all times and in all situations. Cultural and personal factors play a
large role in determining how Christians and the church come to
give expression to their Christian faith in a given setting. Calvin was
alert to this fact and wisely counseled against too rigid and inflexible
a church order.

Calvin puts great store by decorum and propriety in these matters
of church government. "To sum up, the one guiding principle is *to
prepon,* propriety; if that is preserved, Paul asks for no more."[74]
But propriety, being so linked to cultural conditioning, is not in itself
a very adequate or stable guide. Surely it is important always to urge
the influence of Christianity and the power of the gospel on our sense
of propriety. In another place Calvin proposes: "The established
custom of the region, or humanity itself and the rule of modesty, dictate what is to be done or avoided in these matters [of woman's head
covering, silence in church, burial practices]."[75] Once again the
tests are rather general, and not necessarily reflective of Christian influences. Perhaps the "humanity" test comes the closest: do what is
the most humane. Calvin has his most uniquely Christian advice in

73. *Inst.,* IV.x.29, 30.      75. *Inst.,* IV.x.31.
74. *Comm.* on I Cor. 11:4.

this statement: "Love will best judge what may hurt or edify; and if we let love be our guide, all will be safe."[76] But love too must be that Christian love called forth by God's redemptive love toward us. And even that Christian love must sometimes agonize as to what really is the way of Christian love in a certain matter. All these tests—propriety, humaneness, love—suggest that Calvin can indeed conceive of other possibilities for women than the place and role he so consistently assigned them in his day. As Wendel puts it, "Calvin does not . . . advocate any servile imitation of the institutions of the primitive church."[77] Biéler's observation is confirmed: "In principle [Calvin] did not exclude the changes which a new age would effect in the status of women."[78]

### Some troublesome areas in Calvin's scheme

Calvin, however, was not really open to pursuing the implications of the line of thought we have just discovered in him. He admitted that some of Paul's prohibitions were culturally conditioned. He acknowledged that the local situation sometimes occasioned the prohibition. He found that matters of church regulation and of how Christians give expression to their new faith must remain open and free to the changing cultures and times. Propriety, humaneness, love must be observed. But so must the created order of things. And suddenly all thoughts of flexibility, adjustment, adaptation to the times vanish into thin air. The created order is fixed and abiding; it does not change while the earth lasts. Calvin's report of his conversation with John Knox is ever so typical of his approach. The starting point for talking about female government is to note: "It [is] a deviation from the primitive and established order of nature."[79] Any development of the subject of woman must acknowledge her created place and rank. Such an approach had its effect on the interpretation of certain passages and sometimes called for special explanations of the meaning of a text, lest the simple wording of the text lead us to wrong ideas of what the passage was saying.

Galatians 3:28 is a case in point. In this section of his Galatian letter Paul had been giving expression to the marvelous thing that has happened to us by being freed from the law and being made sons of God through faith. He says that Christians "have put on Christ"

76. *Inst.,* IV.x.30.

77. François Wendel, *Calvin, The Origins and Development of His Religious Thought* (New York: Harper and Row, 1963), p. 302.

78. Biéler, *L'homme,* p. 80.

79. Bonnet, *Letters of Calvin,* IV:47.

(v. 27). "There is neither Jew nor Greek, there is neither slave nor free, there is neither male nor female; for you are all one in Christ Jesus" (Gal. 3:28). Calvin captures the heart of Paul's meaning when he comments:

> Whatever other differences there may be, the one Christ suffices to unite them all. Therefore he says, *Ye are one,* and means by this that the distinction is now removed. His object is to show that the grace of adoption and the hope of salvation do not depend on the law but are contained in Christ alone. The one Christ therefore is all.[80]

Calvin's remarks in his commentary on this verse are very brief. The distinction has been removed; no qualifications are added. His sermon makes it much clearer that Calvin finds this new oneness in Christ to be applicable only to a certain limited realm, namely, the spiritual realm. It does not apply to present relationships in this world:

> St. Paul declares that we must be united to Christ in such a way that no one vaunts himself as being more worthy than others. Rather we must recognize that we have everything by the pure grace of God. Men both great and small ought to school themselves together in that outlook. They ought to confess with united voice that they have all they could wish for in our Lord Jesus Christ. They ought to renounce all the fictions and fantasies which are able to seize their minds. However, St. Paul does not mean that in regard to the established order of this world there is no diversity of rank. We know that there are servants and masters; there are magistrates and subjects; in the home there is the man who is head and the woman who must be subject to him. We know then that this established order is inviolable and that our Lord Jesus Christ did not come into the world to cause such confusion that everything which God his Father had established would be abolished.[81]

Does Calvin reflect the real breadth of freedom which Paul here saw? Does putting on Christ and being in Christ not also affect the way we relate ourselves to each other already here in this present world? The early church agonized over this question in terms of the Jew-Greek problem. Later ages of Christians finally developed an uneasy conscience over the slavery question. Calvin assures us there is no occasion for uneasiness in Christians perpetuating woman's subjection to man in this world and in the church, because here there is a divinely ordained relationship involved. Calvin was probably confident that in view of the way Paul had spoken about women in

---

80. *Comm.* on Gal. 3:28.

81. *Sermon on Gal. 3:26-29 (C.O.,* 50:567-68). Cf. also *Comm.* on I Cor. 11:3: "[Paul in Gal. 3:28] is speaking about the spiritual Kingdom of Christ."

other passages, Paul would support him on woman's subjection. And yet in view of the broad freedom which Paul is preaching in this passage and the oneness which he is here so enthusiastically acclaiming, Calvin's exclusion of the present earthly order as an arena to live in freedom and oneness sounds a bit contrived and artificial. Calvin himself sometimes forgets to make the appropriate distinctions. In speaking about the priesthood of all believers Calvin notes Paul's instruction: "If a revelation is made to another sitting by, let the first be silent" (I Cor. 14:30). Calvin explains: "From this it is clear that every member of the church is charged with the responsibility of public edification according to the measures of his grace, provided he perform it decently and in order."[82] Every member? He forgets momentarily that the responsibility for public edification in church belongs only to half of the membership—the men. Or is it that for the moment the thought has surfaced in Calvin that there is no male and female in Christ when Christians are busy edifying each other in the worship services? Calvin's reading of the Biblical materials on women meant he had to keep some definite reins on the freedom that makes for no male and female in Christ.

Calvin has trouble in another spot with the marvelous things that come with Christ. In his sermon on Pentecost Peter saw the coming of the Holy Spirit as the fulfillment of Joel's prophecy: "I will pour out my Spirit upon all flesh, and your sons and your daughters shall prophesy" (Acts 2:17; cf. Joel 2:28). In his lectures on Joel, Calvin immediately notes that the prophet does not exclude women. Calvin therefore clarifies the matter:

> The Prophet [Joel] speaks not here of the public office of teaching, for he calls those Prophets who had not been called to teach, but who were endued with so much of the light of truth, that they might be compared with the Prophets; and certainly the knowledge which flourished in the primitive Church was such, that the meanest were in many respects equal to the ancient Prophets.... Faith then after the coming of Christ, if rightly estimated according to its value, far excels the gift of prophecy. And so the Prophet here, not without reason, dignifies with so honorable a name those who were private men, and to whom was not intrusted the office of teaching among the people, but who were only illuminated; for their light was much superior to the gift of prophecy in many of those who lived under the law.[83]

What has Calvin done here? He has generalized the idea of prophesying until it means something quite different from its ordinary meaning. He says it even more straightforwardly in Acts:

82. *Inst.*, IV.i.12.        83. *Comm.* on Joel 2:28.

The word "prophecy" therefore signifies simply the rare and
excellent gift of understanding: as if Joel should say that under
the Kingdom of Christ there should not be merely a few prophets
to whom God would reveal His secrets, but that all men should
be endowed with spiritual wisdom to the extent of excelling in
prophetic gifts.[84]

Here it is not only Calvin's views of women that are getting in his
way. He also can think of the church only in terms of the institution-
alized form and definite office structure of his day. Women are not
to prophesy, and most men don't hold the teaching office. Hence
prophesying has to mean having wisdom and understanding and at the
same time maintaining silence in the church. One has the unhappy
suspicion that Calvin has not done justice to these passages.[85]

Calvin cannot avoid the fact that at least some women prophesied
in early New Testament times. "[Philip the Evangelist] had four
unmarried daughters, who prophesied" (Acts 21:9). Calvin is faithful
to his whole outlook of what can and what cannot be regarding
women:

> It is not certain how those girls discharged the office of prophesy-
> ing, except that the Spirit of God ruled them in such a way that
> He did not disturb the order that He Himself ordained. But
> since He does not permit women to play a public part in the
> church, one may well believe that they prophesied at home, or
> in a private place, outside the public meeting.[86]

Calvin explains in a sermon that "when [Philip's daughters] were in
the company of women, then did they there lay out the gift that was
given them."[87]

Does Calvin realize the implication of such an explanation? He has
placed the prophetesses of the New Testament in a lower station
than the Old Testament prophetesses, for these latter clearly prophesied before men as well as women. But Calvin finds he can also furnish an explanation for such Old Testament prophetesses as Deb-
orah, Miriam, and Huldah:

> The obvious answer is that God's extraordinary acts do not
> annul the ordinary rules by which He wishes us to be bound.
> Thus, if at some point women held the office of prophets and

84. *Comm.* on Acts 2:17.

85. In his *Comm.* on Joel 2:29 Calvin sees that women again in this text are mentioned alongside the men: "menservants and maidservants." Calvin comments:
"And [Joel] mentions 'handmaids,' for there were, we know, Prophetesses under the
Law. Let us go on—[to verse 30]." No comment from Calvin. Better say nothing,
for there is no room for a great upsurge of prophetesses in the new times!

86. *Comm.* on Acts 21:9.

87. Sermon on I Tim. 2:13-15 (*Trans. L.T.*, p. 226).

teachers and were led to do so by God's Spirit, He who is above all law might do this, but being an extraordinary case, it does not conflict with the constant and accustomed rule.[88]

The answer is neat; but it leaves the problem of finding the line between God's extraordinary, supernatural, peculiar calls to use the gifts of His Spirit and His ordinary and natural calls to do the same. One suspects the distinction between the two may not always be clear to women.

And so Calvin copes with the various data from the Bible. The pattern is formed in his thinking and he remains consistent with it. He admires Paul's modesty in confessing to the Roman congregation that Priscilla was one of his fellow workers in Christ: "This reveals all the more the unassuming nature of the holy apostle, since he does not refuse to have, and is not ashamed to admit that he has, a woman as his associate in the work of the Lord."[89] Calvin also admires the modesty of Apollos:

> Apollos was unusually modest, for he allowed himself to be taught and refined, not only by a manual worker, but also by a woman.... Yet we must remember what I said, that Priscilla carried out this instruction privately, within the walls of her own home, so that she might not destroy the order prescribed by God and by nature.[90]

Calvin does not notice, or at least does not comment on the fact that in the various references to this husband and wife team, Priscilla's name is mentioned first just as many times as Aquila's is—suggestive of the fact that she by no means played an inferior role on the team.

When Paul recommends Phoebe to the church in Rome, he says that she is a *diakonos* (minister, servant, deacon—the Greek form is masculine) in the church of Cenchreae. Calvin calls Phoebe a servant *(ministra)* and tells us what her form of service was. It was that of the order of widows referred to in I Timothy 5:9.[91] He could, of course, be right; but the question is how he knows this. He did not learn it from the title Paul gave her. Elsewhere that title, when found in a context suggesting a church position, is understood as "deacon." But for Calvin, women are not permitted in this church position. So the masculine word *diakonos* refers to the feminine order of widows, and the Bible is once again brought into harmony with Calvin's viewpoint.

Concerning Andronicus and Junias in Romans 16:7, Calvin explains the sense in which these two unknown people can be called "apostles." However, he does not stop to wrestle with the feminine

88. *Comm.* on I Tim. 2:12.
89. *Comm.* on Rom. 16:3.
90. *Comm.* on Acts 18:26.
91. *Comm.* on Rom. 16:1.

sound to the name Junias. In fact, he makes it Junia, even more feminine sounding.[92] The church father Chrysostom saw evidence for a feminine apostle here. The thought never occurred to Calvin, or at least it didn't deserve comment.

One might wish that he could hear Calvin on the prominent role of the Shunnamite woman in her family structure (II Kings 4:8-37; 8:1-6), or the remarkable involvements in society and business of the "good wife" in Proverbs 31:8-31, or the fact that a Christian church would even listen to a prophetess (Rev. 3:20). Calvin did not write commentaries on these portions of Scripture. But there is no reason to believe he could not have worked such passages into harmony with his viewpoint. The basic pattern for Calvin's outlook on the role of women had been set by Paul's allusions to the created structure. The rest of the Biblical material is read through these glasses and made to fit this structure as well as possible. But as we have been noting, sometimes it took some ramming and cramming to make them fit, and sometimes it took an almost high-handed explaining away of the text to keep the structure. Calvin was a prince of exegetes, and he read the Bible's message so well on so many subjects. But the beautifully consistent structure he built on the subject of women has its ragged seams and its threadbare weak spots. It is less than a perfect explanation of the Biblical materials and invites other attempts at putting the Bible all together on this subject.

## The remaining problem and current discussions

Calvin's exposition of the Biblical teachings on the place and role of women was dominated by his belief that he knew God's eternal law on this matter laid down in the created structures. He knew woman's place in the created order. This gave him the confidence to speak absolutely on various matters about woman's place. He was willing to be concessive as long as the creation order was upheld. In fact, sometimes he found reasons for being concessive when it was not clear how this could be harmonized with the creation order. But most of the time the thought of the creation ordinances served as his starting point and his final test of the interpretation of any passage.

As we noted, this zeal for maintaining the creation ordinances had its price. In regard to the freedom and unity which male and female gained in Christ, the woman was not able to gain what the man gained. The man's new freedom and full unity with others applied to both the realm of spiritual things and the present order of earthly life. The woman indeed gained her freedom in the spiritual realm, but it was

92. *Comm.* on Rom. 16:7.

necessary for Calvin to keep explaining to her that this freedom and unity did not apply to the earthly order. She must avoid placing herself on a par with men here and now. The creation order regarding her as a woman had established men over her, and she must be subject and obedient to their rulership. The same price had to be paid in regard to the image of God. God indeed created male and female in His image. But when Calvin had completed his explanation in the light of I Corinthians 11:7, it became apparent that the man's image has to do with both the spiritual order and the present earthly order; the woman's is limited to the spiritual order.

These are quite radical adjustments which have had to be introduced into the Biblical materials on woman. They were necessary adjustments for Calvin in order to maintain what he saw to be "the eternal law of God, which has made the female sex subject to the authority of men."[93] But one must be very sure of his position to be willing to make such radical adjustments. Unity in Christ sounds like such a leveling force and freedom in Christ sounds like such an elevating force that it wrenches one's expectations to hear the qualification added that this is not for women in the present earthly order. Image of God, male and female, sounds so on a par that it comes as a surprise to learn that woman as image is a more limited concept than man as image. Was Calvin really on solid ground in his constant appeal to the created structure regarding women? Recall what difficulties we encountered in following Calvin's demonstration that women had indeed been created subject to men in a divinely appointed order. Calvin needed to import Paul into the Genesis account in order to find it there, and then having read Genesis through Paul's eyes, he turned to Paul and found Paul's statements nicely explicating the Genesis outlook. Several times in our study as we were struggling to follow Calvin's line of reasoning or locate the sources of his ideas, we raised the question why Paul is speaking the way he is about the Genesis materials. Paul appears to be reflecting a view of Genesis which is not implicit in Genesis itself. How is Paul's outlook to be accounted for?

Calvin never asked this question. At one point he was close to seeing it. He noticed that he could not always follow Paul's allusions to the Genesis account for exactly what they said. Thus, in connection with Paul's reference to the woman rather than the man being deceived by the serpent's temptation, Calvin felt free in effect to correct Paul and on the basis of the Genesis materials to point out that Adam was indeed deceived along with his wife. In doing this he

93. *Comm.* on I Cor. 11:10.

very nicely blunted Paul's whole point. Did Calvin at this point have any thoughts on how Paul came to speak of this deception in a way that exonerated the man and blamed only the woman? If he would have pressed on into this area, he might have come to see in regard to all of Paul's allusions to Genesis concerning women's status that Paul's ideas do not appear to be from Genesis itself, but seem to betray a specific way of understanding Genesis. How might Paul have come to understand Genesis in this particular way? One possibility is that Paul had received a new, special revelation from God on how Genesis must be understood. Such a proposal would have placed Calvin in real difficulty, for then how could he dare to discount this new understanding by citing the original Genesis material in explanation of it? Is there any other way of accounting for Paul's particular views?

With this latter question we arrive at the forefront of modern Biblical investigation. Maybe it should be termed the modern battleline for Biblical interpreters. There are those who find Paul reflecting the interpretation of the material he had learned through his training in the Jewish community and among the rabbis. Paul did sometimes make use of the material that went quite beyond the Old Testament account—recall the angels mediating the law at Sinai (Gal. 3:19), the rock following the Israelites through the wilderness (I Cor. 10:4), Jannes and Jambres as names of Pharaoh's magicians (II Tim. 3:8). All of these are later Jewish elaborations on the Biblical account. Does Paul's understanding that the Genesis account itself teaches such definite subjection of women to men result from the way the later Jewish community understood, elaborated, and interpreted this account? Is Paul reflecting Judaistic and rabbinic interpretations here?

Calvin never faced such possibilities. The Judaistic and rabbinic materials were not so available to him as to alert him to such alternatives. However, the ease with which he could sense that Paul had to be explained away on his point that the man was not deceived suggests that Calvin might have been open to seeing new things here. Furthermore, he so readily detected that "nature" has to mean "custom" in regard to men's long hair. He was aware of the cultural conditioning that was back of some of Paul's directives. He foresaw changing times and new situations bringing about new ways of living one's Christianity and of bringing it to expression in church and society. He even was willing in regard to women's role to make important concessions that did not really fit with his principle of her status of subjection by creation. There was an openness about Calvin that shines through even the rigid consistency of his views on women.

He seems to have sensed that his position did not answer all the questions or deal adequately with all situations.

Our study raises a question about Calvin's view concerning woman's created status. Calvin, prince of exegetes that he was, has not paved a really clear and compelling pathway on this issue. Are there creation ordinances regarding women that are clear from Genesis? Does Paul really reflect such creation ordinances, or is something else accounting for the way Paul speaks? Calvin will not give us further help here. The modern struggle to get further Biblical light on women must be with Paul himself to come to clearer understanding of why he speaks the way he does.

In the meantime, Calvin nudges us on. There is room for change with the times. Calvin had the remarkably good sense to comment in regard to Paul's injunction, "Let the women keep silence in the churches" (I Cor. 14:34):

> The discerning reader should come to the decision, that the things which Paul is dealing with here, are indifferent, neither good nor bad; and that they are forbidden only because they work against seemliness and edification.[94]

A new age can bring a new sense of what is seemly. Edification is largely a matter of what one is open to. The fact that in Christ there is no male and female awaits fuller expression in our daily practice of Christianity. The Spirit undoubtedly still has some exciting things in store for the church. Maybe some of them will come through new roles and new freedom for women.

94. *Comm.* on I Cor. 14:35.

Leonard Sweetman, Jr.

CHAPTER **9** THE GIFTS OF THE SPIRIT:

A STUDY OF CALVIN'S COMMENTS ON

I CORINTHIANS 12:8-10, 28;

ROMANS 12:6-8; EPHESIANS 4:11

Since approximately 1960,[1] most of the non-Pentecostal ecclesiastical groups in North America have been engaged in a debate concerning the "gifts of the Spirit" which are listed in I Corinthians 12:8-10, 28; Romans 12:6-8; and Ephesians 4:11. The contemporary debate began as a response to the public operation of the whole spectrum of the "gifts of the Spirit" through individuals who were members of the non-Pentecostal Christian churches. These members of non-Pentecostal churches embraced contemporary gifts of the Spirit as legitimate, and recognized the ability of *some* Christians to function effectively in the "permanent" roles mentioned explicitly in Ephesians 4:11 and I Corinthians 12:28. Mentioned only casually are the gifts found in Romans 12:6-8 and I Corinthians 12:8-10: "pastors," "teachers," and those engaged in the diaconal works which are described under the rubrics "contributing," "giving aid," and "showing mercy."

The contemporary public exercise of "tongues" (*lalōn glōssēi*), "healing," "the working of miracles," and "prophecy" by members of non-Pentecostal churches constituted, at least initially, an irritant in those churches; and in some cases it proved to be divisive.

1. Cf. Dennis J. Bennett, *Nine O'clock in the Morning* (Plainfield, N.J.: Logos International, 1970), p. 61; and Watson Mills, *Understanding Speaking in Tongues* (Grand Rapids: Eerdmans, 1972), p. 14: "On April 3, 1960, Reverend Dennis J. Bennett confessed a belief in tongue-speaking from the pulpit of his Van Nuys, California, Episcopalian Church.... This was the first reported public incident of glossolalia among the so-called non-Pentecostal denominations and it signaled the debut of a phenomenon which undoubtedly had existed for some years in private."

During the last three or four years the strident tones of the debate concerning the legitimacy of the contemporary exercise of the whole spectrum of the gifts of the Spirit, and the polarization of the church, which is involved always in strident debate, have diminished. Perhaps the present moment lends itself to a fruitful discussion of the gifts of the Spirit.

The history of the interpretation of the Biblical passages in which are found the key references to the gifts of the Spirit constitutes a necessary task if a fruitful discussion is to take place. This essay attempts to make a modest contribution to the historical enterprise. I will survey John Calvin's comments on the three passages of the New Testament which are pointed to most frequently in discussions of the gifts of the Spirit: I Corinthians 12—14; Romans 12:4-8; and Ephesians 4:7-8. The survey will be organized around three questions: (1) What function did Calvin attribute to the gifts of the Spirit? (2) What content did Calvin attribute to the gifts of the Spirit? (3) Did the cultural context of the sixteenth century influence Calvin's interpretation of the Biblical material?

## What function did Calvin attribute to the gifts of the spirit?

1. The Spirit distributes a variety of gifts to members of the Christian community,[2] and these gifts are designed to function for their benefit. That is to say, they are designed to promote and maintain the unity of the Christian church in the church's life and work as the agent of God in the world.[3] The "*gifts* should be distinguished from each other just as much as the offices, and . . . they should, nevertheless, be all combined in a unity."[4] Calvin uses the metaphor of a musical composition to illustrate the way in which the diversity of gifts which individuals receive cooperates to promote

2. The term "gifts of the Spirit" is reserved here for the gifts which are given to members of the Christian community. It differentiates these gifts from the gifts which are given to all men. The Spirit does, of course, give to *all* men the gift of rationality, which when exercised makes visible the differentiation between men and animals. Cf. *Inst.*, II.ii.12; and Werner Krusche, *Das Wirken des Heiligen Geistes Nach Calvin* (Göttingen: Vandenhoeck & Ruprecht, 1957), p. 97. The Spirit of God is the sole source of the gifts which Paul lists in I Cor. 12:8-10, 28; Rom. 12:6-8; and Eph. 4:11. The Spirit's distribution of these gifts among men is the way in which the Spirit sends out the power of God and keeps God's power in operation. Cf. also *Comm.* on I. Cor. 12:5.

3. This theme, the use of the individual's gifts for the promotion and maintenance of the unity of the church, is articulated frequently by Calvin: e.g., *Comm.* on I Cor. 12:4, 7, 11, 24, 27, 31; 14:5, 12, 19; *Comm.* on Eph. 4:7, 11. Cf. *Inst.*, III.vii.5-6. Cf. also Wilhelm Niesel, *The Theology of Calvin*, trans. Harold Knight (Philadelphia: Westminster Press, 1956), p. 188.

4. *Comm.* on I Cor. 12:4.

the unity of the Christian church. Individuals in exercising their gifts are "to work harmoniously together for the edification of all," as "in music different parts are adjusted to each other and combined so well that they produce one harmonious piece."[5]

Calvin exhibits an awareness of and a commitment to an organic model of society in all of its structures which, at least, is not congruent with and, perhaps, is antithetical to the voluntaristic and contractual assemblies which characterize many of the structures operative in Western society from the eighteenth to the twentieth centuries. The members of the organism, in Calvin's model of society, are not isolated from one another; rather, they are interrelated and interdependent. The various members of the Christian church, for example, are gifted by the Spirit of God; however, "no-one has so much as to be self-sufficient, and not *need the help of other people*."[6] In Calvin's reading of Paul there is no room for the individual who in the privacy of his own spirit is confronted immediately by God and who in isolation from others answers God in the obedience of faith. The individual Christian functions in the body of Christ with the equipment which the Spirit has given him. He must do this as a member who is related to and dependent on all other members if the organism of Christ is to function properly.

> Even if there are different members in the body, with different functions, yet they are connected together in such a way as to form a unity. Therefore, we who are members of Christ, even if we are equipped with different gifts, ought nevertheless to be concerned about that union with each other, which we have in Christ.[7]

In the Christian community, moreover, because God has distributed gifts as He wills to each member, the members need one another. They cannot function in isolation from one another because one member has received a gift which others have not received and without the exercise of which the others lead, at best, an atrophied life.[8] This makes vivid the interrelation and interde-

---

5. Ibid. Cf. *Comm.* on Eph. 4, introduction to vv. 11-14: "He returns to the dispensation of the graces he had mentioned and declares more fully what he had touched on briefly, that out of this variety arises unity in the Church as various tones in music make a sweet melody."

6. *Comm.* on I Cor. 12:11. Cf. *Comm.* on I Cor. 12:29: "What Paul is after is to show, first of all, that nobody is so fully equipped with everything as to be replete in himself, and not feel the need of other people's help. Secondly, he wants to show that offices, just as much as gifts, are distributed in such a way that no single member constitutes the entire body."

7. *Comm.* on I. Cor. 12:12.

8. *Comm.* on Eph. 4:7. Calvin paraphrases Eph. 4:7: "On no one has God bestowed all things, but each has received a certain measure, so that we need one another; and by bringing together what is given to them individually, they help one another."

pendence of the members of the Christian community. As an isolated
individual, one member of the body is incomplete and is not whole.
In Calvin's reading of Paul, as well as of the Bible as a whole,
Christ calls and unites in the organism of His body the individual
Christians. Organic unity in which the diversity of function among
the members is necessary and beneficial characterizes the body of
Christ. The body is not an aggregate of individuals, each of whom
associates voluntarily with other Christians who have similar commitments and who, consequently, band together. "Since men could
not come into such [an organic] unity by themselves [Christ] Himself became the bond of that union."[9] In this organic union which
Christ generates and maintains, each individual member must "consider what is appropriate to his nature, capacity and calling."[10]

The Christian community, moreover, must use creatively that contribution which each member makes through the exercise of the gifts
with which the Holy Spirit has endowed him.[11] If the Christian community ignores or rejects the contribution made for its benefit by a
specific member through the exercise of the gifts which he has received from the Spirit of God, it ignores and rejects Christ. In his
comments on I Corinthians 12:12 ("So it is with Christ"), Calvin
emphasizes the close relation which exists between Christ and the
church. He understands the substitution of "Christ" for "the
church" in I Corinthians 12:12 as a deliberate, self-conscious act
on the part of the author for the purpose of articulating the interrelation between Christ and the church.

> For Christ invests us with this honour, that He wishes to be
> discerned and recognized, not only in His own Person, but also
> in His members. So... the same apostle says in Ephesians
> 1.23 that the Church is His fullness *(complementum)*, as if He
> would be mutilated in some way, were He to be separated from
> His members.

The dynamic interrelation of the members of the body of Christ
constitutes the technique, the order, God Himself has willed, initi-
ated, and maintained for the purpose of "dispensing His grace."[12]
God wills the differentiation of gifts among the members of the
church in virtue of which it functions as an organism in which the
members are interrelated and interdependent.

9. *Comm.* on Rom. 12:4.

10. Ibid.

11. *Comm.* on Rom. 12:5: "He intimates... how zealous we ought to be in appro-
priating to the common good of the body the powers possessed by individuals."
Cf. *Inst.*, III.vii.4.

12. Ibid.

God guards and preserves the mutual conjunction among us, in that he gives none such perfection as to be sufficient or to be satisfied with himself on his own and apart from others. A certain measure is allotted to each; and it is only by communicating with each other that they have sufficient for maintaining their condition.[13]

In summary, a variety of gifts are distributed to individuals in the Christian community by the Spirit. The criterion determining the distribution of the gifts is the will of the Spirit. One individual receives one gift; another individual, another gift. Whatever gift or gifts an individual receives, however, he must use *solely* for the benefit of his brothers. He *must*, moreover, exercise his gift. He must exercise his gift, furthermore, to build up the Christian church: that is, to promote and maintain the unity of the church as the body of Christ in its life in the world as the agent of God. The church, on the other hand, must recognize that the acts of her gifted members are performed through the exercise of the gifts which the Spirit has given. The church ignores and rejects Christ if the church fails to recognize and accept the gifted members' exercise of their gifts as acts which are beneficial to the Christian community.

2. The gifts of the Spirit differentiate one member of the Christian community from his fellow members. They generate and preserve the individuality of each member.[14] Calvin exhibits a sensitivity to the value of every individual as a functioning member of the Christian community. No Christian has been bypassed by the Spirit in His distribution of gifts. Every Christian, whatever his pedigree may be, is gifted by the Spirit. When Paul writes that "it is the same God who inspires, (*ho energōn*), them all in everyone" (I Cor. 12:6), he is pointing out that God's generosity is expressed here "in thinking everyone worthy of some gift."[15] No member of the Christian community comes from so deprived a background and is so bereft of ability that he has received no gifts of the Spirit. "Even the least significant believer does in fact bear fruit relative to his slender resources, so that there is no such person as a useless member of the Church...."[16] Each member of the church, consequently, has a role

13. *Comm.* on Eph. 4:7.

14. Krusche, *Das Wirken*, p. 97: "Differences arise among the *individual believers* through their being gifted with charismatic gifts...." Ernst Käsemann reaches the same conclusion in his study of Pauline material which Krusche reached in his study of Calvin's comments concerning the Pauline material. See Ernst Käsemann, "Geist, IV, Geist und Geistesgaben im N.T.," *Religion In Geschichte Und Gegenwart*, 3rd ed. (Tübingen: J.C.B. Mohr, Paul Siebeck, 1962), vol. II, col. 1275.

15. *Comm.* on I Cor. 12:6.

16. *Comm.* on I Cor. 12:27.

to play and a contribution to make to his brothers, to the Christian community as a whole.

Playing a necessary and significant role in the orchestration of the total Christian community can prove to be an experience of temptation for individuals whose role in societal structures by virtue of background and training is minimal. The "universal priesthood of all believers"[17] needs to be delineated precisely to avoid the disruption of order and the chaos which Calvin always feared in circumstances which were not regulated clearly. Calvin, consequently, urged the members of the Christian community to recognize and use the gift(s) which the Spirit of God gave to each, and to avoid the temptation to gain the gift(s) which the Spirit had distributed to another.[18] In the discussion of Romans 12:3 concerning the term "according as God hath dealt to each man a measure of faith," Calvin urges each of the members to assess realistically the equipment God has given him. He urges them to posit a realistic self-image. In the discussion of Romans 12:4 Calvin states explicitly, "[God] has determined the order which He desired us to maintain so that each should regulate himself according to the measure of his ability, and not thrust himself into the duties which belong to others." He goes on to add that everyone should "willingly refrain from usurping the offices of others." When he articulates this position, Calvin reflects the historical context of the sixteenth century in which "upward social mobility" did not exist. Societal structures were fixed and relatively inflexible. One's "birthright" served as the primary determinant of one's societal role, status, caste, and class. God located a man; He gave a man his "birthright." Rebellion against one's location, therefore, was rebellion against God. Dissatisfaction with one's location and coveting another's location constituted rebellion against God.[19] Demeaning the gifts one has

---

17. Krusche, *Das Wirken*, p. 322, uses the term in this context. Käsemann, "Geist, IV," col. 1275, uses the term "universal priesthood of all believers" in his study of "the Spirit and the gifts of the Spirit in the New Testament."

18. *Comm.* on I Cor. 12:4: "Paul therefore urges individuals to be content with their gifts, and to make the most of them. He forbids them to overstep their own bounds by selfishly striving to get something else."

19. This perspective comes to expression in the condemnation of the desire for wealth on the part of those who have had little or no wealth entrusted to them which is found in *Inst.*, III.vii.9: "Therefore suppose we believe that every means toward a prosperous and desirable outcome rests upon the blessing of God alone; and that, when this is absent, all sorts of misery and calamity dog us. It remains for us not greedily to strive after riches and honors—whether relying upon our own dexterity of wit or our own diligence, or depending upon the favor of men, or having confidence in vainly imagined fortune—but for us always to look to the Lord so that by his guidance we may be led to whatever lot he has provided for us."

received from the Spirit and coveting or seeking to acquire the gifts which the Spirit has distributed to another member of the Christian community constitutes rebellion against God because this constitutes a threat to the order, the system which God established in creating the universe. The maintenance of that system demands that one subject oneself to the order and processes God has created.

Calvin does not permit the individual Christian to opt for exercising or not exercising the gifts which the Spirit has given him. If one fails to exercise the gifts he has received from the Spirit, he rebels against God and fragments the unity of the Christian church. In refusing to exercise the gifts which he has received, he refuses to subject himself to the system which God established in creation. According to Calvin, Paul, in I Corinthians 12:4,

> is instructing individuals to bring whatever they have as a contribution to the common stock, and not to keep the gifts of God to themselves, which would mean that the benefits of each person's gifts would be restricted to himself alone, instead of being shared with others; but to work harmoniously together for the edification of all.[20]

If one uses the gifts he has received for his own ends rather than for the welfare of the Christian community, he "corrupts the right use of the gifts."[21] He treats as his own possession that which is gift. He assumes that the determination of the use of a gift is his own prerogative. Calvin's warning against the abuse of the gifts of the Spirit stems from the threat to the organic structure of the Christian community which is posed by a member who refuses to play his role for the benefit of the entire organism. Only when the individual member of the Christian community uses his gifts for the benefit of the organism does he retain his unique identity as the one whom God has located in a particular place at a particular time in the framework of specific circumstances for the realization of God's objective.

In summary, every member of the Christian church, the body of Christ, is gifted, for the Spirit has withheld gifts from no member. Each must be satisfied with the gifts he has received, and must use his gifts to benefit the entire Christian community. The gifted member does not have the option to use or not to use his gifts on behalf of the Christian community. To fail to use one's gifts on behalf of the

---

20. Cf. *Comm.* on I Cor. 12:28: "Everyone of us should realize that whatever his gift, it has been given to him for the upbuilding of all the brethren; with that in mind he should devote it to the common good, and not suppress it, burying it within himself so to speak, or use it as if it were his private possession.

21. *Comm.* on Eph. 4:11.

body of Christ is to disobey God and to cripple the body. The body, conversely, must recognize and appropriate the contribution of the gifted members for the unity and welfare of the church. If the church ignores or fails to appropriate the gifts of her gifted members, the church disobeys God and stunts her own development.

3. The gifts of the Spirit serve to qualify and equip individual members of the church for a role in the functioning community. The gifts of the Spirit may not be dissociated from the functioning body of Christ. The gifts of the Spirit, consequently, are related to the "offices" through the exercise of which the Christian community functions. The relation which Calvin discerns between the gifts of the Spirit and the offices of the church comes to concrete, explicit expression in Calvin's discussion of Romans 12:8: "he who contributes, in liberality." In Calvin's comments, the term "he who contributes" does not refer to an individual member of the Christian community who gives of his wealth to support the needy. The term, rather, refers to "the deacons who are charged with the distribution of the public property of the Church." In Romans 12:8 Paul refers, also, to the one "who does acts of mercy." Those who do acts of mercy are "widows and other ministers who were appointed to take care of the sick, according to the custom of the ancient Church." The ease with which Calvin associates these terms with specific offices in the church of his own day, or offices which flourished in the ancient church but which no longer existed in the sixteenth century church, stems from his associating "prophecy" with the proclamation of the gospel and, above all, "service" with the ordained ministry. Calvin finds terms used in Romans 12:6-8 which describe the function of offices in the church.[22] Therefore, he reads descriptions of offices in the church in all the terms which are used, since Paul is writing about the function of the community of believers as the one body in Christ in which a diversity of function is operative.

Calvin does not subordinate the gifts of the Spirit to the offices

22. It would be profitable to study the text which Calvin used in his work. He, quite obviously, works with the Greek text of the New Testament, which was accepted as an authoritative text in his day, in places where the text of the Latin Vulgate constituted a theological problem for him. In other places, however, he evidences an ignorance of the Greek text and bases his interpretation on what is obviously the text of the Latin Vulgate. In his interpretation of Rom. 12:7, he writes, in part, about the ordained minister. He here is basing his interpretation on "he who exhorts, in his exhortation," but, also, on the Latin Vulgate's *sive ministerium in ministrando*. He ignores or has not read the Greek text as he prepares his comments: *eite diakontian en tēi diakoniai*. Had he read the Greek test he would have written about the diaconal office when he commented on the term "if service, in our serving" and not about the ordained minister, the teaching elder.

of the church.[23] The gifts of the Spirit are antecedent to office. The possession of gifts of the Spirit serves as the decisive index of one's having been called by God to serve in an office in the Christian community.[24] The gifts of the Spirit constitute God's act of qualifying a person for office. The gifts of the Spirit, consequently, constitute the prerequisite for office; they are not subordinate to it. "Whenever men are called by God, gifts are necessarily connected with offices. For God does not cover men with a mask in appointing them apostles or pastors, but also furnishes them with gifts, without which they cannot properly discharge their office."[25]

Because, in Calvin's reading of I Corinthians 12—14; Romans 12:4-8; and Ephesians 4:11, the gifts of the Spirit constitute the prerequisite for office, therefore no tension or competition can exist between those who possess the gifts of the Spirit and those who occupy offices in the institutional church. The juxtaposition of "gifts of the Spirit" and "office" results from a reading of the relevant Pauline passages which distorts the content of the passages as such. Dissociating the "gifts of the Spirit" from "office," moreover, tends to isolate the gifts of the Spirit from the processes involved in the functioning of the Christian community: that is, the interdependent, interrelated operation of Christians through which the church plays her role in obedience to Christ, her Lord, as He governs the world and the church in submission to the Father.

The institutional church in the act of her normal operational procedures must exercise a critical function relative to the presence and reality of the gifts of the Spirit in specific members of the Christian community. One of the tools which the Christian community uses in discharging this critical role is that gift of the Spirit which is called "the ability to distinguish between spirits" (I Cor. 12:10). This gift is not constituted of "the normal commonsense, which we make use of in forming judgments; but this is

23. Cf. Krusche, *Das Wirken*, p. 322: "The offices, on the contrary, are subordinate to the charisma."

24. Ibid., p. 323.

25. *Comm.* on Eph. 4, introduction to vv. 11-14. Cf. John Calvin, *Sermons From Job*, trans. Leroy Nixon (Grand Rapids: Eerdmans, 1952), p. 241 (sermon based on Job 32:4-10): "If a man is chosen to proclaim the Word of God, or better, if God wishes to give grace to His Church, He will endow this man by His Spirit, He will give him intelligence of His Word, and dexterity to know how to apply it to the use of the people, and to gather good doctrine from it; He will give him zeal and other things which are required; and God will thereby show Himself so manifestly that we can say He cares for us when He so distributes gifts of grace to men in what is required for our profit."

a special perspicuity, bestowed on a few people ... not simply to prevent their being deceived by the lying faces or false airs." This gift, rather, enables its possessors "to make out the difference between the true ministers of Christ and the false...."[26] The legitimate existence and function of the Christian community, the church as the locus of the presence and operation of the gifts of the Spirit, constitute the framework within which Calvin defines this and all other gifts of the Spirit.[27] The exercise of this gift is not a subjective, irrational, or nonrational act. The Holy Spirit leads the church, rather, to exercise this gift in such a way that she may be led into a new understanding of the apostolic teaching; but the witness of the apostles and the prophets constitutes the only framework in which the ability to distinguish between spirits operates. This gift operates to determine if the teachings, insights, and actions of those who claim to be gifted by the Spirit are located within or without the framework of the apostolic and prophetic witness.[28]

Perhaps the location of Calvin's most explicit discussion of the church's critical function as a gift of the Spirit is found in his *Commentary* on I John 4:1 ("Beloved, do not believe every spirit, but test the spirits[29] to see whether they are of God"). In this comment Calvin distinguishes between a "private" and a "public" testing of doctrine. In the private testing, the individual member recognizes, articulates, and commits himself to that doctrine (= gospel) which has come from God. The public testing refers to that consensus of the members which is achieved through the exercise of the Holy Spirit's gift of discerning the spirits.[30] The con-

---

26. *Comm.* on I Cor. 12:10.

27. Cf. Krusche, *Das Wirken*, p. 325: If the *donum interpretationis* belongs to the office of preacher and teacher, "the corresponding gift of the congregation, *(Gemeinde)*, is the gift of distinguishing between spirits, the *spiritus discretionis*. This gift makes it possible to test all *doctrina* on the touchstone of the Holy Scriptures and to make the judgment about true and false teaching."

28. Ibid., p. 326: "The Holy Spirit never leads the church in such a way that he reveals new teaching to her in addition to or outside of the apostolic and prophetic witness. He, furthermore, does not lead the church in such a way that she, herself, may produce new teaching. He, rather, leads the church in such a way that he helps her gain new understanding of the apostolic teaching.. The same Holy Spirit who gives the church the gift of interpretation, gives her, also, the gift of distinguishing. He leads the church because he gives her *both* gifts."

29. By "spirit" Calvin seems to mean a member of the Christian community who professes to be illuminated, dominated, and led by the Spirit of God in his publicly articulated faith and life.

30. *Comm.* on I John 4:1: "If, then, we are to be fit critics, we must be endowed with and directed by the Spirit of discernment. But, since the apostle would have been commanding this in vain if the faculty of criticism were not supplied, we may

sensus usually is achieved within the framework of the institutional church's structures; however, the situation in the church which necessitated the Reformation in the sixteenth century made Calvin cautious. He will not identify without reservation or qualification the consensus which is achieved in ecclesiastical assemblies and councils of the church as true doctrine.[31]

The conjunction of "word" and "spirit" in the Christian community constitutes the situation in which true "doctrine" emerges; but Calvin refuses to identify specific historical expressions of the Christian community (e.g., the historical episcopate) as the structure of the Christian community in which "word" and "spirit" conjoin.[32]

According to Calvin, the gifts of the Spirit in I Corinthians 12:8-10, 28 do not constitute an exhaustive list. This list, rather, constitutes a list which is sufficient for Paul's purpose there.[33] This is also true of the lists which are found in Romans 12:4-8 and Ephesians 4:11. Does Calvin imply that the Spirit gives to members of a specific community in a particular set of circumstances within the context of a particular historical period the gifts which are necessary if that community is to function effectively as God's agent—gifts which may differ from those mentioned in the lists in the Bible? Calvin never says this. What he does point out is that some gifts and offices seem to have been temporary. Some gifts,

assuredly conclude that the godly will never be left destitute of the Spirit of wisdom as to what is necessary, provided they ask for Him from the Lord. But the Spirit will only guide us to a true discrimination if we subject all our thoughts to the Word. ... The public trial relates to the common consent and *politeia* of the Church. For since there is the danger of fanatical men arising and presumptuously claiming that they are endued with the Spirit of God, it is a necessary remedy that believers shall meet together and seek a way of godly and pure agreement. But the old proverb is true, So many heads, so many viewpoints; and therefore it is a remarkable work of God when He tames our obstinacy and makes us think alike and agree in a pure unity of faith."

31. *Inst.*, IV.ix.13: "But I deny it to be always the case that an interpretation of Scripture adopted by vote of a council is true and certain." "Interpretation of Scripture" does not mean the exegesis of a verse or of a pericope. It means, rather, the perspective within the framework of which one reads the Bible: e.g., the interpretation of Scripture in the period of the Reformation comes to a focus in "justification by faith."

32. Cf. H. Jackson Forstman, *Word and Spirit: Calvin's Doctrine of Biblical Authority* (Stanford: Stanford University Press, 1962), pp. 84-85: "An obstacle appears which requires further handling, issuing in a completely circular argument in which it is difficult to fasten securely on any point. The word must be taught and interpreted. For this the Spirit is necessary, but then the Spirit is tested by the Word. Whenever Calvin introduces another possible criterion, he sooner or later qualifies it and works his way back to the Word or the Spirit."

33. *Comm.* on I Cor. 12:8.

at any rate, were more frequent in one age than in another. The gift of performing miracles was given in the apostolic period "to add light to the new and as yet unknown Gospel." "We see that [the use of miracles] ceased not long after, or at least, instances of them were so rare that we may gather that they were not equally common to all ages."[34]

## What content did Calvin attribute to the gifts of the Spirit?

The list of gifts which is found in Ephesians 4 contains only the rubrics which normally are associated with offices. Calvin suggests that "we might be surprised that when he is speaking of the gifts of the Holy Spirit, Paul should enumerate offices instead of gifts.... Whenever men are called by God, gifts are necessarily connected with offices."[35] Calvin makes the same point as he discusses I Corinthians 12:28. He distinguishes between the gifts mentioned in verses 8-10 and the gifts listed in verse 28: "At the beginning of the chapter Paul had spoken about 'powers' *(facultatibus)*; now he takes up the discussion of the offices."[36] This distinction enables him to state once more that "the Lord only appointed ministers after first providing them with the requisite gifts and making them fit for the duties they had to carry out. We must infer from that that people with absolutely no qualification, who force themselves upon the Church, are fanatics, driven by an evil spirit."[37]

*Apostles and evangelists (Eph. 4:11; I Cor. 12:28)*

"Apostles" and "evangelists" are defined as those who were "to publish the doctrine of the Gospel throughout the whole world, to plant Churches and to erect the Kingdom of Christ. So they had no churches of their own; but they had a common mandate to preach the gospel wherever they went."[38] The distinction between apostle and evangelist is one of rank. Evangelists are subordinate to apostles. "They were next in rank" to apostles.[39]

34. *A Harmony of the Gospels* on Mark 16:17.

35. *Comm.* on Eph. 4, introduction to vv. 11-14.

36. *Comm.* on I Cor. 12, introduction to vv. 28-31.

37. Ibid.

38. *Comm.* on Eph. 4:11. *Inst.*, IV.vii.8, places a more concrete limit on the apostles: "The only thing granted to the apostles was that which the prophets had of old. They were to expound the ancient scripture, and to show that what is taught there has been fulfilled in Christ. Yet they were not to do this except from the Lord, that is, with Christ's Spirit as precursor in a certain measure dictating the words."

39. *Comm.* on Eph. 4:11.

Interestingly enough, when Calvin discusses the replacement of
Judas Iscariot (Acts 1:22), the uniqueness of an apostle does not
consist of his having seen the resurrected Jesus. "All the followers
of Jesus had this experience in common." The uniqueness of the
apostle consisted of his having been chosen to witness to the
resurrection: a symbol for the whole gospel. The chosen apostles
"held first place among those charged with this mission."[40]

### Prophets (Rom. 12:6; I Cor. 12:10, 28; Eph. 4:11)

"Prophets are those who are gifted with extraordinary wisdom"
and "aptitude for grasping what the immediate need of the
Church is." They speak "the right word to meet" that need. That
word cannot be dissociated from the prophet's "outstanding"
interpretation of Scripture, but the word cannot be confined to the
interpretation of Scripture.[41] This Calvin concludes on the basis of
I Corinthians 14:25.

The gifts which have been described so far are also called
offices. These offices, however, were temporary. They were designed "at the beginning for the founding of the Church, and the
setting up of the Kingdom of Christ."[42] What evidence does Calvin
submit to demonstrate the validity of the distinction of "temporary"
and "permanent" offices? The only evidence which Calvin submits
is the empirical observation that these offices died out early in the
church's life. The "permanent" offices, "pastor" and "teacher,"
are the counterpart to "prophet" and "apostle" in the life of the
post-New Testament church.[43] The distinction between pastor and
apostle inheres in their function. The pastor is bound to a particular congregation in a particular place, whereas the apostle's
parish is the world.

In his *Commentary* on Romans 16:7, Calvin deals with the
designation of Andronicus and Junias[44] as apostles. He clarifies his
understanding of the term apostle as it functions in the literature

40. *Comm.* on Acts 1:22. Cf. Calvin's discussion in *Inst.*, IV.iii.4.

41. *Comm.* on I Cor. 12:28. Cf. *Comm.* on Eph. 4:11: Prophets are "outstanding
interpreters of prophecies [i.e., the prophecies recorded in the Bible], who, by a unique
gift of revelation, applied them to the subjects on hand; but I do not exclude the gift of
foretelling, so far as it was connected with teaching."

42. *Comm.* on I Cor. 12:28.

43. Cf. *Inst.*, IV.iii.6.

44. This is a feminine name in the Greek texts of Westcott and Hort, Tischendorf
and Weiss. In p[46], the Sixtine edition of the Vulgate, the Boharic and Ethiopic
translations, the text reads "Julia." Cf. the discussion of this problem in H. N. Ridderbos, "Aan de Romeinen" in *Kommentaar Op Het Nieuwe Testament*, ed. S.
Greijdanus and F. W. Grosheide (Kampen: J. H. Kok, 1959), p. 345.

of the New Testament. When the term is used to designate the
Twelve, the disciples whom Jesus chose, then the term apostle describes an office in the church which was temporary and which disappeared after the New Testament age was closed. This usage Calvin
calls "its proper and generally accepted sense." Paul, however,
uses the term apostle also to refer "in a general way to those who
planted churches by bringing the doctrine of salvation to various
places."[45]

It was not necessary for Calvin to designate the office of apostle
as a temporary office. He indicated in his discussion of Ephesians
4:11 that God provides with the necessary gifts those whom He
chooses as apostles or pastors. One can read "apostle" in Ephesians 4:11 as a functional term, as a description of the role one
plays. God sends the apostle out into the whole world to give witness to the gospel; and God sends the pastor out into the congregation to give witness to the gospel. God sends the apostle out
into the world in much the same way in which God sent Jesus into
the world. (See the analogy in John 20:21—as God sent Jesus, so
Jesus sends out his disciples). One should not ignore the possibility
that "apostle" describes a function in the Bible, and does not name
an office. The definition which Calvin gives to apostle fits well the
function or role, incidentally, of missionary in the modern church.
For pragmatic reasons, the missionary may confine himself to a particular country or "language area." The missionary, however, functions as one whose role is "to publish the doctrine of the Gospel
throughout the whole world, to plant Churches and to erect the
Kingdom of Christ." This is Calvin's description of the role of
the apostle.

The point which has been made relative to apostle can also be
made relative to prophet. Calvin's description of the gift of prophecy, which has been given above, serves as an admirable description of the role of a preacher-pastor in the modern church. The
preacher-pastor should be attuned to the needs of his congregation's members who live in the maelstrom of the contemporary
world, and he should be immersed in Scripture so that he may address
the right word to the congregation in its situation of need.

*"He who contributes," "he who gives aid," "he who does
acts of mercy" (Rom. 12:7, 8)*

When Calvin discusses Romans 12:7, 8 ("he who contributes, in
liberality, he who gives aid, with zeal, he who does acts of
mercy, with cheerfulness"), he understands the three terms as de-

scriptions of offices in the church. As has been pointed out above, because Calvin read the Vulgate text, he understood the term which is translated "of service, in our service" to be descriptive of the minister of the gospel. He read the text *sive ministerium in ministrando.*[46] Calvin, furthermore, understands the term which is translated "he who gives aid, with zeal" as a term which refers to the elders or presbyters who are to rule the congregation zealously.[47] He understands the terms "he who contributes" and "he who does acts of mercy" as terms which describe two kinds of deacons: (1) those "who are charged with the distribution of the public property of the Church"; and (2) "widows and other ministers who were appointed to take care of the sick, according to the custom of the ancient Church."[48]

At this point something can be said about the term "office" as it functions in Calvin's vocabulary. The perspective or framework within which Calvin works is one in which God, the Creator-Lord, and the world which He has created are embraced in a single, unitary system. The human factors or facets present and functioning in the world which God has created are the modes, as it were, through which God exercises His lordship over His creation. God gives people roles to play, functions in the total system created and maintained by God. Furthermore, the societal structures that God has generated, in which people who are interrelated and interdependent are assigned roles, and through which they discharge their roles, have functions also. Instead of referring to roles or functions Calvin refers to "offices." "Office" seems to be a more static term than "function" or "role." This, however, does not prove to be true when one examines Calvin's use of the term. Office is the term descriptive of the mode of God's exercise of His lordship through

46. *Comm.* on Rom. 12:7.

47. Calvin interprets the term in I Cor. 12:28 which the Revised Standard Version translates "administrators" as a term which describes "elders who are responsible for discipline." Cf. *Comm.* on I. Cor. 12:28. The Latin Vulgate reads: *"qui praeest in sollicitudine."* C. H. Dodd, "The Epistle of Paul to the Romans," in *The Moffatt New Testament Commentary* (London: Hodder & Stoughton, 1932), p. 201, translates the term *prohistamenos* as "superintendent," but does not discuss either the term or the location of the term. It is located between two diaconal terms. Charles K. Barrett, "The Epistle to the Romans," in *Black's New Testament Commentaries* (London: Adam & Charles Black, 1957), p. 239, concludes that the term does not describe an office, but, "rather, refers to a function which may have been exercised by several persons, perhaps jointly or in turn." Ridderbos, "Aan de Romeinen," p. 280, opts for the same reading of the term as does Barrett. He, however, does leave room for the meaning which is reflected in the Revised Standard Version: "to assume the responsibility to care for someone."

48. *Comm.* on Rom. 12:8. Cf. *Inst.,* IV.iii.9.

His agents in the church. The various "magistrates" constitute the mode through which God exercises His lordship through His agents in the structure of society which is called the state.

### Pastor and teacher[49] (Rom. 12:8; Eph. 4:11)

These are closely related to one another. The doctor or teacher is not mentioned as one who prepares students to serve as pastor in the church. He, rather, "forms and instructs the Church by the Word of truth." The pastor, of course, also does this; but exhortation seems to characterize his ministry. "No one can exhort without doctrine; yet he who teaches is not at once endowed with the gift of exhortation."[50]

### Helps (I Cor. 12:28)

This term, also, Calvin understands as a title which describes an office and a gift. The "helps" may have functioned in the diaconal work on behalf of the poor.[51] Calvin concludes that we have no concrete knowledge of "helps" now. They disappeared from the life of the church.[52] He comes to a similar conclusion relative to prophets. The term "prophet" constitutes the title of a temporary office which disappeared from the life of the church. Calvin, nevertheless, exercises caution and does not assert apodictically that no prophets or helps have appeared in the life of the church between the completion of the New Testament and the sixteenth century. "It is difficult to make up one's mind about gifts and offices of which the Church has been deprived for so long, *except for mere traces or shades of them which are still to be found*"[53] (italics added).

### Utterance of knowledge and utterance of wisdom (I. Cor. 12:8)

These differ from one another in degree. "Knowledge" refers to an "ordinary grasp" of "holy things," whereas "wisdom" "includes an insight, by their unveiling, into things of a more secret and lofty nature."[54] Calvin's discussion of these particular gifts was too brief to be clear or helpful.

49. Calvin understands Rom. 12:8, "he who exhorts, in his exhorting," to be a description of the preacher-pastor as he functions in his role, his office.

50. *Comm.* on Rom. 12:7. Cf. *Comm.* on I. Cor. 12:27.

51. *Comm.* on I. Cor. 12:28.

52. Ibid.

53. *Comm.* on I Cor. 12:27.

54. *Comm.* on I Cor. 12:8.

## Faith, gifts of healings, working of miracles (I Cor. 12:9-10)

The gift of healings, Calvin states abruptly, needs no explanation. Everyone knows what is meant by the gift of healings.[55] This brusque statement of Calvin reflects the degree to which Calvin's milieu influenced him in his reading of the Bible. In the twentieth century, under the influence of "scientism," both the possibility and character of healings are subject to intense discussion when the claim is made that a specific individual exercises this gift of the Spirit.

"Faith," in I Corinthians 12:9, describes confidence in the exalted Christ's ability to perform miracles at this moment. The term which is translated "working of miracles" means, literally, "the workings of powers." Calvin understands this term to describe the power which God exercises through people over against demons and hypocrites.[56] These three gifts, consequently, are related closely to one another in Calvin's reading of the Biblical text.

The function of these gifts is not discussed in his *Commentary* on I Corinthians 12:9-10. The function of miracles, in general, is discussed in connection with Mark 16:17. ("And these signs will accompany those who believe: in my name they will cast out demons; and they will speak in new tongues; they will pick up serpents, and if they drink any deadly thing it will not hurt them. They will lay their hands on the sick; and they will recover.")[57]

Three points emerge from Calvin's comments on Mark 16:9-20. (1) Calvin does not deal with the individual phenomena of exorcism, tongues, handling serpents, drinking deadly things, and healings. He discusses miracles as acts of the Lord which were designed "to confirm the faith of His Gospel"[58] while Jesus was still in the world and also for the future. (2) Calvin does not assert dogmatically that miracles were designed only for the apostolic age. He states that "it is more likely that miracles were only promised for the time."[59] Calvin prefers this position because of the empirical fact that "instances of them were so rare (historically) that we may

55. *Comm.* on I Cor. 12:9. Calvin read the text in the Latin Vulgate ( = gift of healings), and, therefore, ignored the problem which is posed by the plural forms: gifts of healings.

56. *Comm.* on I Cor. 12:10.

57. The problem of the conclusion of the Marcan gospel is well known. The best text of Mark, established by the criteria of the discipline of textual criticism, ends at Mark 16:8.

58. *A Harmony of the Gospels Matthew, Mark, and Luke* on Mark 16:17.

59. Ibid.

gather that they were not equally common to all ages."[60] Miracles
may have ceased because of the world's ingratitude. More proba-
bility is to be attached to the hypothesis that miracles were designed to complement the proclamation of the Gospel in the apostolic period "to prevent the preaching of the Gospel being vain."[61]
(3) Calvin does not deny categorically that miracles occur in his own
age. Nor does he deny that they will occur in the future. "We certainly see that their use ceased not long after, or at least, that
instances of them were so rare that we may gather that they were
not equally common to all ages."[62] He does leave room, however,
for the possibility of miracle in his own day and in any other day.
Mark 16:20—"And they went forth and preached everywhere, while
the Lord worked with them and confirmed the message by the signs
that attended it. Amen"—"teaches what use we ought to make of
miracles, if we are not to turn them into perverse corruptions; they
must serve the Gospel."[63]

### Discerning of spirits (I Cor. 12:10)

This gift, as has been indicated above, describes something
other than one's "common sense"[64] used in forming judgments.
"Discerning of spirits," rather, is a gift of God to *some* people
which enables them to "make out the difference between the true
ministers of Christ and the false."[65] One can easily appreciate the
divisiveness which the exercise of this gift represents in a specific
church at a specific time. The exercise of this gift in the past—
by a Calvin or a Luther—produced a reformation in the church

60. Ibid.

61. Ibid.

62. Ibid.

63. *A Harmony of the Gospels Matthew, Mark, and Luke* on Mark 16:20. Here one
must be careful that he does not generalize. In the Fourth Gospel, faith in Jesus
which is based on having seen the *sēmeia* of Jesus or on having seen the
*stigmata* of Jesus is juxtaposed to faith in Jesus as a response to hearing the gospel
even though the one exercising faith has not seen (cf. John 20:29). The faith in Jesus
which is based on having *seen* needs correction and modification. The Person of
Jesus as the One whom the Father sent constitutes the appropriate object of faith in
the Fourth Gospel.

64. "Common sense" constitutes one of the factors involved in Calvin's epistemol-
ogy. Cf. *Inst.*, I.xv.6: "Common sense" is the "sort of receptacle" to which the five
sense organs present "all objects." "Fantasy" distinguishes what has been appre-
hended by "common sense"; and, on the basis of these distinctions, "reason" makes
"universal judgments."

65. *Comm.* on I Cor. 12:10.

which many contemporary Roman Catholic historians and theologians judge to have been necessary. But at the moment in which this gift is exercised in the church, the one who is exercising it may be regarded as schismatic, a rebel against God and His order, one who destroys the system. Paul's Corinthian correspondence suggests strongly that his exercise of this gift in the Corinthian situation generated antagonism and resistance among those Christians. In general, the one exercising this gift must be recognized by the Christian community as one who possesses the gift and who, in specific circumstances, is exercising the gift. This generalization makes visible the problems which are involved in the receipt and exercise of this gift in the church, as do the illustrations of Paul in Corinth and Calvin and Luther during the period of the Reformation.

*Tongues and interpretation of tongues (I Cor. 12:10, 14)*

"Tongues" and "the interpretation of tongues" dominate Calvin's discussion of I Corinthians 12—14 because of the space which Paul devotes to tongues in the passage. He expresses concern relative to the use of tongues in the act of worship in Corinth. Calvin scarcely deals with the gift of tongues in his comments concerning I Corinthians 12:10. He mentions that the interpretation of tongues consisted of the act of translating "into the native speech" the "foreign language" which was spoken by those possessing the gift of tongues.[66] Calvin, furthermore, deals briefly with the reference to the "speakers in various tongues" in I Corinthians 12:28. He does not discuss in detail the rhetorical questions posed by Paul in verse 30 of that chapter ("Do all speak with tongues? Do all interpret?"). From his comment relative to verse 28, it is evident that Calvin understands the term "various tongues" to describe various languages which are the verbal mode of communication in specific cultures. "Various tongues" refers to known languages which were spoken in Paul's day. This is consistent with the statement Calvin made concerning the gift of interpreting tongues in his comments on I Corinthians 12:10: "interpreting tongues" = to translate the "foreign languages" of the "speakers in various tongues" into the "native speech" of the auditors. There can be no misunderstanding relative to Calvin's position. "Sometimes a person, *who spoke many languages* (italics added), did not, however, know the tongue of the actual church, that he had to deal with; and interpreters made up for such a deficiency."[67]

66. Ibid.                    67. *Comm.* on I Cor. 12:28.

The position that "speakers in various tongues" describes those who have the ability to communicate effectively and precisely in a variety of known and operational languages is maintained consistently by Calvin. He, consequently, takes seriously Paul's reference to the hypothetical ability of someone to speak the language of the angels. Calvin paraphrases I Corinthians 13:1: "You may have a grasp of all the languages, not only those of all men, but of the angels over and above." "Tongues of angels" does not refer to the language which angels actually speak among one another. The term must be understood, Calvin asserts without further elaboration, as "hyperbole for something remarkable or rare."[68] He presents no linguistic or historical evidence to validate this assertion. He, furthermore, presents no analogical material from the Bible to indicate that this usage of the term "tongues of angels" is a valid usage of the term at a particular time in a particular place.

The comment on I Corinthians 13:8 relative to the temporary character of "knowledge" and of "tongues" indicates that Calvin cannot conceive of a content for tongues which differs from "known languages." "As for tongues they will cease." Calvin, in interpreting this statement, uses "learning" and the "knowledge of languages" as synonyms for "knowledge," the knowledge which will pass away, and "tongues," the tongues which will cease. These "gifts serve the needs of this life," and are not gifts which "will remain in existence" in the life to come.[69]

An investigation of Calvin's comments on the data of Acts 2 reveals that Calvin does not dissociate the phenomenon of the disciples speaking "in other tongues" from the "gift of tongues" to which Paul refers in I Corinthians 12—14. The phenomena are the same. Calvin identifies explicitly the phenomenon of the disciples speaking "in other tongues" (Acts 2:4) with Paul's reference to his own gift of "diverse tongues" in I Corinthians 14:18.[70] If the two phenomena are identified, then, of course, "to speak in other tongues" = "to speak known languages." Calvin does not question the structure and content of Acts 2. He does not raise the question of the relationship between Peter's sermon in which he proclaimed the mighty acts of God and the disciples speaking in other tongues. He does not raise the question of the relationship between the content of Peter's sermon and the previous statement of the auditors: "We hear them telling in our own tongues the mighty works of

68. *Comm.* on I Cor. 13:1.

69. *Comm.* on I Cor. 13:8.

70. *Comm.* on Acts 2:4.

God." If, moreover, "to speak in other tongues" = "to speak known languages," then the problem to which Paul points in I Corinthians 14 focuses on the Corinthian "spirituals" (believers) using tongues in worship services which were unknown languages to unbelievers or outsiders who attended the worship service; and on the failure of the Corinthian "spirituals" to provide interpreters for the auditors. This interpretation of the content of I Corinthians 14, however, does not seem to do justice to the data found there: that is, the unbelieving auditors will judge the Corinthian Christians to be "mad," (*mainesthe,* "to be mad," "to be out of one's mind."). If a group of people who had gathered for worship in Grand Rapids, Michigan, were addressed by one speaker in Urdu and by another speaker in Japanese, visitors from the same area who were present might come to several conclusions: (1) Some of those who were present were "native speakers" of the "foreign languages" which two of the speakers used. (2) These people were impolite because they spoke in public in languages foreign to this particular place. Some of us, at least did not understand the languages in which two speakers addressed us. In addition, the group provided no interpretation of what was said. (3) The speaker did not know English, the language which serves as the primary vehicle of communication in Grand Rapids; and, apparently, no one else present was able to translate those "foreign languages" into English. (4) If the Urdu and Japanese languages' phonology differs radically from the phonology of the visitors' language, English, the visitor could question the character of the sounds he heard. Is this really another language? Or is this merely a jumbled group of unrelated sounds? If the visitors came to the last conclusion, that the sounds were unrelated sounds and not phonemes of a known language, he could question the sanity of the speaker, and, perhaps, of all those who were congregated. The conclusion that the speaker and the congregation were insane is not the first conclusion to which one would come if the speaker was using a known and operational language.

The disciples and other preachers of the gospel, Calvin continues, had need of the ability to communicate in a variety of languages in the first century, A.D., if Christ was to be proclaimed as Lord and Savior throughout the Mediterranean basin. If the Galilean followers of Jesus had not received the gift of the ability to speak effectively and precisely in a variety of known languages, Christ would have been "confined to a small corner of Judaea."[71]

In his comments on Acts 2:2, Calvin at one point seems to suggest

71. *Comm.* on Acts 2:2.

that the disciples and their auditors were given the gift of the language of Canaan, that Pentecost reversed Babel's multiplication of languages: "But now God furnishes the apostles with a diversity of tongues that He may call back lost and wandering men into the blessings of unity. These cloven tongues made every man speak the language of Canaan as Isaiah foretold (Is. 19:18). For whatever language they speak they all with one mouth and one Spirit call upon the same Father in heaven (Rom. 15:8)." The last sentence indicates, however, that in Calvin's analysis Pentecost overcame the disunity of peoples but not the plurality of languages. "The language of Canaan," moreover, is a metaphor for the unity of faith characteristic of the people of God. The term does not refer to a specific language which was spoken by people in a particular place and in a specific era: a language with a recognizable and decipherable phonology and morphology.

Calvin knows, moreover, that there have been those who interpret Pentecost as a miracle of hearing, not a miracle of speaking. He commits himself to a miracle of speaking,[72] but he refuses to make a decision about "a second miracle" being performed "whereby Egyptians and Elamites understood Peter speaking in the Chaldean tongue as if he were uttering diverse voices."[73]

Although Calvin leaves room for a variety of interpretations of the phenomena of Acts 2, three factors cannot be assailed: (1) "The apostles truly changed their speech."[74] (2) The apostles' ability to "speak in other tongues" was not a skill which was gained, at that time, by their "study or industry." This ability was received as a "gift of the Spirit."[75] In Acts 2:11, the auditors were amazed because "the apostles were formerly ignorant and unlearned men, born in a district of no repute, yet now they discoursed profoundly of the things of God and of heavenly lore." (3) The apostles suddenly were "endowed with new tongues."[76] When Calvin indicates that at the time of Pentecost the ability of the apostles to speak in different languages was not the product of their study and diligence, one raises the question of the earlier study of the apostles. Did Calvin think that the apostles, earlier, had engaged in a study of the languages which were heard by the auditors? Calvin's insistence on the suddenness of the disciples' ability to converse in languages different from their native language indicates that his use of the term "at that time" has no special significance.

Calvin understands "tongues" to be the Spirit's gift of the ability

72. *Comm.* on Acts 2:4.
73. Ibid.
74. Ibid.
75. Ibid.
76. *Comm.* on Acts 2:11.

to communicate in a language foreign to the speaker. The speaker, however, uses this gift intelligently. His reason is not shunted out of the process. The speaker uses this new language—a real language which is the communication vehicle of particular people in a particular area—to communicate the mighty acts of God. The Spirit gave the gift of tongues so that the gospel could be preached to foreigners who used a different language, and "for the adornment and honour of the Gospel itself."[77] The mind, the reason of the speaker, operates in the use of the verbal tool of communication as that gift of the right word is articulated, so that the tongue serves the gospel by being a vehicle of prophecy. Calvin's comments in all places in the New Testament where he has dealt with the phenomenon of tongues seem to require the following posture relative to tongues. Although the ability to speak a specific foreign language is a gift of the Spirit to a specific believer, the gifted speaker consciously exercises his rational ability to verbalize, to conceptualize, to differentiate, to classify, to articulate general, universal truths. He does so, however, in the "new" language which he has received as a gift. The same rational processes operate in the gifted speaker's use of his new language as operate in his use of his native language.

The normal function of the new language, the gift of tongues, is the proclamation of the mighty acts of God. When the Corinthian "spiritual" believers used this gift for an ostentatious display of their own abilities to speak "foreign languages" in prayer and praise, Paul spoke sharply about this fault. "There is, therefore, nothing strange about it, if a little later on God took away what He had given, and did not allow it to be vitiated with further abuse."[78] The gift of tongues may not serve the speaker; it must serve the gospel if it is to be a legitimate enterprise.

In his comments on I Corinthians 14, Calvin goes off in two directions. In the first place, he claims that the gift of tongues is a legitimate and necessary gift in his own day when it aids prophecy. The illustrations he uses are the Greek and Hebrew languages.[79] What becomes obvious here is that Calvin is not suggesting that persons who have received the gift of *speaking* Greek and Hebrew proclaim the gospel to the sixteenth century Greeks and Jews in their own language. Nor

77. *Comm.* on Acts 10:46. Cf. *Comm.* on I Cor. 14:22.

78. Ibid. Interestingly enough, although Calvin does deal with tongues in the story of Cornelius the Centurion (Acts 10:46) to make the point which has been mentioned, the manifestation of tongues among the Ephesians who received the Holy Spirit when Paul baptized them in the name of Jesus is passed over without any comment (Acts 19:1-7).

79. *Comm.* on I Cor. 14:27.

is he suggesting that Genevan pastors and members of the Christian church in Geneva witness to Christ in Greek and Hebrew rather than in French. He is not suggesting, moreover, that Christians in Geneva speak Greek and Hebrew in their public prayers. He is suggesting, rather, that the theologians who had received as a gift of the Spirit the ability to use creatively and significantly the Hebrew Old Testament and the Greek New Testament do so. This gift, interestingly enough, operated in cooperation with the individual study of the gifted person. The gifted theologian is obliged to exercise this gift. To fail to use this gift of the Spirit is to cripple the church and to disobey God. In Calvin's comments, the gift of tongues became a tool in his apology over against the Roman Catholic church's insistence on the primacy of the Latin Vulgate.

Calvin goes in another direction, also, in his comments on I Corinthians 14 which superficially seems to be antithetic to his insistence that the gift of tongues was necessary and useful in his own day: that is, he ridicules the use of the Latin language in the prayers of the Roman Catholic liturgy.

> What is clearer than these words of Paul, that an uneducated person cannot take part in public prayer, unless he understands what is being said? What is plainer than this prohibition, "thanksgivings or prayers should not be repeated in public except in the language everyone understands, the native tongue"? When every day they [i.e., Papists] do what Paul says should not or even cannot be done, are they not treating Paul as if he were an uneducated person himself? When they are so scrupulous about observing what He forbids, are they not openly defying God?[80]

Calvin's discussion of the content of the gifts of the Spirit can be summarized in the following points:

1.  He regards the gift of prophecy as the most important and useful gift. This evaluation stems from his understanding of the primacy of exhortation, proclamation, maintaining pure doctrine ( = the pure gospel) in the Christian community.

2.  The offices of the Christian church, or, more precisely, the capability of filling an office in the Christian church, is given to some

---

80. *Comm.* on I Cor. 14:16-17. Calvin's discussion of I Cor. 14:20-24 will not be surveyed. Calvin understands the *apistoi* to be mission objects, those "who were still strangers to Christ." The passage, admittedly, is difficult and seems to be internally self-contradictory. The interpretation of Jean Hering, *The First Epistle of St. Paul to the Corinthians* (London: The Epworth Press, 1962), pp. 152-53, commends itself. He reads *apistoi* as "those who harden their hearts and who remain disbelieving"; whereas *tois pisteuousin* (14:22) "are those in process of becoming Christians." Cf. the similar position in F. J. Pop, *De Eerste Brief van Paulus Aan De Corinthiërs* (Nijkerk: G. F. Callenbach, 1965), pp. 327-31. The function of the "quotation" from Isaiah 28:11 is crucial to the passage.

people as a gift of the Spirit or of Christ. One can also state that God appointed the specific person to this office. All three expressions have the same content. A person, consequently, does not seek an office. The gifted person must use the gift he has received. The Christian community, moreover, must recognize and accept the gift God has given to a specific person.

3. The offices of apostle, evangelist, and prophet were designed to function only in the beginning of the Christian era; the offices of pastor and teacher were designed to be permanent, as were the two diaconal offices and the governing office.

4. The gifts of healing and miracles have occurred only rarely. They were intended to complement and aid the gospel, but have been noticeably absent after the apostolic era. Calvin does not discount the possibility of these gifts appearing; but miracles, if they occur, must serve the gospel.

5. The gift of tongues is the ability to speak effectively, to communicate precisely in a foreign language. This ability is given to specific people by the Spirit of God, and does not result, in the first place, from one's study of the language. In using this gift, one's mind is operative. The speaker may be incapable of translating this speech into the native language of those to whom he addresses himself, but the process of speaking in the foreign language is one in which the rational functions of the speaker are involved. The gift of translating the tongue into the native speech of the auditor is a gift of the Spirit, also. Calvin does not indicate whether this gift is given apart from the study of the language which is interpreted or whether the gift is given along with one's study of a language.

6. The primary gift of the Spirit is the ability to prophesy, to speak the right word in the specific circumstances in which men are located—a word which is continuous with and not antithetical to Scripture. The primacy of this gift reflects Calvin's commitment to God's mediated actions and presence. It also reflects Calvin's commitment to a perspective in which the gifts represent the modes in which God exercises His rule among men as He maintains the creation and brings it to His desired objectives.

## Did the cultural context of the sixteenth century influence Calvin's interpretation of the Biblical material?

Calvin reflects plainly in his discussions of the gifts of the Spirit that the cultural context of the sixteenth century influenced his reading of the Biblical material.

1. In the first place, the illustration of this which stands out most

clearly is Calvin's insistence that when tongues aid in prophecy, tongues are a legitimate and useful gift of the Spirit. In fact, in his own day the Greek and Hebrew languages or tongues served a useful purpose in the prophetic declaration of the gospel. They were not merely a useful and legitimate gift given to some theologians by the Spirit; they were a necessary gift. The exercise of this gift was necessary in order to aid the process of purifying the gospel, of returning to the gospel of Scripture. The plight of the church in the sixteenth century and Calvin's remedy for that plight influenced his reading of I Corinthians 12—14.

2. Calvin, in the second place, reflects the influence of his own cultural context on his reading of I Corinthians 12—14 in discussing Paul's prohibition of the use of tongues in public prayer during the assembly of the church unless an interpretation of what was said in the "foreign language" accompany that which was spoken. Calvin's evaluation of and response to the use of Latin prayers in the liturgy of the church colored his interpretation of Paul's proclamation relative to the prohibition of tongues in the worship of the assembled congregation. Calvin's position stems from his commitment to an intimate relation between language as the vehicle of reason and the system or total comprehensive structure of reality to which all language pointed: the interrelations among God, man, and the rest of the created world. Calvin, consequently, emphasized the verbal character of prayer, thanksgiving, and all other cultic acts. Calvin exhibited no sympathy for nonrational cultic acts. He is able to use Paul's acceptance of the function of tongues in worship services when subject to the two Pauline conditions: (a) the tongue must be interpreted into the language of the auditors; (b) no more than two or three gifted people should speak in a "foreign language" in each worship service of the congregation.

In points 1 and 2, the Roman Catholic insistence on the primacy of the Latin Vulgate text with the theological problems present in that text,[81] and the use of Latin as the liturgical language prompted Calvin to read I Corinthians 12—14 in a specific way—a way which resulted in that passage speaking to the situation of sixteenth-century Geneva.

3. When what seems to be the obvious meaning of the Biblical text conflicts with the intellectual structure of the Reformation, Calvin appeals to the difference between the cultural context of his own day and that of the Biblical author's day. He does this so that the "meaning" of the text may be discerned—something that cannot be done

81. Cf. fn. 22.

until the reader has come to terms with the cultural context which influenced the author. One of the most interesting illustrations of this is found in Calvin's comment on I Corinthians 11:14 ("Does not nature itself teach you that for a man to wear long hair is degrading to him... ?"). Calvin felt compelled to address himself to the question "Does not nature itself teach you... ?" In Calvin's perspective "nature" constitutes the specific structure of created reality over which God exercises His rule through the processes which are embraced by the term "providence." That structure, in Calvin's perspective, did *not* teach that long hair degraded a man. The length of a man's hair in Calvin's day was longer than is thought appropriate among contemporary adult males in positions of responsibility. Calvin, consequently, introduces into his investigation of the Biblical text what today is called "cultural relativity" in order to "understand" Paul's "meaning."

> He means by "natural" what was accepted by common consent and usage at that time, certainly as far as the Greeks were concerned. For long hair was not always regarded as a disgraceful thing in men. Historical works relate that long ago, i.e., in the earliest times, men wore long hair in every country. Thus the poets are in the habit of speaking about the ancients and applying to them the well-worn epithet "unshorn". In Rome they did not begin to use barbers until a late period, about the time of Africanus the Elder, (born 235, B.C.). When Paul was writing these words, the practice of cutting hair had not yet been adopted in Gaul and Germany. Yes, and more than that, indeed, it would have been a disgraceful thing for men, just as much as women, to have their hair shaved or cut. But since the Greeks did not consider it very manly to have long hair, branding those who had it as effeminate, Paul considers that their custom, accepted in his own day, was in conformity with nature.

This expression of cultural relativity becomes more interesting when it is juxtaposed to his discussion of I Corinthians 11:5 ("Any woman who prays or prophesies with her head unveiled dishonors her head"). One would expect Calvin to take seriously the possibility that women were exercising the gift of prophecy in the Corinthian church. That seems to be implied by Paul's statement. Calvin, however, points out that I Timothy 2:12 prohibits women from speaking in the church. In I Corinthians 14:34 ff., moreover, Paul censures women who attempt to prophesy in the church. In 11:5, therefore, Calvin concludes, Paul is addressing himself to the problem of the headdress which women wear. He is not addressing himself to the problem of women exercising a prophetic role. Calvin adds that if this reading of 11:5 does not satisfy one, then it is well to add to what has been written that Paul may be addressing himself to the Corinthian church concerning the act of some women in assemblies which were not official assemblies of the church for worship.

Calvin's reading of I Corinthians 11:5, specifically the possibility that Paul addresses himself to the act of some women in assemblies which were not official assemblies of the church for worship, cannot be sustained for the following reasons.

(1) In I Corinthians 14:33b ff. Paul does not prohibit women from prophesying in the church's service of worship; rather, he prohibits women from speaking. In verse 35, Paul elaborates on the speaking to which he makes reference. "If there is anything they desire to know, let them ask their husbands at home." This certainly differs from the exercise of the prophetic role. One can add to this that in Acts 21:9, Philip's seven unmarried daughters are introduced as those who prophesied. In I Corinthians 14:37 ff., Paul returns once more to his theme relative to the "prophet or spiritual." The prohibited "speaking" in I Corinthians 14:33b ff. cannot be identified with "prophecy" as facilely as Calvin has done.

(2) The problems to which Paul addresses himself in I Corinthians 11—15 seem to be problems which concern the assemblies of the Corinthian church for worship. The problem to which Paul addresses himself immediately after he has finished his discussion of the women's headdress during prayer and prophecy is the problem involved in the celebration of the Lord's Supper in the Corinthian church. The problem to which Paul addresses himself in I Corinthians 11:2-16 does not seem to be concerned with assemblies which differ from those which he discusses in verses 17 and following. There is no indication that Paul has shifted his discussion to a different kind of assembly in which some problems are present also.

(3) The discussion concerning the Lord's Supper which begins at I Corinthians 11:17 is related intimately to the discussion which precedes it through the use of a rhetorical device common to the introduction of both discussions: "I commend you because . . ."; "ordering this I do not commend you because . . . ." The attempt to read verses 2-16 as a description of assemblies which differ fundamentally from the assemblies in verses 17 and following must come to terms with the rhetorical device which Paul uses to relate the two discussions to one another.

(4) When one investigates Calvin's comments on I Corinthians 14:33b and following, the pericope in which Paul prohibits women from speaking in the church, he is surprised to note that Calvin does not maintain unconditionally the necessity of women waiting until they are home to ask their husbands questions relative to what "they desire to know." Calvin qualifies Paul's prohibition. Calvin indicates

that some husbands are ignorant and, consequently, are incapable of answering their wives' questions. These wives must, therefore, ask their questions in church. They must address their questions to men who are capable of giving satisfactory answers.

In the light of the data which have been presented, one is able to conclude that the role of women in sixteenth-century Geneva influenced Calvin's reading of Paul. This role was, of course, traced to the teaching of the Bible; however, a study of Calvin's comments in the relevant sections indicates that the cultural factors operative in his own age caused Calvin to interpret Biblical injunctions in a way which seems to modify them.

Calvin is done an injustice, however, if he is understood to be one who has relativized the Bible and the Christian faith. Calvin is committed to the structure of reality, the system which he finds in the Bible. God the Creator is the Lord of the creation. He exercises His lordship through the structures which He has implanted in the creation: the church, the state, the family. These structures do not operate willy-nilly. God appoints His agents, people through whom He operates mediately in the exercise of His lordship, in discharging His role as God. The structures which God has implanted in the creation and the agents of God through whom these structures operate constitute the modes through which God works as the Lord. As has been indicated earlier, there is less flexibility in this perspective than is deemed appropriate by most twentieth century people.

When Calvin reads a statement such as Paul's in I Corinthians 11:5, he concludes that it must mean something other than the superficial meaning: that is, it must mean something other than that some women are exercising the role of prophet in the worship services of the church. This meaning would be in conflict with the operation of the structured "church" through the agents whom God appoints as that operation is delineated elsewhere in the Bible. Therefore, Calvin does not feel it incumbent on him to give a precise and exhaustive comment on the terms "prayer" and "prophecy" in I Corinthians 11:5. In passages which contain difficulties of this type, Calvin is willing to entertain the possibility that the writer is using hyperbole, and that the writer pictures conditions contrary to fact only as teaching devices.

Calvin is aware of the fact that the environment in which he lives influences him as he reads the Bible. This influence is one of the factors which operates in the prophetic declaration of the gospel. The pastor-preacher must be sensitive to the needs of people in his world, as has been pointed out earlier, and, simultaneously, to Scripture. From out of Scripture he addresses the right word to people living in his world: a word which is peculiarly appropriate to people in their specific need.

This essay has examined Calvin's comments on I Corinthians 12—14; Romans 12:4-8; and Ephesians 4:11. I have concluded that, according to Calvin, the gifts of the Spirit are distributed among individuals who are members of the Christian church so that the exercise of the gifts will promote and maintain the unity of the Church of Christ as she functions in this world as the witness to her Lord. The exercise of the gifts of the Spirit is designed to benefit the body of Christ. It is the gifts of the Spirit, moreover, which generate and preserve the individuality of each member of the Christian church. The gifts of the Spirit, furthermore, constitute the prerequisite for office. One cannot attain office in the church without the gifts of the Spirit; and the gifts of the Spirit must be used in the framework of the body of Christ for the benefit of the body. The gifts must be exercised, consequently, in office, within the operation of the structure which God established and maintains as the locus of God's mediated presence and activity in the world. In this context it may be well to point out that Calvin, in *The Institutes,* introduces the Holy Spirit into his argument at each and every point where the threat of human autonomy intrudes on the gospel. Only through the activity of the Holy Spirit can man discharge his authentic role as the servant-son of God.

In the study of Calvin's descriptions and definitions of the gifts of the Spirit, the influence of his perspective on his understanding of these gifts becomes visible. This influence can be seen most clearly in Calvin's descriptions of tongues as "known languages." The gifts as Calvin describes and defines them, through the use of his "temporary"-"permanent" distinction, can serve effectively as valid descriptions of the roles which specific members of the sixteenth century Christian church in Geneva played for the effective functioning of that church. Calvin, in the context of the needs of the Christian community, has heard the Word of God. His comments constitute his exercise of the gift he received—*doctor*—from the Spirit: a gift which was designed to promote and maintain unity in the Christian community in Geneva, to benefit the church as it discharged its role as witness to Christ, to the gospel.

Calvin has maintained two positions relative to Paul's writings which constitute an important contribution to the contemporary discussion of the gifts of the Spirit. (1) God's presence and activity in the world, including indwelling His saints, is *always* a mediated presence and activity. God does not confront men nor operate in the world directly, immediately. He always uses agents who are His voice and His hands among men. Calvin concludes this on the basis of the Bible. This position differentiates Calvin from those who are involved in the charismatic movement today. (2) The gifts of the Spirit are distributed and function within the framework of the church. Calvin calls attention over and over again to the gifts of the Spirit which are "offices" in the church. Contemporary participants in the charismatic movement can serve to provide a corrective to Calvin at this point. Calvin does not seem adequately sensitive to the argument of Paul in Ephesians 4:11. The gifts are called gifts of Christ (Eph. 4:7); these gifts are *people who function as* apostles, prophets, evangelists, pastors, and teachers. The gifts are not offices as such. Calvin's emphasis on the presence and operation of these gifts in the Christian community—the church—for the benefit of the church in its role as God's servant remains a valuable contribution to the contemporary discussion of the gifts of the Spirit.

*Peter De Klerk*
*Theological Librarian,*
*Calvin Theological Seminary*

# BIBLIOGRAPHY

Due to space limitations this bibliography does not include all the magazine articles and columns written by John Bratt. Those included represent the wide spectrum of subjects which were discussed.

## ABBREVIATIONS

| | | | |
|---|---|---|---|
| *Ban* | *The Banner* | *RJ* | *The Reformed Journal* |
| *CF* | *The Calvin Forum* | *Sfd* | *Springboards for Discussion* |
| *CHS* | *Christian Home and School* | *Sfd 2* | *Springboards for Discussion:* |
| *CTJ* | *Calvin Theological Journal* | | *No. 2* |
| Ed. | Editor/edited | TRA | "The Reader Asks" |
| | *TT* | *Torch and Trumpet* | |

**1938**

*The Southern Presbyterian and Christian Reformed Churches of America: an historical comparison.* ThM. thesis. Decatur, Ga.: Columbia Theological Seminary, 1938, iii, 60 leaves.

**1939**

"Luther on the rostrum" *CF* 5 (1939/40) 43-44.

**1940**

" 'Not many mighty, not many noble' " *CF* 6 (1940/41) 18-19.

**1942**

"Israel and her pagan neighbors" *CF* 7 (1941/42) 141-144, 163-167.

**1946**

*New Testament guide.* Grand Rapids: Wm. B. Eerdmans Publishing Co., 1946. Revised and enlarged edition dated 1961.

"The sun of righteousness" (Malachi 4, 2a) in *Book of sermons, no. 5.* Grand Rapids: Christian Reformed Publishing House, 1946. Pp. 42-51.

**1947**

*New Testament epistles.* A course designed for individual home study. The Back to God Hour courses for home study. Chicago: The Back to God Hour, 1947.

"Reflections on war and peace" *CF* 12 (1946/47) 120-121.

Review of *The story of the faith.* By William Alva Gifford. New York: The Macmillan Co., 1946. *CF* 12 (1946/47) 150.

Review of *Albertus C. Van Raalte and his Dutch settlements in the United States.* By Albert Hyma. Grand Rapids: Wm. B. Eerdmans Publishing Co., 1947. *CF* 12 (1946/47) 223-224.

**1948**

"The church concept in Christian history" *CF* 13 (1947/48) 133-135.

Review of *The glory of the empty tomb.* By Samuel M. Zwemer. New York: Fleming H. Revell Co., 1947. *CF* 14 (1948/49) 29-30.

**1949**

Ed. *Feed my lambs.* A collection of prizewinning essays dealing with improvement of the Sunday School. Grand Rapids: Midwest Sunday School Association, 1949.

Review of *Riches of divine grace.* By Louis Berkhof. Grand Rapids: Wm. B. Eerdmans Publishing Co., 1948. *CF* 14 (1948/49) 125.

"Bible reading in Christian history" *CF* 14 (1948/49) 141-143.

Review of *Hebrew and Chaldee lexicon.* By W. Gesenius. Tr. by S. P. Tregelles. Grand Rapids: Wm. B. Eerdmans Publishing Co., 1949. *CF* 15 (1949/50) 103.

**1950**

Review of *The light in dark ages.* By V. Raymond Edman. Wheaton, Ill.: Van Kampen Press, 1949. *CF* 15 (1949/50) 254.

Review of *Mark in the Greek New Testament for English readers.* By K. S. Wuest. Grand Rapids: Wm. B. Eerdmans Publishing Co., 1950. *Ban* 85 (1950) 1138.

Review of *History of the Christian church.* By Philip Schaff. Grand Rapids: Wm. B. Eerdmans Publishing Co., 1950. 8 vol's. *CF* 16 (1950/51) 74-75.

"The advent gospel in Isaiah" *CF* 16 (1950/51) 81-82.

Review of *The dawn of Christianity.* By Frederick Fyvie Bruce. London: Paternoster Press, 1950. *CF* 16 (1950/51) 97.

Review of *Old Testament studies.* Vol. 1, *Genesis to Job.* By W. R. Newell. Chicago: The Moody Press, 1950. *CF* 16 (1950/51) 99.

Review of *F. B. Meyer on the Psalms.* By F. B. Meyer. Grand Rapids: Zondervan Publishing House, 1950. *Ban* 85 (1950) 1558.

**1951**

Review of *Notes on O. T. history.* Vol. 2, *Exodus to Nehemiah.* By Albertus Pieters. Grand Rapids: Wm. B. Eerdmans Publishing Co., 1950. *CF* 16 (1950/51) 150.

Review of *Expository thoughts on the Gospels* (Matthew—Mark). By J. C. Ryle. Grand Rapids: Zondervan Publishing House, 1951. *Ban* 86 (1951) 499.

Review of *The seed of Abraham.* A biblical study of Israel, the church and the Jew. By Albertus Pieters. Grand Rapids: Wm. B. Eerdmans Publishing Co., 1950. *CF* 16 (1950/51) 221.

Review of *The church in history.* By Barend K. Kuiper. Grand Rapids: Wm. B. Eerdmans Publishing Co., 1951. *CF* 16 (1950/51) 243.

"Albert Schweitzer as theologian: an appraisal" *CF* 17 (1951/52) 9-11.

Review of *A harmony and commentary on the life of St. Paul.* By F. J. Goodwin. Grand Rapids: Baker Book House, 1951. *Ban* 86 (1951) 1042.

"The history of American evangelism" *Ban* 86 (1951) 1447; 87 (1952) 103, 519, 535, 839; 88 (1953) 359, 839.

"The doctrine of the deity of Christ in the early church" *CF* 17 (1951/52) 88-90.

Review of *Introductory guide to the Old Testament.* By M. F. Unger. Grand Rapids: Zondervan Publishing House, 1951. *Ban* 86 (1951) 1583.

**1952**

Review of *Biblical and theological studies.* By Benjamin Breckinridge Warfield. Philadelphia: Presbyterian and Reformed Publishing Co., 1952. *CF* 17 (1951/52) 188.

"Prophets, false and true, in the Old Testament dispensation" *CF* 17 (1951/52) 197-200, 217-222.

**1954**

Review of *Can we trust Bible history?* By Albertus Pieters. Grand Rapids: Wm. B. Eerdmans Publishing Co., 1954. *Ban* 89 (1954) 956.

"The contemporary scene: major religious movements in America during our ecclesiatical history" *Ban* 89 (1954) 1350-1351, 1366, 1606-1607, 1618; 90 (1955) 166-167, 1318-1319; 91 (1956) 358.

**1955**

*The missionary enterprise of the Christian Reformed Church of America.* ThD. dissertation. Richmond, Va.: Union Theological Seminary, 1955. vii, 453, 2 leaves.

**1956**

"John Calvin and ecumenicity" in *Calvinism 301X.* Grand Rapids: Calvin College, 1956. 7 leaves.

Review of *Twentieth century encyclopedia of religious knowledge.* Ed. by L. A. Loetscher. Grand Rapids: Baker Book House, 1955. Vol. 14-15. *CF* 21 (1955/56) 108.

"The Bible major: a new development at Calvin College" *Ban* 91 (1956) 614-615.

**1957**

"The road we have traveled: in retrospect" in *Continuing our onward course.* 1957-58 Christian School Annual. Grand Rapids: The National Union of Christian Schools, 1957. Pp. 130-138.

"Church control of Calvin College" *RJ* 7 (February 1957) 17-20.

"Only one message" (II Timothy 4, 1-2) *Centennial messages* (The Back to God Hour, Chicago, Illinois) 2 (March 1957) 38-42.

Review of *The Christian scholar in the age of the reformation.* By E. Harris Harbison. New York: Charles Scribner's Sons, 1956. *RJ* 7 (September 1957) 30-31.

**1958**

*The life and teachings of John Calvin.* A study manual. Grand Rapids: Baker Book House, 1958.

*Modern ecumenical movements.* Analysis and appraisal. Calvin College Monograph Series. Bible, no. 1. Grand Rapids: Calvin College, 1958.

"Calvinism in America" *Ban* 93 (April 4, 1958) 9, 28, (April 18, 1958) 9, 29, (May 2, 1959) 9, 25, (May 9, 1958) 9, 20, (July 11, 1958) 25.

**1959**

Ed. *The rise and development of calvinism.* A concise history. Grand Rapids: Wm. B. Eerdmans Publishing Co., 1959. Revised edition dated 1964, 1968, and 1971.

"The history and development of calvinism in America" in *The rise and development of calvinism.* A concise history. Ed. by John Harold Bratt. Grand Rapids: Wm. B. Eerdmans Publishing Co., 1959. Pp. 113-134.

"The life and work of John Calvin" in *The rise and development of calvinism.* A concise history. Ed. by John Harold Bratt. Grand Rapids: Wm. B. Eerdmans Publishing Co., 1959. Pp. 9-26.

"John Calvin—our spiritual father" *Ban* 94 (February 13, 1959) 4-5.

"John Calvin and ecumenicity" *RJ* 9 (March 1959) 8-10, (April 1959) 17-18.

"John Calvin and the Genevan schools" *CHS* 37 (March 1959) 12-13.

"Calvinism in America—a tragic story" *Ban* 94 (May 15, 1959) 9, 29.

Review of *The church's ministry to the older unmarried.* By Melvin Dale Hugen. Grand Rapids: Wm. B. Eerdmans Publishing Co., 1959. *RJ* 9 (July-August 1959) 22-23.

**1960\***

"Is this traducianism?" (TRA) *Ban* 95 (January 15, 1960) 11, 23, (January 22, 1960) 11.

"Do Isaiah 45, 7 and Amos 3, 6b teach that God is the author of sin?" (TRA) *Ban* 95 (January 22, 1960) 11, 23.

"What is this Gospel of Thomas that I have been reading about lately?" (TRA) *Ban* 95 (February 12, 1960) 11.

"How long was the 'day' in the creation record?" (TRA) *Ban* 95 (February 19, 1960) 11.

"Should Christians fast?" (TRA) *Ban* 95 (March 4, 1960) 11. Also in *Sfd,* pp. 97-100.

*Beginning in 1960, John Bratt has written a weekly column, "The Reader Asks," in *The Banner.* The bibliography contains only selected samples to indicate the range of topics covered.

"Should we anoint the sick with oil?" (TRA) *Ban* 95 (April 1, 1960) 11. Also in *Sfd,* pp. 104-106.

"Why did Jesus prefer to call himself 'Son of Man'?" (TRA) *Ban* 95 (May 6, 1960) 11.

"Is Genesis 2 a second creation account?" (TRA) *Ban* 95 (June 24, 1960) 11.

"Does the Apostles Creed need revision?" (TRA) *Ban* 95 (July 8, 1960) 11.

"Is cremation compatible with the Christian faith?" (TRA) *Ban* 95 (August 12, 1960) 11. Also in *Sfd,* pp. 19-23.

Review of *The gospel according to Thomas.* Coptic text established and translated by A. Guillamont, et al. New York: Harper and Brothers, 1960. *Ban* 95 (August 19, 1960) 28.

"Why didn't Elisha pray for the mocking children instead of cursing them?" (TRA) *Ban* 95 (September 2, 1960) 11. Also in *Sfd,* pp. 111-114.

"Does footwashing belong with our communion celebration?" (TRA) *Ban* 95 (September 23, 1960) 11. Also in *Sfd,* pp. 101-103.

"What is meant by being 'baptized for the dead'?" (TRA) *Ban* 95 (December 2, 1960) 5.

"May a Christian assign his body after his demise to medical science?" (TRA) *Ban* 95 (December 30, 1960) 11. Also in *Sfd,* pp. 46-48.

**1961**

Ed. *Christian Reformed Church worthies.* A series of biographies. By Jacob Gradus Vanden Bosch. Grand Rapids: Wm. B. Eerdmans Publishing Co., 1961.

"Do the Genesis genealogies give exact chronology?" (TRA) *Ban* 96 (May 5, 1961) 17.

Review of *Institutes of the Christian religion.* By John Calvin. Ed. by John Thomas McNeill, tr. by Ford Lewis Battles. Philadelphia: The Westminster Press, 1961. 2 vol's. *Ban* 96 (May 19, 1961) 28-29.

"How old is our earth?" (TRA) *Ban* 96 (May 26, 1961) 11, (July 28, 1961) 19. Also in *Sfd,* pp. 45-49.

"Are the premillenarians right?" (TRA) *Ban* 96 (June 2, 1961) 9.

"Why did Jesus enjoin silence?" (TRA) *Ban* 96 (July 7, 1961) 13. Also in *Sfd 2,* pp. 118-120.

"Why did the antediluvians live so long?" (TRA) *Ban* 96 (August 18, 1961) 10. Also in *Sfd 2,* pp. 105-107.

"Is death similar to unconsciousness?" (TRA) *Ban* 96 (September 15, 1961) 16. Also in *Sfd,* pp. 119-121.

"Will we know all things in heaven?" (TRA) *Ban* 96 (December 15, 1961) 9. Also in *Sfd,* pp. 129-130.

"Are these millennial events?" (TRA) *Ban* 96 (December 22, 1961) 10.

**1962**

"Were the Bible writers conscious of being inspired?" (TRA) *Ban* 97 (February 2, 1962) 17.

"Is hell a physical state?" (TRA) *Ban* 97 (March 16, 1962) 11. Also in *Sfd,* pp. 134-136.

"Did God threaten immediate death for Adam and Eve?" (TRA) *Ban* 97 (March 30, 1962) 17. Also in *Sfd 2,* pp. 57-59.

"Sabbath or Lord's Day" (TRA) *Ban* 97 (May 25, 1962) 17. Also in *Sfd 2,* pp. 115-117.

"Can capital punishment stand the test of Scripture?" (TRA) *Ban* 97 (June 15, 1962) 17. Also in *Sfd,* pp. 13-15.

"Did Jesus have a human soul?" (TRA) *Ban* 97 (July 6, 1962) 17. Also in *Sfd,* pp. 62-63.

"Is Pentecost repeated?" (TRA) *Ban* 97 (July 13, 1962) 15. Also in *Sfd,* pp. 111-112.

"Could Adam develop before the fall?" (TRA) *Ban* 97 (July 20, 1962) 17. Also in *Sfd 2,* pp. 63-64.

"When did man get headship over woman?" (TRA) *Ban* 97 (August 3, 1962) 17.

"Is there a purgatory?" (TRA) *Ban* 97 (August 31, 1962) 17. Also in *Sfd,* pp. 140-143.

"In what sense was Christ the second or last Adam?" (TRA) *Ban* 97 (September 7, 1962) 17.

"Who were the 'spirits in prison'?" (TRA) *Ban* 97 (September 21, 1962) 17.

"Do we subscribe to a social gospel?" (TRA) *Ban* 97 (October 5, 1962) 17.

"Did the gift of tongues cease?" (TRA) *Ban* 97 (November 23, 1962) 7. Also in *Sfd,* pp. 107-110.

"How is God's justice to be understood?" (TRA) *Ban* 97 (December 7, 1962) 15.

**1963**

"The Christian Reformed Church in American culture" *RJ* 13 (January 1963) 4-8.

"Evangelical ecumenical movements" *TT* 13 (February 1963) 6-8.

"Are socialism and Christianity compatible?" (TRA) *Ban* 98 (February 1, 1963) 15.

"Why don't we join the ICCC?" (TRA) *Ban* 98 (March 8, 1963) 15.

"Did Isaac know that the covenant blessing was to go to Jacob?" (TRA) *Ban* 98 (March 15, 1963) 15.

"Was Jesus' body interred for three days?" (TRA) *Ban* 98 (April 26, 1963) 11.

"Should we have a Christian political party?" (TRA) *Ban* 98 (May 31, 1963) 11.

"What is blasphemy against the Spirit?" (TRA) *Ban* 98 (June 7, 1963) 11. Also in *Sfd 2,* pp. 121-123.

"Is the Heidelberg Catechism outmoded?" (TRA) *Ban* 98 (June 14, 1963) 11.

"Was the American Revolution justifiable?" (TRA) *Ban* 98 (June 28, 1963) 11.

"When did Jesus' flight into Egypt occur?" (TRA) *Ban* 98 (August 2, 1963) 7. Also in *Sfd,* pp. 72-74.

"Is there a case for gambling?" (TRA) *Ban* 98 (October 18, 1963) 11. Also in *Sfd,* pp. 24-27.

"Should women be allowed to hold church offices?" (TRA)*Ban* 98 (October 25, 1963) 11.

"Were the sons of Korah executed for the sin of their father?" (TRA)*Ban* 98 (November 1, 1963) 11.

"Is Sunday the proper day to worship?" (TRA) *Ban* 98 (November 22, 1963) 11.

"Did Jesus envision a restoration of the Jews?" (TRA) *Ban* 98 (December 13, 1963) 15.

"Was the human nature of Jesus omnipotent?" (TRA) *Ban* 98 (December 20, 1963) 17. Also in *Sfd,* pp. 64-65.

**1964**

"Did God actually repent?" (TRA) *Ban* 99 (January 3, 1964) 11.

"Do the dead sleep until the resurrection?" (TRA) *Ban* 99 (January 10, 1964) 15.

"Did Christ die for apostate leaders?" (TRA) *Ban* 99 (January 24, 1964) 15. Also in *Sfd,* pp. 92-94.

"How much free will does man have?" (TRA) *Ban* 99 (February 28, 1964) 15. Also in *Sfd 2,* pp. 60-62.

"Was John Calvin mission-minded?" (TRA) *Ban* 99 (March 20, 1964) 17.

"Why do we bypass the National Council of Churches?" (TRA) *Ban* 99 (April 24, 1964) 15.

"What objections do we have to the International Council of Christian Churches?" (TRA) *Ban* 99 (May 1, 1964) 15.

Review of *The Epistle of Paul the apostle to the Hebrews, and the First and Second Epistles of St. Peter.* By John Calvin. Tr. by William B. Johnston. Ed. by David W. and Thomas F. Torrance. Calvin's Commentaries 12. Grand Rapids: Wm. B. Eerdmans Publishing Co., 1963. *Ban* 99 (May 1, 1964) 24-25.

"What was the tree of knowledge?" (TRA) *Ban* 99 (June 26, 1964) 17. Also in *Sfd 2,* pp. 54-56.

"Must we hold to a 24-hour day in creation?" (TRA) *Ban* 99 (July 17, 1964) 17.

"Did Jesus die also for the body?" (TRA) *Ban* 99 (July 31, 1964) 17. Also in *Sfd 2,* pp. 80-82.

"How do the canonical and apocryphal books differ?" (TRA) *Ban* 99 (September 4, 1964) 15.

"Who are the Thomas Christians?" (TRA) *Ban* 99 (October 2, 1964) 17.

"Will we recognize each other in heaven?" (TRA) *Ban* 99 (October 16, 1964) 11. Also in *Sfd*, pp. 127-128.

"When and how are souls formed?" (TRA) *Ban* 99 (November 20, 1964) 11. Also in *Sfd 2*, pp. 67-69.

## 1965

"Does Paul insist that women wear headgear in church?" (TRA) *Ban* 100 (February 26, 1965) 7.

"What is our position on capital punishment?" (TRA) *Ban* 100 (March 5, 1965) 11.

Review of *Calvin*. Origins and development of his religious thought. By François Wendel. New York: Harper and Row, 1964. *Ban* 100 (March 26, 1965) 24-25.

"Who crucified Christ?" (TRA) *Ban* 100 (April 16, 1965) 7. Also in *Sfd*, pp. 78-80.

"Was Jesus a Nazirite or an Essene?" (TRA) *Ban* 100 (April 30, 1965) 17. Also in *Sfd*, pp. 69-71.

"Did Jesus' resurrected and ascended body differ?" (TRA) *Ban* 100 (May 21, 1965) 7. Also in *Sfd 2*, pp. 86-88.

"Is the final judgment public or private?" (TRA) *Ban* 100 (June 4, 1965) 17. Also in *Sfd*, p. 123.

"What does Satan have to do with sickness?" (TRA) *Ban* 100 (June 18, 1965) 11.

"What is theistic evolution?" (TRA) *Ban* 100 (July 23, 1965) 7.

"When is the new body conferred?" (TRA) *Ban* 100 (September 3, 1965) 7.

"In what sense are we judged according to our deeds?" (TRA) *Ban* 100 (September 10, 1965) 17.

"How did Christ save mankind?" (TRA) *Ban* 100 (October 29, 1965) 17.

"Why bar children from the Lord's Supper?" (TRA) *Ban* 100 (November 5, 1965) 15.

"When did Jesus eat the Passover?" (TRA) *Ban* 100 (November 19, 1965) 11.

"Does Christianity support pacifism?" (TRA) *Ban* 100 (December 3, 1965) 19. Also in *Sfd*, pp. 35-38.

## 1966

Review of *Calvinism and the political order*. Essays prepared for the Woodrow Wilson lectureship of the National Presbyterian Center, Washington, D.C. Ed. by George Laird Hunt, consulting editor, John Thomas McNeill. Philadelphia: The Westminster Press, 1966. *CTJ* 1 (1966) 79-81.

"How long did Jesus' body repose in the tomb?" (TRA) *Ban* 101 (April 8, 1966) 7. Also in *Sfd*, pp. 88-89.

"How did this article of the creed originate?" (TRA) *Ban* 101 (April 15, 1966) 7. Also in *Sfd*, pp. 85-87.

"Will capital punishment yield to new biblical insights?" (TRA) *Ban* 101 (May 20, 1966) 7.

"Is faith-healing real?" (TRA) *Ban* 101 (June 24, 1966) 15. Also in *Sfd*, pp. 113-115.

"May one be a conscientious objector?" (TRA) *Ban* 101 (July 29, 1966) 17. Also in *Sfd*, pp. 16-18.

"Is there a right to revolt?" (TRA) *Ban* 101 (August 19, 1966) 15. Also in *Sfd*, pp. 43-45.

"Can a homosexual be saved?" (TRA) *Ban* 101 (September 30, 1966) 7. Also in *Sfd*, pp. 28-30.

Review of *What about tongue-speaking?* By Anthony Andrew Hoekema. Grand Rapids: Wm. B. Eerdmans Publishing Co., 1966. *CTJ* 1 (1966) 278-279.

**1967**

"How must we appraise Barth?" (TRA) *Ban* 102 (January 6, 1967) 11.

"Is there no lapse from grace possible?" (TRA) *Ban* 102 (January 13, 1967) 7.

"What governs the Christian conscience?" (TRA) *Ban* 102 (January 27, 1967) 15.

"Under what conditions may one risk his life?" (TRA) *Ban* 102 (February 3, 1967) 7. Also in *Sfd 2*, pp. 26-28.

"Did God die on the cross?" (TRA) *Ban* 102 (February 17, 1967) 7. Also in *Sfd*, pp. 81-84.

"Whence the term: limited atonement?" (TRA) *Ban* 102 (March 17, 1967) 7.

"What do we know about demon possession?" (TRA) *Ban* 102 (March 31, 1967) 7.

"Is the creation record a different kind of history?" (TRA) *Ban* 102 (April 28, 1967) 11.

"Did God hate Esau before he appeared on the scene?" (TRA) *Ban* 102 (June 30, 1967) 10. Also in *Sfd 2*, pp. 108-110.

"Could Jesus sin?" (TRA) *Ban* 102 (July 14, 1967) 15. Also in *Sfd*, pp. 75-77.

"How about a fixed date for Easter?" (TRA) *Ban* 102 (August 25, 1967) 11.

"Must the Christian still be judged?" (TRA) *Ban* 102 (September 29, 1967) 7. Also in *Sfd*, pp. 122-123.

"Has the God-concept changed?" (TRA) *Ban* 102 (September 29, 1967) 7.

"Does God change?" (TRA) *Ban* 102 (October 27, 1967) 11.

"Was the death penalty ever commuted in the Old Testament?" (TRA) *Ban* 102 (December 1, 1967) 7.

"Was Mary of the Davidic line?" (TRA) *Ban* 102 (December 15, 1967) 11. Also in *Sfd*, pp. 57-59.

"How complete was Jesus' knowledge when he was here upon earth?" (TRA) *Ban* 102 (December 15, 1967) 11. Also in *Sfd*, pp. 66-68.

**1968**

"Are true believers totally depraved?" (TRA) *Ban* 103 (January 26, 1968) 7, (September 13, 1968) 11.

"What and where is Hades?" (TRA) *Ban* 103 (February 9, 1968) 11. Also in *Sfd,* pp. 137-139.

"Does the Bible intend to give us the date of creation?" (TRA) *Ban* 103 (March 22, 1968) 7.

"Is democracy a Christian concept?" (TRA) *Ban* 103 (April 5, 1968) 7.

"What is a just war?" (TRA) *Ban* 103 (April 19, 1968) 7. Also in *Sfd 2,* pp. 7-10.

"How should we evaluate 'Christian economics'?" (TRA) *Ban* 103 (April 26, 1968) 19.

"What is the proper role of government?" (TRA) *Ban* 103 (June 21, 1968) 6-7.

"What is meant by the number 666?" (TRA) *Ban* 103 (July 19, 1968) 7.

"What was the penalty levied on Eve?" (TRA) *Ban* 103 (July 26, 1968) 7. Also in *Sfd 2,* pp. 65-66.

"Does time hold meaning in the post-death situation?" (TRA) *Ban* 103 (August 16, 1968) 7.

"Did Jesus have in mind an earthly kingdom?" (TRA) *Ban* 103 (August 23, 1968) 7.

"To whom does Isaiah 7, 14 refer?" (TRA) *Ban* 103 (October 18, 1968) 7. Also in *Sfd 2,* pp. 77-79.

"Was Adam an historical figure?" (TRA) *Ban* 103 (October 25, 1968) 7. Also in *Sfd 2,* pp. 50-53.

"Where do we stand now on divorce and remarriage?" (TRA) *Ban* 103 (November 1, 1968) 7.

"What about Jonah?" (TRA) *Ban* 103 (November 8, 1968) 7.

"Is there progress in heaven?" (TRA) *Ban* 103 (December 13, 1968) 6. Also in *Sfd,* pp. 130-131.

"Is the Spirit of Christ distinct from the Holy Spirit?" (TRA) *Ban* 103 (December 13, 1968) 7.

"How must we interpret Genesis?" (TRA) *Ban* 103 (December 27, 1968) 7. Also in *Sfd 2,* pp. 41-44.

**1969**

"Do the Scriptures prohibit racial intermarriage?" (TRA) *Ban* 104 (January 3, 1969) 7.

"What is the soul?" (TRA) *Ban* 104 (January 17, 1969) 7.

"Who are Gog and Magog?" (TRA) *Ban* 104 (January 24, 1969) 7.

"What about the cursings in the Psalms?" (TRA) *Ban* 104 (January 31, 1969) 7.

"Is the Hamitic curse still levied?" (TRA) *Ban* 104 (February 28, 1969) 6. Also in *Sfd 2,* pp. 75-76.

"Who and what was Melchizedek?" (TRA) *Ban* 104 (February 28, 1969) 6-7.

"How must Ecclesiastes be interpreted?" (TRA) *Ban* 104 (March 21, 1969) 6.

"Does the return of the Jews portend the second coming?" (TRA) *Ban* 104 (March 28, 1969) 7.

Review of *Christianity and humanism*. By Quirinus Breen. Grand Rapids: Wm. B. Eerdmans Publishing Co., 1968. *CTJ* 4 (1969) 150-151.

"Is population control acceptable?" (TRA) *Ban* 104 (April 4, 1969) 7. Also in *Sfd*, pp. 39-42.

"Why is the birth control problem ignored?" (TRA) *Ban* 104 (May 9, 1969) 7.

"Did the prophecy of Isaiah have two authors?" (TRA) *Ban* 104 (May 16, 1969) 7.

"Can we interpret the mystic numbers in the Bible?" (TRA) *Ban* 104 (June 6, 1969) 6-7.

"Does the Song of Songs belong in the canon?" (TRA) *Ban* 104 (July 4, 1969) 7.

"Did Jesus advocate resorting to force of arms?" (TRA) *Ban* 104 (September 12, 1969) 7. Also in *Sfd 2*, pp. 89-91.

"Will the 144,000 inhabit the new earth?" (TRA) *Ban* 104 (October 10, 1969) 7.

"May hypnotism be used as a plaything?" (TRA) *Ban* 104 (October 31, 1969) 7. Also in *Sfd*, pp. 31-34.

"Is original sin still a tenable doctrine?" (TRA) *Ban* 104 (November 7, 1969) 7.

"Does Paul advocate celibacy?" (TRA) *Ban* 104 (December 5, 1969) 7. Also in *Sfd 2*, pp. 15-18.

**1970**

*Springboards for discussion*. Contemporary Discussion Series. Grand Rapids: Baker Book House, 1970. Reprinted in 1971, 1972, and 1973.

"Does the Bible insist on monogamy?" (TRA) *Ban* 105 (April 10, 1970) 7. Also in *Sfd 2*, pp. 23-25.

"How did Jesus view the Old Testament?" (TRA) *Ban* 105 (May 1, 1970) 7.

"Did baptism replace circumcision?" (TRA) *Ban* 105 (May 15, 1970) 6.

"Are some lies permissible?" (TRA) *Ban* 105 (May 15, 1970) 7. Also in *Sfd 2*, pp. 11-14.

"Why do we celebrate Christmas on December 25?" (TRA) *Ban* 105 (July 10, 1970) 7. Also in *Sfd 2*, pp. 124-126.

"Is God the author of evil?" (TRA) *Ban* 105 (July 31, 1970) 7.

"Must a Christian hate?" (TRA) *Ban* 105 (August 21, 1970) 7. Also in *Sfd 2*, pp. 96-98.

"Who or what was the rock?" (TRA) *Ban* 105 (September 11, 1970) 11. Also in *Sfd 2*, pp. 99-101.

"When may a church secede?" (TRA) *Ban* 105 (October 9, 1970) 7.

Review of *All one body we*. The doctrine of the church in ecumenical perspective. By John Henry Kromminga. Grand Rapids: Wm. B. Eerdmans Publishing Co., 1970. *CTJ* 5 (1970) 201-203.

"Is not the Christian Reformed Church the product of a dual or triple secession?" (TRA) *Ban* 105 (December 11, 1970) 13.

**1971**

"Will all men get new life in Christ?" (TRA) *Ban* 106 (March 26, 1971) 7, (July 30, 1971) 7.

Review of *The politics of doomsday*. Fundamentalists of the far right. By Erling Jorstad. Nashville: Abingdon Press, 1970. *CTJ* 6 (1971) 120-122.

"What will be the nature of man's resurrected body?" (TRA) *Ban* 106 (April 2, 1971) 7.

"Was Paul prejudiced against women?" (TRA) *Ban* 106 (April 23, 1971) 7.

"Does the Bible advocate prayers to Jesus?" (TRA) *Ban* 106 (May 14, 1971) 17.

"Will we know the approximate date of Christ's return?" (TRA) *Ban* 106 (July 9, 1971) 7.

"Did Calvin hold to the limited atonement doctrine?" (TRA) *Ban* 106 (August 20, 1971) 7.

"What about proper Sabbath observance?" (TRA) *Ban* 106 (December 10, 1971) 7.

"What is the rapture?" (TRA) *Ban* 106 (December 24, 1971) 7.

"Did God really answer Job's question?" (TRA) *Ban* 106 (December 31, 1971) 20.

**1972**

"Are the terms 'soul' and 'spirit' interchangeable in the Scriptures?" (TRA) *Ban* 107 (January 7, 1972) 7.

"Where are Paradise and Hades located?" (TRA) *Ban* 107 (January 14, 1972) 13.

"Where did racial characteristics originate?" (TRA) *Ban* 107 (January 21, 1972) 7. Also in *Sfd 2*, pp. 73-74.

"Did the gift of tongues cease?" (TRA) *Ban* 107 (January 28, 1972) 19, (February 4, 1972) 7, (February 18, 1972) 7, 29, (February 25, 1972) 13.

"What about the context of the virgin birth prophecy?" (TRA) *Ban* 107 (March 24, 1972) 9.

Review of *The Armstrong error*. By Charles F. DeLoach. Plainfield, N.J.: Logos International, 1971. *Ban* 107 (March 24, 1972) 24.

"How can the cultural gap be narrowed or bridged?" (TRA) *Ban* 107 (March 31, 1972) 9.

Review of *Christian faith and modern theology*. Ed. by Carl F. H. Henry. Grand Rapids: Baker Book House, 1971. *CTJ* 7 (1972) 90-91.

"Were the Pentecost tongues identical with the Corinthian tongues?" (TRA) *Ban* 107 (April 21, 1972) 9.

"Is Christ coming in person to rule on this earth?" (TRA) *Ban* 107 (May 5, 1972) 9, (May 12, 1972) 9, (May 19, 1972) 13, (June 2, 1972) 9.

"In what way is Genesis 3,15 messianic?" (TRA) *Ban* 107 (July 14, 1972) 11.

"Is there demon possession today?" (TRA) *Ban* 107 (August 18, 1972) 9, (August 25, 1972) 17, (September 1, 1972) 9. Also in *Sfd 2*, pp. 35-39.

"Are women saved through childbearing?" (TRA) *Ban* 107 (September 15, 1972) 15.

"What items of history are being predicted?" (TRA) *Ban* 107 (October 27, 1972) 9, (November 3, 1972) 9.

"What events must precede the second coming of our Lord?" (TRA) *Ban* 107 (November 10, 1972) 9.

"Did the earth change for the worse after the fall of Adam?" (TRA) *Ban* 107 (November 10, 1972) 9. Also in *Sfd 2*, pp. 70-72.

**1973**

Ed. *The heritage of John Calvin.* Heritage Hall Lectures, 1960-1970. Grand Rapids: Wm. B. Eerdmans Publishing Co., 1973.

"What about state lotteries?" (TRA) *Ban* 108 (January 19, 1973) 14. Also in *Sfd 2*, pp. 19-22.

"For what may we thank God?" (TRA) *Ban* 108 (April 6, 1973) 17.

"Does God at times lead us into temptation?" (TRA) *Ban* 108 (July 27, 1973) 19.

**1974**

"Calvin's indebtedness to others" in *Geneva to Geelong: the ideas and influence of John Calvin.* Ed. by Gordon Oosterman. Grand Rapids: The National Union of Christian Schools, 1974. Pp. 1-8.

*Springboards for discussion. No. 2.* Contemporary Discussion Series. Grand Rapids: Baker Book House, 1974.

Review of *Answers to questions.* By Frederick Fyvie Bruce. Grand Rapids: Zondervan Publishing House, 1973. *CTJ* 9 (1974) 82-83.

"What about these end-time phenomena?" (TRA) *Ban* 109 (April 26, 1974) 9.

"Does Satan still have access to heaven?" (TRA) *Ban* 109 (July 26, 1974) 15.

"How about those who died and were restored to life by Christ during his ministry?" (TRA) *Ban* 109 (August 23, 1974) 15.

"What is the origin of the soul-sleep doctrine?" (TRA) *Ban* 109 (October 11, 1974) 9.

Review of *Herbert W. Armstrong, Garner Ted Armstrong and their worldwide Church of God: a bibliography.* Nashville: St. Paul Publishers, 1974. 3rd edition. *Ban* 109 (October 18, 1974) 25.

"What sort of liberty does a Christian have?" (TRA) *Ban* 109 (November 8, 1974) 19.

**1975**

"Age, aged, old age", "Assassins", "Banishment" in *The Zondervan pictorial encyclopedia of the Bible.* Ed. by Merrill C. Tenney. Grand Rapids: Zondervan Publishing House, 1975. Vol. 1, pp. 69-70, 368, 459-460.

"Sabbath day's journey", "Sackcloth", "Sacrilege", "Saddle", "Sailor", "Sukkuth and Kaiwan", "Salmone", "Salt", "Salutation", "Satrap", "Satyr", "Savory meat, food", "Saw", "Scales, fish", "Scented wood", "Sculptured stones", "Sheepcote, sheepfold", "Sheepskin", "Zealot" in *The Zondervan pictorial encyclopedia of the Bible*. Ed. by Merrill C. Tenney. Grand Rapids: Zondervan Publishing House, 1975. Vol. 5, pp. 189, 192, 211, 216, 217-218, 219, 220, 286, 291, 292, 315, 388, 1036-1037.

"Does regeneration cancel out total depravity?"(TRA) *Ban* 110 (February 14, 1975) 19.

Review of *The Armstrong empire*. By Joseph Hopkins. Grand Rapids: Wm. B. Eerdmans Publishing Co., 1974. *Ban* 110 (February 28, 1975) 24.

"What is the church?" *Ban* 110 (March 7, 1975) 10-11.

"A unique ecumenical experience" *Ban* 110 (July 25, 1975) 20-21.